Molecular crystals: their transforms and diffuse scattering

José Luis and Marisa Amorós

Professor and Associate Professor of Materials Science
Southern Illinois University

John Wiley & Sons, Inc., New York · London · Sydney

Dedicated to our parents and to our son

Foreword to the series

In the 1920's comparatively few people paid much attention to the branch of science known as crystallography, and the only journal devoted to it was circulated to a few hundred subscribers, mostly libraries. Scientists in the classical disciplines hardly recognized crystallography as a science, although each apparently regarded it as a small segment of his own field. No American university boasted a professor of crystallography and any instruction given was adjunct to mineralogy. Nevertheless, papers of interest to crystallographers appeared in journals of mineralogy, physics and chemistry, although not in large numbers. In those days one might claim to have an all-round acquaintance with crystallography because he was able to keep up with the literature.

This is no longer true. In the period between the first and second world wars, science flourished, and scientists not only published more papers, but an increasing proportion of them dealt with solid materials. It was inevitable that the chemists, metallurgists, physicists and ceramists should make increasing use of crystallographic theory and methods, that the journals of many fields should publish more papers of crystallographic interest, and that new journals devoted to crystallography and the "solid state" should arise. Soon the abstracting journals contained hundreds of titles of crystallographic interest with each issue, and now few of us can keep even reasonably well informed about the many aspects of the science of crystals, to say nothing of keeping abreast of the advances in all these aspects. Not only is it out of the question to keep up with the mass of literature that is turned out, but it is even a little difficult to maintain contact with all the advances in one's own speciality. Accordingly, we are tending to become parochial.

In the words of Warren Weaver "...the volume of the appreciated but not understood keeps getting larger and larger." In order to improve this condition to some extent we need the services of those who, having become authorities in some segments of our field, are willing to integrate their understandings of these limited regions. With such help many of us can gain a sufficient understanding of matters whose original literature we have neither the time nor the inclination to study. Such writings exist in several fields, but none, to date, in crystallography. It is to fill this need that the Wiley Monographs in Crystallography are offered.

Martin J. Buerger

Foreword

Some people, including many scientists and a few artists, find a fascination in symmetry and periodicity. The regularity of shape of the snowflake intrigued Kepler three-and-a-half centuries ago, although he was unable to explain it as successfully as he did the motions of the planets. Of the six explanations that he offered to his patron, almost in fun, none satisfied him. But he was sure, as natural philosophers before and after him were sure, that the limited symmetries of crystal shapes must be the consequence of some kind of internal three-dimersional repeating patterns. Just what it was that was being repeated was not known until the idea of the chemical atom took shape in the early part of the nineteenth century. Even then there were no means of finding out whether, for example, the inspired guesses of Wollaston concerning the arrangement in even the simplest crystal structures were correct nor what the actual dimensions of any particular repeat unit were, although the shape of the repeat unit could be deduced from the external interfacial angles of the crystal.

With the discovery of x-rays in 1895 a new means of measuring dimensions of the order of interatomic distances became available; seventeen years later the phenomenon of x-ray diffraction proved to be the key that opened wide the door to knowledge, first of the simpler internal structures of cubic inorganic compounds and then of more complicated ones; and now, only fifty-six years later, the even details of protein structures are becoming clear. Moreover, electron and neutron diffraction techniques have greatly extended the range of phenomena involving elementary patterns that can be studied.

Von Laue, whose intuitive genius inspired the first x-ray diffraction experiments, seemed hardly to be aware that there was then a complete mathematical theory of space groups (due independently to Fedorov, Schœnflies, and Barlow) already at hand to assist the experimental investigator, nor was this theory used in the first few years by W. H. Bragg or W. L. Bragg, who worked out structures of many simple crystals from first principles. W. H. Bragg, in particular, although himself a mathematician of distinction, seemed reluctant to adopt the mathematical crystallography to the practical signifi- cance of which Niggli, Nishikawa, and Wyckoff all drew early atten- tion; he thought that it was better for students and research workers to do their own reasoning from scratch. Possibly he was right, as long as only simple structures were involved, but every kind of tool was needed when crystals with larger and more complicated unit cells were tackled. Even now, however, there is a tendency to describe the basic crystal patterns as if they were static, and whole textbooks can be written which give no hint that atoms and molecules in the solid state are continually in motion.

Yet here again there was, before the discovery of x-ray diffraction in 1912, a remarkably complete theoretical exposition of crystal dynamics as applied to simple cubic crystals. Von Laue was well aware of the work of Debye and of Born and Kármán, and he even wondered whether the thermal vibrations of the atoms in crystals might not be so great as to render the phenomena of x-ray diffraction unobservable. He correctly associated the falling-off of scattering power at high diffraction angles save in the case of diamond with the relatively large mean amplitudes of atomic vibration in all but the diamond structure. W. H. Bragg and W. L. Bragg were able to take up the inquiry at the point at which von Laue had left it, know- ing that since diffraction patterns were obtainable the atomic vibra- tions in general constituted only a second-order complication, which could be neglected in a first consideration of crystal structure as such. They and their research pupils were physicists, however, and therefore they were interested as much in phenomena as in arrangement. Some of the most important of the early publications dealt with the magnitudes of the atomic vibration amplitudes at different temperatures and with the existence of zero-point energy. The name of R. W. James will always be associated with these early studies, just as those of Darwin and Hartree are associated with problems of textural disorder of whatever origin.

So far the phenomenon observed had been that of an extra falling- off of diffraction intensity at high angles, this falling-off being greater the higher the temperature. Faxén and Waller showed theoretically that this diminution of coherent "Bragg" or "Laue" intensity must be accompanied by an increase of diffraction intensity (strictly speaking incoherent) in the general background, and they related the distribution of this diffuse intensity to the elastic constants of simple crystals. Yet again there was a general impression among experimental crystallographers that the effects of which Faxén and Waller were writing were probably unobservable (and this in spite of the fact that we can now see them very clearly on early x-ray photographs), and that they were in any case irrelevant to the main purpose of crystal-structure determination.

Just before the beginning of World War II the Faxén-Waller scattering was rediscovered, empirically, in France, India, the United States, and Great Britain, almost simultaneously. It seemed that it was one of those discoveries for which the time was ripe. At first there was some controversy about its interpretation, and its quantitative observation has been hindered first by the problem of measuring intensity over an extended area or volume of scattering space and second by the problem (solved eventually by neutron diffraction) of frequency measurement in the scattered beam. Many crystallographers do not, even now, realize how much they miss by merely making measurements of average atomic vibration amplitudes or, at the best, of the atomic thermal-ellipsoid axes.

With the need for greater precision, the importance of making a proper allowance for thermal vibration has at last come to be realized. But the difficulties of making measurements of intensity of diffuse scattering over the whole of the observable scattering space, as well as of relating the observations to their various possible causes, have generally discouraged research workers from making more than the most superficial use of background scattering as a means of finding out more about crystal structures and about the deviations of crystal structure from static perfection. Chemists have continued to be satisfied with a stereochemical picture that merely shows the mean relative positions of atoms and molecules in the solid state, and physicists have confined solid-state physics very largely to a study of the properties of the simplest of elements or compounds, modified by inclusions that may drastically alter those properties. An immense field of knowledge has thus been virtually ignored.

A monograph on the subject of diffuse scattering has long been wanted, but there are few research workers who would be qualified to write one. The authors of the present book have made an intensive study of this subject, and therefore they are quite the best people to write about it. They do so with a keen interest in the subject which shows throughout the work, and they are able to take many examples from their own papers. At the same time, the impressive list of references shows that they have taken full account of all the work done by others in this field and ensures that their outlook is a balanced one. The story is not finished, they would be the first to admit that, but this only makes the investigation a more exciting and rewarding one.

Kathleen Lonsdale

University College, London

Preface

One of the main concerns of X-ray crystallography has been the accurate determination of crystal structures. The calculation of the atomic coordinates is only a first-order approximation in the study of crystals; a further approximation is the measurement of the vibration parameters of their atoms (and molecules). A crystal, however, is a dynamical system of vibrating units, and therefore a further step toward understanding it is a knowledge of crystal dynamics. X-ray diffuse scattering is a tool for this study, the problem with which this book deals.

Molecular crystals are well suited to this kind of study. First of all, several crystal structures of molecular compounds are known with a reasonably high degree of accuracy, their thermal parameters are known, and the average vibration scheme has been determined. This provides a starting point toward an understanding of the crystal dynamics of these compounds. Besides, molecular crystals show intense and complicated patterns of X-ray diffuse scattering, which makes their study highly attractive. Yet the esthetic approach in science is not always justifiable. Molecular compounds are the materials studied by a whole branch of chemistry, solid-state physicists are becoming more and more interested in their properties, and life itself is based on their dynamics. Therefore the study of crystal dynamics of molecular compounds will be mandatory in the future.

Much of our contribution to the field was published in Spanish and difficult for the non-Spanish speaking scientist to obtain. We felt that something was needed to incorporate our work into the common scientific literature. In addition, the only existing book on diffuse scattering is one by W. A. Wooster, in which, however, many aspects of the behavior of thermal diffuse scattering of molecular crystals are not treated. This book has been written to supply a fuller account.

Our subject matter falls naturally into three broad sections. The basic concepts needed to understand diffuse scattering are described in the first three chapters. The method of the Fourier transform has been widely used, and special emphasis has been given to the use of optical analogs, both Fraunhofer diffraction of light by circular apertures and optical Q-functions. This procedure is intended to clarify concepts whose answers can be obtained readily by optical experiments. The actual X-ray diffuse scattering, as it is observed in molecular crystals, and its application are discussed in Chapters 4 and 5. The continuous diffuse scattering typical of molecular crystals is analyzed by the difference Fourier transform (DFT) method and its relations with the crystal structure are described. The method is also extended to crystal structure determination. The theory of thermal waves is logically included, and the application of the theory to the determination of the elastic constants and molecular forces is given. In this respect the case of hexamine is examined at length. Temperature dependence of the diffuse scattering is treated in the last chapter and the inversion phenomenon of the diffuse scattering with temperature is discussed. The effect of polymorphic transitions is analyzed and critical scattering appearing at the transition temperature of a continuous transition is theoretically and experimentally treated. We have purposely omitted any description of the actual gathering of experimental data.

MOLECULAR CRYSTALS is intended for crystallographers and solid-state physicists with some experience in X-ray diffraction. Mathematics has been kept to the lowest possible level necessary to clarify the complex problem of crystal dynamics. The reader will find that only a few basic principles, given in the first part of the book, are necessary to a comprehension of continuous diffuse scattering.

The text is far from being exhaustive. We have dealt mainly with our own work; however, the references will allow the interested reader to extend his own study in ampler fields. We very much hope that we shall have introduced more researchers to an exciting field that has held our attention for many years.

We are grateful to our pupils and colleagues with whom we have worked since 1954 during our stay at the Universities of Barcelona and Madrid. Reference to their work is fully acknowledged in the book. We must also extend our deep appreciation to Professor Martin J. Buerger whose constructive criticism, patience, and understanding helped us so much during the difficult task of preparing the manuscript. We are indebted as well to the Air Force Office of Scientific Research, Solid State Sciences Division, for their continuous and generous support of our work over ten years in this and related fields. Last, but not least, we wish to thank Miss Janice Lindenberg for her patient and skillful work in preparing the typed manuscript.

José Luis and Marisa Amorós

Carbondale, Illinois
March 1968

Contents

Contents

Molecular crystals:
their transforms and diffuse scattering

1

Scattering by atoms and molecules

Diffraction by an arbitrary object

Any atomic structure can be described in terms of a function $\rho(\mathbf{r})$, which gives the electron density of scattering matter. The space where the density function is defined is called physical space, which is defined by its metrics, the three base vectors $\mathbf{a}$, $\mathbf{b}$, $\mathbf{c}$. A vector $\mathbf{r}$ defines the distance from the origin to a point whose coordinates are x, y, z:

$$\mathbf{r} = x\mathbf{a} + y\mathbf{b} + z\mathbf{c}. \tag{1}$$

A volume element of this space is

$$dv = \mathbf{a}(\mathbf{b} \times \mathbf{c})\, dx\, dy\, dz. \tag{2}$$

The x-rays are scattered by the electrons. Suppose that an x-ray monochromatic plane wave, defined by its wave vector $\mathbf{k}_0$ where $|\mathbf{k}_0| = 1/\lambda$, is incident on an element of volume dv located at a distance given by the vector $\mathbf{r}$ relative to the origin O (Fig. 1). The number of electrons in dv are $\rho(\mathbf{r})\, dv$. The phase of the wave at $\mathbf{r}$ is equal to $\mathbf{k} \cdot \mathbf{r}$, where $\mathbf{k}$ gives the direction of the wave front, the phase being zero at the origin of coordinates O. The phase of the wave on leaving dv is given by the phase difference between the two scattered wavelets arriving at a point P at a distance very large compared with $\mathbf{r}$ (Fraunhofer-diffraction case). The phase difference ψ is obtained from the path difference times $2\pi/\lambda$:

$$\psi = 2\pi(\mathbf{k}_0 \cdot \mathbf{r} - \mathbf{k} \cdot \mathbf{r}). \tag{3}$$

The amplitude of the diffracted wave is expressed in terms of that scattered under the same conditions by the single classical Thomson

1

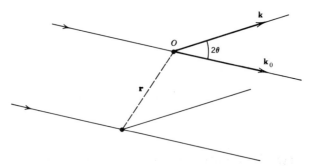

Fig. 1. Path difference of x-rays diffracted by two atoms. k_0 = Unit vector of incident radiation; k = Unit vector of diffracted radiation; 2θ = Diffraction angle (the deviation angle); r = Interatomic distance.

electron situated at the origin. This amplitude is proportional to $\rho(\mathbf{r})\,dv$. Accordingly, the expression for the amplitude of the wave scattered at a point $\mathbf{r}$ is proportional to

$$\rho(\mathbf{r})\exp\left(2\pi i(\mathbf{k}_0-\mathbf{k})\mathbf{r}\right)dv.$$

Let us introduce the vector

$$\mathbf{r}^* = \mathbf{k} - \mathbf{k}_0 \tag{4}$$

which is determined by the directions of incidence and scattering and by the wavelength. This vector has the dimensions of the reciprocal of length, and can be represented in a reciprocal space of base vectors $\mathbf{a}^*, \mathbf{b}^*, \mathbf{c}^*$ related to those of physical space through the equations

$$\begin{aligned}
\mathbf{a}\cdot\mathbf{a}^* &= 1 & \mathbf{a}\cdot\mathbf{b}^* &= 0 & \mathbf{b}\cdot\mathbf{c}^* &= 0 \\
\mathbf{b}\cdot\mathbf{b}^* &= 1 & \mathbf{a}\cdot\mathbf{c}^* &= 0 & \mathbf{c}\cdot\mathbf{a}^* &= 0 \\
\mathbf{c}\cdot\mathbf{c}^* &= 1 & \mathbf{b}\cdot\mathbf{a}^* &= 0 & \mathbf{c}\cdot\mathbf{b}^* &= 0
\end{aligned} \tag{5}$$

The vector $\mathbf{r}^*$, drawn from the origin of coordinates of the space defined by the metrics $\mathbf{a}^*, \mathbf{b}^*, \mathbf{c}^*$, is given by

$$\mathbf{r}^* = h\mathbf{a}^* + k\mathbf{b}^* + l\mathbf{c}^*. \tag{6}$$

A volume element dv^* in this space is given by

$$dv^* = \mathbf{a}^*(\mathbf{b}^*\times\mathbf{c}^*)\,dh\,dk\,dl. \tag{7}$$

It follows that

$$\mathbf{a}^*(\mathbf{b}^*\times\mathbf{c}^*) = \frac{1}{\mathbf{a}(\mathbf{b}\times\mathbf{c})} \qquad \text{or} \qquad v^* = 1/v. \tag{8}$$

It can easily be seen that the modulus of the vector $\mathbf{r}^*$ is

$$|\mathbf{r}^*| = 2\sin(\theta/\lambda). \tag{9}$$

The angle of diffraction, i.e., the angle between the directions of incidence and scattering, is 2θ. In Fig. 2 point P is such that the straight line CO corresponds in magnitude and direction to the incident wave vector $|k_0| = 1/\lambda$, and PO to the diffracted vector $|k|$. Since $|k| = |k_0| = 1/\lambda$ it is possible to represent any diffracted vector k as a radius vector in a sphere of radius $1/\lambda$, constructed with the point C as a center. This sphere evidently passes through the point O, and it is called the sphere of reflection or the Ewald sphere. More precisely it can be named the sphere of diffraction.

Any vector $\mathbf{r}^*$, whose origin is at O and whose tip lies on the sphere, satisfies (4). This vector is the so-called diffraction vector, or reciprocal vector, since it is given in units reciprocal to the units of physical space. If, in direct space, we express the r vectors in terms of Å, the $\mathbf{r}^*$ vectors will be given in $Å^{-1}$. An element of volume of an object scatter x-rays with an amplitude proportional to

$$\rho(\mathbf{r}) \exp (-2\pi i\, \mathbf{r} \cdot \mathbf{r}^*)\, dv.$$

Similar conditions appear in electron and neutron diffraction. In these cases, the electron density $\rho(\mathbf{r})$ is substituted by the potential

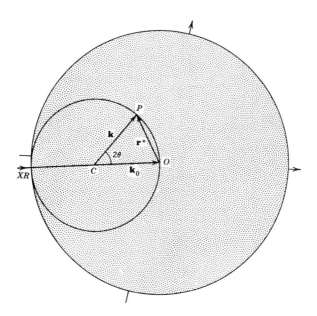

Fig. 2. Ewald sphere and reciprocal space. O = Origin of the reciprocal space; C = Center of the Ewald sphere; XR = Direction of the incident x-ray beam; 2θ = Diffraction angle; $\mathbf{r}^*$ = Reciprocal vector; k = Diffracted ray.

$\psi(\mathbf{r})$ in the case of electron diffraction, and by $\delta(\mathbf{r})$, the density distribution of the atomic nuclei in neutron (nuclear) diffraction. Figure 3 represents schematically the different density functions for a monoatomic structure. The electron density $\rho(\mathbf{r})$ and the potential functions $\phi(\mathbf{r})$ are continuous functions of similar shape, the latter being of lower intensity. The density distribution $\delta(\mathbf{r})$ in nuclei, however, is a discontinuous function resulting from the sum of individual point-like functions. In optical diffraction a two-dimensional pattern of apertures or transparent "disks" is often used. The density function $\rho_d(\mathbf{r})$ here is again discontinuous, and it is schematically represented in Fig. 3.

If we do not consider the interaction with other electrons by a wave scattered by the electrons $\rho(\mathbf{r})\,dv$, the amplitude of the wave scattered coherently by the object is the algebraic sum of the amplitudes of the waves scattered by each of the electrons

$$F(\mathbf{r}^*) = \int_v \rho(\mathbf{r})\exp(-2\pi i\mathbf{r}\cdot\mathbf{r}^*)dv. \qquad (10)$$

The integration is to be taken throughout the volume v occupied by the scattering matter. The distribution $F(\mathbf{r}^*)$ corresponds to the diffraction amplitude, whose corresponding intensity can be produced under any conditions of incidence and scattering, and with any wavelength, by the distribution of the scattering matter $\rho(\mathbf{r})$.

Relation (10) holds in the Fraunhofer diffraction phenomenon of x-rays, electrons, and neutrons. If the Fraunhofer diffraction with

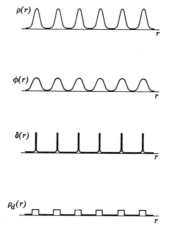

Fig. 3.   Density functions of a monoatomic structure: Electron density $\rho(\mathbf{r})$; Potential density $\phi(\mathbf{r})$; Nuclear density $\delta(\mathbf{r})$; Uniform disks, $\rho_d(\mathbf{r})$.

ordinary monochromatic light by a given transparency is considered, $\rho(\mathbf{r})$ is a two-dimensional function, and the integration in (10) is taken over the area A of the transparency.

The intensity $I(\mathbf{r}^*)$ scattered by a whole object for a given $\mathbf{r}^*$ can be calculated in terms of the amplitude times its complex conjugate, when the amplitude is given by a complex number:

$$I(\mathbf{r}^*) = F(\mathbf{r}^*) \cdot F^*(\mathbf{r}^*). \tag{11}$$

It is also given by the square of the modulus of the complex amplitude

$$I(\mathbf{r}^*) = |F(\mathbf{r}^*)|^2. \tag{12}$$

The function $I(\mathbf{r}^*)$, called the intensity function, is

$$I(\mathbf{r}^*) = \int\int \rho(\mathbf{r})\rho(\mathbf{r}') \exp\left[-2\pi i(\mathbf{r}-\mathbf{r}') \cdot \mathbf{r}^*\right] dv\, dv'$$

$$= \int\int \rho(\mathbf{r})\rho(\mathbf{r}') \exp(-2\pi i\mathbf{r}^* \cdot \mathbf{r}) \exp(2\pi i\mathbf{r}^* \cdot \mathbf{r}')\, dv\, dv'. \tag{13}$$

It depends only on the structure of the object that does the scattering.

From the preceding we can conclude that the amplitude F and the intensity I can be defined as functions of position in reciprocal space. The amplitudes and intensities of scattering are functions of the vector $\mathbf{r}^*$, whose length is governed by the magnitude of the scattering angle, as given in (9), while its direction depends on the orientation of the object with respect to the incident beam, according to (4). Thus the scattering intensity can be considered to be located in a hypothetical space, variously called reciprocal space, diffraction space, or Fourier space.

In principle, to construct the scattering intensity or amplitude functions we could choose an arbitrary coordinate system. However, there is great advantage in relating the coordinate systems of the object space and reciprocal space according to (5), because with such a choice the amplitude of the scattered wave is mathematically the Fourier transform T of the electron density of the object,

$$F(\mathbf{r}^*) = T\{\rho(\mathbf{r})\}, \tag{14}$$

and reciprocally the electron density is the inverse Fourier transform T^{-1} of the scattering amplitude,

$$\rho(\mathbf{r}) = T^{-1}\{F(\mathbf{r}^*)\} \tag{15}$$

$$\rho(\mathbf{r}) = \int_{v*} F(\mathbf{r}^*) \exp(2\pi i\mathbf{r} \cdot \mathbf{r}^*)\, dv^*. \tag{16}$$

The integration now extends to infinity in reciprocal space. The operators T and T^{-1} can be defined by the equations

$$T = \int \exp(-2\pi i r^* \cdot r) \, dv, \tag{17}$$

$$T^{-1} = \int \exp(2\pi i r^* \cdot r) \, dv^*. \tag{18}$$

It follows that if we knew $F(r^*)$ for the whole reciprocal space it would be possible to determine $\rho(r)$ by the integral given in (16).

Symmetry properties of scattering functions

The symmetry of the scattering functions obviously depends on the symmetry of the density distribution that gives rise to the scattering. However, the knowledge of such relations is of interest because they help in the understanding of more complex problems such as the scattering by a molecular crystal.

The electron density is positive and real. For noncentrosymmetrical distributions of $\rho(r)$ the amplitude $F(r^*)$ is complex, so it must be defined in terms of either its real and imaginary parts $A(r^*)$ and $B(r^*)$,

$$F(r^*) = A(r^*) + iB(r^*), \tag{19}$$

or in terms of its modulus $|F(r^*)|$ and the phase angle ψ,

$$F(r^*) = |F(r^*)| \exp(i\psi). \tag{20}$$

The phase angle is determined by the common solution of the two following equations

$$\psi = \cos^{-1} \frac{A(r^*)}{|F(r^*)|},$$

$$\psi = \sin^{-1} \frac{B(r^*)}{|F(r^*)|}. \tag{21}$$

Since $\rho(r)$ is real, (16) can be written

$$\rho(r) = \int A(r^*) \cos 2\pi(r^* \cdot r) \, dv^* + \int B(r^*) \sin 2\pi(r^* \cdot r) \, dv^*, \tag{22}$$

and the following relation holds:

$$A(r^*) = \int \rho(r) \cos 2\pi(r^* \cdot r) \, dv. \tag{23}$$

It follows that the real part of the diffraction amplitude is a centro-symmetric function,

$$A(\mathbf{r}^*) = A(-\mathbf{r}^*), \tag{24}$$

like the cosine function (Fig. 4), having positive and negative regions and zero surfaces as the sign changes. It is very unlikely, however, that an extended region exists, or an isolated value of $\mathbf{r}^*$ where the real part is zero. At $|\mathbf{r}^*| = 0$, $A(0) > 0$. Similarly

$$B(\mathbf{r}^*) = \int \rho(\mathbf{r}) \sin 2\pi(\mathbf{r}^* \cdot \mathbf{r})\, dv. \tag{25}$$

The imaginary part of the diffracted amplitude is antisymmetric, i.e.,

$$B(\mathbf{r}^*) = -B(-\mathbf{r}^*) \tag{26}$$

like the sine function (Fig. 4). At the origin of Fourier space (26) becomes $B(0) = 0$.

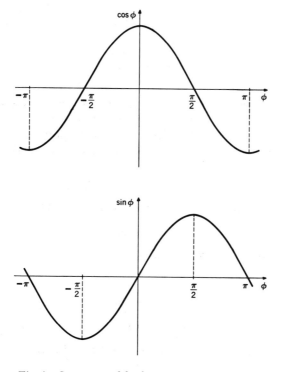

Fig. 4. Symmetry of the functions $\cos \phi$ and $\sin \phi$.

On the other hand, the modulus of the amplitude is centrosymmetric about the origin of Fourier space, i.e.,

$$|F(\mathbf{r}^*)| = |F(-\mathbf{r}^*)|. \qquad (27)$$

It becomes zero only when the real and imaginary parts are simultaneously zero, so the most common fact is that there exist isolated values of $\mathbf{r}^*$ where $|F(\mathbf{r}^*)| = 0$, which lie on the intersections of the zero surfaces of the real and imaginary parts. $F(0)$ is always a positive real number.

The phase angle is antisymmetrical,

$$\psi(\mathbf{r}^*) = -\psi(-\mathbf{r}^*), \qquad (28)$$

and not, in general, discontinuous since each value of ψ depends on the variation of both the real and imaginary parts. In many cases it has singular points where it is indeterminate, that is, at the points where $|F(\mathbf{r}^*)| = 0$; on a circular path surrounding any of these points the ψ function passes through all values from zero up to 2π, i.e., it again becomes zero. At the origin of reciprocal space (28) becomes $\psi(0) = 0$.

The intensity function is real and centrosymmetric, and positive or zero,

$$I(\mathbf{r}^*) = I(-\mathbf{r}^*)$$
$$I(\mathbf{r}^*) \geq 0. \qquad (29)$$

It has isolated points or sometimes surfaces or lines where $I(\mathbf{r}^*) = 0$, which occur where the amplitude function is zero.

A real function like the electron density $\rho(\mathbf{r})$ can always be split into an even function $\rho_1(\mathbf{r})$ and an odd function $\rho_2(\mathbf{r})$ (Fig. 5),

$$\rho(\mathbf{r}) = \rho_1(\mathbf{r}) + \rho_2(\mathbf{r}). \qquad (30)$$

The even function is centrosymmetric, i.e., it satisfies

$$\rho_1(\mathbf{r}) = \rho_1(-\mathbf{r}), \qquad (31)$$

and the odd function antisymmetric,

$$\rho_2(\mathbf{r}) = -\rho_2(-\mathbf{r}). \qquad (32)$$

We have

$$\rho_1(\mathbf{r}) = \tfrac{1}{2}[\rho(\mathbf{r}) + \rho(-\mathbf{r})]$$
$$\rho_2(\mathbf{r}) = \tfrac{1}{2}[\rho(\mathbf{r}) - \rho(-\mathbf{r})]. \qquad (33)$$

$F(\mathbf{r}^*)$ is, in general, complex, however. Recalling that

$$\exp(-2\pi i\,\mathbf{r}\cdot\mathbf{r}^*) = \cos 2\pi(\mathbf{r}\cdot\mathbf{r}^*) - i\sin 2\pi(\mathbf{r}\cdot\mathbf{r}^*), \qquad (34)$$

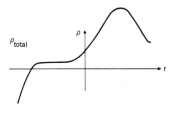

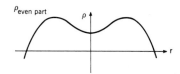

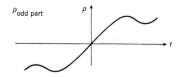

Fig. 5. Components of the electron-density function.

(10) can be written

$$F(\mathbf{r}^*) = \int \rho(\mathbf{r}) \cos 2\pi(\mathbf{r} \cdot \mathbf{r}^*) \, dv - i \int \rho(\mathbf{r}) \sin 2\pi(\mathbf{r} \cdot \mathbf{r}^*) \, dv$$

$$= F_1(\mathbf{r}^*) - iF_2(\mathbf{r}^*). \tag{35}$$

Condition (31) can only hold if $B_1(\mathbf{r}^*) = 0$. Hence the transform of the even part of the density function is real and even.

$$T\{\rho_1(\mathbf{r})\} = A_1(\mathbf{r}^*). \tag{36}$$

Equation (32) can only hold if $A_2(\mathbf{r}^*) = 0$; therefore, the transform of the odd term of the electron density is imaginary and odd,

$$T\{\rho_2(\mathbf{r})\} = B_2(\mathbf{r}^*). \tag{37}$$

In the general case we have

$$T\{\rho_1(\mathbf{r}) + \rho_2(\mathbf{r})\} = A_1(\mathbf{r}^*) + iB_2(\mathbf{r}^*). \tag{38}$$

The transform of the electron-density function is, in general, complex: the real part $A(\mathbf{r}^*)$ is even, the transform of the even part of $\rho(\mathbf{r})$; the imaginary part $B(\mathbf{r}^*)$ is odd, the transform of the odd part of $\rho(\mathbf{r})$.

If $F(\mathbf{r}^*)$ is the transform of $\rho(\mathbf{r})$, (14),

$$T\{\rho(\mathbf{r})\} = F(\mathbf{r}^*),$$

then

$$T\{\rho(-\mathbf{r})\} = F(-\mathbf{r}^*). \tag{39}$$

Since $\rho_1(\mathbf{r})$, $\rho_2(\mathbf{r})$, $A(\mathbf{r}^*)$, and $B(\mathbf{r}^*)$ are real, we have

$$F(-\mathbf{r}^*) = F^*(\mathbf{r}^*). \tag{40}$$

This is known as *Friedel's law* in x-ray crystallography.

When, in physical space, there exist two identical and parallel distributions of scattering matter, both the real and imaginary parts are zero along the same given surfaces. Therefore the modulus and the intensity functions must also be zero along these surfaces.

When the symmetry operation of inversion is applied to an electron-density distribution $\rho(\mathbf{r})$, the real part $A(\mathbf{r}^*)$ of the diffracted amplitude, its modulus $F(\mathbf{r}^*)$, and the intensity function $I(\mathbf{r}^*)$ remain unchanged because these functions have a center of symmetry in the origin of Fourier space. On the other hand, the imaginary part $B(\mathbf{r}^*)$ and the phase angle $\psi(\mathbf{r}^*)$ change only in sign on inversion in the origin. Thus we have

$$T\{\rho(\mathbf{r})\} = A(\mathbf{r}^*) + iB(\mathbf{r}^*) = F(\mathbf{r}^*), \tag{41}$$

$$T\{\rho(-\mathbf{r})\} = A(\mathbf{r}^*) - iB(\mathbf{r}^*) = F^*(\mathbf{r}^*),$$

or

$$T\{\rho(\mathbf{r})\} = |F(\mathbf{r}^*)|e^{i\psi},$$

$$T\{\rho(-\mathbf{r})\} = |F(\mathbf{r}^*)|e^{-i\psi}. \tag{42}$$

When the distribution of the scattering matter is centrosymmetric and the center of symmetry is the origin of $\mathbf{r}$, then $\rho(\mathbf{r})$ is an even function. The imaginary part of the asymmetric distribution cancels with the other asymmetric part, and the amplitude becomes real and even. Thus if

$$\rho(\mathbf{r}) = \rho(-\mathbf{r}),$$

we have

$$F(\mathbf{r}^*) = A(\mathbf{r}^*); \qquad B(\mathbf{r}^*) = 0. \tag{43}$$

The positive regions of $A(\mathbf{r}^*)$ have phase angles equal to zero, while the negative regions of $A(\mathbf{r}^*)$ correspond to a phase angle equal to π; values different from 0 or π can be disregarded. There exist surfaces of discontinuity in the phase angle corresponding to an abrupt change from zero to π. Also, $A(0) > 0$ and $\psi(\mathbf{r}^*) = \psi(-\mathbf{r}^*)$. In this case there exist surfaces where the modulus of the amplitude is equal to zero, coinciding with the surfaces where the real part vanishes. Consequently the intensity along these surfaces is zero. These surfaces correspond to a change of sign in the $A(\mathbf{r}^*)$ part, from positive to negative:

$$A(\mathbf{r}^*) \geqslant 0, \qquad \psi(\mathbf{r}^*) = 0,$$
$$A(\mathbf{r}^*) < 0, \qquad \psi(\mathbf{r}^*) = \pi. \tag{44}$$

The intensity function is again real, centrosymmetric, and positive or zero. In this case the surfaces of $I(\mathbf{r}^*) = 0$ coincide with the surfaces of $A(\mathbf{r}^*) = 0$.

If the electron-density distribution has a central plane as a plane of symmetry, its transform has a parallel central plane as a plane of symmetry (Wrinch, 1946). This means that the real part, imaginary part, the amplitude, and the phase all have this symmetry plane. The intensity function also has the same symmetry plane.

If an electron-density distribution has an n-fold symmetry axis or an n-fold axis of rotatory inversion through its origin, its transform (comprising both the real and imaginary parts, or the amplitude and phase) has the same symmetry element with respect to the parallel line through its origin, and so has the intensity function. Hence when a rotation or rotatory inversion is applied to a given electron density, an identical operation takes place in the transform.

If two density distributions $\rho_1(\mathbf{r})$ and $\rho_2(\mathbf{r})$ satisfy

$$\rho_2(\mathbf{r} + \mathbf{t}) = \rho_1(\mathbf{r}), \tag{45}$$

i.e., $\rho_2(\mathbf{r})$ corresponds to $\rho_1(\mathbf{r})$ translated by a vector $\mathbf{t}$, the transform of $\rho_2(\mathbf{r})$ is related to $\rho_1(\mathbf{r})$ by

$$F_2(\mathbf{r}^*) = F_1(\mathbf{r}^*)\exp(2\pi i\, \mathbf{r}^* \cdot \mathbf{t}). \tag{46}$$

It follows that translation by $\mathbf{t}$ in physical space corresponds to multiplication by $\exp(2\pi i\, \mathbf{r}^* \cdot \mathbf{t})$ in Fourier space.

The Q function

To calculate $\rho(\mathbf{r})$ from (16) we need to know $F(\mathbf{r}^*)$. The diffraction experiment, however, does not provide $F(\mathbf{r}^*)$, but only the intensity function $I(\mathbf{r}^*)$, whose square root is $|F(\mathbf{r}^*)|$. Therefore the information gathered directly from diffraction experiments does not contain all the necessary data to calculate directly the electron-density distribution.

Now, the convolution theorem in Fourier-transformation theory states that the Fourier transform of the product of two functions is the convolution of their Fourier transforms. After applying this theorem to (11), and then using (14), (39), and (40), it follows that

$$T^{-1}\{I(\mathbf{r}^*)\} = \rho(\mathbf{r}) * \rho(-\mathbf{r}). \tag{47}$$

(The symbol $*$ is discussed in the next paragraph.)
This is the only function of the electron density that can be obtained from the intensity function.

The mathematical operation called convolution or folding product (symbol $*$) of two functions $g_1(\mathbf{r})$ and $g_2(\mathbf{r})$ of a given space is defined (Doetsch, 1961) as

$$g_1(\mathbf{r}) * g_2(\mathbf{r}) = \int g_1(\mathbf{r}') \cdot g_2(\mathbf{r}-\mathbf{r}')\, dv'. \tag{48}$$

Both sides of (48) obviously belong to the same space. In this integral $\mathbf{r}'$ is to be varied throughout the entire space, and $\mathbf{r}$ appears as a parameter. The integrand is the product of one function by the second function translated and inverted at the origin. The symbol looks like a product, and in fact the convolution behaves like a product. It is commutative, that is,

$$g_1(\mathbf{r}) * g_2(\mathbf{r}) = g_2(\mathbf{r}) * g_1(\mathbf{r}), \tag{49}$$

or

$$\int g_1(\mathbf{r}') \cdot g_2(\mathbf{r}-\mathbf{r}')\, dv' = \int g_2(\mathbf{r}') \cdot g_1(\mathbf{r}-\mathbf{r}')\, dv'. \tag{50}$$

It is also associative,

$$[g_1(\mathbf{r}) * g_2(\mathbf{r})] * g_3(\mathbf{r}) = g_1(\mathbf{r}) * [g_2(\mathbf{r}) * g_3(\mathbf{r})], \tag{51}$$

so that the convolution of several functions is independent of the order in which the convolution is calculated.

When the two functions g_1 and g_2 are identical, the convolution is called a self-convolution (Buerger, 1962),

$$g(\mathbf{r}) * g(\mathbf{r}) = \int g(\mathbf{r}') \cdot g(\mathbf{r}-\mathbf{r}')\, dv' \tag{52}$$

If the integrand of (48) is the product of one function by a second function translated (but not inverted) with respect to the origin, i.e.,

$$g_3(\mathbf{r}) = \int g_1(\mathbf{r}') \cdot g_2(\mathbf{r}+\mathbf{r}') \, dv', \tag{53}$$

this function is not equal to (48). For, substituting in (53) the variable of integration $\mathbf{r}'$ by $-\mathbf{r}'$, we have

$$g_3(\mathbf{r}) = \int g_1(-\mathbf{r}') \cdot g_2(\mathbf{r}-\mathbf{r}') \, dv'. \tag{54}$$

Integral (54) is the convolution of two functions of which one has first been inverted

$$g_1(-\mathbf{r}) * g_2(\mathbf{r}) = \int g_1(\mathbf{r}') \cdot g_2(\mathbf{r}+\mathbf{r}') \, dv' \tag{55}$$

Buerger (1962) calls this integral an image function, the image of g_1 in g_2.

When the two functions $g_1(\mathbf{r})$ and $g_2(\mathbf{r})$ are identical, i.e., $g_1(\mathbf{r}) = g(\mathbf{r})$, $g_2(\mathbf{r}) = g(\mathbf{r})$, (55) becomes

$$g(\mathbf{r}) * g(-\mathbf{r}) = \int g(\mathbf{r}') \cdot g(\mathbf{r}+\mathbf{r}') \, dv'. \tag{56}$$

This function is called the self-image by Buerger (1962), or convolution square or Q function by Hosemann and Bagchi (1962). This function is of great importance in diffraction theory because, according to (47), the inverse transform of the intensity function yields the self-image of the density function. We shall write

$$Q(\mathbf{r}) = \rho(\mathbf{r}) * \rho(-\mathbf{r}). \tag{57}$$

This function has the striking property of atomicity. Comparison of (55) and (56) shows that

$$Q(\mathbf{r}) = Q(-\mathbf{r}), \tag{58}$$

i.e., the Q function is always centrosymmetric with respect to the origin, $\mathbf{r} = 0$. Another interesting property of the Q function is that it is unaffected by a parallel displacement of $\rho(\mathbf{r})$ by any arbitrary vector $\mathbf{a}$;

$$\rho'(\mathbf{r}) = \rho(\mathbf{r}-\mathbf{a}),$$
$$Q'(\mathbf{r}) = Q(\mathbf{r}) \tag{59}$$

Moreover, the Q function is also unaffected by the change of sign of the ρ function:

$$Q(\mathbf{r}) = \rho(\mathbf{r}) * \rho(-\mathbf{r}) = \rho(-\mathbf{r}) * \rho(\mathbf{r}). \tag{60}$$

The great interest of the Q function in diffraction phenomena is that it is related to the electron-density function $\rho(\mathbf{r})$ by (57). It is defined in physical space; for an ideal crystal it degenerates into the Patterson function, which is much used in crystal-structure analysis. From (47) and (57) it follows that

$$Q(\mathbf{r}) = T^{-1}\{I(\mathbf{r}^*)\}. \tag{61}$$

The operation which would lead us to $\rho(\mathbf{r})$ in terms of $Q(\mathbf{r})$ is called by Hosemann and Bagchi (1962) the convolution square root, and is represented by

$$\rho(\mathbf{r}) = \sqrt{\widetilde{Q(\mathbf{r})}}. \tag{62}$$

The greater part of the fine structure of the function $Q(\mathbf{r})$ is lost in the case of the ideal crystal, but we shall see how a detailed study of the function Q can yield important information in the study of real crystals, particularly when there is thermal disorder.

Repeated Fourier transformations

The Fourier integral theorem applied to the Fourier mates $\rho(\mathbf{r})$ and $F(\mathbf{r}^*)$ states that if these functions are piece-wise continuous and its volume integral is absolutely convergent, then

$$\rho(\mathbf{r}) = \int_{v^*} \exp(2\pi i \mathbf{r} \cdot \mathbf{r}^*) \, dv^* \int_v \rho(\mathbf{r}') \exp(-2\pi i \mathbf{r} \cdot \mathbf{r}^*) \, dv, \tag{63}$$

or

$$\rho(\mathbf{r}) = \int_{v^*} \int_v \rho(\mathbf{r}') \exp[-2\pi i (\mathbf{r} - \mathbf{r}') \cdot \mathbf{r}^*] \, dv \, dv^*, \tag{64}$$

and

$$F(\mathbf{r}^*) = \int_v \int_{v^*} F(\mathbf{r}'^*) \exp[2\pi i \mathbf{r} \cdot (\mathbf{r}^* - \mathbf{r}'^*)] \, dv^* \, dv, \tag{65}$$

i.e., the direct and inverse transformations applied in either order to either $\rho(\mathbf{r})$ or $F(\mathbf{r}^*)$ leave any of these functions unchanged. Hence a function can be found by applying the T^{-1} transformation to its transform T. Equations (64) and (65) can be written as

$$\rho(\mathbf{r}) = T^{-1}\{T\{\rho(\mathbf{r}')\}\} \tag{66}$$

$$F(\mathbf{r}^*) = T\{T^{-1}\{F(\mathbf{r}'^*)\}\}. \tag{67}$$

In a similar way application of the direct or inverse transformation twice in succession to either $\rho(\mathbf{r})$ or $F(\mathbf{r}^*)$ merely inverts any of these functions in the origin

$$\rho(-\mathbf{r}) = T\{T\{\rho(\mathbf{r}')\}\} \tag{68}$$

$$F(-\mathbf{r}^*) = T^{-1}\{T^{-1}\{F(\mathbf{r}^*')\}\}. \tag{69}$$

We then see that the direct or the inverse transformation, applied twice, lead to a function that differs from the original one only by an inversion in the origin.

Because $Q(\mathbf{r})$ and $I(\mathbf{r}^*)$ are also a pair of Fourier transforms, we can apply the Fourier integral theorem to those mates if these functions satisfy the conditions stated in the Fourier integral theorem and write

$$Q(\mathbf{r}) = T^{-1}\{T\{Q(\mathbf{r}')\}\} \tag{70}$$

$$I(\mathbf{r}^*) = T\{T^{-1}\{I(\mathbf{r}'^*)\}\}, \tag{71}$$

Since both $Q(\mathbf{r})$ and $I(\mathbf{r}^*)$ are centrosymmetric, application of either TT or $T^{-1}T^{-1}$ to the Q and intensity functions will give the same result as (66) and (67), respectively.

Projections and sections of the transforms $\rho(\mathbf{r})$ and $F(\mathbf{r}^*)$

Let us consider a section of the function $F(\mathbf{r}^*)$ by a plane passing through the origin of Fourier space, for example, the main plane defined by $\mathbf{a}^*$ and $\mathbf{b}^*$, or the $hk0$ plane. We then have

$$F(hk0) = v \int \int \int \rho(xyz) \exp(-2\pi i(hx+ky)) \, dx \, dy \, dz. \tag{72}$$

We can write

$$F(hk0) = A_0 \int \int \left[\int \rho(xyz) \, dz \right] \exp(-2\pi i(hx+ky)) \, dx \, dy \tag{73}$$

where $A_0 = \mathbf{a}_0 \times \mathbf{b}_0$ is the unit area in the plane $xy0$. The function inside the brackets is the projection of the electron-density function along the z direction, and dz is the element of length in that direction. Obviously, such a function is the projection of the density function on a plane normal to the given direction. By definition of the reciprocal axes, the plane of projection is parallel to the $hk0$ plane. According to (72), $F(hk0)$ and $\int \rho(xyz) \, dz$ are a pair of Fourier transforms. In other words, the plane section of the diffracted amplitude function passing through the origin is the transform of the electron-density function projected on a plane parallel to that section, i.e.,

$$F(hk0) = T\{\text{proj}_{\parallel c}\, \rho(xyz)\} \tag{74}$$

and

$$\text{proj}_{\parallel c}\, \rho(xyz) = T^{-1}\{F(hk0)\}. \tag{75}$$

Conversely, a plane section of the electron density passing through the origin

$$\rho(xy0) = A_0^* \int \int \left[\int F(hkl)\, dl \right] \exp\left(2\pi i(hx + ky)\right) dh\, dk \tag{76}$$

is the Fourier transform of the diffracted amplitude function projected on a plane passing through the origin and parallel to that section, i.e.,

$$\rho(xy0) = T\{\text{proj}_{\parallel c} \cdot F(hkl)\}. \tag{77}$$

The above relations lead to very important results. To calculate a section of the density function, information about the whole diffraction space is needed. However to calculate a two-dimensional projection of the density function, knowledge of a section of the diffraction space alone is needed. Conversely, once the projection of the density function is known, the corresponding section of the diffraction space can be calculated. In the last two cases the information required is reduced to a two-dimensional problem. This allows us to study x-ray diffraction by optical analogues that use two-dimensional models and produce two-dimensional results.

Since $Q(\mathbf{r})$ and $I(\mathbf{r}^*)$ are also a pair of Fourier transforms, the above results are also valid for these mates,

$$I(hk0) = T\{\text{proj}_{\parallel c}\, Q(xyz)\} \tag{78}$$

and

$$Q(xy0) = T^{-1}\{\text{proj}_{\parallel c} \cdot I(hkl)\}. \tag{79}$$

The limiting sphere of diffraction

For a given x-ray wavelength, the region of reciprocal space accessible to observation lies inside a limiting sphere of radius $2/\lambda$. Thus the maximum value of the diffraction vector $\mathbf{r}^*$ is given by

$$|\mathbf{r}^*_{\max}| = 2/\lambda. \tag{80}$$

The bounding of the diffraction space by the limiting sphere is just an artificial limitation due to the experimental conditions, set by the selected wavelength λ. In fact we can extend the information gathered from the diffraction space by selecting a shorter wavelength. The functions $F'(\mathbf{r}^*)$ and $I'(\mathbf{r}^*)$, as limited by a finite λ, will be different than $F(\mathbf{r}^*)$ and $I(\mathbf{r}^*)$, which are not so limited, this difference being greater for longer wavelengths. This effect can be mathematically expressed by introducing the shape function of the limiting sphere.

A *shape function* (Ewald, 1940) is a function that has value unity everywhere within a given volume and is identically zero outside:

$$s(\mathbf{r}^*) = 1 \quad \text{for all values of } \mathbf{r}^* \text{ inside } v^*,$$

$$= 0 \quad \text{everywhere else.} \tag{81}$$

This function is properly called a shape function because it depends only on the exterior shape of the volume and not on the function defined inside. Its integrated value is equal to the volume

$$\int_{v^*} s(\mathbf{r}^*)\, dv^* = v^*. \tag{82}$$

We then have
$$F'(\mathbf{r}^*) = F(\mathbf{r}^*) \cdot s(\mathbf{r}^*), \tag{83}$$

and
$$I'(\mathbf{r}^*) = I(\mathbf{r}^*) \cdot s(\mathbf{r}^*). \tag{84}$$

Due to this limitation of the diffraction space, the electron density $\rho'(\mathbf{r})$ or the self-image $Q'(\mathbf{r})$ obtained by inverse transformation of $F'(\mathbf{r}^*)$ and $I'(\mathbf{r}^*)$, respectively, will be different from the true $\rho(\mathbf{r})$ and $Q(\mathbf{r})$ if the information outside the limiting sphere is not negligible. Application to (83) and (84) of the convolution theorem yields, respectively,

$$\rho'(\mathbf{r}) = T^{-1}\{F'(\mathbf{r}^*)\} = \rho(\mathbf{r}) * S(\mathbf{r}) \neq \rho(\mathbf{r}) \tag{85}$$

and
$$Q'(\mathbf{r}) = T^{-1}\{I'(\mathbf{r}^*)\} = Q(\mathbf{r}) * S(\mathbf{r}) \neq Q(\mathbf{r}), \tag{86}$$

where
$$S(\mathbf{r}) = T^{-1}\{s(\mathbf{r}^*)\} \tag{87}$$

is the inverse transform of the shape function, called the *shape amplitude*.

The shape function of the limiting sphere is defined by

$$s(\mathbf{r}^*) = 1 \quad \text{for} \quad |\mathbf{r}^*| \leqslant R$$
$$\phantom{s(\mathbf{r}^*)} = 0 \quad \text{for} \quad |\mathbf{r}^*| > R, \tag{88}$$

where R is given in Å^{-1} units. Its shape amplitude, defined in this case in physical space, also has spherical symmetry, and its radial distribution is given (Hosemann and Bagchi, 1962) by

$$S(|\mathbf{r}|) = \frac{4}{3}\pi R^3 \cdot 3\frac{\sin 2\pi(R|\mathbf{r}|) - 2\pi R|\mathbf{r}| \cos 2\pi(R|\mathbf{r}|)}{(2\pi R|\mathbf{r}|)^3}. \tag{89}$$

The function shows a principal maximum at $|\mathbf{r}| = 0$ and subsidiary maxima of weights decreasing with $1/|\mathbf{r}|^2$, that appear at

$$|\mathbf{r}| = \frac{n + \frac{1}{2}}{R} \tag{90}$$

i.e., the distances between successive maxima are inversely proportional to the radius.

In practice convolution of the shape amplitude with either $\rho(\mathbf{r})$ or $Q(\mathbf{r})$ translates $s(\mathbf{r})$ to each maximum of these functions. The effect shown in $\rho(\mathbf{r})$ or $Q(\mathbf{r})$ is a series of ripples surrounding each main maximum. According to (90), these surrounding ripples are closer to each center of the maximum the shorter the wavelength of the experiment (Fig. 6).

For CuKα x-radiation, where $\lambda = 1.54\,\text{Å}$, the limiting sphere has a radius of $1.29\,\text{Å}^{-1}$ so that the maximum value of the diffraction vector is

$$|\mathbf{r}_{max}^*| = 1.29\,\text{Å}^{-1} \qquad (\lambda = 1.54\,\text{Å}).$$

The resolving power for this radiation is $0.38\,\text{Å}$. For MoKα x-radiation, we have

$$|\mathbf{r}_{max}^*| = 2.81\,\text{Å}^{-1} \qquad (\lambda = 0.71\,\text{Å}),$$

with a resolving power of $0.195\,\text{Å}$. In x-ray diffraction experiments, the entire range of the glancing angle θ from 0 to 90° can, in principle, be recorded because the Ewald sphere has a significant curvature inside the volume under observation.

The equivalent wavelength band of the thermal neutrons used in neutron-diffraction experiments is of the same order of magnitude

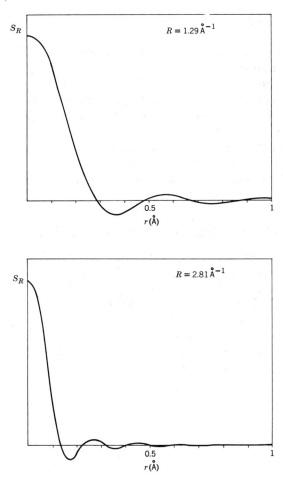

Fig. 6. Shape function of the limiting sphere.

as the characteristic x-ray radiation from Cu. Therefore the limiting sphere for neutron diffraction corresponds to a radius of about 1.3 Å^{-1}, and the diffraction sphere has again a significant curvature inside the volume of observation.

   In electron diffraction, the value of the wavelength for an accelerating potential of 50 kv is about $\lambda_{el} = 0.05 \text{ Å}$, i.e., about 30 times smaller than the wavelength of the characteristic x-radiation of Cu. The above value would, in principle, correspond to a $|r^*_{max}|$ of about 40 Å^{-1}. The electron-diffraction experiments with crystals, however, show no appreciable intensity for glancing angles θ larger than $3°$, in which case the reciprocal vector has a modulus, which, in practice, does not exceed about $1.5\ \text{Å}^{-1}$. This means that, for the accessible volume in electron-diffraction experiments, the curvature of the diffracting sphere is practically planar (Fig. 7).

A similar situation occurs in the diffraction of ordinary light by given transparencies. The wavelength of the yellow D line of Na is $5890\ \text{Å}$. If a diffracting mask is built of transparent disks at distances apart of the order of $10^{-1}\ \text{mm}$, the wavelength is about 10^3 times smaller than the distances in the grating. In this case the curvature of the diffracting sphere inside the region of observation is practically planar, and the Fraunhofer pattern corresponds to a plane in reciprocal space passing through the origin.

Electron density and Q function of an atom

From x-ray diffraction experiments it is known that an atom can be described in terms of its electron-density distribution. The wave mechanics leads to the same picture of the atom, in such a way that an individual electron can be described as a stationary, time-averaged distribution of the electron through the space. In the case of a multi-electron atom the electron-density can be described as the sum of the individual time-averaged distributions of the different electrons. The resulting electron density of the free atom extends to infinity.

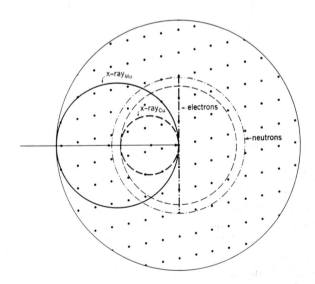

Fig. 7.   Accessible regions of reciprocal space for different experimental conditions.

We can always speak of the atom, however, as having a definite size if we take into account that the electrons are at finite distances from the nucleus of the atom most of the time. For instance, we can refer to the mean radius of the outer electron orbital state and we can define a boundary at which the electron cloud should vanish. That the atoms have a definite size is an experimental fact deduced from crystal-structure determination. In ionic and molecular crystals it is found, for instance, that the electron density of an atom attains very small values (less than $0.2\, e/\text{Å}^3$) at short distances, of the order of 1.5Å, of the nucleus. The electron density of the free atom has spherical symmetry, i.e., it depends only on the modulus of **r**. In this case it can be analytically represented by a sum of spherically symmetric Gaussian functions,

$$\rho(r) = \sum_{s=1}^{S} \rho_s(r) = \sum_{s=1}^{S} G_s \exp\left[-g_s^2 r^2\right], \tag{91}$$

where G_s and g_s are the parameters of the Gaussian. Each Gaussian represents the electron density of an electron shell of the atom, and the summation (91) is extended over its S shells. In the case of the carbon atom, the K and L shells are the only components (Fig. 8i), and four Gaussian parameters G_K, g_K, G_L, and g_L, describe the total electron density. It is seen in Fig. 8i that the contribution of the L shell to the total electron density is very small. The electron density is a very poor representation when the components of the different shells are sought.

A very meaningful representation of the atomic functions is the radial distribution of the electron density

$$U(r) = \sum_{s=1}^{S} U_s(r) = 4\pi r^2 \sum_{s=1}^{S} \rho_s(r), \tag{92}$$

where $U_s(r)$ is the radial distribution of the density of the electron shell s. Figure 8ii represents the radial distribution of the electron density of an atom of carbon for the two electrons of the $K(1s)$ shell and for the four electrons of the $L(2s2p)$ shell, as well as their sum.

The maximum of $U_K(r)$ appears at about 0.15 Å, and that of $U_L(r)$ at about 0.75 Å. Above 0.40 Å the contribution of the K shell to the total radial distribution is negligible, and the total distribution is always practically negligible for $r > 2\text{Å}$. The radial distribution representation of the electron density is very meaningful because it contains ready information on the distribution of the electrons into shells for a given atom.

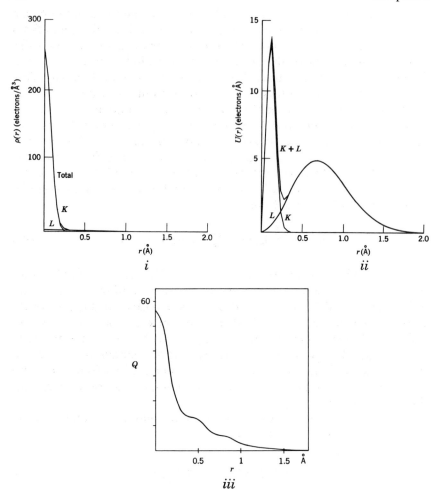

Fig. 8. Carbon atom. (*i*) Shell components of the electron density; (*ii*) shell components of the radial distribution of the electron density; (*iii*) Q-function.

The spherical symmetry of the free atom is lost when bonded to others with covalent bonds. However, the alteration of the spherical symmetry of the atom is very small, and we can still speak about spherical atoms as a first approximation.

The Q function of the electron density of an atom is merely the self-image of the atomic density, given by

$$Q_{at}(\mathbf{r}) = \rho_{at}(\mathbf{r}) * \rho_{at}(-\mathbf{r}).\tag{93}$$

This is also a spherically symmetric function and for practical purposes is finite (Fig. 8iii).

The coherent diffraction by an atom

The x-ray waves are scattered by the electrons. The simplest case is the scattering by a free electron. The scattered intensity is given by the Thomson formula

$$I_e = r_e^2 I_0 \frac{1 + \cos^2 2\theta}{2}, \tag{94}$$

where I_0 is the intensity of the incident x-ray beam, r_e the classical radius of the electron, and θ the glancing angle. In the model that we have described, instead of independent electrons we have an electron cloud. The scattering of x-rays by an isolated atom is proportional to Z, the atomic number, and it is determined by the Fourier transform of this electron-density cloud:

$$f_X(\mathbf{r}^*) = \int_v \rho_{at}(\mathbf{r}) \exp\left(-2\pi i \mathbf{r} \cdot \mathbf{r}^*\right) dv. \tag{95}$$

If the atomic electron density is assumed to have spherical symmetry, and if $\rho(r)$ is the atomic density distribution, the coherent amplitude diffracted by the atom can be expressed in spherical coordinates as

$$f_X(r^*) = 4\pi \int_0^\infty \rho(r) r^2 \frac{\sin 2\pi r \cdot r^*}{2\pi r \cdot r^*} dr, \tag{96}$$

where $f_X(r^*)$ is known as the *atomic scattering factor* for x-rays; it corresponds to the ratio of the amplitude scattered by an atom and by a free electron under the same conditions. The function $f_X(\mathbf{r}^*)$, or the Fourier transform of the atomic electron density, is centered at the origin of reciprocal space and has spherical symmetry, so that it can also be represented radially (Fig. 9). As can be seen, we have a Gaussian-like curve that decreases with increasing magnitude of the reciprocal vector, and the ordinate at the origin coincides with the atomic number Z. When $|\mathbf{r}^*| = 0$, all the electrons of the atom scatter in phase.

We have seen that the electron density of an atom can analytically be expressed by the Gaussian functions describing its electron-shell components. Since the Fourier transform of a Gaussian of width g is again a Gaussian, of width $1/\pi g$ (Ewald, 1938), the atomic scattering

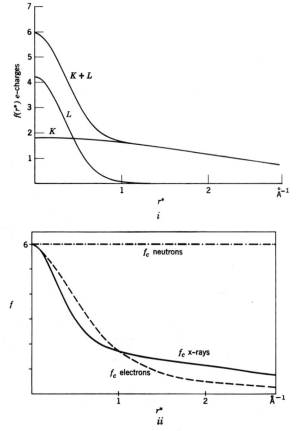

Fig. 9. Carbon atom. (*i*) Shell components of the x-ray scattering; (*ii*) comparison of the x-ray, electron, and neutron scattering factors.

factor of a Gaussian atom can also be written as a sum of the S Gaussian terms

$$f(r^*) = \sum_{s=1}^{S} G'_s \exp(-\pi^2 g'^2_s r^{*2}), \tag{97}$$

where $G'_s = G_s(\pi g_s^2)^{3/2}$ and $g'_s = 1/g_s^2$. In the case of the carbon atom, the x-ray atomic scattering factor as given in the International Tables of Crystallography (1952) can be nicely approximated by two Gaussians, of constants $G'_K = 1.80$ *e* charges, $g'_K = 0.108$ Å units, and $G'_L = 4.20$ *e* charges, $g'_L = 0.680$ Å units, respectively (Fig. 9*i*). It can be seen that the *L*-shell scattering factor practically vanishes for $r^* > 1$ Å^{-1}, and that the *K*-shell scattering factor is the only contribution at high values of the reciprocal vector.

On the other hand, the scattering of electrons by an isolated atom is determined by the Fourier transform of the potential $\psi(\mathbf{r})$ of the atom, and it is given (Vainshtein, 1964) by

$$f_{el}(\mathbf{r}^*) = K \int_0^\infty \psi_{at}(\mathbf{r}) \exp(-2\pi i \mathbf{r} \cdot \mathbf{r}^*) \, dv, \tag{98}$$

where $K = 2\pi m e/h^2$, in which m and e are the mass and electron charge, and h is Planck's constant. The potential $\psi(\mathbf{r})$ is related to the electron-density function $\rho(\mathbf{r})$ by

$$\psi(\mathbf{r}) \sim \rho^{2/3}(\mathbf{r}).$$

Hence $\psi(\mathbf{r})$ is more diffuse than the electron-density distribution. The maxima of the $\rho(\mathbf{r})$ function are sharper than those of the $\psi(\mathbf{r})$ function, but the ratio between the heights of the ψ peaks is less than between the ρ peaks.

Expression (98) is analogous to (95) for x-ray diffraction, where the factor K is omitted, since f_X is expressed in electron units, i.e., relative to scattering by the Thomson electron. If the atom is assumed to have spherical symmetry, (98) can be expressed in terms of spherical coordinates, and we have

$$f_{el}(r^*) = 4\pi K \int_0^\infty \psi(r) r^2 \frac{\sin 2\pi r \cdot r^*}{2\pi r \cdot r^*} \, dr. \tag{99}$$

The atomic scattering factor for electrons and for x-rays may be calculated from equations (95) and (98), respectively, if the potentials and electron distributions of the corresponding atoms are known. Conversely, once the corresponding atomic scattering factors are known, the atomic electron-densities or the atomic potentials can be obtained through an inverse Fourier transformation,

$$\rho_{at}(\mathbf{r}) = T^{-1}\{f_X(\mathbf{r}^*)\} \tag{100}$$

$$\psi_{at}(\mathbf{r}) = T^{-1}\{f_{el}(\mathbf{r}^*)\}. \tag{101}$$

The atomic scattering factors for x-rays fall off more slowly with the modulus of the reciprocal vector than the f_{el} curves (Fig. 9).

The atomic scattering functions of electrons and x-rays obviously depend on the atomic number Z. On the average, the atomic scattering for x-rays is given by

$$f_X \sim Z^\alpha, \tag{102}$$

where α is approximately equal to unity (roughly 1.2). In the case of electron diffraction

$$f_{el} \sim Z^{1/3}. \tag{103}$$

In the case of neutron scattering the fundamental scattering matter in most atoms is the nucleus and not the electron or the potential density function, except for magnetic materials where the electron scattering is also appreciable. Since neutron scattering is dependent on the nucleus, it shows no clear relation with Z. Within a factor of two or three, most atoms scatter neutrons equally well, in contrast with the rapid increase of the x-ray scattering amplitude with atomic number. For example, the neutron scattering amplitude of a lead atom is only about 50 per cent greater than that of a carbon atom, in contrast with a ratio of about 20:1 for the x-ray scattering amplitude of the two atoms (Bacon, 1962). On the other hand, the dimensions of the nucleus, unlike those of the cloud of extranuclear electrons, are small in comparison with the wavelength of 1 Å. Consequently the atomic scattering factor for nuclear neutron diffraction shows no variation with the reciprocal vector. Another distinctive feature is that atomic scattering by neutrons can have positive or negative amplitudes, in contrast with the always positive amplitudes in the cases of x-ray and electron diffraction by an atom.

In Fig. 9*ii* the atomic scattering factors of x-rays, electrons, and neutrons corresponding to the carbon atom are represented radially. It is seen that the decreasing of f with the modulus of the reciprocal vector is higher for electrons than for x-rays. In the case of neutrons no variation is detected.

In principle the scattering theory is the same for all radiations. The peculiarities of each case determine the most suitable radiation for specific cases. The most universal method, however, is x-ray diffraction, and in this book we shall refer primarily to it. In order to visualize the diffraction phenomenon of x-rays by atoms, extensive use of diffraction of light by disks simulating atoms will be made throughout this book, in which case we restrict the problem to a two-dimensional one.

The Q function or self-image of a disk

Since atoms in a two-dimensional structure can be easily represented in a drawing by disks, it is important to know the self-image or Q function of a disk-like atom. A disk of radius R can be represented mathematically in terms of a shape function

$$\rho_{\text{disk}}(\mathbf{r}) \quad \begin{aligned} &= 1 \quad \text{for } |\mathbf{r}| \leqslant R \\ &= 0 \quad \text{for } |\mathbf{r}| > R, \end{aligned} \qquad (104)$$

where **r** is a vector in the plane of the disk. Since the disk is centro-symmetric, the self-image coincides with the self-convolution. It has circular symmetry, and is given by

$$Q_{disk}(\mathbf{r}) = \begin{cases} 2R^2\left[\cos^{-1}\dfrac{|\mathbf{r}|}{2R} - \dfrac{|\mathbf{r}|}{2R}\sqrt{1 - \left(\dfrac{|\mathbf{r}|}{2R}\right)^2}\right] & \text{for } |\mathbf{r}| < 2R \\[2mm] 0 & \text{for } |\mathbf{r}| > 2R. \end{cases} \tag{105}$$

Figure 10 gives the radial distributions of a disk-like atom and of its Q function.

For two-dimensional functions the convolutions and image functions can be obtained optically with the aid of a device called a folding machine or Q integrator. If the functions to be convolved are supposed to correspond to electron-density functions $\rho_1(\mathbf{r})$ and $\rho_2(\mathbf{r})$, the atoms of the structure can be represented in a drawing by disks, and the microfilms (negatives) of these two drawings will have holes at the positions of each atom, the other portions of the negative being opaque to light. The negatives should have transparencies $T_1(\mathbf{r})$ and $T_2(\mathbf{r})$ proportional to $\rho_1(\mathbf{r})$ and $\rho_2(\mathbf{r})$, respectively. The two negatives

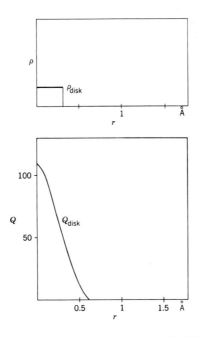

Fig. 10.   Radial density and Q functions of a disk atom.

are placed (Fig. 11) parallel to one another, and behind a ground-glass plate that diffuses ordinary light. The light rays parallel to the optical axis of the apparatus pass through the two microfilms at the same position $\mathbf{r'}$, and the light rays that are inclined to the optical axis pass through the first microfilm at $\mathbf{r'}$ and through the second one at $\mathbf{r'} - \mathbf{r}$, $\mathbf{r}$ being constant for all parallel individual rays. A lens located after the second microfilm concentrates the rays on its focal plane, where a receiving screen or a photographic film can be placed to obtain either the optical convolution product or image functions. The intensity $I(\mathbf{r})$ at each point on the focal plane is given by

$$I(\mathbf{r}) = \int T_1(\mathbf{r'}) \cdot T_2(\mathbf{r'} - \mathbf{r}) \, dv_{r'}. \qquad (106)$$

We obtain the self-image or Q function (Fig. 12i) any time we use two identical negatives in the same orientation, $T_1(\mathbf{r'}) = T_2(\mathbf{r'})$ (Fig. 11i). If the two transparencies are different, we obtain the image function.

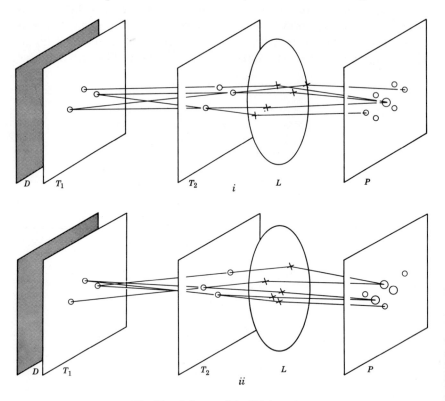

Fig. 11.   Scheme of the Q integrator.

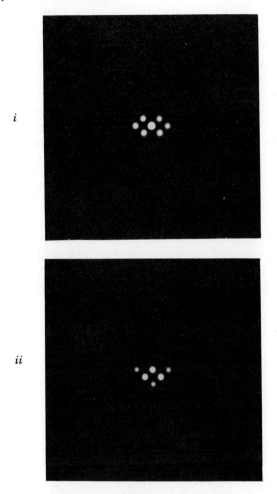

Fig. 12. Optical self-image and self-convolution of a given structure of transparent disks.

When two identical negatives are placed in a centrosymmetric positions, i.e., $T_2(\mathbf{r}') = T_1(-\mathbf{r}')$ (Fig. 11ii), we obtain the self-convolution (Fig. 12ii). If the two transparencies are different, we obtain the convolution product.

Fraunhofer diffraction by a disk: Airy rings

In the phenomenon of Fraunhofer diffraction the light source and the observer are at infinity. The Fraunhofer diffraction pattern, produced when a beam of monochromatic light is incident on a circular aperture whose plane is perpendicular to the wave front, is the well-known Airy pattern (Fig. 13). A circular aperture centered at the origin of physical space can be described as a disk function, $\rho_{\text{disk}}(\mathbf{r})$, which has the value d in the interior of a circle of radius R and is zero outside the disk. The radial distribution of the "electron"-density function of a disk was given in Fig. 10. The amplitude of the Fraunhofer diffraction by a disk is also a radially symmetrical function and therefore is expressed as a function of distance from the origin. This radial distribution is given by Born and Wolf (1959) as

$$F(r^*) = C\pi R^2 \frac{2J_1(kRw)}{kRw}, \tag{107}$$

where C is a constant depending on the position of the light source and on the position of the observer, $k = 2\pi/\lambda$, and $w = 2\sin\theta$. This function is actually the section of the three-dimensional transform of the aperture in a plane perpendicular to its axis, and is the same for all such sections.

The radial distribution of the intensity function is expressed by

$$I(r^*) = I_0\left[\frac{2J_1(kRw)}{(kRw)}\right]^2 \tag{108}$$

where $I_0 = C^2(\pi R^2)^2$. This formula was first derived by Airy (1835).

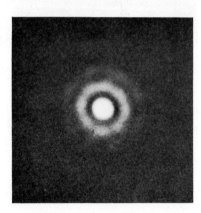

Fig. 13.   Airy pattern, or Fraunhofer diffraction by a disk.

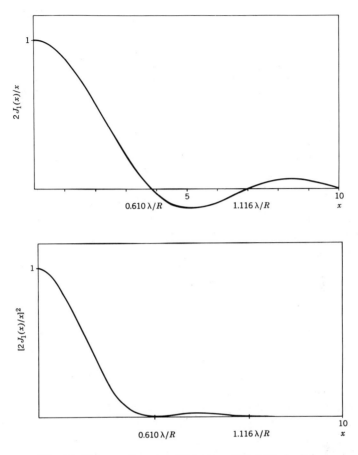

Fig. 14. Universal functions $2J_1(x)/x$ and $[2J_1(x)]^2$ of a disk.

The amplitude and intensity distribution near the line that is normal to the plate at its center are described by the functions (Fig. 14)

$$y = \frac{2J_1(x)}{x} \quad \text{and} \quad y^2 = \left[\frac{2J_1(x)}{x}\right]^2 \tag{109}$$

where

$$x = 2\pi R\, 2\frac{\sin\theta}{\lambda}. \tag{110}$$

The principal maximum of y and y^2 occurs when $y = 1$, at $x = 0$, and as x increases, y fluctuates from positive to negative with gradually

Table 1   The first few maxima and minima of the functions $2J_1(x)/x$
and $[2J_1(x)/x]^2$

x	$2J_1(x)/x$,	Type	$[2J_1(x)/x]^2$,	Type
0	1	maxima	1	maxima
$1.220\,\pi = 3.832$	0	from + to −	0	minima
$1.635\,\pi = 5.136$	−0.1320	minima	0.0175	maxima
$2.233\,\pi = 7.016$	0	from − to +	0	minima
$2.679\,\pi = 8.417$	0.0643	maxima	0.0042	maxima
$3.238\,\pi = 10.174$	0	from + to −	0	minima
$3.699\,\pi = 11.620$	−0.0031	minima	0.0016	maxima

decreasing amplitude (Table 1). The intensity y^2 is zero (minimum) for values of x satisfying $J_1(x) = 0$. The minima are not strictly equidistant (Table 2). The secondary maxima occur at values of x satisfying equation

$$\frac{d}{dx}\left(\frac{J_1(x)}{x}\right) = 0.$$

With increasing x the separation between two successive minima or two successive maxima approaches the value π.

   The Fraunhofer diffraction pattern of a circular aperture thus consists of a bright spot centered on the geometrical image of the source, surrounded by concentric rings, alternately bright and dark (the Airy rings). The intensity of the bright rings decreases rapidly with their radius, and even the first is so small that it is not generally seen unless the central area appear to be overexposed (Fig. 13). Rayleigh (1881) calculated that more than 90 per cent of the light is found within the circle bounded by the second dark ring.

   The radii of the dark rings can easily be obtained in terms of $2\sin\theta$. From Table 2, by substituting x for 3.832, 7.016, and 10.174, one obtains from (110)

$$(2\sin\theta)_{1st} = 0.610\frac{\lambda}{R}, \;(2\sin\theta)_{2nd} = 1.116\frac{\lambda}{R}, \;(2\sin\theta)_{3rd} = 1.619\frac{\lambda}{R}, \dots$$

$$(111)$$

respectively. The separation between two consecutive rings assymtotically approaches $\lambda/2R$. The effective size of the diffraction image is inversely proportional to the diameter of the disk.

   In order to represent, in Fourier space, both the amplitude diffracted by a disk and its intensity function in terms of the reciprocal vector

Table 2 Values of $2J_1(x)/x$ for $0 \leqslant x \leqslant 10.2$

x	$2J_1(x)/x$	x	$2J_1(x)/x$	x	$2J_1(x)/x$
0.0	1.0000	3.8	.0067	7.0	−.0013
0.1	.9980				
0.2	.9950	3.832	zero	7.016	zero
0.3	.9886				
0.4	.9800	3.9	−.0139	7.1	.0070
0.5	.9692	4.0	−.0330	7.2	.0150
0.6	.9556	4.1	−.0503	7.3	.0226
0.7	.9400	4.2	−.0660	7.4	.0296
0.8	.9220	4.3	−.0799	7.5	.0360
0.9	.9020	4.4	−.0921	7.6	.0418
1.0	.8802	4.5	−.1027	7.7	.0470
1.1	.8561	4.6	−.1115	7.8	.0516
1.2	.8305	4.7	−.1187	7.9	.0554
1.3	.8030	4.8	−.1243	8.0	.0586
1.4	.7741	4.9	−.1284	8.1	.0611
1.5	.7438	5.0	−.1310	8.2	.0629
1.6	.7123	5.1	−.1321	8.3	.0640
1.7	.6797			8.4	.0644
1.8	.6461	5.136	min		
1.9	.6117			8.417	max
2.0	.5767	5.2	−.1320		
2.1	.5412	5.3	−.1305	8.5	.0642
2.2	.5054	5.4	−.1278	8.6	.0634
2.3	.4694	5.5	−.1241	8.7	.0620
2.4	.4335	5.6	−.1193	8.8	.0600
2.5	.3976	5.7	−.1137	8.9	.0575
2.6	.3621	5.8	−.1072	9.0	.0545
2.7	.3271	5.9	−.1000	9.1	.0510
2.8	.2926	6.0	−.0922	9.2	.0472
2.9	.2588	6.1	−.0839	9.3	.0430
3.0	.2260	6.2	−.0751	9.4	.0386
3.1	.1941	6.3	−.0660	9.5	.0339
3.2	.1633	6.4	−.0567	9.6	.0290
3.3	.1337	6.5	−.0473	9.7	.0240
3.4	.1054	6.6	−.0378	9.8	.0189
3.5	.0785	6.7	−.0284	9.9	.0138
3.6	.0530	6.8	−.0191	10.0	.0087
3.7	.0290	6.9	−.0101	10.1	.0035
				10.174	zero
				10.2	.0032

$\mathbf{r^*}$ for a given radius R of the disk, let us write (107) and (108) as follows:

$$f_R(\mathbf{r^*}) = C\pi R^2 \frac{2J_1(2\pi R|\mathbf{r^*}|)}{2\pi R|\mathbf{r^*}|}, \tag{112}$$

and

$$I_R(\mathbf{r^*}) = C^2(\pi R^2)^2 \left[\frac{2J_1(2\pi R|\mathbf{r^*}|)}{2\pi R|\mathbf{r^*}|}\right]^2. \tag{113}$$

Since J_1 is a function not only of the reciprocal vector but of R, the positions of the maxima and minima of the diffraction rings depend

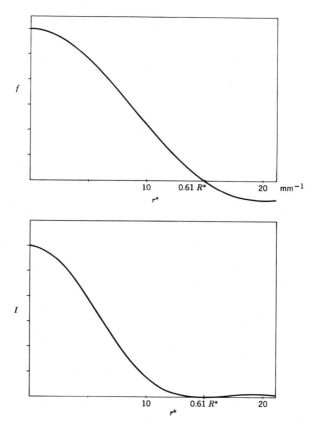

Fig. 15. Amplitude and intensity functions of the Fraunhofer diffraction of a disk of $R = 0.04$ mm.

on the size of the disk. In Fourier space the radii of the dark rings in reciprocal units $[L^{-1}]$ in terms of the reciprocal vector are given by

$$\begin{aligned}
|\mathbf{r}^*_{1st}| &= 0.610\, R^*, \\
|\mathbf{r}^*_{2nd}| &= 1.115\, R^*, \\
|\mathbf{r}^*_{3rd}| &= 1.519\, R^*
\end{aligned} \tag{114}$$

where $R^* = 1/R$. For a disk of an actual radius size of 0.04 mm, the first dark ring is defined by a radius of 15.25 mm^{-1} (Fig. 15). On the other hand, from (112) we learn that the first maximum of the diffracted amplitude, which is located at the origin of Fourier space, has a value proportional to the square of the radius of the disk:

$$f_R(0) = C\pi R^2. \tag{115}$$

Also from (113) it can be seen that at the origin of Fourier space the intensity diffracted by a disk is proportional to the square of the area of the disk.

Optical simulation of x-ray diffraction by atoms

The diffraction of x-rays by real atoms can be simulated in two dimensions by using the Fraunhofer diffraction of monochromatic light by suitable models. In practice it is difficult to obtain a model such that the density of shading corresponds to the electron density of the projection. Nevertheless, we are lucky that this difficulty can be avoided by representing the atoms of a structure by disks of uniform density, due to the strong analogy between the Fourier transform of the two-dimensional projection of a real atom scattering x-rays and the central part of the transform of a disk (circular aperture) diffracting ordinary monochromatic light. Two things must be taken into account: that x-ray diffraction cannot be observed outside the limiting sphere, and that the x-ray scattering factors are proportional to the atomic number Z at the origin of Fourier space. In Fig. 16 the solid line is the Fourier transform of a disk, hereafter the disk scattering factor of radius R, $f_R(|\mathbf{r}^*|)$, which we have seen has maxima and minima, though they are not sharp, and are removed from the origin of the diffraction space. The broken line is the x-ray atomic scattering factor of carbon f_C, which is a continuous function, decreasing with $|\mathbf{r}^*|$. We can easily impose the condition that for small and moderate values of the modulus of the reciprocal vector $\mathbf{r}^*$ the scattering of x-rays by real atoms be simulated by the diffraction by disks of

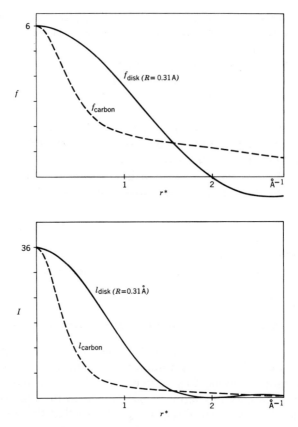

Fig. 16. Comparison between the amplitude and intensity scattering functions of a disk of $R = 0.31$ Å and of a carbon atom.

ordinary light. In order to do this we can simply choose the radius R of the disk of the mask such that the first zero of $f_R(|\mathbf{r}^*|)$ falls outside of the limiting sphere of the x-rays used in the experiment we want to simulate. In such a case both curves are quite similar in a central region of Fourier space. The two curves have been normalized at the origin. If the model represents a molecule or group of atoms, the proper size of the disk must be determined in relation to the separation of the disks in the model. These distances can be given in Å, and therefore the radius of the disks can be also expressed in Å. Accordingly, the corresponding dimensions in the Fraunhofer pattern can be expressed in terms of Å^{-1}. Obviously, the actual dimensions are mm and mm^{-1}, respectively. In order to simulate optically the x-ray diffraction by carbon atoms we have selected a disk of 0.31 Å radius.

By introducing $C = 19.91$ in (115), the disk scattering factor at the origin of Fourier space is scaled to the value 6, the atomic number of the carbon atom.

The problem becomes less simple when atoms of different atomic number occur together in a given structure. This can be solved in the following way. From (115) we see that at the origin of Fourier space the disk scattering factor is proportional to R^2. We have seen also that, at the origin of Fourier space, the x-ray scattering factors are proportional to Z, the atomic number. If we want a direct relation between the two functions, we must use disks of area proportional to Z, i.e. radii proportional to $\sqrt{Z}$. However, the solution is not so simple because the positions of the rings of the Airy pattern strongly depend upon the radius of the disk. In Table 3 the appropriate radii of the

Table 3   Radii of disks simulating atoms of
Z = 1 to 11

Atom	R^a	$Z = f_R(0)$	$|\mathbf{r}^*_{1st}|^b$
H	0.12	1	4.6
He	.18	2	
Li	.22	3	
Be	.25	4	
B	.28	5	
C	.31	6	1.96
N	.33	7	
O	.36	8	
F	.38	9	
Ne	.40	10	
NH₄, Na	.42	11	1.45

[a] 1 unit length representing 1 Å.
[b] 1 unit length representing 1 Å⁻¹.

disks simulating atoms of atomic number up to 11 are given, together with the modulus of the reciprocal vector defining the radius of the first dark ring. The table has been calculated based on the radius of 0.31 Å and $C = 0.127$ for carbon. One can see in Fig. 17 that, for disks larger than 0.42 Å, the first zero of the Bessel function becomes nearer to 1.3 Å⁻¹, and reasonable comparison inside the limiting sphere of Cu radiation can no longer be made. For other kinds of atoms, a different set of radii must be adopted. If the radii of the disks are very small we can speak of a point-like atom having constant scattering factors. The radius of the disk having an almost constant scattering factor inside of the Cu-radiation sphere has a relative value

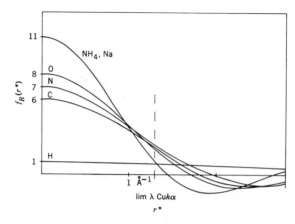

Fig. 17.   Atomic scattering factors for disks of different radii.

of about 0.17 Å. However, it follows that for organic compounds built up mainly of carbon atoms, the x-ray diffraction in a zero section of reciprocal space can be nicely simulated optically.

The light used in this kind of Fraunhofer experiment has been mainly the mercury green light $\lambda_{Hg} = 5461$ Å (Buerger, 1950; Taylor and Lipson, 1965; Hosemann and Bagchi, 1962) or the yellow line of sodium $\lambda_{Na} = 5890$ Å (Amorós and Canut, 1965). The recent development of lasers with highly coherent beams calls for the use of lasers (Françon, 1964). The wavelength in this case is $\lambda = 6328$ Å. We then see that all these lights have quite similar wavelengths.

All the Fraunhofer patterns illustrating this book have been obtained with sodium light. The masks are microfilms of a drawing that, after reduction, have the holes of an effective radius of about 0.04 mm. By substituting this value of the radius in (114) one obtains a value of 15.24 mm^{-1} for the modulus of the reciprocal vector defining the first dark ring. On the other hand, application of (111) to this case yields $2 \sin \theta = 0.00848$, which implies a diffraction angle of $2\theta = 30'$.

The radial distance r from the center of the Fraunhofer pattern to the first zero is given by

$$r_{\text{first zero}} = D \cdot \tan 2\theta_{\text{first zero}} . \qquad (116)$$

By using the above equation we obtain $r = 8$ mm for lenses of focal length $D = 1000$ mm. Under these experimental conditions, the scale of the Fraunhofer pattern is 2 mm $\sim$ 1 mm^{-1}.

If the Buerger optical synthesizer is used at this respect, since the focal lengths of this apparatus are 1800 mm (Buerger, 1950), we find, that the area inside the first dark ring has a radius of about 16 mm. In this case the scale is practically 1 mm film $= 1$ mm^{-1} for holes of 0.04 mm radius.

The size of the Fraunhofer pattern strongly depends on the radius of the holes. Thus application of (111) to a hole of 0.5 mm radius yields a diffraction angle of about 1'. In this case r is of only about 0.6 mm for focal lenses of 1000 mm, and of about 1.1 mm for $D = 1800$ mm. Under these conditions the Fraunhofer patterns need to be observed with a microscope, and the photographic copies must be substantially enlarged.

Taylor and Lipson (1965) have pointed out that most of the optical transforms illustrating their book were obtained from diffracting masks punched with 1-mm holes. Since the apparatus frequently used by Lipson and Taylor has a lens of focal length 1500 mm, the useful part of the pattern has a radius of about 1 mm only.

The molecule as a group of atoms

One of the characteristics of the electron-density function of a molecular crystal is that it shows concentrations only in the molecule, and drops to near zero in the region in between the molecules. Figure 18 gives an example of the electron density of anthracene projected on (010). The individuality of the molecules is very well shown by the concentration of the electron-density function. This fact is most remarkable, and allows us to treat x-ray diffraction by molecular crystals as a function of the molecular transform of its molecular electron density.

The electron density is not merely the sum of the individual electron densities of the several atoms involved in the molecule. In reality the sizes and shapes of the molecules are determined by geometrical factors, namely bond lengths, valence angles, and intermolecular radii. The bonds in the molecule are strongly covalent in type, characterized by electron wave functions resulting from the linear combination of the wave functions of the two electrons shared in the bond. In the molecule, however, it seems also proper to speak of molecular wave functions or molecular orbitals. The fact that the electron density is concentrated in the molecule, and is zero outside it, is in accordance with the idea of stable molecular orbitals for the electrons in the molecule.

Accordingly we can define the molecule as a stable group of atoms, whose electrons have their wave functions combined in molecular orbitals. These stable molecules cohere by their mutual van der

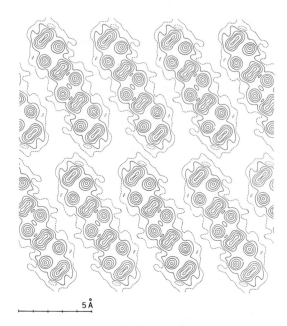

Fig. 18. Electron density of the molecular (crystal) structure of anthracene projected on (010).

Waals attraction. In some cases hydrogen bonds are also present in which the forces between molecular groups are taken through a shared proton.

In order to express mathematically the electron-density function of a molecule let us make use of Ewald's (1940) *peak function* of content 1, a function that is zero everywhere except at one point defined by the vector $\mathbf{r} = \mathbf{r}_p$, where it is infinity in such a way that its integrated value is the weight 1. A peak function is represented by

$$z_p{}^1(\mathbf{r}) = z^1(\mathbf{r} - \mathbf{r}_p), \tag{117}$$

where

$$\int z^1(\mathbf{r} - \mathbf{r}_p) \, dv = 1 \quad \text{for } r = r_p + \delta \ (\delta \text{ an infinitesimal quantity})$$
$$= 0 \quad \text{for all other values.} \tag{118}$$

A peak function of content m has a volume integral equal to m, instead of one:

$$\int z^m(\mathbf{r} - \mathbf{r}_p) \, dv = m \quad \text{for } r = r_p + \delta$$
$$= 0 \quad \text{for all other values.} \tag{119}$$

Let us consider an atomic function $\rho_{at}(\mathbf{r})$ whose maximum at $r = 0$ defines the center of the atom. Suppose now that the center of the atom is given by the vector $\mathbf{r}_j$. The convolution of the atomic function $\rho_{at}(\mathbf{r})$ with the peak function $z^1(\mathbf{r} - \mathbf{r}_j)$ is simply $\rho_{at}(\mathbf{r})$ with its origin translated to $\mathbf{r}_j$:

$$\rho_{at}(\mathbf{r}) * z^1(\mathbf{r} - \mathbf{r}_j) = \rho_{at}(\mathbf{r} - \mathbf{r}_j). \tag{120}$$

The electron density of a molecule of J atoms can be treated as a superposition of J atomic electron densities $\rho_{at}(\mathbf{r})$ having spherical symmetry, and the centers of the atoms can be expressed in terms of a sum of J peak functions

$$\sum_{j=1}^{J} z_{\mathbf{r}_j}^{\ 1}(\mathbf{r}) = \sum_{j=1}^{J} L(\mathbf{r} - \mathbf{r}_j). \tag{121}$$

As before,

$$\sum_{j=1}^{J} \rho_j(\mathbf{r}) * z\ (\mathbf{r}) = \sum_{j=1}^{J} \rho_j(\mathbf{r} - \mathbf{r}_j), \tag{122}$$

that is,

$$\rho_{mole}(\mathbf{r}) = \sum_{j=1}^{J} \rho_j(\mathbf{r} - \mathbf{r}_j). \tag{123}$$

A molecule can thus approximately be described as the convolution of the atomic density functions with a set of peak functions defining the atomic centers. The convolution of a function with a sum of peak functions propagates the first function. Figure 19 illustrates this point. The density function of a molecule is thus characterized by the presence of n discrete peaks, corresponding to the centers of the n atoms of the molecule.

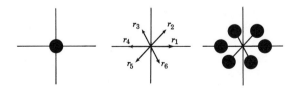

Fig. 19. Scheme of the convolution of the density function of a disk with a peak function, to generate the density function of a molecule.

The Q function of a molecule

If the electron density of a molecule is represented by (123), the Q function is given by

$$Q_{\text{mol}}(\mathbf{r}) = \sum_{j}^{n} \sum_{j'}^{n} \int \rho_j(\mathbf{r}' - \mathbf{r}_j) \cdot \rho_{j'}(\mathbf{r}' - \mathbf{r} - \mathbf{r}_{j'}) \, dv', \qquad (124)$$

where the integral

$$\chi_{jj'}(\mathbf{r}) = \int \rho_j(\mathbf{r}' - \mathbf{r}_j) \cdot \rho_{j'}(\mathbf{r}' - \mathbf{r} - \mathbf{r}_{j'}) \, dv' \qquad (125)$$

is an interatomic function of the atoms j and j' (Kitaigorodskii, 1961). Since the $\rho_j(\mathbf{r})$'s are Gaussian-like functions, the integral must have maximum values at the positions given by the

$$\mathbf{r} = \mathbf{r}_j - \mathbf{r}_{j'}, \qquad (126)$$

that is, when the $\mathbf{r}$ vector equals an interatomic vector.

Thus the Q function of a molecule is a sum of interatomic functions

$$Q_{\text{mol}}(\mathbf{r}) = \Sigma_j \Sigma_{j'} \chi_{jj'}(\mathbf{r} - \mathbf{r}_{jj'}). \qquad (127)$$

We can isolate the terms with $j = j'$ to give

$$Q_{\text{mol}}(\mathbf{r}) = \Sigma_j \chi_{jj}(\mathbf{r}) + \Sigma_j \underset{j \neq j'}{\Sigma_{j'}} \chi_{jj'}(\mathbf{r} - \mathbf{r}_{jj'}). \qquad (128)$$

The term χ_{jj} is the inverse Fourier transform of the intensity function of the atom j:

$$\chi_{jj}(\mathbf{r}) = T^{-1}\{|f_j|^2\}. \qquad (129)$$

$\Sigma_j \chi_{jj}(\mathbf{r})$ is called the zero peak of the Q function. Also

$$\chi_{jj'}(\mathbf{r}) = T^{-1}\{f_j f_{j'}\}. \qquad (130)$$

An interatomic function is the transform of the product of atomic scattering factors; $f_j f_{j'}$ can be considered as the scattering factor for the interatomic function $\chi_{jj'}$.

The Q function or self-image of the molecule has $n(n-1)$ peaks arising whenever both factors within the integral sign in (125) have a large value. This happens when $\rho_j(\mathbf{r})$ and $\rho(\mathbf{r} + \mathbf{r}_j - \mathbf{r}_{j'})$ coincide respectively with the atomic centers of any pair of atoms in the molecule. Therefore the distance from the origin of the Q function to any of its peaks corresponds to interatomic distances in the molecule.

Because the interatomic vectors r_{ij} and r_{ji} have equal modulus but opposite directions, the Q function is always centrosymmetric. The heights of the peaks, on the other hand, are proportional to the product of the peak heights in $\rho(r)$ of the pair of atoms concerned, i.e., approximately proportional to the product of their atomic numbers. Apart from the $n(n-1)$ interatomic peaks, there are n peaks more arising from the distances of the atoms to themselves. These peaks are superimposed at the origin of the Q function, forming a very high peak of height approximately proportional to ΣZ_j^2, the sum extending to all the atoms in the molecule.

The two-dimensional Q functions of molecules can be obtained optically with the Q integrator (Fig. 11) by using two identical microfilms of the negative of the model of the molecule composed of disk atoms. Figure 20 shows the disk-like atoms models of a

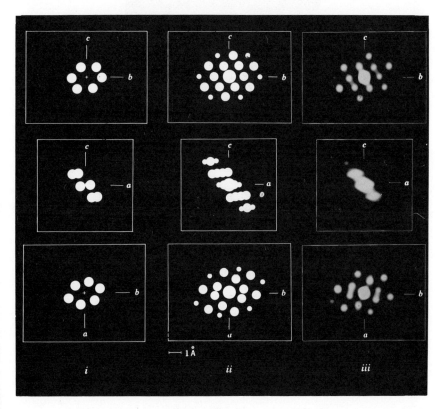

Fig. 20. Benzene. (*i*) Scheme of the molecules projected on (100), (010), and (001); (*ii*) its calculated Q function; (*iii*) its optical Q function.

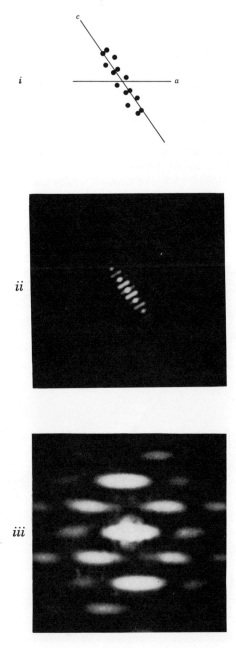

Fig. 21. Anthracene. (*i*) Molecule projected on (010); (*ii*) Q function; (*iii*) Fraunhofer pattern.

benzene molecule as projected on the three main planes of the benzene crystal, together with the calculated and optical Q functions. Figure 21 shows the Q function of a single molecule of anthracene projected on $(0\dot{1}0)$. The atoms are represented by disks in the same figure. The radius of the disks relative to the carbon-to-carbon distance in the benzene ring has been chosen as $R = 0.31$ Å. Even though all the atoms in the models have the same area and density, different peaks of the Q functions have different intensities due to the number of equal interatomic distances in the model. Such peaks are known as multiple peaks.

Diffraction by a molecule or a group of atoms

The Fourier transform of a peak function z_j^1 is

$$T\{z^1(\mathbf{r}-\mathbf{r}_j)\} = \int z^1 \exp\left(2\pi i \mathbf{r} \cdot \mathbf{r}^*\right) dv = \exp\left(2\pi i \mathbf{r}^* \cdot \mathbf{r}_j\right). \quad (131)$$

By applying the convolution theorem, and by using (120) and (123), we obtain the amplitude diffracted by a molecule or the molecular Fourier transform

$$F_{\text{mole}}(\mathbf{r}^*) = \sum_{j=1}^{J} f_j(\mathbf{r}^*) \exp\left(2\pi i \mathbf{r}^* \cdot \mathbf{r}_j\right), \quad (132)$$

and the molecular intensity transform

$$I_{\text{mole}}(\mathbf{r}^*) = \sum_{j} \sum_{j'} f_j(\mathbf{r}^*) f_{j'}(\mathbf{r}^*) \exp\left[2\pi i \mathbf{r}^* \cdot (\mathbf{r}_j - \mathbf{r}_{j'})\right]. \quad (133)$$

The functions $F_{\text{mole}}(\mathbf{r}^*)$ and $I_{\text{mole}}(\mathbf{r}^*)$ are defined throughout reciprocal space. Such functions are continuous and characteristic of the structure (geometry) of the group (Hettich, 1935).

By optical diffraction we can easily simulate the intensity $I_{\text{mol}}(\mathbf{r}^*)$ that would be diffracted by a molecule in a given section of reciprocal space, by using as the diffracting grating a microfilm of a drawing of the corresponding projection of the molecule in which the atoms have been represented by disks (Bragg, 1944). Figure 21iii gives the Fraunhofer pattern of the anthracene molecule of Fig. 21i acting as a diffracting object.

Figure 22i shows the models of the principal projections of a single molecule of benzene as it is oriented in a unit cell. Figure 22ii represents the corresponding Fraunhofer patterns of a single molecule. The radius of the disks relative to the carbon-to-carbon distance in the benzene ring is again 0.31 Å.

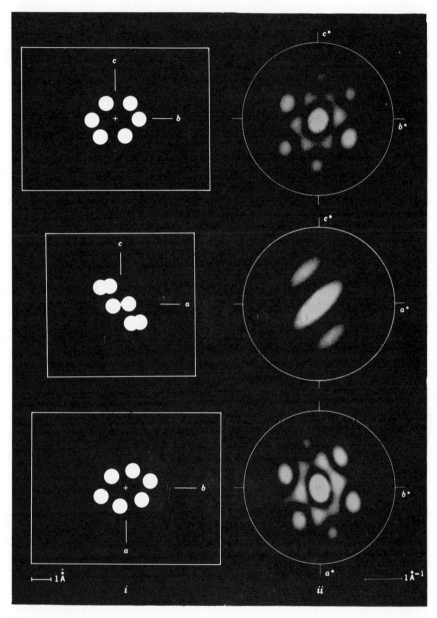

Fig. 22. Benzene. (i) Scheme of a molecule projected on (100), (010), and (001); (ii) its Fraunhofer pattern.

Computation of molecular Fourier transforms

The Fourier transform $F_{mole}(hkl)$ of a single molecule with atoms at (x_j, y_j, z_j) with scattering factors $f_j(\mathbf{r}^*)$ is a continuous function in the space reciprocal to (xyz). It can be calculated at a set of discrete points (hkl), where h, k, l, can take on integral or fractional values. Here x_j, y_j, z_j, are the fractional coordinates with respect to the basic vectors $\mathbf{a}, \mathbf{b}, \mathbf{c}$ in physical space, and hkl define the $\mathbf{r}^*$ vector in Fourier space. We have

$$F_{mole}(hkl) = \sum_{j=1}^{J} f_j(hkl) \exp[2\pi i(hx + ky + lz)]. \tag{134}$$

The summation is over all J atoms of the molecule. When the $\rho(\mathbf{r})$ is real but noncentrosymmetric, $F(\mathbf{r}^*)$ is a complex number. It is common to compute the real and imaginary parts separately, as follows:

$$A(hkl) = \sum_{j=1}^{J} f_j(hkl) \cos 2\pi(hx_j + ky_j + lz_j), \tag{135}$$

$$B(hkl) = \sum_{j=1}^{J} f_j(hkl) \sin 2\pi(hx_j + ky_j + lz_j). \tag{136}$$

The complex number $F(\mathbf{r}^*)$ can also be specified in terms of its modulus

$$|F(hkl)| = \sqrt{|A(hkl)|^2 + B(hkl)|^2}, \tag{137}$$

and the phase angle $\psi(\mathbf{r}^*)$, which is given by the common solution of the two following equations:

$$\psi(hkl) = \cos^{-1}\frac{A(hkl)}{|F(hkl)|}, \tag{138}$$

$$\psi(hkl) = \sin^{-1}\frac{B(hkl)}{|F(hkl)|}. \tag{139}$$

The solution of (138) and (139) can be solved by applying

$$\psi(hkl) = \tan^{-1}\frac{B(hkl)}{A(hkl)}, \tag{140}$$

and adding the conditions given in Table 4 in terms of the signs of both A and B.

Table 4 Value of the phase angle ψ

B	A	ψ
	$A > 0$	$0 < \psi < \pi/2$
$B > 0$	$A = 0$	$\pi/2$
	$A < 0$	$\pi/2 < \phi < \pi$
	$A > 0$	0
$B = 0$	$A = 0$	Indeterminate
	$A < 0$	π
	$A > 0$	$-\pi/2 < \phi < 0$
$B < 0$	$A = 0$	$-\pi/2$
	$A < 0$	$-\pi/2 < \psi < -\pi$

The intensity transform $I(\mathbf{r}^*)$ of a single molecule is given by

$$I(hkl) = F(hkl) \cdot F^*(hkl), \tag{141}$$

where $F^*(hkl)$ is the complex conjugate of $F(hkl)$, and by

$$I(hkl) = |F(hkl)|^2, \tag{142}$$

i.e.,

$$I(hkl) = |A(hkl)|^2 + |B(hkl)|^2. \tag{143}$$

The functions A, B, $|F|$, ψ, and I can easily be calculated by a high-speed computer (Caruso, Richards, and Canut-Amoros, 1966). If complete three-dimensional calculations are done for any of the molecular functions described, separate diagrams need to be given of the contours at different levels or sections of reciprocal space.

It is important to recall that a change of origin of the xyz coordinates in physical space implies a change of both the values of the A and B functions, hence the phase angle ψ will also change, but this change will not affect the modulus $|F|$ or the intensity function I. On the other hand, since the functions A and B are dependent upon the choice of origin, there is not much physical meaning in the variation of the real and imaginary parts.

Computations of Fraunhofer patterns

The Fraunhofer patterns of molecules of disk-like atoms can also be calculated by using a high-speed computer. The difference between calculations of intensity functions of atoms as diffracted by x-rays or of disks by ordinary light differ only in the atomic scattering factors, $f_X(\mathbf{r}^*)$ for x-rays and $f_R(\mathbf{r}^*)$ with light. The function $f_R(\mathbf{r}^*)$ reaches negative values, whereas $f_X(\mathbf{r}^*)$ is always positive (see Fig. 16). Besides, (134) is restricted to two dimensions. We have

$$F_{\mathrm{mole}}(hk0) = \sum_{j=1}^{J} C\pi^2 R_j^2 \frac{2J_1(2\pi R_j|\mathbf{r}_{hk0}^*|)}{2\pi R_j|\mathbf{r}_{hk0}^*|} \exp\left[2\pi i(hx_j + ky_j)\right]. \quad (144)$$

Figure 23 shows the calculated Fraunhofer intensity transform of the three projections of a molecule of benzene, calculated in terms of the disk-scattering factor equivalent to $R = 0.31$ Å.

In order to show the strong analogy between the optical and x-ray diffraction phenomena the molecular transforms have been calculated in terms of both $f_R(\mathbf{r}^*)$ with $R = 0.31$ Å^{-1} and $R \rightarrow 0$, and $f_{\mathrm{carbon}}(\mathbf{r}^*)$; the results are represented in Figs. 24–26. Due to the fact that the benzene molecule is centrosymmetric, the transform is real so the real part only needs to be represented.

The circle in the transform of the Fraunhofer patterns (Figs. 24i and 25i) corresponds to the first zero of the first-order Bessel function. It can easily be seen how, for values beyond this circle, the real part changes in sign. However, the values beyond the circle are quite small for both the Fraunhofer pattern and the calculated x-ray pattern. If we limit the comparison to a radius of 1.3 Å^{-1}, i.e., the limit for CuKα x-radiation, we can see the striking analogy between the optical and x-ray results. A change in radius of the disk would evidently tend to spoil the analogy. If point atoms are assumed, the transform no longer decreases with the reciprocal vector (Fig. 26).

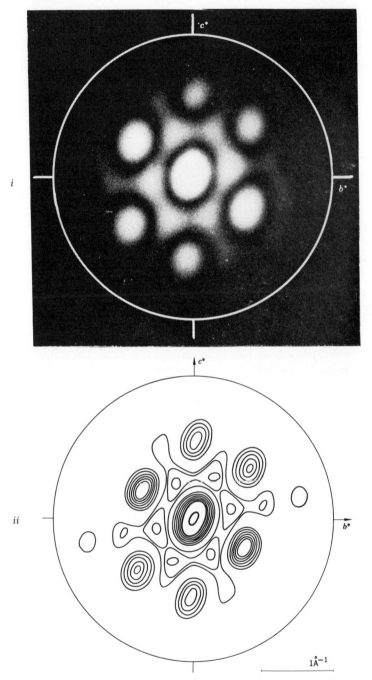

Fig. 23. Benzene. Fraunhofer patterns of a molecule projected on (100), (010), and (001). (*i*) optical; (*ii*) calculated.

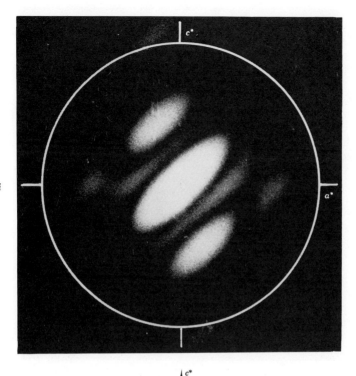

i

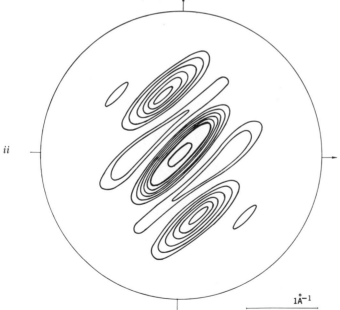

ii

1Å⁻¹

Fig. 23. *(continued)*.

51

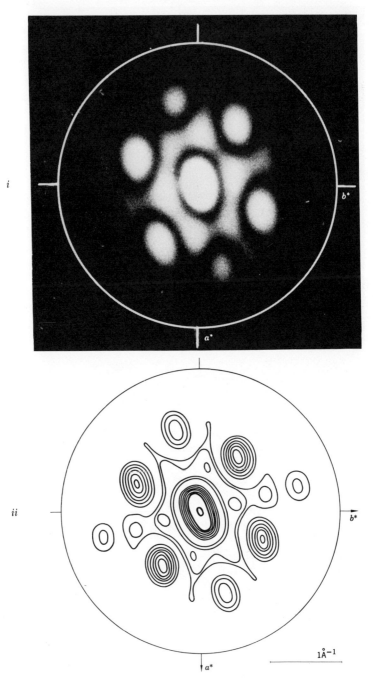

Fig. 23. (continued).

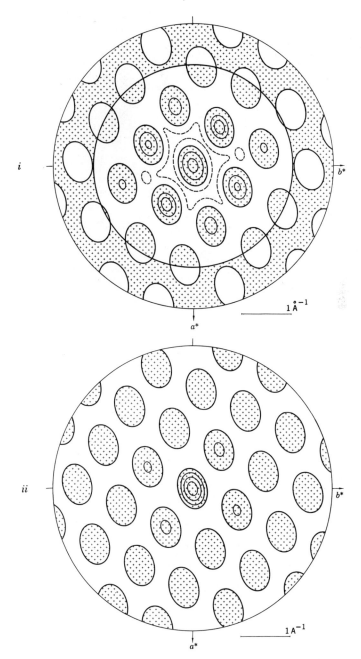

Fig. 24. Benzene, $(001)_0^*$. Real part of the transform of the molecule centered at the origin (i) in terms of $f_{\mathrm{disk}}(\mathbf{r}^*)$; (ii) in terms of the x-ray $f_{\mathrm{carbon}}(\mathbf{r}^*)$.

53

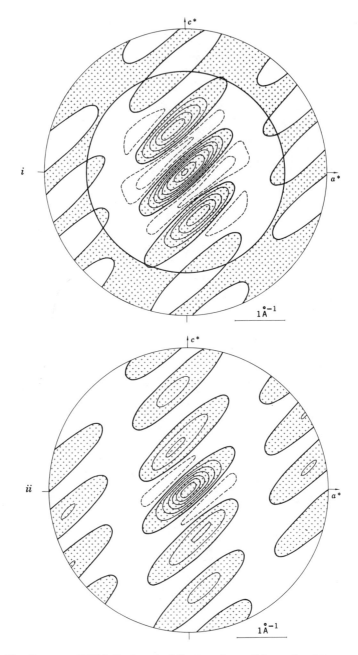

Fig. 25. Benzene, $(010)_0^*$. Real part of the transform of the molecule centered at the origin (i) in terms of $f_{\text{disk}}(\mathbf{r}^*)$; (ii) in terms of the x-ray $f_{\text{carbon}}(\mathbf{r}^*)$.

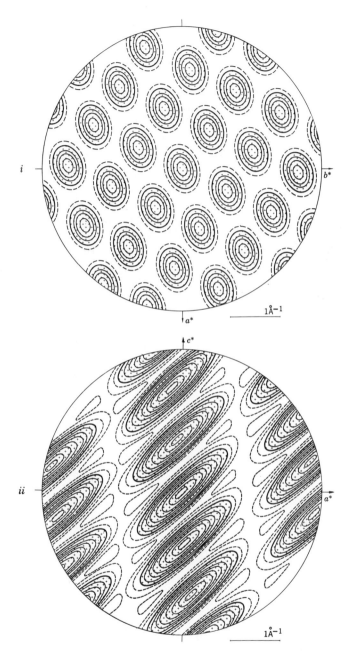

Fig. 26. Benzene. Real part of the transform of the molecule centered at the origin calculated with point atoms. (i) $(001)_0^*$; (ii) $(010)_0^*$.

Molecular transform and molecular geometry

The molecular transform is directly related to the molecular geometry, that is, to the pattern of the atoms that form the molecule. It is interesting, therefore, to refer here to simple cases. The molecule of benzene is a clear example. The carbon atoms are at the vertices of a hexagon whose side is 1.40 Å. The molecule is planar (Fig. 27i). Prominent spacings of 1.21 Å in the molecule are apparent when the molecule is viewed from a direction parallel to one of the sides. A less well-defined spacing of 2.12 Å is evidenced when the molecule is viewed perpendicular to one of its sides. The essential feature of the transform of benzene is an hexagonal arrangement of peaks (Fig. 28). The six prominent peaks around the central peak P_0 are the principal maxima P_1 that are at a distance from P_0 equal to 0.82 Å^{-1}, and therefore correspond to the prominent spacings of the benzene ring. A second set of peaks having lower intensity form the secondary maxima S_1 of the transform. The distance between P_0 and S_1, 0.47 Å^{-1}, and the maxima, correspond to the secondary spacing in the benzene ring. At each of those maxima the molecular transform shows columns

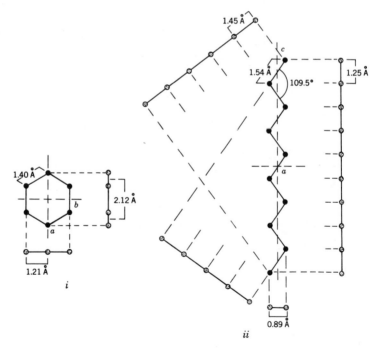

Fig. 27. (i) Scheme of a benzene ring. (ii) Scheme of an aliphatic chain.

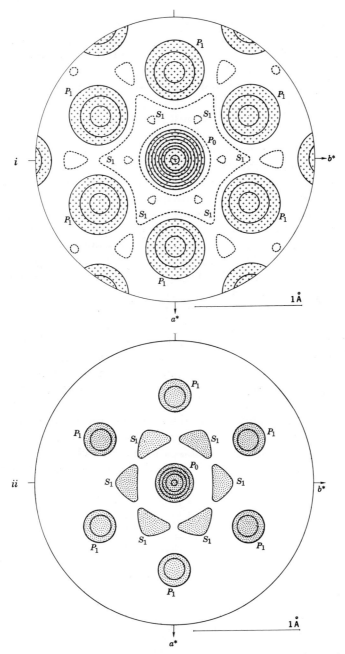

Fig. 28. Benzene molecular transforms. Section parallel to the plane of the ring. (*i*) Real part. (*ii*) Intensity function.

57

of intensity perpendicular to the plane of the molecule. The whole picture is represented in Fig. 29. The molecular transforms obtained for different projections of benzene shown in Fig. 23 are just sections of this three-dimensional pattern by planes that form an angle equal to the inclination of the molecule in the respective projection and pass through the origin of the reciprocal space. In the projection (100) the molecule of benzene is almost parallel to the plane of projection. The intensity transform clearly shows the six principal maxima. The distortion of the hexagon in the projection is shown in the intensity transform. The secondary peaks are not quite resolved but form a ring of peaks at the centroids of the triangles formed by the central peak and two neighboring principal peaks. A similar situation is observed in the intensity transform of the projection (001); this shows a higher distortion of the hexagon of principal peaks and of the ring of secondary peaks. An extreme distortion is observed in the projection (010) in which the plane of projection forms a large angle with the plane of the molecule. The principal peaks coalesce in pairs, with the result of forming elongated regions of high intensity, and the secondary peaks are scarcely shown. The relation between the orientation of the molecule and the section of the molecular transform is no longer straightforward. We can generalize the results of the benzene molecule and say that the molecular intensity transform of a planar molecule is a set of columns perpendicular to the plane of the molecule and whose geometrical arrangement and intensity depends on the intramolecular spacings.

Another nice example of a single correlation between molecular transform and molecular geometry is the case of chain molecules. Long-chain hydrocarbons, mono- and dicarboxylic acids, and many others, fall in this category. For our example we have selected an

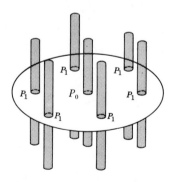

Fig. 29. Benzene. Three-dimensional scheme of the molecular intensity transform.

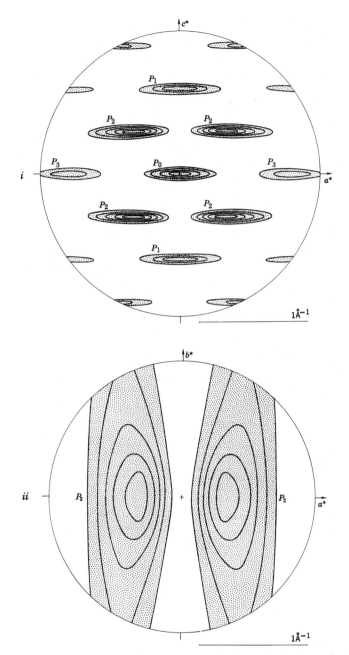

Fig. 30. Intensity transform of the chain molecule: (*i*) parallel to the molecular plane (*ii*) *hk*5 section.

aliphatic chain (Knott, 1940) with a carbon-carbon distance of 1.54 Å and a bond angle of 109° 27′ (Fig. 27ii). It is assumed here that the molecule has ten atoms of carbon, and the hydrogens have been disregarded. Also, we have assumed that all the carbon atoms are coplanar. The longest axis of the molecule has been taken parallel to the c direction. The principal spacings in this molecule are as follows: 1.25Å along the direction of the chain, 0.89 Å along the perpendicular to the chain direction, and 1.45 Å along a direction perpendicular to the shortest distance between carbon atoms in the chain. All these directions are contained in the plane of the molecule. In this case, again, the molecular transform shows columns of intensity perpendicular to the plane of the molecule (Fig. 30). The intersections of the columns with the plane $(010)_0^*$ of reciprocal space are located at the reciprocal spacing of the principal spacings of the molecule, and are labeled P_1, P_2, and P_3, respectively (Fig. 30i). The columns are thin in the direction of the chain, elongated along the perpendicular to this direction in the plane of the molecule, and extend to infinity along the direction perpendicular to the plane of the molecule. Two P_2 columns are shown in their own plane in Fig. 30ii. Due to the extension of the columns along the direction parallel to a^* and their relatively thin section along the c^* direction, the molecular transform of the chain can be also described as consisting of a set of sheets of nonuniform intensity perpendicular to the chain direction, and whose spacing depends on the fundamental spacing along the direction of the chain molecule. The intensity in the sheets is anisotropic and shows concentrations along bands perpendicular to the plane that contains the chain.

Symmetry properties of some molecular Fourier transforms

Since $\rho(\mathbf{r})$ is real, if the molecule is centrosymmetrical, and the atomic coordinates are referred to the center of symmetry, the imaginary part B of the transform becomes zero. For each atom at the point xyz there is a corresponding atom at the point $\bar{x}\bar{y}\bar{z}$, and the expression (134) becomes

$$F(hkl) = A(hkl) = 2\sum_{j=1}^{J/2} f_j(hkl)\cos 2\pi(hx_j + ky_j + lz_j),$$
$$B(hkl) = 0, \tag{145}$$

the summation now being made over half of the molecule; any atom related to an atom already considered is not included in the summation. The phase angle ψ is, in this case, either zero or π. Positive values of $A(hkl)$ correspond to phase angles equal to zero, and negative values of $A(hkl)$ correspond to phase angles equal to π:

$$A(hkl) > 0 \qquad \psi = 0$$

$$A(hkl) < 0 \qquad \psi = \pi.$$

The nodal surfaces are the loci of $I = 0$; these are boundary surfaces between regions of positive A where the phases have values of zero, and regions of negative A, where the phases are π. They correspond to a change in phase from 0 to π.

As an example of a centrosymmetric molecule, let us consider one of the molecules of adipic acid, projected on (010) plane, as it is oriented in the crystal. The transform of this projection corresponds to the zero section $(010)_0^*$ in reciprocal space. The map of the real part A shows (Fig. 31i) positive and negative areas, separated by zero lines. This function is centrosymmetric. Notice that the area in the origin of Fourier space is a positive one because $A(0) > 0$.

The imaginary part, B, is obviously zero. Consequently, the zero lines of the A function are also zero lines on the $|F|$ map (Fig. 31ii) and of the I function.

The phase map would show areas $\psi = 0°$ corresponding with the positive areas of the A function, and areas of $\psi = \pi$ corresponding with the negative areas of the real part. The zero lines of A, $|F|$, and I correspond in the phase map to discontinuity lines of the phase function because the phase angle goes from zero to π. Notice that the phase function is centrosymmetric in the origin of Fourier space for the case of a centrosymmetric electron-density distribution.

When the molecule is not centrosymmetric, or its center is not at the origin of coordinates, the phase angle may have any value from 0 to 360°. In order to illustrate this point the functions A, B, F, and ψ have been calculated by displacing the molecule half the distance of the basic vector **a**. The real part, in this case, also has positive and negative areas and zero lines (Fig. 32i). Apart from the zero lines that appeared at identical positions in the map of the molecule centered at the origin, there exist systematic zero straight lines satisfying the condition $h + n = \frac{1}{2}$, which split the areas of the former map in a checkerboard pattern. These straight lines are called "fringes."

The imaginary part of the molecule displaced with respect to the origin is no longer zero, and its map is shown in Fig. 32ii. Zero straight lines satisfying $h = n$ are present, crossing also the former

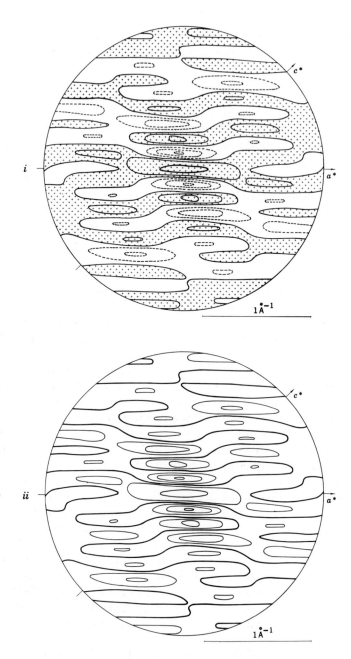

Fig. 31. Adipic acid, $(010)_0^*$. (*i*) Real part and (*ii*) modulus of the transform of the molecule with the origin of coordinates at the center of symmetry.

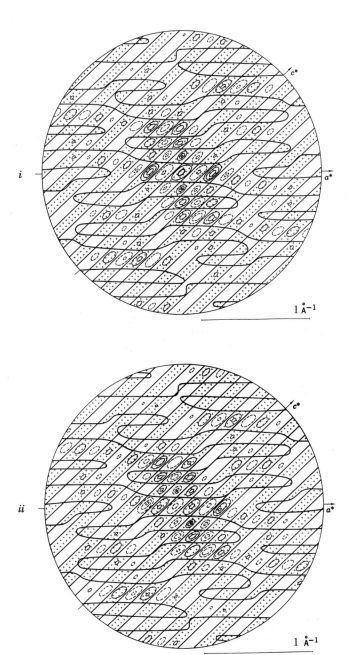

Fig. 32. Adipic acid, $(010)_0^*$. (i) Real and (ii) imaginary parts of the transforms of the molecule shifted a/2 from the origin.

63

Chapter 1

lines of the zero real part of molecule 1. Notice the antisymmetry
center at the origin of Fourier space.

   The phase map of the molecule displaced (Fig. 33i) shows the iso-
phase lines of $0°$, $\pi/2$, π, $-\pi/2$, $-\pi$, and the lines of indeterminacy of
the phase angle. It can easily be seen how the lines of $-\pi$, $-\pi/2$, 0, $\pi/2$,
π are repeated again and again inside of each region having as boundaries the lines of indeterminate phase. The variation of ψ with the
reciprocal vector $\mathbf{a}^*$ is linear, so that, in one dimension, it could be
represented as in Fig. 33ii. Notice the antisymmetry center that
characterizes the phase function.

   The map of the modulus of the transform of the molecule displaced
is identical to the map of the molecule centered at the origin (Fig.
31i) and, of course, the intensity diffracted by the two molecules is

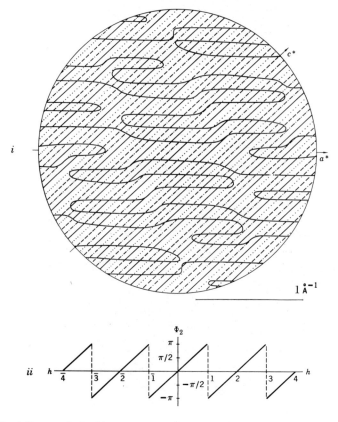

Fig. 33. Adipic acid, $(010)_0^*$. (i) Phase-angle map of the molecule shifted $a/2$ from the
origin: (ii) variation of Φ along the straight line $h00$.

the same. Both functions are always centrosymmetrical in the origin of Fourier space. From the above example we can conclude that the modulus of the transform and the intensity function is insensitive to a translational displacement of the molecule with respect to the origin of coordinates, but that the real and imaginary parts and the phase angle are affected by the displacement.

Pentaerythritol is another interesting example, since the molecule has a fourfold axis. In the crystal the molecules are tilted with respect to a about 12°. Figure 34 clearly shows the fourfold symmetry of the real part transform at $(001)^*_0$ of Fourier space. Figure 35 shows the real and imaginary parts of the transforms of pentaerythritol molecule as projected on (100). The phase-angle map is given in Fig. 36. Since the projection on (100) of the molecule does not differ very much from centrosymmetric, the imaginary part has low values.

In order to provide an example in which the molecule is very far from centrosymmetric real and imaginary parts of the transform of a nitrite group are shown in Fig. 37. In Fig. 38 the modulus of the transform and the phase angle are given. In this case the calculations have

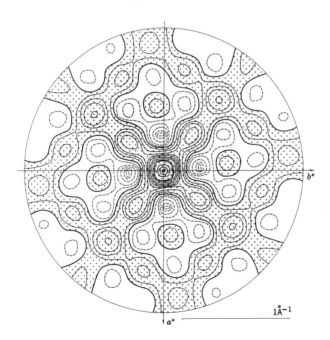

Fig. 34. Pentaerythritol, $(001)^*_0$. Real part of the molecular transform showing the 4-fold symmetry.

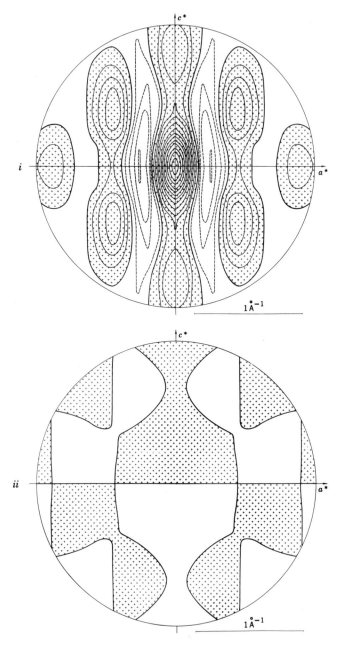

Fig. 35. Pentaerythritol, $(010)_0^*$. (i) Real and (ii) imaginary parts of the molecular 4-fold symmetry.

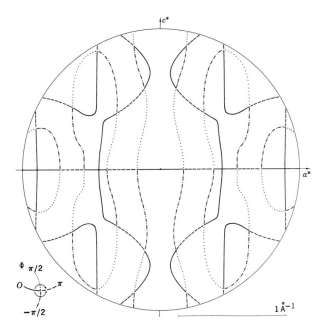

Fig. 36. Pentaerythritol, $(100)_0^*$. Phase-angle map. Contour lines are zero: ―――――

$$\pi: ― ― ―$$
$$\tfrac{1}{2}\pi: \ldots\ldots$$
$$-\tfrac{1}{2}\pi: ―\cdot―\cdot―\cdot$$

67

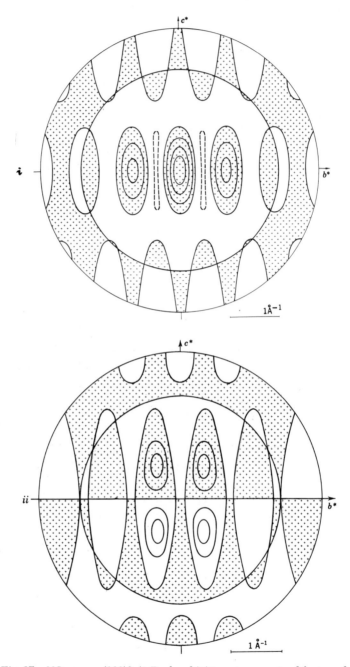

Fig. 37. NO$_2$ group, $(100)^*_0$. (i Real and (ii) imaginary parts of the transform.

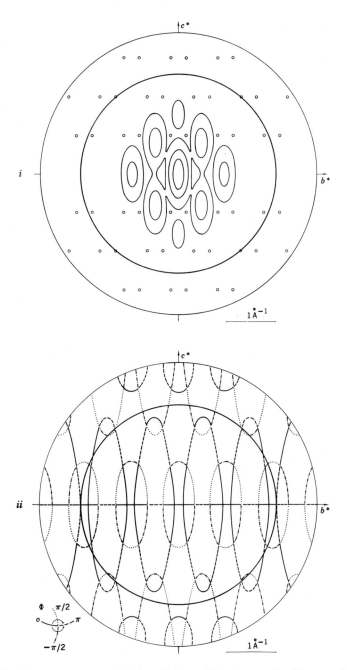

Fig. 38. NO$_2$ group, $(100)_0^*$. (i) Modulus and (ii) phase angle of the transform.

been made in terms of the atomic-scattering factors of disks of $R =$ 0.31 Å, and we can see in the phase-angle map how the Φ isolines change when crossing the circle where f_R changes in sign. An interesting feature of the phase-angle map is that, if only the angles $-\pi, -\pi/2$, 0, $\pi/2$, and π are represented, these lines are just built up of the zero lines of the real and imaginary parts. The intersection lines of $A(\mathbf{r}^*) = 0$ and $B(\mathbf{r}^*) = 0$ are points where $\Phi =$ indeterminate, and these points have been marked in the map of the modulus of the transform with small circles (Fig. 38i).

2

Diffraction by an ideal periodic structure

The periodic nature of the crystal and the lattice-peak function

Crystals are known to be homogeneous, symmetric, and anisotropic solids. These properties are consequences of the periodic nature of the crystal on an atomic or molecular scale. This means that the most striking feature of the ideal crystal is that the electron density is a triperiodic function. It follows that

$$\rho(\mathbf{r}) = \rho(\mathbf{r}+\mathbf{r}_1), \tag{1}$$

where

$$\mathbf{r}_1 = l\mathbf{a} + m\mathbf{b} + n\mathbf{c}, \qquad (l, m, n \text{ integers}), \tag{2}$$

$\mathbf{a}, \mathbf{b}, \mathbf{c}$ being three noncoplanar vectors, the base vectors. It is customary to select as base vectors the three smallest noncoplanar translations in the crystal. These three vectors are called the fundamental translations. The set of points generated from an initial point by the vectors defined by (2) is a lattice, the points are called lattice points, and the vectors $\mathbf{r}_1$ are lattice vectors.

The lattice is just one abstraction useful in describing the periodic reality of the crystal. Mathematically, we can write a peak function that defines the points of a lattice:

$$z_{\text{cr}}(\mathbf{r}) = \sum_{l=-\infty}^{+\infty} \sum_{m=-\infty}^{+\infty} \sum_{n=-\infty}^{+\infty} L(\mathbf{r} - l\mathbf{a} - m\mathbf{b} - n\mathbf{c}) = \sum_1 L(\mathbf{r} - \mathbf{r}_1). \tag{3}$$

This function is zero everywhere in physical space, except at the lattice points located at r_l, where it becomes infinite, but in such a way that its integrated value is equal to unity:

$$L(\mathbf{r}-\mathbf{r}_l) = 0 \quad \text{for all } |\mathbf{r}-\mathbf{r}_l| > \delta \text{ (δ an infinitesimal).}$$

$$\int L(\mathbf{r}-\mathbf{r}_l)\, dv_r = 1 \tag{4}$$

The lattice-peak function was introduced by Ewald (1940) and is a useful concept that allows the formulation of any periodic function in either physical or reciprocal space. The set of lattice points defined by the lattice-peak function is unique for a given crystal; it is known as the lattice-peak function of that crystal. It can be easily seen, however, that the same set of lattice points can be defined by using different triads of fundamental vectors $\mathbf{a}'$, $\mathbf{b}'$, $\mathbf{c}'$, the only requirement being that the volume of the primitive cell defined by the fundamental vectors,

$$v_c = (\mathbf{a} \times \mathbf{b})\mathbf{c} = (\mathbf{a}' \times \mathbf{b}')\mathbf{c}' = \text{constant,} \tag{5}$$

must be a constant. The vectors $\mathbf{a}'$, $\mathbf{b}'$, $\mathbf{c}'$ are called conjugate. Of the many choices of conjugate vectors, it is customary to use the three shortest for the fundamental vectors $\mathbf{a}$, $\mathbf{b}$, $\mathbf{c}$ as the reference vectors defining a primitive lattice.

It can easily be seen that any triad of nonconjugate translation vectors defines a parallelepiped whose volume is a multiple of the volume of the primitive cell. Such a cell is called a multiple cell. For reasons of orthogonality, a multiple cell is usually chosen in the description of certain lattices.

In dealing with problems of crystal dynamics, however, it is convenient, for the sake of simplicity, to use the primitive cell instead of the multiple one. When the crystal structure is described in terms of the multiple Bravais cell, it is necessary to transform it into the primitive cell in order to deal with groups that are symmetry equivalent but not translation equivalent. The corresponding transformation matrices can be found in books like the "International Tables of Crystallography," vol. 1 (1952).

The reciprocal lattice

The Fourier transform of the lattice-peak function is a set of evenly spaced peaks in Fourier space at the nodes of a three-dimensional lattice, which is called the reciprocal lattice. We call

$$Z_{cr}(\mathbf{r}^*) = T\{z_{cr}(\mathbf{r})\}. \tag{6}$$

$Z_{cr}(\mathbf{r}^*)$ has sharp peaks when $\mathbf{r}^*$ simultaneously satisfies

$$\begin{aligned}
\mathbf{r}^* \cdot \mathbf{a} &= h \\
\mathbf{r}^* \cdot \mathbf{b} &= k \\
\mathbf{r}^* \cdot \mathbf{c} &= l
\end{aligned} \tag{7}$$

When $\mathbf{r}^*$ satisfies this triple condition, $Z_{cr}(\mathbf{r}^*)$ is infinite and its integrated value becomes (Ewald, 1940)

$$\int_{\mathbf{r}^*=\mathbf{r}_h^*} Z_{cr}(\mathbf{r}^*)\,dv^* = v_c^* = \frac{1}{v_c}, \tag{8}$$

where v_c^* is the volume reciprocal to v_c. The points satisfying (7) form, in Fourier space, a three-dimensional lattice, which is the reciprocal of the primitive direct lattice. It is related to the direct lattice through the following equations:

$$\begin{aligned}
\mathbf{a} \cdot \mathbf{a}^* &= 1, & \mathbf{a} \cdot \mathbf{b}^* = \mathbf{a} \cdot \mathbf{c}^* &= 0, \\
\mathbf{b} \cdot \mathbf{b}^* &= 1, & \mathbf{b} \cdot \mathbf{a}^* = \mathbf{b} \cdot \mathbf{c}^* &= 0, \\
\mathbf{c} \cdot \mathbf{c}^* &= 1, & \mathbf{c} \cdot \mathbf{a}^* = \mathbf{c} \cdot \mathbf{b}^* &= 0.
\end{aligned} \tag{9}$$

We have seen in Ch. 1 that the scattering functions are defined in Fourier or reciprocal space, and that the three standard vectors of reciprocal space are related to the base vectors of physical space through (5), Ch. 1. In the case of a crystal lattice the standard vectors are chosen to coincide with the fundamental lattice vectors, and in this case the corresponding reciprocal base vectors as given by (9) define, in Fourier space, the reciprocal lattice. Any reciprocal-lattice point is at the end of a vector

$$\mathbf{r}_h^* = h\mathbf{a}^* + k\mathbf{b}^* + l\mathbf{c}^*, \qquad (h, k, l, \text{ integers}), \tag{10}$$

where the vectors $\mathbf{a}^*, \mathbf{b}^*, \mathbf{c}^*$ are the standard vectors of this reciprocal lattice. The Fourier transform of the lattice-peak function, is another lattice peak function

$$Z_{cr}(\mathbf{r}^*) = v_c^* \sum_{h=-\infty}^{+\infty} \sum_{k=-\infty}^{+\infty} \sum_{l=-\infty}^{+\infty} L(\mathbf{r}^* - h\mathbf{a}^* - k\mathbf{b}^* - l\mathbf{c}^*) = v_c^* \sum_h L(\mathbf{r}^* - \mathbf{r}_h^*) \tag{11}$$

This obviously represents the reciprocal lattice, but with weight v_c^* instead of unit weight.

The reciprocal lattice has interesting properties (Ewald, 1933) that can be found in current books dealing with the subject. In Ch. 1 we have seen that the vector diffraction condition

$$\mathbf{k} - \mathbf{k}_0 = \mathbf{r}^* \qquad |\mathbf{r}^*| = \frac{2\sin\theta}{\lambda} \tag{12}$$

can be geometrically expressed in terms of the Ewald representation of the diffraction sphere of radius $1/\lambda$. In the reciprocal space of the ideal crystal the only meaningful vectors are those from the origin to reciprocal-lattice points. These can be defined by the reciprocal-lattice peak function, all other points having weight zero. The diffraction condition in this case requires that $\mathbf{r}^*$ (Fig. 1) in (12) to be a vector of the reciprocal lattice

$$\mathbf{k}_{hkl} - \mathbf{k}_0 = \mathbf{r}^*_{hkl} \qquad \text{(Laue condition)}. \qquad (13)$$

Wigner-Seitz and Brillouin zones

The periodic nature of the crystal means that we can build the whole crystal by applying the lattice translations to a volume equal to the volume of the unit cell of the lattice, but no a priori provision need be made for the form of that volume. Obviously, the simplest way of

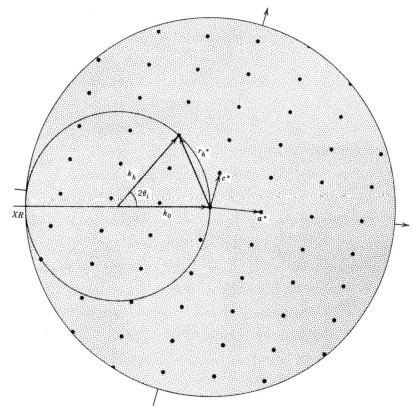

Fig. 1.   Reciprocal lattice and Ewald sphere.

selecting such a volume is to choose it identical to the parallelepiped defined by the primitive cell. This simple method has the disadvantage that it does not automatically display the point symmetry of the lattice. The point symmetry of the lattice is contained in the neighborhood of every lattice point in accordance with the homogeneity of the lattice. Therefore the point symmetry of the lattice is displayed by the region consisting of all those points that lie closer to a given lattice point than to any other. This simple volume can be obtained by drawing the planes that are the perpendicular bisectors of the translation vectors from a given lattice point to the nearest lattice points. The volume limited by the bisector planes is obviously equal to the volume of the primitive cell; the shape is unique for a given lattice but, in general, it is not a parallelepiped. Such figures are the Veronoi bodies, better known to physicists as the Wigner-Seitz zones. It is easy to see that there is a one-to-one correspondence between that primitive Bravais cell and Wigner-Seitz zone. The latter contains only one lattice point and has the point symmetry of the crystal. Obviously the whole crystal can be generated by just applying to the Wigner-Seitz zone the translation defined by the lattice. The Veronoi bodies or Wigner-Seitz zones corresponding to the 14 Bravais lattices are represented in Figs. 2 and 3. Other types of zone are not often used.

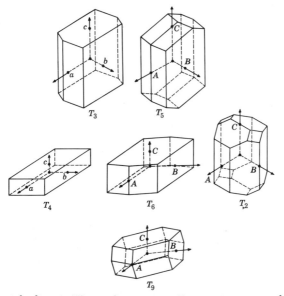

Fig. 2. Verenoi bodies or Wigner-Seitz zones. T_3: primitive monoclinic; T_5: base-centered monoclinic; T_4: primitive orthorhombic; T_6: base-centered orthorhombic; T_2: face-centered orthorhombic; T_9: body-centered orthorhombic.

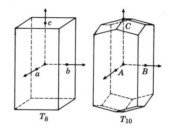

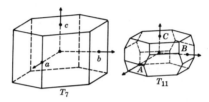

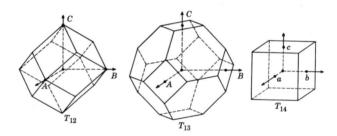

Fig. 3. Verenoi bodies or Wigner-Seitz zones. T_8: primitive tetragonal; T_{10}: body-centered tetragonal; T_7: hexagonal; T_{11}: rhombohedral; T_{12}: face-centered cubic; T_{13}: body-centered cubic; T_{14}: primitive cubic.

The same procedure can be applied in reciprocal space. The volume corresponding to the Veronoi body is equal to the volume of the reciprocal primitive cell; this is known as the first Brillouin zone. The first Brillouin zone of a given lattice is again unique. A two-dimensional lattice with its Wigner-Seitz zones and the corresponding reciprocal lattice with its first Brillouin zones are given in Figs. 4 and 5, respectively. It is easy to see that the Wigner-Seitz zone and the first Brillouin zone are reciprocals. Brillouin zones are very convenient when dealing with the study of the dynamics of the crystal structures, and several important examples are given in Fig. 6.

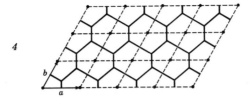

Fig. 4. Two-dimensional lattice with the corresponding Wigner-Seitz zones.

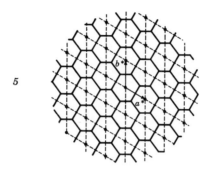

Fig. 5. Reciprocal lattice and Brillouin zones corresponding to Fig. 4.

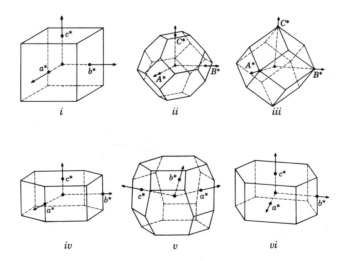

Fig. 6. Some important Brillouin zones. (*i*) primitive cubic; (*ii*) face-centered cubic; (*iii*) body-centered cubic; (*iv*) hexagonal; (*v*) rhombohedral (as in bismuth); (*vi*) primitive monoclinic (as in α uranium).

The electron density of a unit cell and the symmetry of the motif

We started our description of the crystal by referring to the electron-density function as a continuous, periodic function. The lattice merely describes the fact that the electron density is periodic. The electron density is not monotonously uniform, but shows maxima at the loci of the atoms in the structure. The total electron density of the crystal is, in fact, the sum of the individual electron densities of the different atoms, and it can be said that it has the property of atomicity.

We can describe the electron density of the crystal by defining first the electron density of the unit cell

$$\rho_{cell}(r) = \sum_{j=1}^{J} \rho_j(\mathbf{r} - \mathbf{r}_j), \tag{14}$$

as formed by the electron densities of the different atoms contained in the unit cell.

The motif is given by the electron density that fills up the unit cell, and is known also as the unit-cell content. The unit cell, therefore, defines the smallest volume of the electron density that, by repetition through the lattice translations generates the whole crystal. We can select an infinite number of motifs just by shifting the lattice in the continuous electron-density function, and cutting this function by the planes that limit the parallelepiped that define the unit cell of the lattice. The spacial distribution of the different atoms of the motif is known to have a symmetry consistent with a given space group, which implies the presence of symmetry operators other than the trivial translations. Because of this, it is customary to select as the origin of the unit cell a singular point on a given element of symmetry, ordinarily a center of symmetry if the electron-density function is centrosymmetric.

The electron density of a molecule is practically zero outside the volume of the molecule; that is, there is no overlapping of the electron-density functions of the different molecules. If there is only one molecule per unit cell, the unit cell can be chosen as to have an electron density practically identical to that of the molecule. If there are several identical molecules in the unit cell, these molecules will not, in general, be translation equivalent but rather equivalent by some other symmetry operation. The electron density of the unit cell can be calculated by adding the electron densities of the molecules at each molecular site, provided the different orientations of these molecules are considered. The electron density of the cell can then be expressed as

$$\rho_{\text{cell}}(\mathbf{r}) = \sum_{p}^{P} \rho_p(\mathbf{r} - \mathbf{r}_p), \tag{15}$$

where the summation is extended to the P molecules of the unit cell.

The Q function of a unit cell of a molecular crystal

Using the Q functions of an individual molecule given by (127) of Ch. 1, we can express the Q function of a single unit cell containing several molecules by

$$Q_{\text{cell}}(\mathbf{r}) = \sum_{p} \sum_{p'} \rho_p(\mathbf{r} - \mathbf{r}_p) * \rho_{p'}(-\mathbf{r} + \mathbf{r}_{p'}) \tag{16}$$

The Q function of a unit cell that contains P identical molecules of n atoms has $(Pn)^2$ peaks, of which Pn^2 are due to the self-images of the P molecules and correspond to intramolecular atomic distances. Of those, Pn peaks correspond to the self-images of the individual atoms of the molecules and give rise to the high peak at the origin of the Q function. The remaining $(Pn)^2 - P_n^2$ peaks correspond to intermolecular atomic distances, arising from the images of each molecule on every other. Figure 7 represents schematically the case of a unit cell containing two molecules, each with two atoms. The atoms belonging to the second molecule are labelled with primes. The peaks of the type (n, m) (n', m') correspond to the self-images of molecules 1 and 2, respectively. The peaks with mixed indices correspond to the images of molecule 1 in molecule 2 and vice versa.

We can show explicitly the above facts by splitting the double summation of (16) into two terms, i.e.,

$$Q_{\text{cell}}(\mathbf{r}) = \sum_{\substack{p \\ p=p'}} \rho_p(\mathbf{r}) * \rho_p(-\mathbf{r})$$
$$+ \sum_{p} \sum_{\substack{p' \\ p \neq p'}} \rho_p(\mathbf{r} - \mathbf{r}_p) * \rho_{p'}(-\mathbf{r} + \mathbf{r}_{p'}). \tag{17}$$

The first summation corresponds to intramolecular Q functions of the individual molecules in the unit cell, and represents the sum of the self-images of the molecules of the unit cell; the second sum corresponds to the intermolecular Q functions. Relation (17) can be written

$$Q_{\text{cell}}(\mathbf{r}) = \sum_{p} Q_p(\mathbf{r}) + \sum_{p} \sum_{p'} \rho_p(\mathbf{r} - \mathbf{r}_p) * \rho_{p'}(-\mathbf{r} + \mathbf{r}_{p'}). \tag{18}$$

The peaks of the first term are located at and around the origin of the physical space. The peaks of the second term are located at and

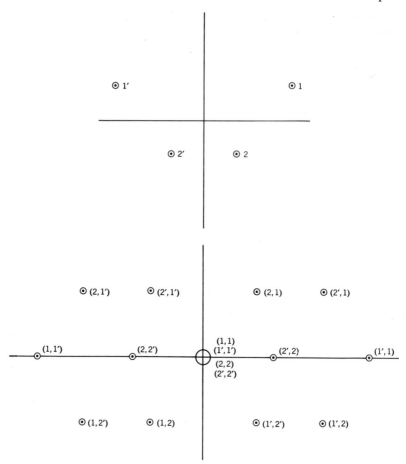

Fig. 7. Schematic two-dimensional Q function of a bimolecular unit cell of diatomic molecules.

around $\mathbf{r}_p - \mathbf{r}_{p'}$, which is the vector distance between the sites of the two molecules being considered. In other words the second term is translation dependent. Two-dimensional examples that correspond to the Q functions of the unit cell of benzene projected on (010), (100), and (001) can be seen in Fig. 8. The three-dimensional unit cell of benzene contains four molecules that project on the selected planes in two different orientations only. A unit cell in these projections can be selected that contains only two molecules with symmetrical orientations (Fig. 8i). The molecules have been represented schematically by substituting disks for the carbon atoms. The two-dimensional

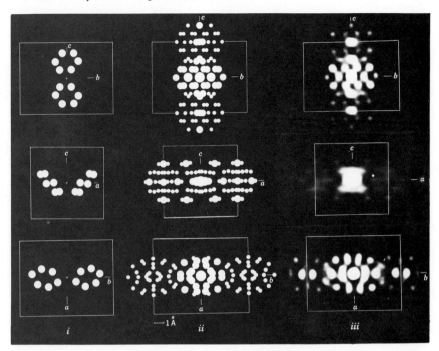

Fig. 8. Benzene. Q functions of the unit-cell projected on (100), (010), and (001); (*i*) scheme of the unit-cell content; (*ii*) calculated Q-function; (*iii*) optical Q function.

Q functions are represented in Fig. 8*ii*. The interatomic peaks are clearly seen, and have been represented by disks of different radii depending on the number (multiplicity) of equal interatomic distances. Comparing this calculated Q functions with the optical Q functions (Fig. 8*iii*) obtained with the same models, we can see the agreement of both types of Q functions.

The interpretation of such Q functions is straighforward when compared with the scheme of Fig. 7, especially in the case of the projection (010). The central motif of the Q function corresponds to

$$Q_1(\mathbf{r}) + Q_2(\mathbf{r}),$$

and shows a symmetry directly related to the two symmetrical orientations of the two molecules in the unit cell. The motifs at $\frac{1}{2}0$ and $-\frac{1}{2}0$ are identical, but different from the motif at 00; they correspond to the image function of molecule 1 in molecule 2,

$$\rho_1(\mathbf{r}-\mathbf{r}_1) \ast \rho_2(-\mathbf{r}+\mathbf{r}_2)$$

and vice versa.

The lower intensity of the external part of the optical Q functions is due mainly to the fact that most of the intermolecular atomic peaks are simple, in contrast with the multiple peaks of the intramolecular region of the total Q function. It can be seen in Fig. 8 that the Q function of a unit cell extends over the geometrical limits of the unit cell. This fact has important consequences when dealing with the Q function of a crystal, because the sum of the overlapping regions of the Q function must be taken into account.

Diffraction by the content of a single unit cell of a molecular crystal

The amplitude diffracted by the content of a unit cell of a crystal is the Fourier transform of the electron density of a single unit cell, and can be simply expressed as

$$F_{cell}(\mathbf{r^*}) = \sum_{j=1}^{n} f_j(\mathbf{r^*}) \exp(2\pi i\,\mathbf{r^*} \cdot \mathbf{r}_j), \tag{19}$$

where the summation extends over all n atoms inside the unit cell. The Fourier transform $F_{cell}(\mathbf{r^*})$ of the electron density of the unit cell of a crystal is a continuous function in reciprocal space, as is the molecular Fourier transform. It can be shown, however, that the scattering pattern of a unit cell is too weak to be observed. In practice the smallest crystals studied by x-rays have dimensions on the order of 0.01μ on a side, and contain on the order of 10^9 cells, in which case the crystal is large enough to give observable diffraction.

In a molecular crystal where molecules have individuality, it is of interest to express the Fourier transform of the unit cell as a function of the transforms of the different molecules referred to their centers; thus:

$$F_{cell}(\mathbf{r^*}) = \sum_{p}^{P} \sum_{j}^{J} f_{p,j}(\mathbf{r^*})\ \exp\left\{2\pi i[\mathbf{r^*} \cdot (\mathbf{r}_{j,p}+\mathbf{r}_p)]\right\}. \tag{20}$$

The summation over j is extended to the atoms of each molecule and the summation over p to their "centers." This is of particular interest because normally more than one molecule is contained in the primitive cell, yet such molecules are often related by the symmetry operations of the space group. It is understandable that the diffraction amplitude of the unit-cell content can easily be derived in terms of the amplitudes diffracted by the different molecules of the unit cell, taking into account the phase differences between all atoms in the unit cell. If the individual molecules are related by symmetry operations, there are also specific relations between the corresponding transforms.

If the transform of the molecule whose location in the unit cell is given by r_p is called $F_p(r^*)$,

$$F_p(r^*) = \sum_{j=1}^{J} f_j \exp(2\pi i \, r^* \cdot r_{p,j}), \tag{21}$$

where $r_{j,p}$ are the atomic positions, r_p being considered as its origin, then

$$F_{\text{cell}}(r^*) = \sum_{p=1}^{p} F_p(r^*) \exp(2\pi i r^* \cdot r_p). \tag{22}$$

The intensity function of the content of a unit cell is given by

$$I_{\text{cell}}(r^*) = F_{\text{cell}}(r^*) \cdot F_{\text{cell}}^*(r^*)$$
$$= |F_{\text{cell}}(r^*)|^2, \tag{23}$$

and for a molecular crystal

$$I_{\text{cell}}(r^*) = \sum_{p=1}^{p} F_p(r^*) \cdot F_{p'}^*(r^*). \tag{24}$$

By splitting the summation into two parts, $p = p'$ and $p \neq p'$, we have

$$I_{\text{cell}}(r^*) = \sum_{p=p'}^{p} I_p(r^*)$$

$$+ \sum_{p \neq p'}^{P} \sum^{P} F_p(r^*) \cdot F_{p'}^*(r^*) \exp[2\pi i r^* \cdot (r_p - r_{p'})]. \tag{25}$$

As an example let us consider a monoclinic molecular crystal belonging to the space group $P2_1/a$, such as adipic acid. The unit cell contains two centrosymmetric molecules, molecule 1 having its symmetry center at the origin, and molecule 2 having its center at $\frac{1}{2}\frac{1}{2}0$. For sake of simplicity let us consider the projection of the structure on (010) where the two molecules project identically. In Ch. 1 we discussed the molecular transform functions of the molecule at the origin (Fig. 31, Ch. 1) and the case of the molecule shifted from the origin of coordinates (Fig. 32, Ch. 1). In this case

$$F_2(hkl) = F_1(hkl) \exp[2\pi i \, (r^*_{hkl} \cdot a/2)]. \tag{26}$$

The factor $\exp[2\pi i \, (r^*_{hkl} \cdot a/2)]$ is a fringe interference function, whose modulus is always unity. This function modifies the transform F_1 by a *fringe function* giving rise to F_2. In the unit cell both molecules diffract together, and the amplitude of the diffraction is given by

$$F_{\text{cell}}(r^*) = F_1(h0l)(1 + \exp[2\pi i \, (r^*_{h0l} \cdot a/2)]). \tag{27}$$

Since here there enter not only the relative phases due to the different atoms of a single molecule, but also the relative phases due to the atoms of both molecules, the transform map of the unit cell has regions

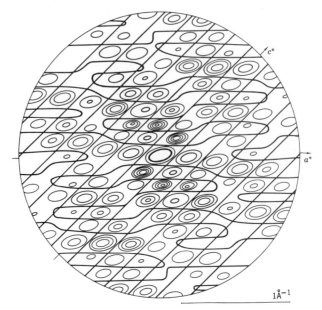

Fig. 9. Adipic acid. $(010)_0$ Map of the modulus of the transform of the content of a unit cell.

where the diffraction-amplitude function vanishes because the diffraction from related atoms has opposite phases. This effect is seen clearly in Fig. 9.

The factor $1 + \exp[2\pi i(\mathbf{r}^*_{hkl} \cdot \mathbf{a}/2)]$ is also a fringe function that modifies the diffraction amplitude. Its modulus is 2 for $h = 2n$. The transform of the unit cell at $(010)^*_0$ is built up of the transform of molecule 1 multiplied by 2, crossed by a set of planar fringes.

As an optical example, Fig. 10 shows the Fraunhofer pattern of two molecules (the unit-cell content) of benzene projected on (100), (010), and (001). The pattern is not merely the sum of the intensities diffracted by the two individual molecules, but shows some fine structure due to the phase relations between the two molecules of the unit cell.

The ρ and Q functions of an infinite, ideal crystal

We have seen that the electron-density function of an ideal crystal is an ideal periodic function. It can be expressed in terms of the electron density $\rho_{\text{cell}}(\mathbf{r})$ of a single unit cell, the motif function, convolved with the crystalline-lattice peak function $z_{\text{cr}}(\mathbf{r})$

$$\rho_\infty(\mathbf{r}) = \rho_{\text{cell}}(\mathbf{r}) * z_{\text{cr}}(\mathbf{r}). \tag{28}$$

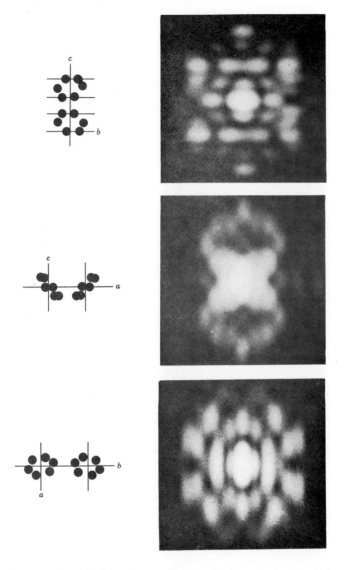

Fig. 10. Benzene. Fraunhofer patterns of the unit-cell content projected on (100), (010), and (001).

We can define a solitary function as a periodic component of a periodic function. We can derive an infinite number of solitary functions from the electron-density function. Let us consider, for instance, a mono-molecular crystal generated by the triperiodic repetition of a given molecule. We can derive a solitary function by selecting a given atom in each molecule of the crystal. Obviously we can define as many solitary functions as there are single atoms in the molecule, or pairs of atoms, or any other groups of atoms in the molecule. None of these solitary functions will reproduce the total electron density of the crystal. The total electron density can be generated by the sum of the solitary functions defining each atom of the molecule. In this case we can visualize the crystal as formed by as many identical, inter-penetrating lattices as there are atoms in the molecule. This concept is very useful when the contribution of an atom or a group of atoms of the crystal structure to diffraction is analyzed.

Solitary functions that generate the total electron density of the crystal can also be defined. In our example we can select the electron density of the whole molecule as a solitary function that fulfills such a condition. In this case the electron-density function of monomolecular crystals can be given by

$$\rho_\infty(\mathbf{r}) = \rho_{\mathrm{mole}}(\mathbf{r}) * z_{\mathrm{cr}}(\mathbf{r}), \tag{29}$$

where $\rho_{\mathrm{mole}}(\mathbf{r})$ is the electron density of the molecule. If the crystal contains P molecules per unit cell, we have an analogous expression

$$\rho_\infty(\mathbf{r}) = [\ \textstyle\sum_p^P \rho_p(\mathbf{r}-\mathbf{r}_p)\,] * z_{\mathrm{cr}}(\mathbf{r}). \tag{30}$$

The electron density of the crystal is just the sum of P solitary functions, each one including the electron density of a molecule.

The Q function of an infinite, ideal crystal is also a periodic function in physical space, which can be generated in terms of the self-image of a single unit cell convolved with the lattice-peak function:

$$Q_{\mathrm{cr}}(\mathbf{r}) = \frac{1}{v_c} Q_{\mathrm{cell}}(\mathbf{r}) * z_{\mathrm{cr}}(\mathbf{r}). \tag{31}$$

The self-image of the motif now defines the solitary function.

Similarly, the Q function of a monomolecular crystal is given by

$$Q_{\mathrm{cr}}(\mathbf{r}) = \frac{1}{v_c} Q_{\mathrm{mole}}(\mathbf{r}) * z_{\mathrm{cr}}(\mathbf{r}), \tag{32}$$

which is equivalent to generating the whole Q function by a solitary function, the self-image of the molecule. As the self-image of the molecule extends over the limits of the unit cell, some overlapping of the solitary function takes place.

A two-dimensional example of a monomolecular crystal is given in Fig. 11i where the projection on (010) of the anthracene molecule is schematically given as built up by disk atoms. The Q function of this

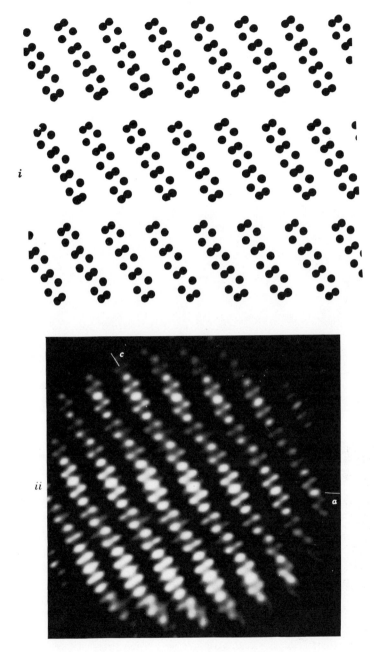

Fig. 11. Anthracene. (*i*) Periodic electron density projected on (010) of the molecular structure of disk atoms; (*ii*) optical Q function.

two-dimensional structure is just the solitary function formed by the
self-image of the molecule. Since this is the Q function of a perfect
crystal, the same distribution of maxima is found in all the unit cells.

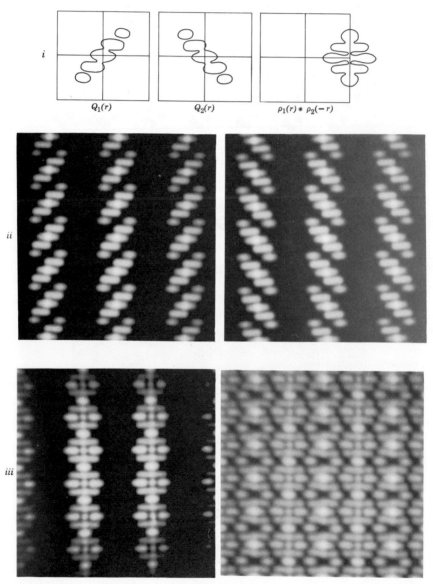

Fig. 12.   Benzene. Projection on (010). (*i*) Motifs; (*ii*) solitary functions Q_1 and Q_2; (*iii*)
solitary image function of molecule 1 on molecule 2 and Q function of the crystal.

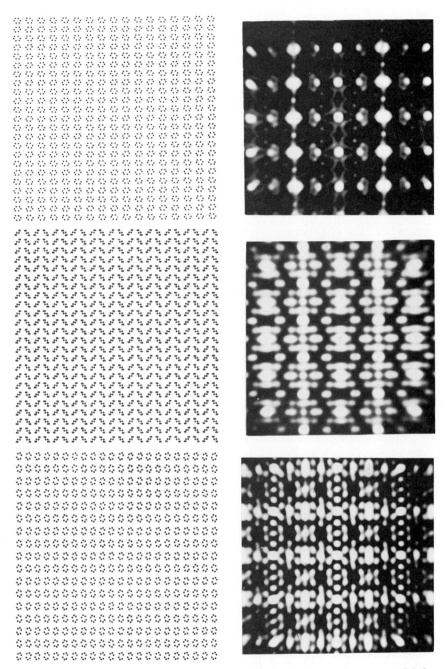

Fig. 13. Benzene. Projections on (100), (010), and (001) of the ideal structure of disk-like atoms and the corresponding two-dimensional Q functions.

If there are several molecules per unit cell, the expression for the Q function takes the form

$$Q_{cr}(\mathbf{r}) = \frac{1}{v_c}[\Sigma_p Q(\mathbf{r}) + \sum_p \sum_{p'} \rho_p(\mathbf{r}-\mathbf{r}_p) * \rho_{p'}(-\mathbf{r}+\mathbf{r}_{p'})] * z_{cr}(\mathbf{r}). \quad (33)$$

The Q function is in this case generated by several solitary functions, namely the solitary functions each containing the self-image of each individual molecule and the solitary functions each containing the image of each molecule in every other. The total Q function is the result of the sum of the different solitary functions. To make this clear let us examine the Q function of benzene projected on (010). As there are only two different projected molecules per unit cell, the components of the Q function are three solitary functions (Fig. 12i). Two correspond respectively to the self-images of the two differently oriented molecules, and the third one corresponds to the image of one molecule in the other. In the figure the motifs of the three solitary functions are referred to the same origin. The solitary function of the self-image of each molecule is given in Fig. 12ii. The total Q function (Fig. 12iii) is just the sum of the three solitary functions.

The Q functions of the three main projections of benzene have similar features. The projections on (100), (010), and (001) of the ideal structure in which the atoms have been replaced by disk-like atoms are given in Fig. 13, together with the corresponding optical Q functions. From comparison of these two-dimensional Q functions and the ones reproduced in Fig. 8 corresponding to the Q functions of a unit cell alone it can easily be deduced that the self-image of the perfect crystal results from taking the Q function of a single unit cell as the solitary function. The higher intensity of the intermolecular atomic peaks in the Q functions of the infinite crystal with respect to the Q function of a single unit cell results from the overlapping of the Q functions of single unit cells. This overlap affects mainly the part due to intermolecular interaction. In the (010) projection the intra- and intermolecular components are well separated. In the other two projections some overlap of the two functions exist.

Diffraction by an infinite, ideal crystal

We obtain the amplitude diffracted by the crystal by performing a Fourier transformation to (28) and by applying the convolution theorem:

$$F_{cr}(\mathbf{r}^*) = T\{\rho_{cell}(\mathbf{r}) * z_{cr}(\mathbf{r})\}. \quad (34)$$

Since $Z_{cr}(r^*)$, the Fourier transform of $z_{cr}(r)$, is the reciprocal-lattice peak function, giving peaks of content v_c^* at the lattice points r_h^*, (8), we see that each individual discrete value of $F_{cell}(r_h^*)$ can be expressed in terms of $F_{cell}(r^*) \cdot Z_{cr}(r^*)$. We have

$$F_{cr}(r^*) = v_c^* \sum_h^\infty F_{cell}(r_h^*) \cdot L(r^* - r_h^*). \tag{35}$$

For the amplitude diffracted by the ideal, infinite crystal, we obtain a function that is zero everywhere except at the nodes of the reciprocal lattice, where it has the values of the Fourier transform of a single unit cell. We meet with a discrete function, sampled in reciprocal space at the reciprocal lattice points. The discrete values of this function are called, in x-ray crystallography, the structure factors $F(hkl)$ associated with the crystal plane of indices hkl, so that

$$F_{cr}(r^*) = v_c^* \sum_{hkl} F(hkl) \cdot L(r^* - r_{hkl}^*). \tag{36}$$

The structure factor $F(hkl)$ is given by

$$F(hkl) = v_c \int \int \int_0^1 \rho(r) \exp[2\pi i(hx + ky + lz)] \, dx \, dy \, dz, \tag{37}$$

where the integration is over the volume of the unit cell. One structure factor is particularly interesting:

$$F(000) = v_c \int \int \int_0^1 \rho(r) \, dx \, dy \, dz. \tag{38}$$

This integral represents the total mass of the unit-cell content, or the projection on the origin of the unit-cell content.

In an analogous way we can perform a Fourier transformation to the $Q_{cr}(r)$ of (31), and obtain

$$I_{cr}(r^*) = T\{Q_{cell}(r^*) * z_{cr}(r)\} \tag{39}$$

Since $Z_{cr}(r^*)$ is the Fourier transform of $z_{cr}(r)$, we finally obtain, by applying the convolution theorem:

$$I_{cr}(r^*) = I_{cell}(r^*) \cdot Z_{cr}(r^*), \tag{40}$$

and

$$I_{cr}(r^*) = v_c^* \sum_{hkl}^\infty I_{cell}(hkl) \cdot L(r^* - r_h^*), \tag{41}$$

which has discrete values at the reciprocal-lattice points, corresponding to the diffracted intensity of a single unit-cell content, and is zero everywhere else.

We have seen now that if the physical space is periodic, its transform is discrete. We are able to observe and measure the intensities scattered by a crystal, while losing the information about the continuous scattering from the unit cell. In other words information is lost about the diffraction space lying between the reciprocal-lattice points.

When proper use of the symmetry of the motif is made, we can talk about the scattering pattern of the assymmetrical part of the unit cell, that is, of the minimum stereochemical group of atoms that corresponds to the chemical formula of the substance. In mathematical language we refer to the patterns of continuous scattering as Fourier transforms. We can speak of the Fourier transforms of a molecule, of the content of a unit cell, and of the whole crystal.

In spite of everything, the information outside the reciprocal lattice points is not completely lost, for the very reason that the crystal is not perfect. The objective of this book is the detailed study of Fourier space of molecular crystals outside the reciprocal-lattice points.

Fraunhofer pattern of perfect crystal

We have established the analogy between the Fourier transform of a disk illuminated by ordinary light and the Fourier transform of a real atom by x-ray scattering; now we can use the disk atoms or transparent disks (in our drawings, black circles) to represent the atoms of our model of the two-dimensional projection of the crystal structure to be investigated.

Let us first treat the simple case of a two-dimensional, monoatomic, rectangular crystal, whose atoms are represented by disks (Fig. 14i). The "electron"-density of this model can be defined as the convolution of the disk function $\rho_d(\mathbf{r})$ with the lattice peak function $z_{cr}(\mathbf{r})$.

The function $Q_d(\mathbf{r})$ of a disk is the self-image of $\rho_d(\mathbf{r})$, and the function $Q(\mathbf{r})$ of the ideal crystal is given by (31). Because we are dealing with a perfect lattice, the maximum of the $Q(\mathbf{r})$ function at the origin has the same shape and intensity as the rest, and we do not reproduce it here.

In a photographic negative of the model drawn the black disks appear as circular apertures that can diffract monochromatic light. The intensity function $I(\mathbf{r}^*)$ of the image obtained with the optical diffractometer with a transparency as a diffraction grating, is shown in Fig. 14ii.

The intensity function has well-defined maxima (Bragg reflections) at the lattice points of the corresponding zero level of the reciprocal lattice. The figure shows clearly the first dark ring and the first bright ring, which distinguish it from an x-ray photograph. This Fraunhofer pattern clearly shows the intensity distribution of the Airy pattern through the "windows" of the reciprocal lattice.

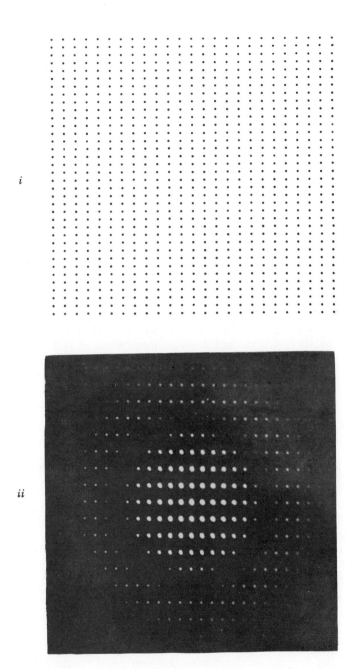

i

ii

Fig. 14. Two-dimensional lattice and its Fraunhofer photograph. The Airy pattern of a disk can be recognized.

In order to compare the intensity function of a zero level of the reciprocal lattice of a given crystal diffracting x-rays with the intensity of the diffraction obtained by the incidence of ordinary light on a model corresponding to the plane projection of the crystal it is necessary that the first dark ring of the optical pattern fall outside the sphere of reflection of the x-rays used in the experiment. The experimental conditions are easily obtained if we take into account that, for a one-dimensional diffraction grating, the maxima appear at $2 \sin \theta = \lambda/d, 2\lambda/d, \ldots, n\lambda/d$, where d is the spacing of the slits, n is an integer, and λ is the wavelength of the light used (Fig. 15i). The first minimum of intensity of the diffraction of a disk of radius R lies at a distance from the origin equal to $2 \sin \theta = 0.610 \, \lambda/R$ (Fig. 15ii). With a diffraction grating of spacing d, the number n of maxima included between the origin and the first minimum due to the diffraction by a single disk (Fig. 15iii) must satisfy

$$\frac{0.615\lambda}{R} = \frac{n\lambda}{d}. \tag{42}$$

This allows us to choose the radius R of the disk in relation to the spacing d in such a way that a given number n of reflections will appear along a radial line of the sphere of reflection corresponding to the x-ray wavelength used. That is the criterion followed in this book. In many of the Fraunhofer patterns reproduced here we can see, from the scale in reciprocal units, that the number of reflections appearing is more or less the number of those lying inside of the limit of the sphere of reflection for the wavelength of $CuK\alpha = 1.54$ Å. In the model of Fig. 14i, given the spacings in the two principal directions and the radius of the disks, application of (42) shows that within the first dark ring there should appear four to six orders of reflections (Fig. 14ii) along the two principal directions.

An example of the intensity diffracted by a monomolecular crystal of anthracene (Fig. 16i) is given in Fig. 16ii. Comparison of the Fraunhofer patterns of a single molecule (Fig. 21iii, Ch. 1) and the one corresponding to the crystal, clearly shows that the molecular transform is seen through the "windows" of the reciprocal lattice.

Another interesting example is given by the Fraunhofer diffraction of the two-dimensional projections of the crystal structure of benzene. The Fraunhofer patterns (Fig. 17) correspond to the diffraction of the perfect crystal structure projected on (100), (010), and (001), respectively. In the bottom of the figure the weighted reciprocal lattices for optical diffraction have been plotted, where the circles have areas proportional to the intensity maxima.

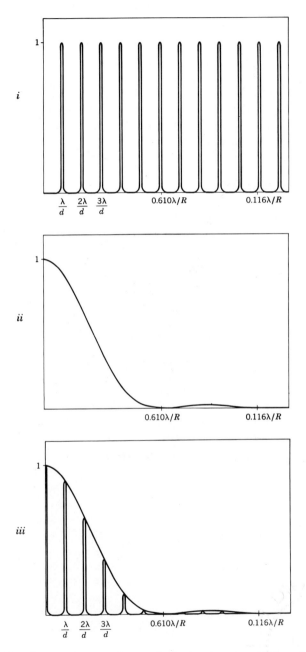

Fig. 15. (*i*) Diffraction maxima of a one-dimensional grating; (*ii*) form factor of a disk; (*iii*) composite effect.

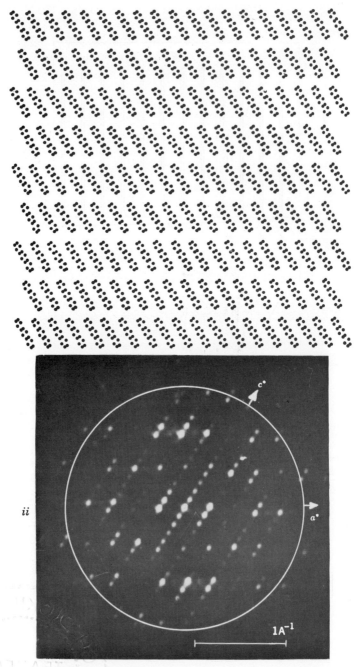

_i_

_ii_

Fig. 16. Anthracene. (_i_) Periodic electron density, projected on (010), of the molecular structure of disk atoms; (_ii_) Fraunhofer pattern.

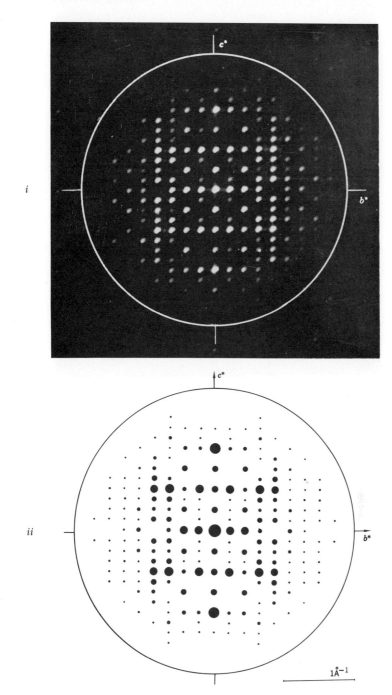

Fig. 17. Benzene. (*i*) Fraunhofer patterns of the two-dimensional structures given in Fig. 16*i*, (*ii*) weighted reciprocal lattices.

97

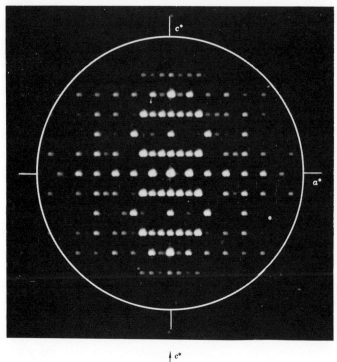

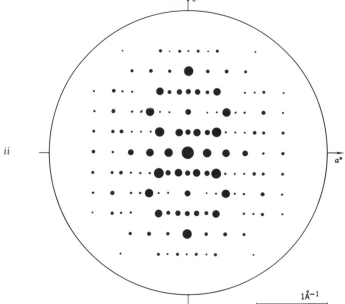

Fig. 17. (continued).

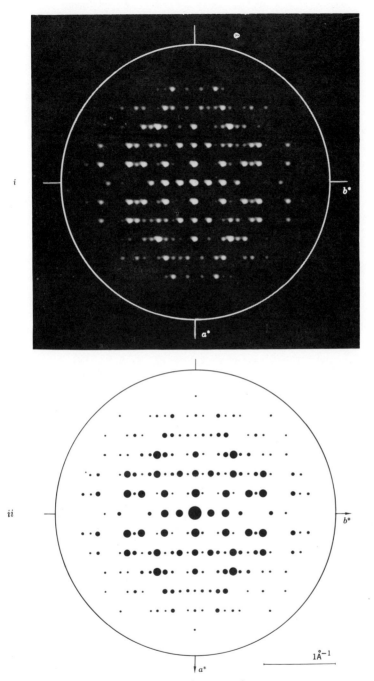

Fig. 17. (continued).

99

Scattering by a perfect but finite crystal: shape factor

When the crystal is ideal but finite, we must introduce a shape function $s(\mathbf{r})$ equal to unity inside this finite volume v, and vanishing identically outside it. Mathematically, it is expressed as follows:

$$s(\mathbf{r}) = \begin{array}{ll} 1 & \text{for r values inside } v \\ 0 & \text{everywhere else} \end{array} \qquad (43)$$

where

$$\int_{v} s(\mathbf{r}) \, dv_r = v. \qquad (44)$$

In the two-dimensional case, v represents the area. The electron-density function of a finite crystal is expressed then as

$$\rho(\mathbf{r}) = \rho_0(\mathbf{r}) * [z_{cr}(\mathbf{r}) \cdot s(\mathbf{r})], \qquad (45)$$

and its function $Q(\mathbf{r})$ as

$$Q(\mathbf{r}) = \frac{1}{v_c} Q_0 * [z_{cr}(\mathbf{r}) \cdot Q_s(\mathbf{r})]. \qquad (46)$$

The Fourier transform of the shape function $s(\mathbf{r})$ is the shape amplitude $S(\mathbf{r}^*)$,

$$S(\mathbf{r}^*) = T\{s(\mathbf{r})\}. \qquad (47)$$

On the other hand, $|S(\mathbf{r}^*)|^2$ is called the shape factor whose inverse transform is

$$T^{-1}\{|S(\mathbf{r}^*)|^2\} = Q_s(\mathbf{r}). \qquad (48)$$

Finally, the intensity function of a perfect, finite crystal is then given by

$$T^{-1}\{Q(\mathbf{r})\} = I(\mathbf{r}^*) = v^* \cdot I_{cell}(\mathbf{r}_c^*) \cdot Z_{cr}(\mathbf{r}^*) * |S(\mathbf{r}^*)|^2. \qquad (49)$$

Expression (49) tells us that the effect in diffraction space of the size of the crystal consists of a repetition of the transform of the shape function at each reciprocal-lattice point (Ewald, 1940).

The influence of the shape factor $s(\mathbf{r})$ is evident when one or more dimensions of the three-dimensional crystal are markedly limited. In the case of a needle-shaped crystal, for instance, the reciprocal-lattice points are plates normal to the direction of the needle, while with a plate-like crystal the Bragg reflections are needle shaped and elongated along the normal to the plane of the plate. The effect of the crystal shape can be seen in Fig. 18, which shows the Fraunhofer diffraction pattern for only three rows of atoms of the model. The reciprocal of the shape of the model is clearly seen in the diffraction pattern.

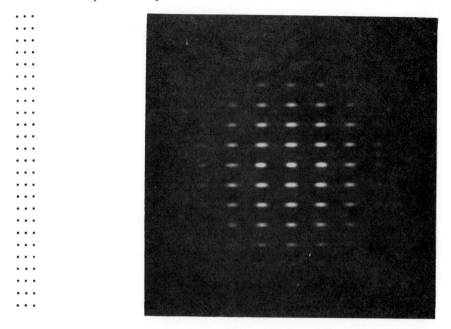

Fig. 18. Fraunhofer pattern of only three rows of disk-like atoms, showing the shape-factor effect.

· The Fourier and Patterson syntheses

Since, in an ideal crystal, the density function is a periodic function, the Fourier integral can be replaced by Fourier series. We can represent the density function of this ideal crystal by a Fourier series whose coefficients are the structure factors. In fact, by inverse transformation of the diffracted amplitude we obtain

$$
\begin{aligned}
\rho_\infty(\mathbf{r}) &= T^{-1}\{F(\mathbf{r^*}) \cdot Z_{\mathrm{cr}}(\mathbf{r^*})\} \\
&= T^{-1}\Big\{\sum_h^\infty F(\mathbf{r_h^*}) \cdot L(\mathbf{r}-\mathbf{r}_h)\Big\} \\
&= \int_v \sum_h^\infty F(\mathbf{r_h^*}) \cdot L(\mathbf{r}-\mathbf{r}_h) \, \exp(2\pi i \mathbf{r} \cdot \mathbf{r^*}) \, dv^*.
\end{aligned}
\tag{50}
$$

Since $F(\mathbf{r_h^*})$ is a discrete function we can replace the Fourier integral by a Fourier series

$$
\rho(xyz) = v_c^* \sum_{h=-\infty}^{+\infty} \sum_{k=-\infty}^{+\infty} \sum_{l=-\infty}^{+\infty} F(hkl) \exp\left[2\pi i \left(hx + ky + lz\right)\right].
\tag{51}
$$

This is equivalent to saying that the periodic electron density of an infinite perfect crystal is the sum of an infinite set of static, harmonic electron-density waves whose amplitudes are equal to $v^* \cdot F(hkl)$, whose wavelengths are $1/|\mathbf{r}^*_{hkl}|$ and whose wavefronts are parallel to the plane (hkl). Each pair of waves $\mathbf{r}^*_{hkl}$ and $\mathbf{r}^*_{hkl}$ correspond to a certain sinusoidal electron-density distribution, and the sum in (51) includes the term $F(000)$ with a uniform distribution of the average electron density of the cell. This term insures that the total electron density at every point of the crystal is positive.

A very elegant way of showing that a Fourier synthesis is built up by the sum of harmonic density waves is provided by the von Eller *photosummateur harmonique* (von Eller, 1951). This machine contains a periodic mask that corresponds to the function $(1 + \cos 2\pi hr)$ (Fig. 19i). With such a mask, density waves can be generated whose wavelength, phase, amplitude, and orientation can be adequately varied. As an example, four components of the Fourier synthesis are shown in Fig. 19ii as plane waves of intensity. The Fourier synthesis of anthracene projected on (010) is given in Fig. 20. The individual molecules are clearly shown as well as the atoms that form the molecule.

From (51) we can now define the structure factor associated with the reciprocal-lattice point hkl as the coefficient of the hkl term of the Fourier series that represents the electron density in the crystal divided by the volume of the unit cell. The coefficients $F(hkl)$ contain not only the amplitude but the phase $\phi(hkl)$. Equation (51) can be written so as to contain explicitly the phase, as follows:

$$\rho(xyz) = v_c^* \sum_h \sum_k \sum_l^{+\infty} |F(hkl)| \exp[2\pi i(hx + ky + lz) + \phi(hkl)]. \quad (52)$$

We have seen in Ch. 1 that the modulus of the diffracted amplitude is a centrosymmetric function, and that the phase angle ϕ is antisymmetric, i.e.

$$|F(hkl)| = |F(\bar{h}\bar{k}\bar{l})|, \qquad \phi(hkl) = -\phi(\bar{h}\bar{k}\bar{l}). \quad (53)$$

With these relations into account, equation (52) becomes

$$\rho(xyz) = v_c^* F(000) + v_c^* \sum_{h=0}^{+\infty} \sum_{k=0}^{+\infty} \sum_{l=0}^{+\infty} |F(hkl)| \cos 2\pi [hx + ky + lz \pm$$
$$\phi(hkl)], \quad (54)$$

where $v_c^* F(000) = \rho_0$ is the average electron density of the unit cell. Since it is not possible to determine from experiment the phase $\phi(hkl)$ but only the modulus of the amplitude $|F(hkl)|$, the direct calculation of the electron density from experimental data is, in general, impossible, giving rise to the so-called phase problem in crystal-structure analysis. The discussion of this problem is outside the scope of this book.

The simplest example of a Fourier synthesis is the calculation of the electron density of a monoatomic hypothetical structure. As the

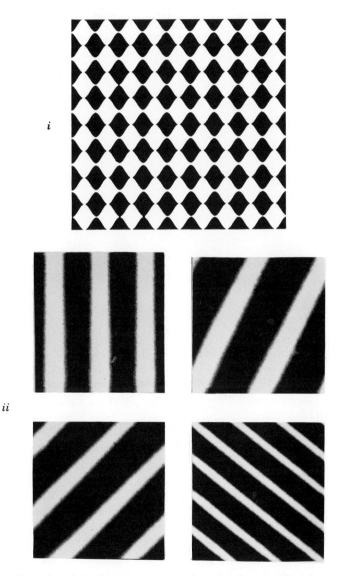

Fig. 19. (*i*) Mask with the function $1 + \cos 2\pi rh$ used in the von Eller photosummateur; (*ii*) four components of the Fourier series.

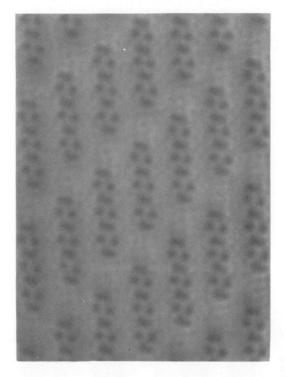

Fig. 20. Anthracene projected on (010). Two-dimensional Fourier obtained with the von Eller machine.

centers of the atoms of the structure coincide with the lattice points, the position of the atom can be selected as lying at th origin of coordinates. Because of this, and because the electron density of the atom has spherical symmetry (Ch. 1), there is no phase problem because all the Fourier coefficients have the same phase angle $\phi = 0$. The Fourier coefficients can be easily obtained by sampling the atomic scattering factor of the corresponding atom at the reciprocal-lattice points. If these coefficients are introduced into (54) the electron density of the atom can be calculated.

The atomic scattering factors are functions decreasing with the magnitude of the reciprocal vector; for x-ray or electron waves these functions have only been calculated out to about $3.8\ \text{Å}^{-1}$ [see "International Tables of Crystallography," vol. 3, (1962), and in the case of carbon atom the value of the functions at this limit ($|\mathbf{r}^*| = 3.8\ \text{Å}^{-1}$) is $f_c = 0.419$, so that no big error arises by cutting off the Fourier series at the above limit, or even at $2.8\ \text{Å}^{-1}$, which is the radius of the limiting sphere for Mo$K\alpha$ x-ray radiation. In (50) the integral in the operator of T^{-1} is extended over all reciprocal space, and hence the summation in (51) is extended to all hkl values different from zero. Whenever, by setting artificial limits, some Fourier coefficients that are not zero are cut off from the Fourier synthesis, there arises the *series-termination effect*. The new Fourier synthesis

$$\rho'_{\text{exp}}(\mathbf{r}) = v^* \sum_{\mathbf{r}_h^* = 0}^{|\mathbf{r}_h^*| \leqslant 2/\lambda} F(\mathbf{r}_h^*) \exp(-2\pi i \mathbf{r} \cdot \mathbf{r}_h^*) \tag{55}$$

is different than the complete synthesis although, for practical purposes, this difference, in general, is of no major importance.

The effect of cutting off the experimental values beyond a certain value, $|\mathbf{r}_n^*| = 2/\lambda$, is equivalent to introducing the shape function of the limiting sphere (see Ch. 1). Its transform, the shape amplitude, was said to show a principal maximum at $|\mathbf{r}| = 0$ and subsidiary minima and maxima decreasing with $1/|\mathbf{r}|^2$. The whole shape amplitude has spherical symmetry. This shape amplitude is reflected at each maximum of the Fourier synthesis, giving rise to ripples surrounding the atoms (see Buerger, 1960).

According to (39), the Q function of an ideal, infinite crystal can be calculated by inverse Fourier transformation of the intensities obtained from diffraction experiments:

$$Q_{\text{cr}}(\mathbf{r}) = T^{-1}\{I_{\text{cell}}(\mathbf{r}^*) \cdot Z_{\text{cr}}(\mathbf{r}^*)\} = T^{-1}\left\{ \sum_{h=0}^{\infty} I(\mathbf{r}_h^*) \cdot L(\mathbf{r}^* - \mathbf{r}_h^*) \right\} \tag{56}$$

Since $I(\mathbf{r}_h^*)$ is a discrete function, the Q_{cr} function of the ideal, infinite crystal can be calculated in terms of a Fourier series,

$$P(\mathbf{r}) = v_c^* \sum_{h=-\infty}^{+\infty} \sum_{k=-\infty}^{+\infty} \sum_{l=-\infty}^{+\infty} I(hkl) \exp[-2\pi i(hx + ky + lz)], \tag{57}$$

known as the Patterson function.

It has been shown in Ch. 1 that (assuming there is no anomalous-dispersion effect) the intensity function is always centrosymmetric, i.e.,

$$I(hkl) = I(\bar{h}\bar{k}\bar{l}) \tag{58}$$

a fact that it is known as the Friedel law. Equality (58) allows one to reduce the computation in (57) to a sum of cosine functions, which are centrosymmetric. In this case the Patterson series can be expressed as

$$P(\mathbf{r}) = v_c^* |F(000)|^2 + 2v_c^* \sum_{h=0}^{+\infty} \sum_{k=0}^{+\infty} \sum_{l=0}^{+\infty} I(hkl) \cdot \cos 2\pi(hx + ky + lz), \quad (59)$$

where $|F(000)|^2 v_c^* = \rho_0^2$ is the square of the average electron density of the unit cell. This term insures that the density of the Patterson synthesis is positive everywhere in physical space.

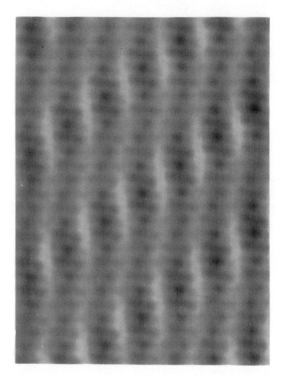

Fig. 21. Anthracene. Patterson function projected on (010), obtained with the von Eller machine.

As the Patterson function and the Q function of an ideal, infinite crystal are identical, everything discussed for the Q function applies here, and we shall not discuss it further. Ample information can be obtained from Buerger (1959).

As the Patterson function can be calculated by (59), it can be obtained with the photosummateur of von Eller. As an example of a Patterson function of a monomolecular crystal, Fig. 21 reproduces the function of anthracene projected on (010) as obtained with the von Eller photosummateur. We can see clearly the overlap of the intra-molecular Q functions by the continuity of the function along the c axis. The optical Q function of Fig. 11ii has been obtained using disk atoms. In order to compare the optical Q function with the Patterson function, this function has been calculated using as Fourier co-efficients the $I(\mathbf{r}^*_{hkl})$ calculated introducing a Bessel function of order one instead of the x-ray atomic scattering factor of carbon, and using

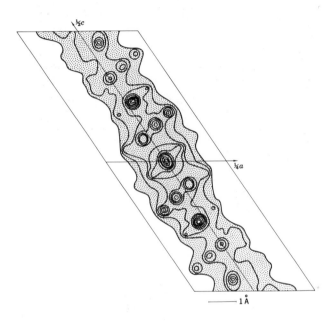

Fig. 22.   Anthracene. Calculated Patterson function projected on (010).

the atomic coordinates given by Sinclair, Robertson and Mathieson (1950). The result (Fig. 22) is the counterpart of the optical Q function reproduced in Fig. 11ii. As an example of a dimolecular crystal, the same procedure has been applied to benzene projected on (010). The result (Fig. 23i) is the calculated counterpart of the optical Q function represented in Fig. 13. The central part of Fig. 23i corresponds to the intramolecular Q function of the two symmetrical molecules in the unit cell. The rest correspond to the overlapping of intermolecular Q functions. Notice that the intensity of both intra- and intermolecular Q functions are very similar, but they differ greatly in Fig. 8iii due to the nonoverlapping in this latter case.

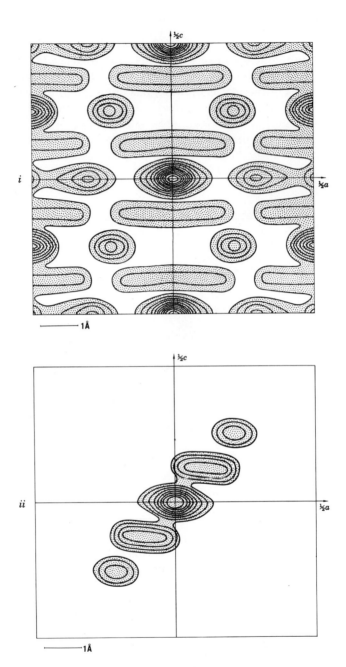

Fig. 23. Benzene. Patterson function of (*i*) the structure of disk-like atoms projected on (010), (*ii*) one molecule.

Inverse Fourier and Patterson synthesis

The concepts developed in the last section can also be applied to performing Fourier summations, whose coefficients are functions of physical space, in order to obtain the corresponding transforms in Fourier space. Since the electron density and the Q function of the motif are continuous functions, it is not possible, in principle, to use Fourier series to yield $F(\mathbf{r}^*)$ or $I(\mathbf{r}^*)$ in Fourier space by using values of $\rho(\mathbf{r})$ and $Q(\mathbf{r})$, respectively, as coefficients of the series. However, we can define a function of the continuous electron density such as

$$\rho_s'(\mathbf{r}) = \rho_{\text{cell}}(\mathbf{r}) \cdot Z_s^{v'}(\mathbf{r}), \tag{60}$$

where $Z_s^{v'}(\mathbf{r})$ is a lattice peak function, describing a sampling lattice of fundamental vectors $\mathbf{a}'\mathbf{b}'\mathbf{c}'$ and volume v' inside the unit cell. For simplicity, let us choose $\mathbf{a}', \mathbf{b}', \mathbf{c}'$ such that

$$\mathbf{a}' = \frac{\mathbf{a}/2}{L}, \qquad \mathbf{b}' = \frac{\mathbf{b}/2}{M}, \qquad \mathbf{c}' = \frac{\mathbf{c}/2}{N}, \tag{61}$$

Any lattice point of the sampling lattice is defined in terms of the vector

$$\mathbf{r}_{h'} = h'\mathbf{a}' + k'\mathbf{b}' + l'\mathbf{c}' \tag{62}$$

where h', k', l' are integers with $-L \leqslant h' \leqslant L$, and so on.

The sampling-lattice peak function is then given by

$$Z_s^{v'}(\mathbf{r}) = v' \sum_{h'=-\infty}^{+\infty} \sum_{k'=-\infty}^{+\infty} \sum_{l'=-\infty}^{+\infty} L(\mathbf{r} - h'\mathbf{a}' - k'\mathbf{b}' - l'\mathbf{c}') = v' \sum_{h'} L(\mathbf{r} - \mathbf{r}_{h'}). \tag{63}$$

Therefore

$$\rho_s'(\mathbf{r}) = v' \sum_{h'} \rho_{\text{cell}}(\mathbf{r}) \cdot L(\mathbf{r} - \mathbf{r}_{h'}). \tag{64}$$

The transform of the $\rho_{\text{cell}}(\mathbf{r})$ (or of a molecule) is not periodic. However, the transform of $\rho_s'(\mathbf{r})$ is periodic and it can easily be obtained by applying the convolution theorem to (60):

$$T\{\rho_s'(\mathbf{r})\} = F_{\text{cell}}(\mathbf{r}^*) \ast z_s(\mathbf{r}^*), \tag{65}$$

where the transform of the sampling lattice $z_s(\mathbf{r}^*)$ is given by

$$z_s(\mathbf{r}^*) = \sum_{l'=-\infty}^{+\infty} \Sigma\Sigma \, L(\mathbf{r}^* - l'\mathbf{a}'^* - m'\mathbf{b}'^* - n'\mathbf{c}'^*) = \sum_{l'} L(\mathbf{r}^* - \mathbf{r}_{l'}^*), \tag{66}$$

with

$$\mathbf{r}_{l'}^* = l'\mathbf{a}'^* + m'\mathbf{b}'^* + n'\mathbf{c}'^*, \qquad (l', m', n' \text{ integers}). \tag{67}$$

The term $z_s(\mathbf{r}^*)$ defines a new lattice peak function in Fourier space whose inverse transform has the character of its reciprocal lattice in direct space:

$$Z_s^{v'}(\mathbf{r}) = T^{-1}\{z_s(\mathbf{r}^*)\}. \tag{68}$$

The vectors $\mathbf{a}'$, $\mathbf{b}'$, $\mathbf{c}'$ and $\mathbf{a}'^*$, $\mathbf{b}'^*$, $\mathbf{c}'^*$ satisfy the following reciprocal conditions

$$\mathbf{a}' \cdot \mathbf{a}'^* = 1$$
$$\mathbf{a}' \cdot \mathbf{b}'^* = \mathbf{a}' \cdot \mathbf{c}'^* = 0, \tag{69}$$

and so on. The lattice peak function $z_s(\mathbf{r}^*)$ repeats the continuous function $F_{\text{cell}}(\mathbf{r}^*)$ over and over through all reciprocal space with the translations $\mathbf{a}'^*$, $\mathbf{b}'^*$, $\mathbf{c}'^*$. With rising L, M, N, the reciprocal-lattice peak function becomes larger and larger and therefore the function $F_{\text{cell}}(\mathbf{r}^*)$, expanding around each of the reciprocal-lattice points $\mathbf{r}_h^*$, overlap each other less and less [see (65)]. Now $F_{\text{cell}}(\mathbf{r}^*)$ is the solitary function associated to the reciprocal sampling lattice. Inside the volume defined by a parallelepiped of sides $\mathbf{a}'^*$, $\mathbf{b}'^*$, $\mathbf{c}'^*$, centered at the origin of the reciprocal space, the transforms of $\rho_s(\mathbf{r})$ and $\rho_{\text{cell}}(\mathbf{r})$ are identical, i.e., for L, M, N large enough

$$T\{\rho_s(\mathbf{r})\} = T\{\rho_{\text{cell}}(\mathbf{r})\} \tag{70}$$

This is equivalent to stating

$$F_s(\mathbf{r}^*) = F_{\text{cell}}(\mathbf{r}^*) \tag{71}$$

and if no overlapping of the solitary function occurs.

As $\rho_s'(\mathbf{r})$ is discrete, and its transform periodic, $F_s(\mathbf{r}^*)$ can be calculated by means of a Fourier series whose coefficients are the values of $\rho_s(\mathbf{r}_{h'})$, i.e.,

$$F(\mathbf{r}^{*\prime}) = v' \sum_{h'=-L}^{+L} \sum_{k'=-M}^{+M} \sum_{l'=-N}^{+N} \rho_s(\mathbf{r}_{h'}) \exp\left[2\pi i (h'X^* + k'Y^* + l'Z^*)\right] \tag{72}$$

where X^*, Y^*, Z^* are fractional coordinates inside the reciprocal unit cell defined by $\mathbf{a}'^*$, $\mathbf{b}'^*$, $\mathbf{c}'^*$.

The density function is a positive and real function which, in the most general case, is noncentrosymmetrical. The transform of a real noncentrosymmetrical function has real and imaginary parts that must be synthesized separately. In (29) of Ch. 1 we have seen that the electron-density function can be split into an even and an odd function that are centrosymmetrical and anticentrosymmetrical, respectively. The real part of the transform is an even function [the transform of the even part of $\rho'_s(\mathbf{r})$]:

$$A(X^*Y^*Z^*) = \tfrac{1}{2} \sum_{h'} \sum_{k'} \sum_{l'} [\rho_s(h'k'l') + \rho_s(\bar{h}'\bar{k}'\bar{l}')]$$

$$\cos 2\pi(h'X^* + k'Y^* + l'Z^*) \qquad (73)$$

while the imaginary part of the transform is an odd function [the transform of the odd part of $\rho'_s(\mathbf{r})$]:

$$B(X^*Y^*Z^*) = -\tfrac{1}{2} \sum_{h'} \sum_{k'} \sum_{l'} [\rho_s(h'k'l') - \rho_s(\bar{h}'\bar{k}'\bar{l}')]$$

$$\sin 2\pi(h'X^* + k'Y^* + l'Z^*). \qquad (74)$$

We have

$$F(X^*Y^*Z^*) = A(X^*Y^*Z^*) + iB(X^*Y^*Z^*). \qquad (75)$$

If the electron-density function is centrosymmetric, and the origin of coordinates is the center of symmetry, only the cosine function is needed in the Fourier summation:

$$A(X^*Y^*Z^*) = 2 \sum_{h'} \sum_{k'} \sum_{l'} \rho_s(h'k'l') \cos 2\pi(h'X^* + k'Y^* + l'Z^*). \qquad (76)$$

We have seen that it is possible from the theoretical standpoint (although, in general, it is not practical) to calculate the transforms of the electron density of the unit cell or of a molecule by making an adequate sampling of the lattice and using as coefficients of a Fourier series the values obtained from the sampling of the continuous electron-density function. Sayre (1951) suggested the computation of structure factors by sampling the electron density of the unit cell. He introduced the concept of hypothetical atoms, or atoms whose transforms coincide with the value of the atomic scattering factor inside the limit of the sphere of reflection, but identically zero outside the sphere. This is a way to overcome the difficulty of overlap in Fourier space.

Figure 24i represents the electron density of one molecule of anthracene as it is projected on (010). This density corresponds to the overlap of the individual atomic electron densities of the hypothetical carbon atoms as obtained from the radial distribution of Fig. 8, Ch. 1. The sampling lattice used has $a' = 0.14$ Å and $c' = 0.15$ Å, n' max along a' is 25 and n' along c is 50. Since the molecule is centrosymmetric, the sampling was carried out for the assymmetric part alone.

Figure 24ii gives the transform of the sampled electron-density function of anthracene calculated from (76). The transform is real,

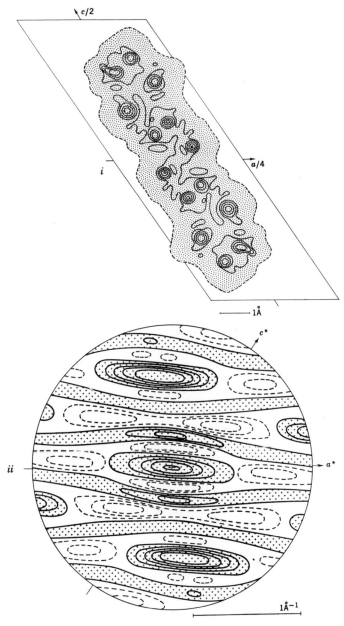

Fig. 24. Anthracene (010). (i) Sampled electron density; (ii) central part of the molecular transform obtained by sampling; (iii) molecular transform computed in the conventional way.

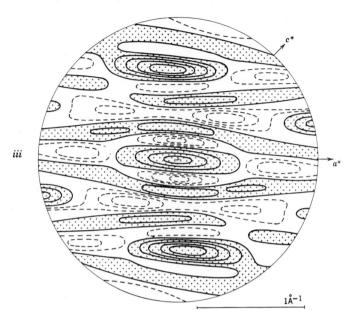

Fig. 24. (*continued*).

and it has positive and negative values and zero lines. The transform of the continuous electron density is repeated over and over, building up the whole transform of the sampled density function. The repetition of the transform occurs at $a'^* = 9.10\ \text{Å}^{-1}$, so that overlap has been avoided. The limiting sphere for CuKα x-radiation is shown. Figure 24iii represents the molecular transform of anthracene, calculated in the conventional way. It can be seen that both methods give similar results.

The same concepts can be applied to obtain the intensity function in terms of a Fourier summation, using as coefficients the sampled values of the Q function of a unit cell. From similar considerations, and substituting the density function by the Q function in (65) we have

$$T\{Q'_s(\mathbf{r}_{h'})\} = I(\mathbf{r}^*) \ast z_s(\mathbf{r}^{*'}). \tag{77}$$

However, since the Q function of a unit-cell content extends outside the cell, in this case we must introduce the shape function of the unit cell.

The molecular intensity transform is a continuous function in Fourier space, and coincides with the intensity function of a single unit cell of a crystal containing only one molecule. Unfortunately, $I_{cell}(\mathbf{r}^*)$ cannot be obtained directly from x-ray diffraction experiments. We have seen that the Patterson function can be calculated directly from the observed Bragg x-ray intensities. $P(\mathbf{r})$ is an infinite periodic function in physical space, but we can consider one unit cell only of the Patterson function by introducing the shape function of the cell $s_{cell}(\mathbf{r})$ given by

$$s_{cell}(\mathbf{r}) = 1 \quad \text{for} \quad \begin{aligned} -\frac{a}{2} \leqslant x \leqslant \frac{a}{2} \\ -\frac{b}{2} \leqslant y \leqslant \frac{b}{2} \\ -\frac{c}{2} \leqslant z \leqslant \frac{c}{2}, \end{aligned} \tag{78}$$

$$= 0 \quad \text{everywhere else.}$$

The transform of this shape function is called the shape amplitude by Hosemann and Bagchi (1962), and is given by

$$S_{cell}(\mathbf{r}^*) = v_c \frac{\sin \pi h}{\pi h} \frac{\sin \pi k}{\pi k} \frac{\sin \pi l}{\pi l}, \tag{79}$$

where v_c is the volume of the parallelepiped defining the unit cell. In the case of a two-dimensional projection, the parallelepiped becomes a parallelogram, and v_c is replaced by the area of the unit cell. For simplicity we shall consider the two-dimensional case. The shape amplitude of the parallelogram, defined by the vectors $\mathbf{a}$, $\mathbf{c}$ of the unit cell of anthracene, is shown in Fig. 25i. It has a central maximum whose peak value is equal to the area, and successive alternating minima and maxima along the two reciprocal axes. The height of the first minimum is on the order of 20 per cent of the central maximum, while the second peak (positive) is only of the order of about 10 per cent, the others being practically negligible. The Patterson function, limited to a single-unit cell, is given in terms of the shape function of this cell by

$$P_{cell}(\mathbf{r}) = P(\mathbf{r}) \cdot s_{cell}(\mathbf{r}). \tag{80}$$

Its transform,

$$T\{P(\mathbf{r}) \cdot s_{cell}(\mathbf{r})\} = I_{cell}(\mathbf{r}^*) \ast S_{cell}(\mathbf{r}^*), \tag{81}$$

is the intensity of the unit cell convolved with the transform of the shape function of the unit cell. In order to compute (81) by using Fourier series, we can map the Patterson function of the unit cell by calculating $P(\mathbf{r})$ at the points of an adequate sampling $\mathbf{r}_{h'}$ inside a unit

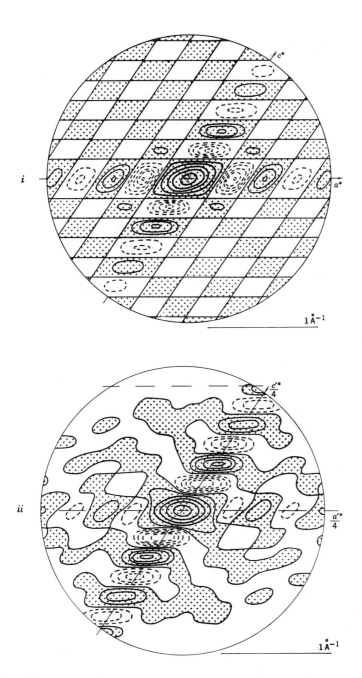

Fig. 25. Anthracene. (*i*) Shape amplitude $S(h0l)$ of the unit cell; (*ii*)$T^{-1}\{P(\mathbf{x})\}$.

cell alone. Let us choose the sampling fine enough that the reciprocal of this sampling is coarse enough to define a reciprocal parallelepiped containing our volume of interest. Let us set up a new Fourier synthesis from values inside a unit cell alone with the $P(\mathbf{r}_{h'})$ as coefficients, in order to go back to reciprocal space. Since the new transform can be calculated at any fractional value of the cell reciprocal to $\mathbf{a}'$, $\mathbf{b}'$, $\mathbf{c}'$, these two repeated Fourier syntheses, namely

$$\Sigma_h \Sigma_k \Sigma_l \; I(hkl) \cos 2\pi (hx + ky + lz) = P(xyz) \qquad (82)$$
$$\underset{\text{discrete}}{} \qquad\qquad\qquad \underset{\text{continuous + periodic}}{}$$

$$\Sigma_{h'} \Sigma_{k'} \Sigma_{l'} \; P(h'k'l') \cdot S_{\text{cell}}(h'k'l') \cos 2\pi (h'X^* + k'Y^* + l'Z^*) =$$
$$\underset{\text{discrete in a single period}}{}$$

$$I(X^*Y^*Z^*) \ast S_{\text{cell}}(X^*Y^*Z^*) \ast z_s(l'm'n'), \qquad (83)$$
$$\underset{\text{continuous + periodic}}{}$$

give us a method of "interpolating" the observed values of the intensities diffracted by the ideal crystal between the reciprocal lattice points, without any knowledge of the crystal structure, provide the transform of the shape function of the unit cell, $S_{\text{cell}}(\mathbf{r}^*)$, does not blurr the results and provide that overlap of the transforms is avoided.

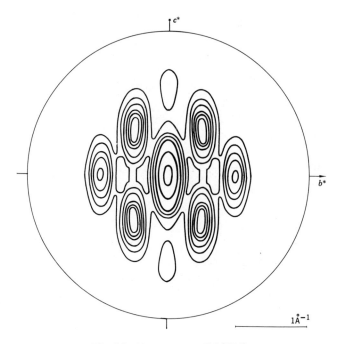

Fig. 26. Nitrite group $T^{-1}\{P(\mathbf{x})\}$.

At the origin of Fourier space the function $I_{cell}(\mathbf{r}^*)$ has the highest peak whose value is $\Sigma_j Z_j^2$, and this central peak is several orders of magnitude greater than the others. Convolution of this origin peak with the shape amplitude gives rise to spurious minima and maxima (similar to the ripple effect in electron-density and Patterson maps), which may be higher than important maxima of the molecular intensity transform, and therefore the intensity transform of the molecule obtained from (83) can hardly be recognized. Fig. 25ii shows the intensity transform of anthracene, and we can see that the convolution of the origin peak with the shape amplitude is big enough to blurr the shape and intensity of the molecular transform.

Figure 26 represents the intensity transform of the NO_2 group obtained by sampling of the Patterson function. In this case, since this function is not extended outside the unit cell, the effect of the shape function is negligible.

In Ch. 3 we shall see that, due to the thermal agitation, we can apply (83) to some special kind of Patterson function to obtain a special kind of intensity function in Fourier space.

Relationships between the optical methods

Figure 27 gives a summary of the various possible operations that can be performed by optical instruments used in the study of problems arising from the scattering of x-rays by crystals, i.e., the Q integrator, the optical diffractometer (OD) and the von Eller machine. We have seen that we can obtain through Fourier summation the electron-density function $\rho(\mathbf{r})$ from the discrete function $F(\mathbf{r}_h^*)$ by means of the von Eller photosummateur (Fig. 20), and that we can also obtain through a Fourier summation the $Q(\mathbf{r})$ or Patterson function from the function $I(\mathbf{r}_h^*)$ (Fig. 21). It is obvious that we can likewise obtain through a Fourier summation the functions $F(\mathbf{r}^*)$ and $I(\mathbf{r}^*)$ by means of a Fourier synthesis, using as coefficients in the Fourier series an adequate sampling in the unit cell of the functions $\rho'(\mathbf{r})$ and $Q'(\mathbf{r})$, respectively. In the photographic method inherent in the von Eller machine, however, the negative regions of $A(\mathbf{r}^*)$ in a centrosymmetric crystal must be deduced by observation of the zero line, a procedure that is not practical, and with Pepinsky's X-RAC two separate maps of negative and positive contours need to be given (Pepinsky, 1951). When the $I(\mathbf{r}_h^*)$ coefficients are used, no problem arises due to the photographic method inherent in the von Eller machine, since the Patterson function is either zero or positive at any point of physical space.

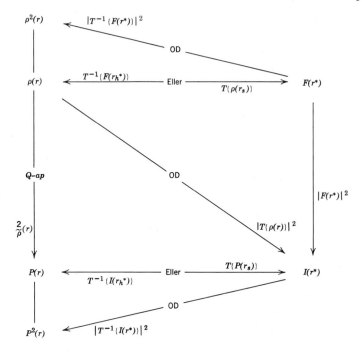

Fig. 27. Relationships between the different optical methods.

What is clear is that the von Eller machine permits us to obtain, in principle, with values of the discrete functions $F(r_h^*)$ and $I(r_h^*)$ defined in reciprocal space, the values of their Fourier transforms $\rho(r)$ and $P(r)$ in physical space. Reciprocally, from the functions $\rho'(r)$ and $Q'(r)$ sampled in direct space, the former can be obtained by adequate Fourier syntheses in reciprocal space.

The role of the Q integrator, on the other hand, is totally different. In this case, from two identical masks of the density function $\rho(r)$, we obtain optically the self-image or $Q(r)$ function defined in the same physical space, which (for an ideal periodic mask) is the Patterson function (Fig. 11ii).

Finally, the role of the optical diffractometer, in simulating the scattering of x-rays by a crystal, is to give the Fraunhofer pattern or intensity function $I(r^*)$ directly from the function $\rho(r)$ (Fig. 16ii). Therefore, this device gives rise to a Fourier-transform operation and simultaneously squares it to $(T)^2$; in the squaring lies the limitation of the optical diffraction phenomenon for, by giving only squares of the values of the function, information about the phase is lost, thus giving rise to the well-known phase problem of crystal-structure analysis.

It is clear, in principle, that if instead of representing a density function by disks, the diffracting object is some kind of representation by disks of the discrete amplitude function of a crystal with its accompanying phase, the Fraunhofer pattern will simulate, reciprocally, the periodic electron-density function defined in the other space. The resulting Fraunhofer patterns show the general distribution of the electron density of the crystal when we start with $F(\mathbf{r}_h^*)$. If the diffracting object is a mask representing the intensity function $I(\mathbf{r}_h^*)$ of an ideal periodic crystal, the Fraunhofer pattern will simulate $P(\mathbf{r})$. The method, applied to obtaining a projection of the electron-density function, was first described by Bragg in 1939. He applied it to diopside, for which most $F(h0l)$'s have equal phases. The method was called x-ray microscopy by Bragg. In 1939 Buerger also suggested that the method was directly useful for obtaining the Patterson synthesis, and that mica could be used for the control of the phase in obtaining the electron density. Buerger (1941) developed this idea that was applied by Bragg (1942) again to diopside to take into account of the fact that F_{202} was negative. Between those years and 1950 the apparatus was greatly improved by Buerger (1950) even allowing the direct use of an x-ray diffraction photograph as diffracting grating. This was in fact a simulation of image reconstruction, and called the whole procedure "the two wave-length microscope." The basic ideas and techniques known, the method was later applied to several special cases (see for instance, Dunkerly and Lipson, 1955; Hanson and Lipson, 1952; Harburn and Taylor, 1962).

3

Scattering by a real crystal

Thermal vibrations and its symmetry

Real crystals are far from perfect. Not only are real crystals finite, i.e. they have a size and shape, but they also show many imperfections such as dislocations, vacancies, isomorphous substitution, and disorder of the atomic building groups. Independent of such imperfections, the real crystal has an intrinsic and constant disorder due to the thermal vibrations of the atoms that form the crystal. We shall discuss in further detail in Ch. 5 the implications of such vibrations in the crystal. In this chapter we shall deal with the general picture of the influence of thermal vibrations in x-ray scattering.

Thermal motion of the atoms or molecules in the crystal can be described as vibrations of their structural units about their equilibrium, or average, positions in the unit cell. Accordingly, the position of the atoms or the molecules, considered as rigid bodies in the unit cell, must be described by a time-averaged function, the probability function of its location in space.

During one period of vibration the atom describes a complicated curve about its equilibrium position because it is subject to a field of anisotropic restoring forces. In a monoatomic crystal structure the thermal vibrations of all the atoms can be described by the same figure. If the crystal contains more than one atom per unit cell the thermal vibrations of each one are, in general, different, and they are described by different figures. It is clear that for a substance to belong to a given space group it is necessary for its atoms to occupy positions (in the unit cell) whose symmetries are contained in that particular space group. Thermal motion cannot alter, at least when integrated in time, the symmetry requirements of the given space group. The instant symmetry of the structure is in reality different from the time-average space-group symmetry; in order to take care of this fact we must distinguish between the static (time-averaged) space group and the dynamic (instantaneous) space group. The difference between these two space groups gives rise to the thermal disorder of the real crystal. Thermal motion of the atoms in the crystal must be compatible with the point symmetry of the atomic locus in the crystal (Amorós, 1960). In molecular crystals the rigid-body motion of the molecules also must be consistent with the symmetry of the molecular locus. The study of the symmetry of the atomic or molecular thermal motion is reduced therefore to the study of the point symmetries of the equivalent positions occupied by each atom.

The point symmetries of the equivalent positions of the 230 space groups are the point groups, that is the 32 crystal classes. The occurrence of an atom on a glide plane or a screw axis does not add new point symmetries, since a point located on one of these symmetry elements has symmetry 1, that is, the lowest symmetry. The vibrations of an atom in the crystal, however, always have a higher symmetry than the point-group symmetry of the corresponding locus, and, in general, this symmetry has at least a mirror plane or a center of symmetry. The possible symmetries are further reduced by assuming that rotation axes of higher order than 2 behave as axes of infinite symmetry for thermal vibrations.

In general the surfaces (Fig. 1) that describe the amplitudes of vibration of the atom are quadrics (Waser, 1955); in the most common

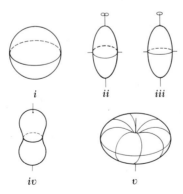

i   *ii*   *iii*

iv   *v*

Fig. 1. Different surfaces describing atomic thermal motion in crystals. (*i*) Sphere; (*ii*) rotation ellipsoid; (*iii*) triaxial ellipsoid; (*iv*) prolate (peanut-shaped) surface of revolution; (*v*) oblate surface of revolution.

cases this is an ellipsoid whose orientation and type depends on the symmetry of the atomic locus. The vibrations of an atom in a harmonic anisotropic potential field can therefore be characterized by a symmetrical tensor $\mathbf{U}$ with six independent components, such that the mean square amplitude of vibration in the direction of a unit vector $\mathbf{l}$ (whose components are l_i) is (Cruickshank, 1956a)

$$\overline{\mathbf{u}^2} = \sum_{i=1}^{3} \sum_{j=1}^{3} U_{ij}l_il_j. \tag{1}$$

The matrix that describes the tensor $\mathbf{U}$ is simplified according to the symmetry of the atomic locus. If the point symmetry of the locus is 1 or $\bar{1}$, the matrix has the maximum generality, specifically

$$\begin{vmatrix} U_{11} & U_{12} & U_{13} \\ U_{12} & U_{22} & U_{23} \\ U_{13} & U_{23} & U_{33} \end{vmatrix}$$

and the ellipsoid is a triaxial ellipsoid with no predetermined orientation with respect to the crystal axes.

For a locus with $2/m$ symmetry, the corresponding matrix is

$$\begin{vmatrix} U_{11} & 0 & U_{13} \\ 0 & U_{22} & 0 \\ U_{13} & 0 & U_{33} \end{vmatrix},$$

showing that one of the principal planes of the triaxial ellipsoid coincides with m (defined by $\mathbf{a}$ and $\mathbf{c}$), and that the axis normal to that plane coincides with 2 (along $\mathbf{b}$). In the case of loci with symmetry mmm, we have

$$\begin{vmatrix} U_{11} & 0 & 0 \\ 0 & U_{22} & 0 \\ 0 & 0 & U_{33} \end{vmatrix},$$

showing that each of the three principal planes of the ellipsoid coincides with one of the three mirrors of vibration symmetry.

In the loci with point symmetries $4/m$, $4/mmm$, 3, $3m$, $6/m$, and $6/mmm$, the matrix is reduced to

$$\begin{vmatrix} U_{11} & 0 & 0 \\ 0 & U_{11} & 0 \\ 0 & 0 & U_{33} \end{vmatrix},$$

showing that the ellipsoid is one of revolution whose c axis coincides with the 3-, 4-, or 6-fold axis of the point group. Thus, an atom whose locus has the symmetry of these point groups is subject to isotropic vibration in the plane normal to the higher-order axis, but the vibration along that axis is, in general, different from that in the plane.

For loci of symmetries $m3$ and $m3m$, the matrix is reduced to

$$\begin{vmatrix} U_{11} & 0 & 0 \\ 0 & U_{11} & 0 \\ 0 & 0 & U_{11} \end{vmatrix},$$

which corresponds to a sphere. The atom in such a locus is subject to isotropic vibrations.

The matrices given are further modified in accordance with the orientation of the symmetry operators in the crystal. The symmetries of the ellipsoids that have been discussed are the minimum symmetries compatible with the point symmetry of the locus. It is obvious that a given atom can show vibrations with higher symmetry than the locus, but not lower. For instance, the carbon atoms in hexamethylentetramine (Becka and Cruickshank, 1963a) occupy a locus with point group symmetry $2mm$. The expected ellipsoid was a triaxial ellipsoid, yet the vibrations correspond to a rotation ellipsoid of high symmetry.

Relationships between the vibration ellipsoids of the atoms in a cell

The atoms contained in the unit cell are related by the symmetry elements of the space group. The number of equivalent atoms is given by N/m, where N is the number of operations in the space group (the multiplicity of the general position) and m the multiplicity of the position (locus) occupied by the atom. Equivalent atoms have the same properties, and therefore they have identical vibration ellipsoids whose axes have different orientations relative to the crystallographic axes. These relative orientations are conditioned by the existence of certain symmetry operations in the space group, and therefore are not mutually independent. Finally, the number of equivalent atoms is determined by the multiplicity of the locus. Therefore, the final relationship between homologous atoms is conditioned by the point symmetry of the locus. The vibration ellipsoids of atoms equivalent by symmetry can be found, therefore, by calculating the new set of U_{ij} in (1) by taking into account the change in

Table 1 Components of the vibration tensor (from Trueblood, 1965, modified)

System	Direction of the axis	Order of the axis	U'_{11}	U'_{22}	U'_{33}	U'_{12}	U'_{13}	U'_{23}
Monoclinic and tri-rectangular systems	a	2	U_{11}	U_{22}	U_{33}	$-U_{12}$	$-U_{13}$	$+U_{23}$
	b	2	U_{11}	U_{22}	U_{33}	$-U_{12}$	$+U_{13}$	$-U_{23}$
	c	2	U_{11}	U_{22}	U_{33}	$+U_{12}$	$-U_{13}$	$-U_{23}$
	a+b	2	U_{22}	U_{11}	U_{33}	$+U_{12}$	$-U_{23}$	$-U_{13}$
	b+c	2	U_{11}	U_{33}	U_{22}	$-U_{13}$	$-U_{12}$	$+U_{23}$
	c+a	2	U_{33}	U_{22}	U_{11}	$-U_{23}$	$+U_{13}$	$+U_{12}$
	a+b+c	3	U_{33}	U_{11}	U_{22}	$+U_{13}$	$+U_{23}$	$+U_{12}$
	a	4	U_{11}	U_{33}	U_{33}	$-U_{13}$	$+U_{12}$	$-U_{23}$
	b	4	U_{33}	U_{22}	U_{11}	$+U_{23}$	$-U_{13}$	$-U_{12}$
	c	4	U_{22}	U_{11}	U_{33}	$-U_{12}$	$-U_{23}$	$+U_{13}$
Hexagonal system — Referred to P cell	a	2	$U_{11}+U_{22}-U_{12}$	U_{22}	U_{33}	$2U_{22}-U_{12}$	$U_{23}-U_{13}$	$+U_{23}$
	b	2	U_{11}	$U_{11}+U_{22}-U_{12}$	U_{33}	$2U_{11}-U_{12}$	$+U_{13}$	$U_{13}-U_{23}$
	a+b	2	U_{22}	U_{11}	U_{33}	U_{12}	$-U_{13}$	$-U_{13}$
	2a+b	2	U_{11}	$U_{11}+U_{22}-U_{12}$	U_{33}	$2U_{11}-U_{12}$	$U_{13}-U_{23}$	$U_{23}-U_{13}$
	2b+a	2	$U_{11}+U_{22}-U_{12}$	U_{22}	U_{33}	$2U_{22}-U_{12}$	$U_{13}-U_{23}$	$-U_{23}$
	c	6	$U_{11}+U_{22}-U_{12}$	U_{11}	U_{33}	$2U_{11}-U_{12}$	$+U_{13}$	$+U_{13}$
Hexagonal system — Referred to R cell	a+b+c	3	U_{33}	U_{11}	U_{22}	$+U_{13}$	$+U_{23}$	$+U_{12}$
	a−b	2	U_{22}	U_{11}	U_{33}	$+U_{12}$	$+U_{23}$	$+U_{13}$
	a+b−2c	2	$\tfrac{1}{3}(4U_{11}+U_{22}+4U_{33}-2U_{12}+4U_{13}-2U_{23})$	$\tfrac{1}{3}(U_{11}+4U_{22}+4U_{33}-2U_{12}-2U_{13}+4U_{23})$	$\tfrac{1}{3}(4U_{11}+4U_{22}+4U_{12}-2U_{13}-2U_{23})$	$\tfrac{1}{9}(-4U_{11}-4U_{22}+8U_{33}+5U_{12}+2U_{13}+2U_{23})$	$\tfrac{1}{9}(8U_{11}+4U_{22}-4U_{33}+2U_{12}+2U_{13}+5U_{23})$	$\tfrac{1}{9}(-4U_{11}+8U_{22}-4U_{33}+2U_{12}+5U_{13}+2U_{23})$

coordinates. The complete description of the thermal vibrations of the atoms in the crystal must take into account the double aspect of the motion and the equivalence of the loci. The atomic positions can be found in the "International Tables of Crystallography", Vol. 1 (1952). The best way to consider the equivalence is to consider the effect of the individual elements of symmetry relating equivalent atomic locus. Simple translations and inversions do not affect the general expression for the vibration ellipsoid, since the ellipsoids so related must be parallel to each other. The preceding is true because the vibration ellipsoid is itself centrosymmetric. Therefore, a mirror plane and a glide plane produce the same effect on the orientation of the ellipsoid as a 2-fold axis normal to the symmetry plane. On the other hand, screw axes and 3, 4, and 6 axes produce the same effect as pure rotation axes of the same order. By applying individually the different elements of symmetry to the original set of U_{ij}, a new set U'_{ij} is obtained. Table 1 contains such information for different elements of symmetry in crystals belonging to the monoclinic system and the various systems with orthogonal axes (Trueblood, 1956). Table 1 also contains information for hexagonal crystals.

Anisotropic thermal motion in a molecular crystal

If a crystal is built up of molecules, the above also holds, i.e., each individual atom of the molecule has a definite ellipsoid of vibration. One example can be seen in Fig. 2 where the ellipsoids of vibrations (including a peanut-shaped surface) of the different atoms of the citric acid in magnesium citrate decahydrate (Johnson, 1965) are represented. Not all the vibrations performed by the individual atoms, however, are independent, but an important part of the thermal motion can be described in terms of the vibrations of the molecules.

It is meaningful, therefore, to talk about molecular vibrations and intramolecular atomic vibrations. The problem in molecular crystals is thus simplified considerably, whereas the complete analysis of thermal vibration would otherwise be very difficult. Since the bonds between molecules are considerably weaker than interatomic intramolecular bonds, the vibration frequencies of the molecules are lower and, in general, the vibrations of the molecules as rigid bodies are of decisive importance in the dynamics of these crystals. The simplest hypothesis that can be made is that the rigid-body molecular motion can be expressed as a function of two symmetric tensors (Cruickshank, 1956a), each one with six independent components. One of the tensors describes the translational vibrations

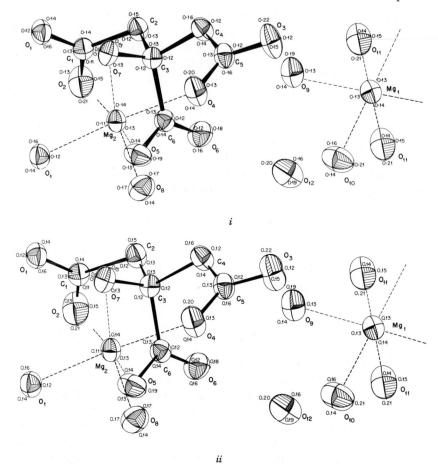

Fig. 2. Vibration surfaces of the different atoms of the citric acid molecule in magnesium citrate decahydrate. (*i*) RMS displacement surfaces; (*ii*) thermal motion probability ellipsoids. O_3 has a peanut-shape RMS displacement surface (from Johnson, 1965).

of the center of equilibrium of the molecule, while the other refers to the angular oscillations or librations about certain axes through the center, the molecule axes.

If **T** is the tensor that gives the mean square amplitude of the translational vibrations, the translational contribution to the vibrational motion of an atom in that molecule is

$$\overline{u_t}^2 = \sum_{i=1}^{3} \sum_{j=1}^{3} T_{ij} l_i l_j. \tag{2}$$

In the case of librations the mean square amplitude of libration about an axis defined by a unit vector t passing through the center of the molecule is given by

$$\bar{u}_t^2 = \sum_{i=1}^{3} \sum_{j=1}^{3} \omega_{ij} t_i t_j. \tag{3}$$

For a given atom at a distance $r \equiv (x,y,z)$ from the center of the molecule, motion in the direction l due to a libration is possible only if the molecule rotates about the axis parallel to $l \times r$, what is equivalent to saying that there should be no angular momentum with respect to the translating-rotating coordinate system. If the libration is small, the mean square amplitude of vibration of the atom in the direction l is

$$\bar{u}_l^2 = \sum_{i=1}^{3} \sum_{j=1}^{3} \omega_{ij} (l \times r)_i (l \times r)_j. \tag{4}$$

Therefore, assuming rigid-body vibrations, each atomic tensor U_{ij}^r can be expressed as

$$\sum_{i=1}^{3} \sum_{j=1}^{3} U_{ij} l_i l_j = \sum_{i=1}^{3} \sum_{j=1}^{3} [T_{ij} l_i l_j + \omega_{ij} (l \times r)_i (l \times r)_j]. \tag{5}$$

In simple cases complete thermal motion can be interpreted as a function of the tensors T and ω, and in such cases it is of little interest to talk about the vibrations of isolated atoms.

Following Higgs (1955), we can suppose that the different molecular vibrations are independent of phase, and that the resultant mean square amplitude of vibration in an arbitrary direction is the sum of the mean square amplitudes of atomic vibrations of all types, rigid-body or internal, in that given direction. For each molecule we can take three principal directions of vibration; for example, along the long, short, and medium axes of the molecule. The selection of the center of libration is easy in the case of centrosymmetric molecules: the origin of the molecular axes must be at the center of symmetry, and the rotational tensors are therefore in the inertial coordinate system, describing librations about the center of symmetry. In the case of molecules without a center of symmetry the determination of the actual center of libration of the molecule is more difficult. Azulene (Pawley, 1963) furnishes a very good example. The molecule has no center of symmetry, but the crystal is built up by a random distribution of molecules in two orientations related to each other by the center of symmetry of the space group. The center of libration is the center of gravity of the molecule, which is near to, but not at, the center of symmetry of the averaged crystal structure. In other cases the origin of ω_{ij} may not necessarily coincide with the center of gravity of the molecule. Translational and librational amplitudes of some molecular crystals are given in Ch. 4.

The separation of translational and librational motions is not real, but it is useful in that it simplifies the description of the vibrational motion of the molecule as a rigid body. On the other hand, the molecule is made up of atoms, and each one of them has a vibrational motion defined by the symmetric tensor U^r. It is useful, however, to consider the rigid-body vibrational component and the internal (nonrigid-body) vibrational component separately, since at least part of the molecule can be assumed to vibrate as a whole. There are cases where the nonrigid-body vibrations may be quite large compared with the rigid-body vibrational amplitudes, and to neglect such intramolecular vibrations is not justified (Lonsdale and Milledge, 1959, 1961). The translational components of the rigid-body vibrations of the molecules are likely to be mainly governed by intermolecular forces, that is, by the packing of the molecules in the crystal. The librational vibrations are perhaps more likely to be closely related to the molecular geometry and conditioned by the axes of inertia of the molecules. The intramolecular vibrations certainly are conditioned by the bond system of the molecule itself.

Atomic vibrations, electron density, and the Q function

The displacements due to the thermal vibrations of the atoms or molecules in the crystal are small compared with the interatomic or intermolecular distances. The instantaneous configurations define an instantaneous distorted structure that differs little of the time-averaged structure. The thermal disorder introduces fluctuations in the distances between corresponding atoms, preserving the long-range order, which is less disturbed than the short-range order. The instantaneous configurations cannot be known, and only the mean (averaged) atomic and molecular positions can be known; the obvious consequence of this is that the effective electron-density function of the vibrating atom is different from the one for the atom at rest.

If the atoms vibrate as rigid bodies about their equilibrium positions at sites $r_j + r_l$, which correspond to the ideal structure, any instantaneous configuration of an atom can be expressed in terms of the vector $r_j + r_l + u_{jl}$ where the displacements u_{jl} are now functions of time. The time average of the value u_{jl} can then be set equal to zero for any l and j. It is justifiable to replace time averages by the corresponding spatial averages over the instantaneous configuration of the crystal structure, and we can write

$$\overline{\mathbf{u}}_{jl} = 0, \tag{6}$$

the bar indicating either the average over time for given l, j, or the average l for given j and time.

Due to this averaging of the instant positions of the center of the atom, the electron-density function of the vibrating atom is smeared out, and the sharp strong peak of the stationary atom becomes a broad, weaker maximum as the whole average electron-density function spreads out. Not only the height of the peak, but also the whole average electron density of the crystal depends quite strongly on the mean amplitude of vibration.

Let $\rho_0(\mathbf{r})$ be the electron distribution in the atom at rest, and suppose the atom vibrates at a given temperature T in an isotropic harmonic potential field. The probability that the atomic center lies within a volume element dv is given by a Gaussian function

$$p_T(\mathbf{r}) \, dv = (2\pi\overline{u}^2)^{-3/2}\exp(-r^2/2\overline{u}^2)dv, \tag{7}$$

where $\overline{u}^2$ is the mean square vibrational amplitude in any direction at the temperature T. The resulting average electron-density distribution $\rho_T(\mathbf{r})$ may be described as the convolution of $\rho_0(\mathbf{r})$ with $p_T(\mathbf{r})$:

$$\overline{\rho_T}(\mathbf{r}) = \rho_0(\mathbf{r}) * p_T(\mathbf{r}). \tag{8}$$

The electron-density distribution of an atom in the crystal is therefore temperature dependent. The average electron-density function of a crystal containing several atoms in the motif can be given by the sum of the solitary functions defining the average electron density of each individual atom of the motif, and therefore is also temperature dependent. This fact is of paramount importance in understanding the x-ray scattering by crystals as a function of temperature.

According to (8), the effect of temperature is to replace the actual instantaneous electron density of the atom by an averaged Gaussian distribution of its electron-density cloud (Ewald, 1940). We have seen in Chapter 1 that it is a good approximation to express analytically the electron density of an atom by a sum of Gaussian functions, each one describing an electronic shell of the atom. The effect of temperature on the atom is then to convolve each electron shell with the appropriate Gaussian function describing the corresponding vibration. If the atom is vibrating as a rigid body, the whole electron cloud is modified by the same Gaussian distribution. The product of a pair of

Gaussians is again a Gaussian, and therefore the time averaged effect of thermal vibrations in the analytical expression of the electron shells is just to modify the parameter a_j of the corresponding Gaussians. Accordingly, the time averaged electron density at the temperature T is then given by

$$\bar{\rho}_T(r) = \sum_{j=1}^{J} \frac{A_j}{(\pi a_{Tj}^2)^{3/2}} \exp\left(-\frac{1}{a_{Tj}^2} r^2\right), \tag{9}$$

where A_j, the number of electrons in the j shell is obviously constant, but a_{Tj} now is different from a_j describing the shell at rest. This temperature modified Gaussian parameter is given by

$$a_{Tj} = \sqrt{a_j^2 + 2\bar{u}^2}, \tag{10}$$

where $\bar{u}^2$ is the mean square amplitude of oscillation of the atom at the temperature T. If the atomic temperature oscillations are anisotropic, the spherical Gaussian is substituted by an ellipsoidal Gaussian that can be taken into account by substituting

$$\frac{x}{\alpha^2} + \frac{y}{\beta^2} + \frac{z}{\gamma^2} \quad \text{for} \quad \frac{r^2}{a^2}$$

in (9).

As an example, Fig. 3 represents the electron density and its radial distribution of an atom of carbon under isotropic thermal vibrations, of mean square amplitudes of 0.15 and 0.20 Å. The K- and L- shells have the following parameters

$$
\begin{aligned}
&\bar{u} = 0.15 \text{ Å} \quad A_K = 1.8 \text{ electrons} \quad a_K = 0.24 \text{ Å} \\
&\qquad\qquad\quad\ A_L = 4.2 \text{ electrons} \quad a_L = 0.72 \text{ Å} \\
&\bar{u} = 0.20 \text{ Å} \quad A_K = 1.8 \text{ electrons} \quad a_K = 0.30 \text{ Å} \\
&\qquad\qquad\quad\ A_L = 4.2 \text{ electrons} \quad a_L = 0.74 \text{ Å}
\end{aligned}
\tag{11}
$$

The self-image of the atom is similarly affected by the thermal motion because the electron density is modified by such motion:

$$Q_T(\mathbf{r}) = \bar{\rho}_T(\mathbf{r}) * \bar{\rho}_T(-\mathbf{r}). \tag{12}$$

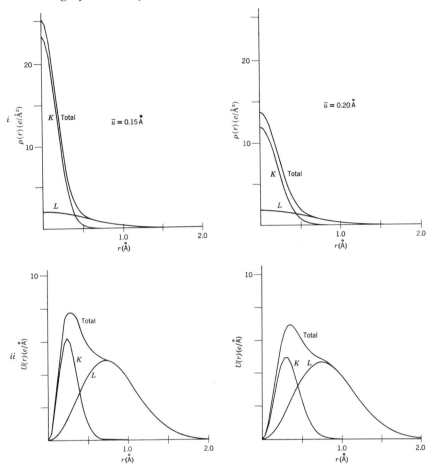

Fig. 3. Effect of the *rms* amplitude of 0.15 and 0.20 Å in the electron cloud of the carbon atom. (*i*) Electron density; (*ii*) radial distribution.

Due to the centrosymmetry of vibration, this is equivalent to

$$\overline{Q}_T(\mathbf{r}) = Q(\mathbf{r}) * p_T(\mathbf{r}). \tag{13}$$

Figure 4*i* shows the self-image of the atom of carbon at rest (continuous line) and the average self-image at *T* (broken line).

Since the Patterson function can be obtained optically with the *Q*-integrator apparatus, where density functions of atoms are simulated by disks, it is of interest to represent the self-image of a disk.

Figure 4*ii* shows the self-image of the disk-like atom at rest (continuous line) and the average self-image at T(broken line).

The isotropic Debye-Waller temperature factor

The frequency of the x-rays is several orders of magnitude higher than the frequency of the atomic vibrations, and the diffraction is a function of the instantaneous configurations of the dynamic crystal structure. However, the time used in the observation of the diffracted intensity is also several orders of magnitude greater than that of the frequency of the atomic vibrations. The diffracted intensity observed in the experiment is the time-averaged intensity of the instant configurations, and therefore is temperature dependent. The effect of the thermal vibrations on the diffracted intensity can be deduced directly from the distortion of the electron density of the corresponding atom by thermal motion.

The Fourier transform of a Gaussian function is also a Gaussian function. The transform of $p(\mathbf{r})$ in (10) is given by

$$D(\mathbf{r}^*) = T\{p(\mathbf{r})\} = \exp\left(-2\pi^2\bar{u}^2|\mathbf{r}^*|^2\right).$$
$$= D(\mathbf{r}^*), \tag{14}$$

the Debye-Waller temperature factor for isotropic thermal vibrations. The application of the convolution theorem to (11) yields

$$T\{\rho_T(\mathbf{r})\} = f_T(\mathbf{r}^*) = f_0(\mathbf{r}^*)\exp\left(-2\pi^2\bar{u}^2|\mathbf{r}^*|^2\right). \tag{15}$$

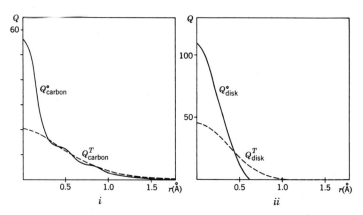

Fig. 4. Radial distribution of two-dimensional Q functions for atoms at rest and in motion. (*i*) Carbon atom; (*ii*) disk atom.

It will be convenient later to use a term B, which is given by

$$8\pi^2 \, \bar{u}^2 = B. \tag{16}$$

Since u^2 is given in Å^2, B is also expressed in Å^2. If this is substituted in the temperature factor (14), it becomes

$$D(\mathbf{r}^*) = \exp\left(-\tfrac{1}{4}B|\mathbf{r}^*|^2\right). \tag{17}$$

In (10) of Ch. 1 it was seen that

$$|\mathbf{r}^*| = \frac{2\sin\theta}{\lambda},$$

so that the temperature factor can also be written

$$D = \exp\left(-B\frac{\sin^2\theta}{\lambda^2}\right). \tag{18}$$

Sometimes the entire exponential is abbreviated as M, that is,

$$M = 8\pi \, u^2 \, \frac{\sin^2\theta}{\lambda^2}. \tag{19}$$

and D can be written as

$$D = \exp\left(-M\right). \tag{20}$$

From (15) it can easily be seen that the effect of atomic vibration on the scattering is to diminish the amplitude function f_0 and, therefore, to weaken the intensity function with respect to that which it would have if the atom were at rest. This effect is increasingly significant at increasing distances from the origin of the reciprocal space. The effect of the atomic vibration ($u = 0.20$ Å) of a carbon atom on both the $f(\mathbf{r}^*)$ and $I(\mathbf{r}^*)$ are shown in Fig. 5i and ii. The Debye-Waller factor curve is given in Fig. 5iii.

The Debye-Waller anisotropic temperature factor

As indicated before, in an anisotropic, harmonic, potential field the vibrations of an atom can be described by the symmetrical tensor $\mathbf{U}$. For anisotropic vibrations, the probability $p_T(\mathbf{r})$ that at the temperature T the center of the atom lies within a volume element dv is given by

$$p_T(\mathbf{r}) \, dv = (2\pi)^{-3/2} \, (\det \mathbf{U})^{-1/2} \exp\left[-\tfrac{1}{2}(\textstyle\sum\sum U_{ij}^{-1} r_i r_j)\right] dv, \tag{21}$$

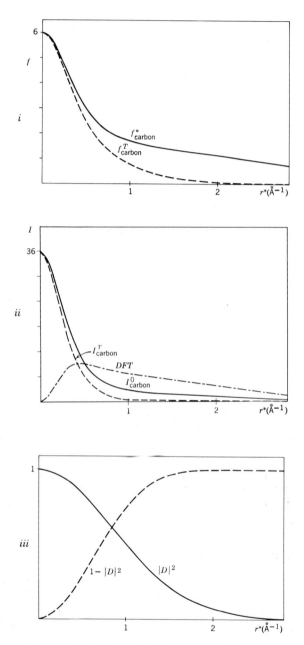

Fig. 5. (*i*) Atomic scattering factor of carbon at rest and at T; (*ii*) intensity scattering factor of carbon at rest and at T and DFT; (*iii*) variation of the Debye-Waller factor with the reciprocal vector, continuous line: $|D|^2$; broken line: $1-|D|^2$.

where $\mathbf{U}^{-1}$ is the matrix inverse to $\mathbf{U}$. The Fourier transform of $p(\mathbf{r})$ is

$$D(\mathbf{r}^*) = \exp\left[-2\pi^2(\sum\sum U_{ij}\, r_i^*r_j^*)\right], \tag{22}$$

where r_i^* are the components of the reciprocal vector $\mathbf{r}^*$.

By applying the convolution theorem to (11) in obtaining the transform, we have, for anisotropic motion,

$$T\{\rho_0(\mathbf{r}) * p_r(\mathbf{r})\} = f_j(\mathbf{r}^*)\exp\left[-2\pi^2(\sum\sum U_{ij}r_i^*r_j^*)\right]. \tag{23}$$

The vibration exponential of the scattering factor for anisotropic motion in (22) can be expanded to give

$$D(\mathbf{r}^*) = \exp\left[-2\pi^2(U_{11}h^2a^{*2} + U_{22}k^2b^{*2} + U_{33}l^2c^{*2} + 2U_{12}ha^*kb^*\right.$$
$$\left. + 2U_3ha^*lc^* + 2U_3kb^*lc^*)\right]. \tag{24}$$

Notice that ha^*, kb^*, and lc^* are the main components of $\mathbf{r}^*$ along the reciprocal axes. Equation (16) relates $\bar{u}^2$ with B for isotropic motion. For anisotropic vibrations $\mathbf{B}$ is a symmetrical tensor related to $\mathbf{U}$ by

$$\mathbf{B} = \frac{\mathbf{U}}{8\pi^2}. \tag{25}$$

Therefore we can write

$$D(\mathbf{r}^*) = \exp\left[-(\sum\sum B_{ij}m_im_j)\,\frac{\sin^2\theta}{\lambda^2}\right] \tag{26}$$

In this expression $\mathbf{m}$ is a unit vector in reciprocal space and $\sum\sum B_{ij}\,m_im_j$ can be considered as the value of B in the direction of $\mathbf{m}$. In terms of the reciprocal vector, (17)—which was valid for isotropic motion—becomes, for anisotropic thermal motion,

$$D = \exp\left[-\tfrac{1}{4}(B_{11}h^2a^{*2} + B_{22}k^2b^{*33} + B_{33}l^2c^{*2} + 2B_{12}ha^*kb^* + 2B_{13}ha^*lc^*\right.$$
$$\left. + 2B_{23}kb^*lc^*)\right]. \tag{27}$$

The temperature factor M is dimensionless. The anisotropic temperature factor D in (27) can also be expressed in terms of dimensionless quantities β_{ij} as follows

$$D = \exp\left[-(\beta_{11}h^2 + \beta_{22}k^2 + \beta_{33}l^2 + 2\beta_{12}hk + 2\beta_{13}hl + 2\beta_{23}kl)\right]. \tag{28}$$

Although the magnitudes β_{ij} are the most convenient for performing the calculations, they do not give an immediate idea of the magnitude of the motion or of the degree of anisotropy (Cruickshank, 1965). From a table of the β_{ij}, the corresponding U_{ij} or B_{ij} can be deduced as follows:

$$U_{11} = \frac{\beta_{11}}{2\pi^2 a^{*2}}, \qquad U_{22} = \frac{\beta_{22}}{2\pi^2 b^{*2}}, \qquad U_{33} = \frac{\beta_{33}}{2\pi^2 c^{*2}},$$

$$\tag{29}$$

$$U_{12} = \frac{\beta_{12}}{2\pi^2 a^* b^*}, \qquad U_{13} = \frac{\beta_{13}}{2\pi^2 a^* c^*}, \qquad U_{23} = \frac{\beta_{23}}{2\pi^2 b^* c^*},$$

$$B_{11} = \frac{4\beta_{11}}{a^{*2}}, \qquad B_{22} = \frac{4\beta_{22}}{b^{*2}}, \qquad B_{33} = \frac{4\beta_{33}}{c^{*2}},$$

$$\tag{30}$$

$$B_{12} = \frac{4\beta_{12}}{a^* b^*}, \qquad B_{13} = \frac{4\beta_{13}}{a^* c^*}, \qquad B_{23} = \frac{4\beta_{23}}{b^* c^*}.$$

We can also express the anisotropic temperature factor in terms of M_{r^*} analogous to equation (20) for isotropic motion

$$\exp(-M_{r^*}) = \exp\left[-\left(\sum_{i=1}^{3}\sum_{j=1}^{3}\beta_{ij} h_i h_j\right)\right] \tag{31}$$

where

$$\mathbf{r}^* = \sum_{i=1}^{3} h_i \mathbf{r}_i^*.$$

Average Fourier and Patterson syntheses at temperature T

It is well known that the Bragg intensities of a crystal at a given temperature T correspond to the whole intensity function of the average electron density of an ideal crystal. If $\overline{F}$ is the structure factor of the average crystal structure, we have

$$I_T(hkl) = |\overline{F}_T(hkl)|^2, \tag{31}$$

where the structure factor at the reciprocal-lattice point hkl is given by

$$\overline{F}_T(hkl) = \sum_{j=1}^{J} f_j \exp\left(-B_j \frac{\sin^2\theta}{\lambda^2}\right) \exp(2\pi r_j \cdot r_h^*). \tag{32}$$

The summation is extended over the J atoms of the unit cell, while the r_j's define the mean positions of the atoms; B_j is the well-known Debye-Waller temperature factor for the atom j.

Any Fourier map calculated by using as coefficients the observed structure factors $|F_{obs}|$ and the calculated phases, corresponds to the electron-density map of the average crystal structure at the given temperature T. Its detailed form is

$$\bar{\rho}_T(xyz) = v_c^* \sum_{h=-\infty}^{+\infty} \sum_{k=-\infty}^{+\infty} \sum_{l=-\infty}^{+\infty} \overline{F_T(hkl)} \exp\left[2\pi i(hx + ky + lz)\right]. \qquad (33)$$

Similarly, any Patterson function calculated by using the observed Bragg intensities as coefficients corresponds to the Q function of the average crystal structure at the given temperature T. It provides a map that may be called average Patterson map at T. Its detailed form is

$$P_T(xyz) = v_c^* \sum_{h=-\infty}^{+\infty} \sum_{k=-\infty}^{+\infty} \sum_{l=-\infty}^{+\infty} |\overline{F_T(hkl)}|^2 \exp\left[2\pi i(hx + ky + lz).\right] \qquad (34)$$

The Patterson map at the temperature T differs from the one that would correspond to the Patterson map of the crystal structure at rest $(T = 0)$. The detailed form of this calculation is

$$P_0(xyz) = v_c^* \sum_{h=-\infty}^{+\infty} \sum_{k=-\infty}^{+\infty} \sum_{l=-\infty}^{+\infty} |F_0(hkl)|^2 \exp\left[2\pi i(hx + ky + lz)\right]. \qquad (35)$$

The difference between the two maps is caused by the smearing of the interatomic peaks at T, which is more severe for increasing temperatures. For an ideal infinite crystal at rest, the Q function degenerates into the Patterson function (Hosemann and Bagchi, 1962)

$$\lim_{N\to\infty} \frac{1}{N} Q_{cro}(\mathbf{r}) = P_0(\mathbf{r}) = Q_{cell_0}(\mathbf{r}) * z_{cr}(\mathbf{r}). \qquad (36)$$

For an hypothetical average crystal at T we can also write

$$\lim_{N\to\infty} \frac{1}{N} Q_{av_T}(\mathbf{r}) = P_T(\mathbf{r}) = \overline{Q}_{cell_T}(\mathbf{r}) * z_{cr}(\mathbf{r}) \qquad (37)$$

i.e. the Q function of the hypothetical average ideal crystal at T is also ideally periodic.

Both the Fourier and Patterson maps at T differ from the ones that would correspond to the electron density and Patterson maps of the crystal structure at rest in that the peaks of the electron density and of the self-image function of the ideal crystal are smeared; this becomes more severe for increasing temperatures. The effect of thermal motion in the Fourier and Patterson maps of a molecular crystal is represented in Fig. 6. This shows the two-dimensional electron-density and Patterson maps of anthracene projected on (010) at 95°K and 290°K, using as coefficients $|F_{obs}|$ and $|F_{obs}|^2$ for CuKα radiation, respectively, as given by Mason (1964). It can be seen that at high temperature the maps have the less sharp peaks.

The Fourier and Patterson syntheses given in Fig. 6 were calculated from observed x-ray diffraction data using CuKα radiation, thus leaving out all the possible reflections outside the limiting sphere of such radiation. The maps can therefore be affected by the shape factor of the limiting sphere. This effect, if real, would be more intense in the Patterson synthesis where the height of the peaks is higher. In order to minimize this effect and to compare the Patterson synthesis of the ideal crystal at rest with the corresponding one at the average structure at a given temperature, the maps have been computed, using as coefficients the calculated squared structure factors up to 2.8 Å^{-1}. We used the atomic coordinates of anthracene given by Mathieson, Robertson, and Sinclair (1950), and mean temperature factors of $B = 0$ Å^2 and $B = 3.2$ Å^2. The resulting maps are shown in Fig. 7. Comparison of the Patterson map calculated at $T = 0$°K with the one observed at 95°K shows that even at the temperature of liquid nitrogen vibrations are still not negligible.

An interesting example of the effect of thermal motion on the Patterson function is shown in Fig. 8, which corresponds to the projection on (010) of benzene. Only the calculated coefficients using the atomic coordinates given by Cox, Cruickshank, and Smith (1958) were employed. The structure factors were calculated up to 2.8 Å^{-1}, by using, instead of the x-ray atomic scattering factors of the carbon atom, the Fourier transform of the atom disk of 0.31 Å radius. In this way the calculated values correspond to the intensity expected from a Fraunhofer pattern of a two-dimensional structure with disk-like atoms of benzene. For the calculation of the structure factors at a given temperature, a Debye-Waller factor was introduced that corresponds to isotropic motion vibrations of $\bar{u} = 0.20$ Å. Figure 8 shows the Patterson maps of the ideal structure at rest (i) and the Patterson of the average structure in motion (ii). It can be seen that a thermal vibration of $u = 0.20$ Å has strong effect for disk-like atoms.

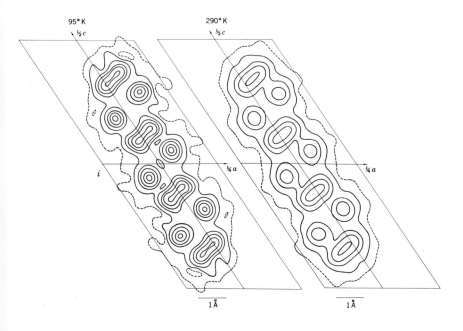

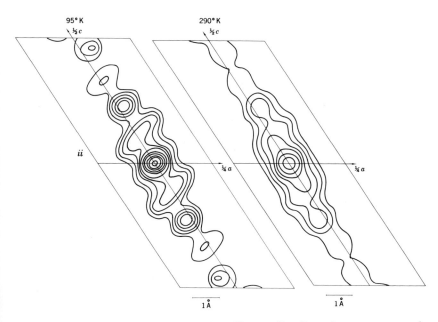

Fig. 6. Anthracene. Projections on (010). Half unit cell. Effect of temperature on the electron density (*i*) and Patterson (*ii*).

139

The Patterson maps of one molecule of benzene at rest and in motion are given in Fig. 9*i* and *ii*, respectively. It can be seen that the central regions of the Patterson maps given in Fig. 8*i* and *ii* correspond to the sum of the self-images of the Patterson of individual molecules symmetrical in a vertical mirror, showing that this region arises from the intramolecular vectors and corresponds to $Q_1 + Q_2$. The areas outside the zig-zag zone of low density arise from the intermolecular images, i.e., they correspond to the image of molecule 2 in molecule 1. The Patterson function in this case can be described as formed by three solitary functions; two of them have as their motif

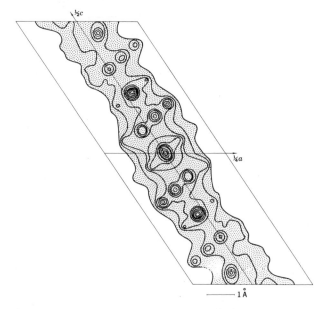

Fig. 7. Anthracene. Projections on (010). Half unit cell. Left, without temperature factor; right, with $\overline{u} = 0.20$ Å.

the self-images of the average molecules 1 and 2 respectively, while the third solitary function corresponds to the image of one molecule in the other.

Q function and Fraunhofer pattern of a monoatomic lattice array subject to thermal vibrations

The hypothetical average crystal is a good model for crystal-structure analysis at a given temperature. The model fails, however, when a more detailed study of the diffraction by a thermally agitated crystal is needed. For instance, since the model deals with an ideal crystal, no diffraction other than the Bragg intensities could be generated. It is a fact, however, that in diffracting x-rays, thermally agitated crystals give rise to some diffuse scattering beside the Bragg intensities. This can be shown in a very dramatic way by the Fraunhofer patterns of a simple two-dimensional model.

Optical methods in the study of crystalline disorder were introduced by Bragg and Lipson (1943), who, in view of the good results obtained in structure analysis, applied the optical diffractometer to simple models of one-dimensional disorder. The results obtained stimulated further development. Taylor, Hinde, and Lipson (1951) had used optical methods in the study of the mechanism of alloy

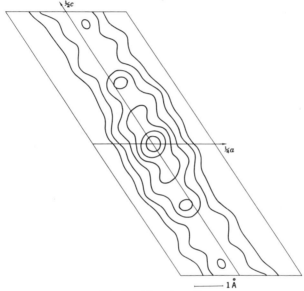

Fig. 7. *(Continued).*

ordering, and Chayes (1957) applied such methods to the study of diffuse scattering caused by packing disorder. Hosemann and his school have applied the optical diffractometer to certain problems of statistical disorder, analyzing the results from a general point of view within the theory of the paracrystal (Hosemann and Bagchi, 1962). With a different approach, but still using the same type of instrument, Wooster (1954) undertook the study of the effect of "thermal" waves on diffuse scattering, and a general view of the problem is found in his recent book (Wooster, 1962).

A wide use of the optical diffractometer in the study of thermal diffuse scattering of molecular and other crystals has been recently

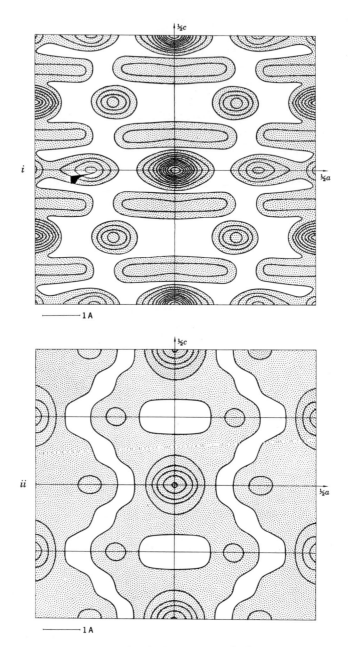

Fig. 8. Benzene. Projection on (010). (i) Patterson calculated with disk atoms at rest; (ii) the same with $\overline{u} = 0.20$ Å.

142

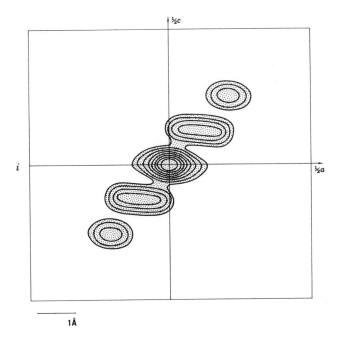

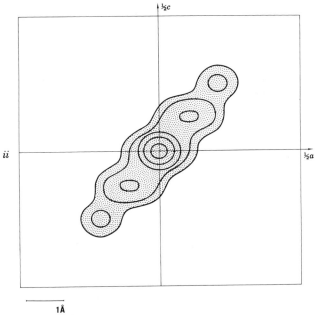

Fig. 9. Benzene. Projection on (010). (i) $Q_{\text{mol 1 at rest}}$. (ii) $Q_{\text{mol 1 in motion}}$.

143

made by Amorós and coworkers (1963, 1965). We shall first explain certain general considerations that are necessary to understand the scope and use of the method.

The simulation of thermal vibrations in a two-dimensional model of a structure can be achieved in a simple manner if we use the practical, but unrealistic, model of thermal motion of the atoms in the form of isotropic and independent vibrations (translations), so that it is supposed that there is no interaction between the vibrations of neighboring atoms, and that the amplitudes of vibration have the same magnitude and are equally probable in all directions. Motion of this type can be simulated in a model (Fig. 10i) where the centers of the different disks ("atoms") are displaced in different directions by amounts equal to the square root of the mean square displacement ($\bar{u} = 0.20$ Å), simulating the same probability in each direction. This model corresponds to a "frozen" configuration of the structure, and is actually equivalent to a static positional disorder. Nevertheless, as we shall see, the resulting effect is that which would be expected in the case of isotropic and independent thermal vibrations.

If the centers of the atoms have been displaced by Δr_l from their equilibrium positions r_l in the cell l, the distribution function of the displacement vectors can be given by the function (Hosemann and Bagchi, 1962)

$$H_l(\mathbf{r}) = H(\mathbf{r}) \neq L(\mathbf{r}-0). \tag{38}$$

The electron density in any cell l is given by

$$\rho_l(\mathbf{r}) = \rho_{\text{disk}}(\mathbf{r}-\Delta\mathbf{r}_l) = \rho_{\text{disk}}(\mathbf{r}) * L(\mathbf{r}-\Delta\mathbf{r}_l), \tag{39}$$

and the crystal electron density by

$$\rho_{\text{cr}}(\mathbf{r}) = \sum_{l=-\infty}^{+\infty} \rho_{\text{disk}}(\mathbf{r}) * L[\mathbf{r}-(\mathbf{r}_l+\Delta\mathbf{r}_l)] \tag{40}$$

If the crystal model is limited, one must introduce the shape function $s(\mathbf{r})$. If the $\Delta\mathbf{r}_1$ is small, (40) is an almost periodic function. In this case the Q function is expressed by

$$Q(\mathbf{r}) = \frac{1}{A_c} Q_{\text{disk}} * Q_H * (z_{\text{cr}} \cdot Q_s) - NQ_{\text{disk}} * Q_H + NQ_{\text{disk}}. \tag{41}$$

where $Q_H(\mathbf{r})$ is the self-image of $H(\mathbf{r})$, N is the number of disk atoms, and A_c is the area of the cell. Let us introduce the average value Q_{disk}, and $Q_s(\mathbf{r})$, the self-image of the shape function:

$$\overline{Q}_{\text{disk}}(\mathbf{r}) = Q_{\text{disk}}(\mathbf{r}) * Q_H(\mathbf{r}). \tag{42}$$

If this is substituted in (41) it becomes

$$Q(\mathbf{r}) = \frac{1}{A_c}\,\overline{Q}_{\text{disk}} * (z_{cr} \cdot Q_s) - N\overline{Q}_{\text{disk}} + NQ_{\text{disk}}. \tag{43}$$

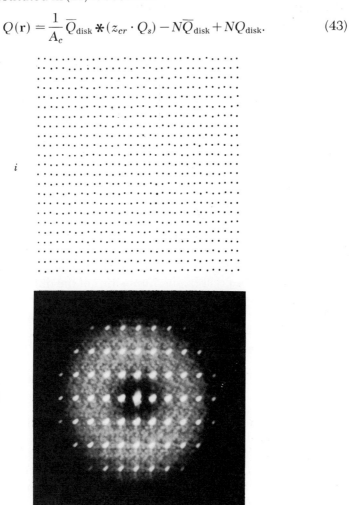

Fig. 10. Effect of isotropic vibrations in a monoatomic (disk) structure. (*i*) Negative of the model stimulating random thermal vibrations of the atoms; (*ii*) Fraunhofer pattern.

The third term in (43) gives the central spot at $\mathbf{r} = 0$, which is proportional to the self-image of the disk, while the other two terms are proportional to $\overline{Q}_{disk}(\mathbf{r})$. All the peaks of the Q function are equal, except the one at the origin. The Q function is no longer a solitary function, but is very similar to it. We shall call this new function a pseudosolitary function. Since the difference is very small, the optical Q function is not reproduced here.

The Fourier transform of (43) gives the total intensity (Fig. 10ii):

$$I(\mathbf{r}^*) = A^* I_{disk}(\mathbf{r}^*) |D|^2 (Z_{cr} * |S|^2) + N I_{disk}(\mathbf{r}^*)(1 - |D|^2) \qquad (44)$$

where $|S|^2 = T\{Q_s\}$ is the shape factor of the model of disks and $D(\mathbf{r}^*) = T\{H(\mathbf{r})\} \neq 1$. The first term gives the Bragg reflections, all of which have the same shape and size, and differ from those of a crystal at rest (Fig. 17ii, Ch. 2) only by the factor $|D|^2$, which can be identified with the Debye-Waller temperature factor for isotropic motion

$$|D|^2 = \exp(-1/2B|\mathbf{r}^*|^2). \qquad (45)$$

Comparing the Fraunhofer pattern of Figs. 9ii with the one reproduced in 17ii, Ch. 2, we see that as the distance from the origin of reciprocal space increases, the intensities of the diffraction maxima of the structure with thermal motion decrease with respect to the intensities of the maxima of the model composed of atoms at rest. This is because they now obey the condition

$$I^T(\mathbf{r}^*) = (C\pi R^2)^2 \left[\frac{2J_1(2\pi R r^*)}{2\pi R r^*}\right]^2 \exp\left(-\tfrac{1}{2}B|\mathbf{r}^*|^2\right). \qquad (46)$$

The distribution of the amplitude and intensity functions are shown in Fig. 11. Besides this effect on the diffraction maxima, there appears in the Fraunhofer pattern a diffuse background in the form of a ring (Fig 10ii), which corresponds to the effect predicted by Debye (1914) in the case of independent atomic motion. The distribution of the diffuse background (Fig. 11ii) is given by

$$I_{dif}(\mathbf{r}^*) = (C\pi R^2)^2 \left[\frac{2J_1(2\pi R r^*)}{2\pi R r^*}\right]^2 (1 - \exp[-\tfrac{1}{2}B|\mathbf{r}^*|^2]). \qquad (47)$$

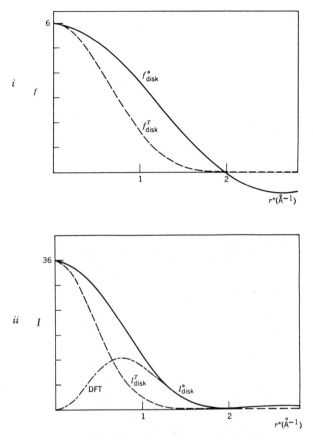

Fig. 11. Amplitude (*i*), and intensity (*ii*) functions of a disk atom of radius 0.31 Å. Continuous line: atoms at rest; broken line: at temperature T; - · - · - DFT.

The function inside the parenthesis is called the Debye (as contrasted with the Debye-Waller) temperature factor and is given in Fig. 5*iii* (broken line).

The fact that in the Q function the central motif Q_{disk} is different from the others given by $\overline{Q}_{disk}$ implies the appearance of a certain amount of diffuse scattering.

If instead of an isotropic vibration, the atoms are subject to aniso-tropic vibrations, this anisotropic effect is reflected in the Fraunhofer pattern. Figure 12 shows the extreme case where the vibration is in a single direction.

The similarity between the distributions of diffuse intensity with independent atomic motion in the cases of real atoms and of disk

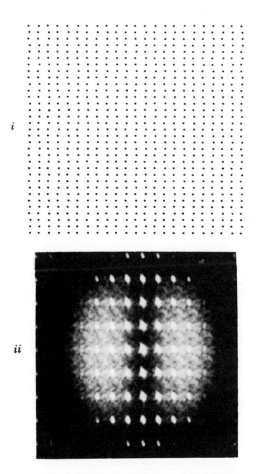

Fig. 12. Fraunhofer pattern showing the effect of vibration along only a single direction.

atoms can be seen in Fig. 13. It is evident that for values not far from the origin of reciprocal space, independent atomic motion can be simulated optically by an appropriate model of disk atoms.

The Q function of the thermally disordered unimolecular crystal

For an infinite real crystal with no other defect but thermal agitation, the Q function is distinct from the Patterson function. Patterson functions derived from experimental data correspond, as we have emphasized, to the self-image of the electron density of an ideal hypothetical crystal in which the electron density corresponds to its time-average. The Patterson so defined is always a periodic function. In contrast, the Q function of the ideal crystal is a quasiperiodic function and is therefore different from the Patterson function.

Let us consider the simplest model of a unimolecular infinite crystal with thermal agitation consisting of rigid-body independent translational motions of the molecules. Let us consider, for example, the projection on (010) of the anthracene crystal, in which the two molecules of the unit cell are translation-equivalent; the projection is equivalent to a monomolecular crystal. In the model of Fig. 14i thermal vibration has been simulated in the form of independent translational motion as follows: the rigid molecule was placed parallel to itself and with its center of gravity displaced by approximately 0.20 Å from the positions 000 and $\frac{1}{2}, \frac{1}{2} 0$ along six radial directions, giving to the radial positions and the equilibrium position an equal probability.

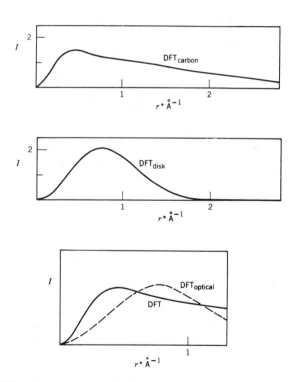

Fig. 13. Comparison of DFT functions of a carbon atom and a disk atom.

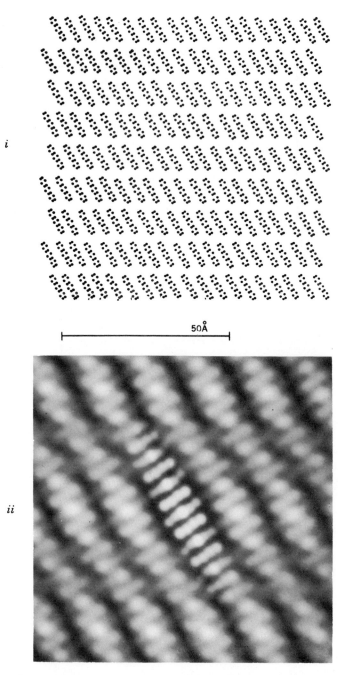

i

ii

Fig. 14. Anthracene. Projection on (010). (*i*) Negative of the model simulating random rigid-body translational motion; (*ii*) optical Q function.

In this case the centroid of the molecule in the cell l does not lie at the lattice point r_l but is displaced by a vector Δr_l from its ideal position. The density function of any cell l of the model simulating thermal motion can be expressed by

$$\rho_l(\mathbf{r}) = \rho_{\text{mole}}(\mathbf{r} - \Delta \mathbf{r}_l) = \rho_{\text{mole}}(\mathbf{r}) * L(\mathbf{r} - \Delta \mathbf{r}_l). \tag{48}$$

The total density function of the model is again an almost periodic function:

$$\rho_{\text{cr}}(\mathbf{r}) = \sum_{l=-\infty}^{+\infty} \rho_{\text{mole}}(\mathbf{r}) \quad L[\mathbf{r} - (\mathbf{r}_l + \Delta \mathbf{r}_l)]. \tag{49}$$

The average over all $L(\mathbf{r} - \Delta \mathbf{r}_l)$ gives a distribution function $H(\mathbf{r})$

$$H(\mathbf{r}) = H_l(\mathbf{r}) = \overline{L(\mathbf{r} - \Delta \mathbf{r}_l)}, \tag{50}$$

and the average electron-density distribution may be described as $\rho_{\text{mole}}(\mathbf{r})$ convolved with $H(\mathbf{r})$:

$$\overline{\rho}_{\text{mole}}(\mathbf{r}) = \rho_{\text{mole}}(\mathbf{r}) * H(\mathbf{r}). \tag{51}$$

This function is the motif of the solitary function defining the whole electron density of the hypothetical average crystal, which can also be expressed as

$$\overline{\rho}_{\text{cr}}(\mathbf{r}) = \sum_{l=-\infty}^{+\infty} \overline{\rho}_{\text{mole}}(\mathbf{r}) \cdot L(\mathbf{r} - \mathbf{r}_l). \tag{52}$$

The Q function of a primitive unit cell of the hypothetical average ideal crystal is given by

$$\overline{Q}_{\text{cell}}(\mathbf{r}) = Q_{\text{mole}}(\mathbf{r}) * Q_H(\mathbf{r}) = \overline{Q}_{\text{mole}}(\mathbf{r}) \tag{53}$$

If this is substituted in (37), it becomes

$$\lim_{N \to \infty} \frac{1}{N} \overline{Q}_{T\text{cr}}(\mathbf{r}) = Q_{\text{cell}_0}(\mathbf{r}) * Q_H(\mathbf{r}) * z_{\text{cr}}(\mathbf{r}). \tag{54}$$

The convolution of $Q_{\text{cell}_0}(\mathbf{r})$ with $Q_H(\mathbf{r})$ merely smears the function $Q_{\text{cell}_0}(\mathbf{r})$. This smeared function is the motif of a solitary function and corresponds to the Patterson of the average structure at temperature T.

In computing the self-image of the density function of the whole model two different kinds of terms arise. First of all, at the origin of the physical space there appears a motif due to the sum of the self-images of the molecules of each cell l. Since the self-image function is unaltered by the change Δr_l of origin, the central motif has high values, corresponding to N times the self-images of a single molecule at rest, $N Q_{\text{mole}}(\mathbf{r})$, N being the total number of molecules in the crystal. Obviously (since the model is built of rigid molecules), this term is free from vibration effect.

The image functions of every molecule in another one give rise to motifs $\overline{Q}_{\text{mole}_T}(\mathbf{r})$ repeated by lattice translations r_l. This term is obviously affected by the molecular displacements. In terms of the lattice peak function $z_{\text{cr}}(\mathbf{r})$ the motifs of this kind can be expressed by (53) if the motif at the origin is adequately subtracted.

Finally, the Q function of this thermally agitated unimolecular crystal is given by

$$Q(\mathbf{r}) = \overline{Q}_{\text{mole}_T}(\mathbf{r}) * z_{\text{cr}}(\mathbf{r}) + Q_{\text{mole}}(\mathbf{r}) - \overline{Q}_{\text{mole}_T}(\mathbf{r}) \qquad (55)$$

$$= P_T(\mathbf{r}) + Q_{\text{moleo}}(\mathbf{r}) - \overline{Q}_{\text{mole}_T}(\mathbf{r}).$$

This equation shows that the Q function of a unimolecular crystal is a pseudosolitary function in which all the motifs are given by $\overline{Q}_{\text{mole}_T}$ except the motif at the origin that corresponds to Q_{mole} (Fig. 14ii). These two motifs correspond respectively to those of the Patterson functions of the crystal at rest and of the average crystal in motion. These motifs can be therefore easily calculated from only two Patterson syntheses. The Q function is a pseudosolitary function which can be constructed just by repeating the motif of the average Patterson over and over in the framework of the crystal lattice except at the origin, where the motif of the Patterson of the ideal structure at rest must be added. Figure 15 shows the calculated Q function of the (010) projection of anthracene at rest and in motion.

The difference Fourier transform (DFT) of a unimolecular crystal

The Fourier transform of (55) is equivalent to the total intensity of the Fraunhofer pattern of Fig. 16i,

$$I(\mathbf{r}^*) = I_{\text{mole}}(\mathbf{r}^*)|D|^2 Z_{\text{cr}}(\mathbf{r}^*) + I_{\text{mole}}(\mathbf{r}^*)(1 - |D|^2). \qquad (56)$$

The first term gives rise to the Bragg reflections, all of which have the same shape and size and differ from the reflections of the crystal at

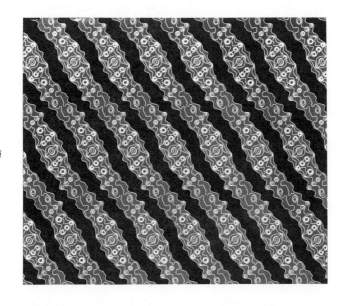

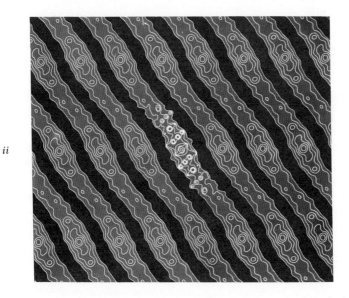

Fig. 15. Anthracene. Projection on (010). Calculated Q functions of (i) ideal structure at rest; (ii) structure with thermal motion ($\bar{u} = 0.20$ Å).

153

rest only by the factor $|D|^2$, which can be identified as the well known Debye-Waller factor. The second term is responsible for the continuous diffuse scattering. Equation (56) can be written

$$I(\mathbf{r}^*) = I_{\mathrm{mole}_T}(\mathbf{r}^*)Z_{\mathrm{cr}}(\mathbf{r}^*) + I_{\mathrm{mole}_0}(\mathbf{r}^*) - I_{\mathrm{mole}_T}(\mathbf{r}^*), \qquad (57)$$

where the first term stands for the Bragg intensities at the temperature T, while the continuous diffuse scattering, given by the second term, is expressed as the difference between the molecular intensity transforms at rest and in motion. This coincides with the difference Fourier transform function as given by Amorós, Canut, and de Acha (1960), and is hereafter abbreviated the *DFT* function:

$$I_{\mathrm{DFT}}(\mathbf{r}^*) = I_{\mathrm{mole}_0}(\mathbf{r}^*) - I_{\mathrm{mole}_T}(\mathbf{r}^*). \qquad (58)$$

Comparison of the Fraunhofer patterns corresponding to the structure at rest (Fig. 16, Ch. 2) and the structure with thermal vibrations (Fig. 16*i*) reveals two basic differences:

1. The diffraction maxima of the structure subject to thermal vibrations (Bragg reflections) evidence a weakening of intensity with increasing reciprocal vector and correspond to the first term of (57), where $|D|^2$ is the Debye-Waller factor.
2. A certain amount of continuous diffuse scattering appears in the Fraunhofer pattern corresponding to the thermal-vibration model. This diffuse scattering is distributed in elongated areas parallel to $\mathbf{a}^*$. The intensity function of the continuous diffuse part of the diffraction pattern is given by the second term of (57), where $(1-|D|^2)$ corresponds to the Debye factor of independent atomic motion.

Comparison of the diffraction pattern of independent molecular motion in anthracene (Fig. 16*i*) and the pattern from a single molecule (Fig. 16*ii*) shows that the continuous diffuse scattering is distributed in reciprocal space in a way analogous to the diffraction by a single molecule. Nevertheless there is a fundamental difference that is manifested in the region near the origin of reciprocal space. In the diffraction pattern of a single molecule there is an intense elongated maximum surrounding the origin. In contrast, this maximum disappears in the model of the crystal with molecular vibrations. The second term of (57) accounts for this phenomenon too, since in this case the intensity transform I_{mole} of the molecule is multiplied by the Debye factor $(1-|D|^2)$. The resulting effect is equivalent to multiplying the intensity of the diffraction pattern of a single molecule by

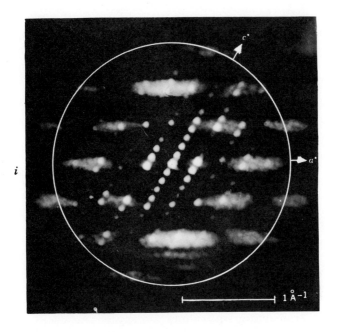

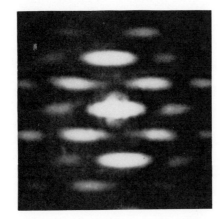

Fig. 16. Anthracene. Fraunhofer patterns of projections on (010) of (*i*) the thermal disordered crystal; (*ii*) a single molecule.

the intensity of the ring of continuous diffuse scattering of Fig. 10ii, which corresponds to the diffuse-intensity function of independent atomic motion. Because this function vanishes near the origin, a decrease in the continuous intensity is produced in this region.

The Q function of the thermally disordered dimolecular crystal

The Q function of a dimolecular crystal subject to rigid-body thermal vibrations is also quasiperiodic, and can be given by

$$Q(\mathbf{r}) = N(Q_1 + Q_2) - N(\overline{Q}_1 + \overline{Q}_2) + \frac{1}{v_c}[\overline{Q}_1 + \overline{Q}_2$$
$$+ \overline{\rho}_1(\mathbf{r} - \mathbf{r}_1) * \overline{\rho}_2(-\mathbf{r} + \mathbf{r}_2)] * z_{cr}(\mathbf{r})$$
$$= Q_1 + Q_2 - \overline{Q}_1 - \overline{Q}_2 + P_T(\mathbf{r}). \tag{59}$$

The first term, located at the origin, arises from the sum of the self-images of each molecule of the crystal and is therefore proportional to $Q_1 + Q_2$. Obviously this term is free from vibration effect. The last term contains two parts, one proportional to $\overline{Q}_1 + \overline{Q}_2$; it corresponds to images of translation-equivalent molecules in each other. It is affected by the thermal vibrations and is equivalent to the intramolecular images of the Patterson of the average structure. The other part is proportional to $\overline{\rho}_1(\mathbf{r} - \mathbf{r}_1) * \overline{\rho}_2(-\mathbf{r} + \mathbf{r}_2)$; it corresponds to the intermolecular images of the Patterson of the average structure. In expression (59) a term proportional to $\overline{Q}_1 + \overline{Q}_2$ is subtracted in the origin in a way analogous to the subtraction of a term in the Q function of a unimolecular crystal. It is clear therefore that the Q function of a dimolecular crystal can be described in terms of two pseudosolitary functions corresponding to the self-images of the molecules 1 and 2, respectively, and a solitary function whose motif is the image of one molecule in the other.

Benzene has been chosen as an example of a molecular crystal with more than one molecule per unit cell. The unit cell has four molecules; on each principal plane, however, every two molecules project identically, so that on each projection we can define a smaller cell containing only two molecules. The models (Fig. 17) were constructed in a similar way to that described for anthracene. For our study we have selected the projection on (010). One of the two pseudosolitary functions corresponding to the self-images of one molecule has been represented in Fig. 18i. The total Q function (Fig. 18ii) is the sum of two symmetrical pseudosolitary functions like 18i and a solitary function corresponding to the image of one molecule on the other. As a

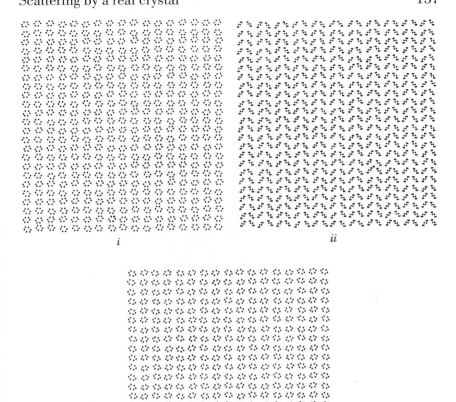

Fig. 17. Benzene. Negatives of the models simulating rigid-body random translational motion. (*i*) Projection on (100); (*ii*) projection on (010); (*iii*) projection on (001).

result, the motif of the origin is different of the others, and is proportional to $Q_1 + Q_2$. All the motifs at the lattice points defined from the origin correspond to $\overline{Q}_1 + \overline{Q}_2$, and appear in Fig. 18*ii* along rows parallel to **c**, at integer multiples of **a**. The motif of the solitary function corresponds to $\overline{p}_1(\mathbf{r}) * \overline{p}_2(-\mathbf{r})$; it is located at the lattice points of a lattice shifted $\frac{1}{2}$**a**, 0 from the origin. Those motifs appear along columns parallel to **c** but shifted $\frac{1}{2}a$.

In a similar way as is done for anthracene, the Q function can be

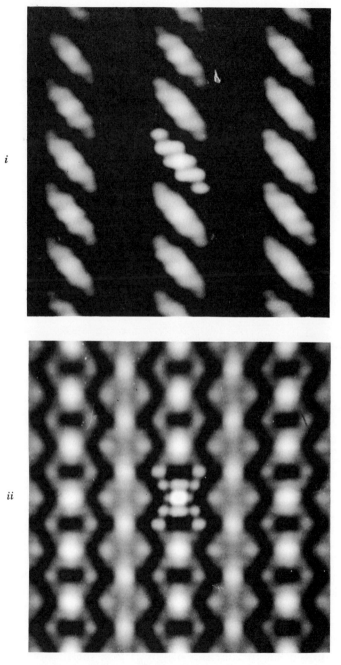

i

ii

Fig. 18. Benzene. Projection on (010). Optical Q function. (*i*) Pseudo solitary function of one molecule; (*ii*) total Q function.

calculated from Patterson syntheses. Figures 19i and ii show the calculated Q functions of the structure at rest and in motion, respectively. The Q function of the structure at rest is merely the Patterson whose unit-cell content was given in Fig. 8i. The Q function of the structure in motion is built up of the motifs of the Patterson average whose unit-cell content was given in Fig. 8ii. At the origin of this Q function the motif of the self-images of the molecules in motion (see Fig. 9ii) is substituted by the corresponding motif of the self-images of the molecules at rest (Fig. 9i).

If the unit cell contains more than two molecules (59) can be easily extended to

$$Q = N \sum_p Q_p - N \sum_p \overline{Q}_p + \frac{1}{v'}\left[\sum_p \overline{Q}_p + 2 \sum_{p \neq p'} \overline{\rho}_p(\mathbf{r} - \mathbf{r}_p) * \overline{\rho}_{p'}(-\mathbf{r} + \mathbf{r}_{p'})\right]$$

$$* z_{cr}(\mathbf{r}). \qquad (60)$$

From (60) we can easily deduce that the Q function of a polymolecular crystal is built up of solitary functions whose motifs are the images of one molecule in the other, and pseudosolitary functions whose central motifs are the self-images of the different molecules at rest and the other motifs the self-images of the average molecules.

The DFT function of a thermally disordered dimolecular crystal

The total intensity function of a thermally disordered dimolecular crystal can be obtained by Fourier inversion of (59), namely

$$I(\mathbf{r}^*) = [I_{1_0}(\mathbf{r}^*) + I_{2_0}(\mathbf{r}^*)] - [I_{1_T}(\mathbf{r}^*) + I_{2_T}(\mathbf{r}^*)]$$

$$+ v_c^* \sum_h \{|F_{1_T}(\mathbf{r}^*)|^2 + |F_{2_T}(\mathbf{r}^*)|^2 + 2F_{1_T}(\mathbf{r}^*) \cdot F_{2\,T}^*(\mathbf{r}^*)$$

$$\cos 2\pi[\mathbf{r}^* \cdot (\mathbf{r}_p - \mathbf{r}_{p'})]\}L(\mathbf{r}^* - \mathbf{r}_h^*). \qquad (61)$$

The transform of the difference between the first and second terms of (59) is merely the difference between the intensities diffracted incoherently by two molecules at rest and in motion, and the result is a continuous diffuse-intensity function in reciprocal space. This diffuse-scattering intensity reflects the shape and orientation of the individual molecules through their intensity Fourier transforms.

The transform of the last term of (59), on the other hand, has discrete values at the points of the reciprocal lattice, and is proportional to the intensity diffracted by a single unit cell; i.e., here the two individual molecules diffract coherently, due to the term $2F_{1_T}(\mathbf{r}_h^*) \cdot F_{2\,T}^*(\mathbf{r}_h^*) \cos 2\pi[\mathbf{r}^* \cdot (\mathbf{r}_p - \mathbf{r}_{p'})]$. Moreover, the intensity maxi-

Fig. 19. Benzene. Projection on (010). Calculated Q functions. (*i*) For molecules at rest; (*ii*) in motion.

mum contains implicitly the Debye-Waller factor, and (61) can be written as

$$I(\mathbf{r}^*) = [I_{1_0}(\mathbf{r}^*) + I_{2_0}(\mathbf{r}^*)] - [I_{1_T}(\mathbf{r}^*) + I_{2_T}(\mathbf{r}^*)] + v_c^* \sum_h I_{\text{cell}_T}(\mathbf{r}^*) \cdot$$
$$L(\mathbf{r}^* - \mathbf{r}_h^*). \qquad (62)$$

For a crystal with several molecules, the Bragg intensities are given by the squares of the structure factors of the average crystal structure; these intensities are different from the sums of the intensities that would be diffracted by the molecules of the unit cell independently. This indicates that, while the Bragg intensities are obtained by taking into account the phase differences between the different molecules of the unit cell, the diffuse scattering, as given by the DFT function, corresponds to the superpositions of intensities diffracted by different molecules incoherently.

We call the function

$$I_{\text{DFT}}(\mathbf{r}^*) = \sum_{p=1}^{P} [I_{p_0}(\mathbf{r}^*) - I_{p_T}(\mathbf{r}^*)] \qquad (63)$$

the difference Fourier transform, or simply DFT. The simplest DFT function arises when all the atoms of the molecule are considered to be subject to the same translational motion, and the motion is isotropic. In this case the expression for the DFT is considerably simplified, and takes the form

$$I_{\text{DFT}} = \sum_{p=1}^{P} I_{p_0}(\mathbf{r}^*)\{1 - \exp(-\tfrac{1}{2}B|\mathbf{r}^*|^2)\}. \qquad (64)$$

The fundamental characteristic of the DFT in this case is that it is proportional to $1 - \exp(-\tfrac{1}{2}B|\mathbf{r}^*|^2)$. In all cases the DFT function has the property of being zero at the origin of Fourier space, i.e.,

$$I_{\text{DFT}}(0) = 0. \qquad (65)$$

In order to interpret the diffuse bands observed in the scattering of electrons by a crystal of anthracene, Charlesby, Finch, and Wilman (1939) obtained the following expression on assuming independent, harmonic, rigid-body vibrations of the molecules about their average positions in the structure:

$$I = I_1 + I_2 = (A^2 + B^2)\frac{\sin^2 \pi Lh \sin^2 \pi Mk \sin^2 \pi Nl}{\sin^2 \pi h \sin^2 \pi k \sin^2 \pi l}\exp\left[-16\pi^2\frac{\sin^2\theta}{\lambda^2}\frac{fT}{f}\right.$$

$$\left. + N\sum_p (A_p^2 + B_p^2)\right]\left[1 - \exp\left(-16\pi^2\frac{\sin^2\theta}{\lambda^2}\frac{fT}{f}\right)\right]. \qquad (66)$$

I_1 consists of three factors: the structure factor of the crystalline cell, the Laue interference function, and the temperature factor. I_1 therefore accounts for the Bragg reflections. The second term explains the intensity of the diffuse bands, in agreement with the experimental results obtained by electron diffraction. This expression, obtained by Charlesby, Finch, and Wilman after laborious calculations, is the same as that derived in Debye's primitive theory of independent atomic motion extended to the molecular case. It is easily seen that the second term of (66) corresponds to our DFT function in the special case where all the atoms are subject to the same isotropic vibrational amplitude.

Computation of DFT functions

In Ch. 1, we described how to calculate the molecular transforms at rest at any point hkl in the space reciprocal to the physical space given by some reference vectors. When dealing with a crystal, either ordered or disordered, the points in reciprocal space for which hkl are integers are the reciprocal-lattice points. The transforms can obviously be calculated at fractional values of hkl. The points hkl are defined in terms of the vector r^*_{hkl}.

The Fourier transform of a molecule or unit cell undergoing isotropic motion can be defined in a way similar to the structure factor of a crystal at a given temperature by introducing the Debye-Waller isotropic temperature factor in the different atomic scattering factors of the molecule or of the unit cell, thus:

$$\overline{F}_T(hkl) = \sum_{j=1}^{J} f_j(hkl) \exp(-B_j \sin^2 \theta/\lambda^2) \exp[2\pi(hx_j + ky_j + lz_j)]. \quad (67)$$

We can also express $\overline{F}_T$ in terms of the real and imaginary parts of the transform:

$$A_T(hkl) = \sum_{j=1}^{J} f_j(hkl) \exp(-B_j \sin^2 \theta/\lambda^2) \cos 2\pi (hx_j + ky_j + lz_j), \quad (68)$$

$$B_T(hkl) = \sum_{j=1}^{J} f_j(hkl) \exp(-B_j \sin^2 \theta/\lambda^2) \sin 2\pi(hx_j + ky_j + lz_j). \quad (69)$$

The amplitude $|\overline{F}_T|$ is given by

$$|\overline{F}_T| = \sqrt{A_T^2 + B_T^2}, \quad (70)$$

where the phase angle ϕ is the same as for the molecule at rest [see (23), Ch. 1]. Finally, the intensity transform of the molecule or unit cell undergoing thermal motion can be defined as

$$I_T(hkl) = |\overline{F}_T(hkl)|^2. \tag{71}$$

The contribution of a given molecule p to the total DFT can be calculated just in terms of

$$I^p_{\mathrm{DFT}}(hkl) = I_{p_0}(hkl) - I_{p_t}(hkl), \tag{72}$$

while the total DFT function is given by

$$I_{\mathrm{DFT}}(hkl) = \sum_{p=1}^{P} I^p_{\mathrm{DFT}}(hkl). \tag{73}$$

Complete three-dimensional calculations can easily be made by using high-speed computers (Caruso, Richards, and Canut-Amorós, 1966), and the iso-DFT contours can be plotted along different sections of reciprocal space. As an example of the calculations of DFT functions along different sections of reciprocal space the benzene crystal has been selected. The computations have been made by using $f_{\mathrm{disk}}(\mathbf{r}^*)$ in order to compare the results with the Fraunhofer patterns simulating the DFT optically. From what follows we shall see that for $(100)^*_0$, $(010)^*_0$, and $(001)^*_0$, the contribution of only two molecules need to be considered, but the final results must be multiplied by two.

Benzene is an orthorhombic crystal that belongs to space group *Pbca*; the unit cell contains four molecules that lie on centers of symmetry at 000, $0\frac{1}{2}\frac{1}{2}$, $\frac{1}{2}0\frac{1}{2}$, and $\frac{1}{2}\frac{1}{2}0$, giving rise to a pseudoface centering (Cox, Cruickshank, and Smith, 1958). In the unit cell there are two sets of molecules differently oriented. The molecule whose center is at 000 is denoted molecule 1. Molecule 2 is related to 1 by reflection in the plane at $x = \frac{1}{4}$ followed by a translation of $\frac{1}{2}\mathbf{b}$; molecule 3 by reflection in the plane at $y = \frac{1}{4}\mathbf{b}$ and by a translation of $\frac{1}{2}\mathbf{c}$; and 4 by reflection in $z = \frac{1}{4}\mathbf{c}$ and by a translation of $\frac{1}{2}\mathbf{a}$.

On the (100) plane, molecules 1 and 3 project identically, as do 2 and 4. Then the following relations hold for the molecular transforms:

$$I_1(0kl) = I_4(0kl), \qquad |F_1| = |F_4|,$$

$$I_3(0kl) = I_2(0kl), \qquad |F_3| = |F_4|,$$

$$|A_1| = |A_4|,$$

$$|A_3| = |A_4|.$$

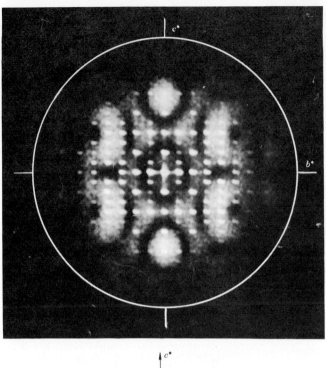

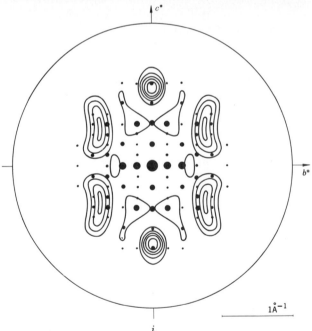

Fig. 20. Benzene. Top: Fraunhofer patterns of the models of Fig. 17. Bottom: Calculated DFT with the weighted reciprocal lattice superimposed.

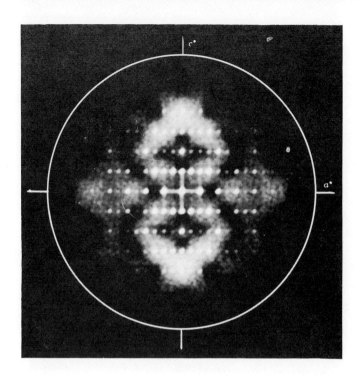

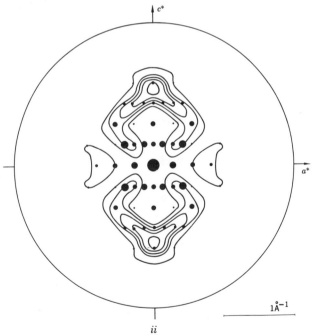

ii

Fig. 20. (*Continued*).

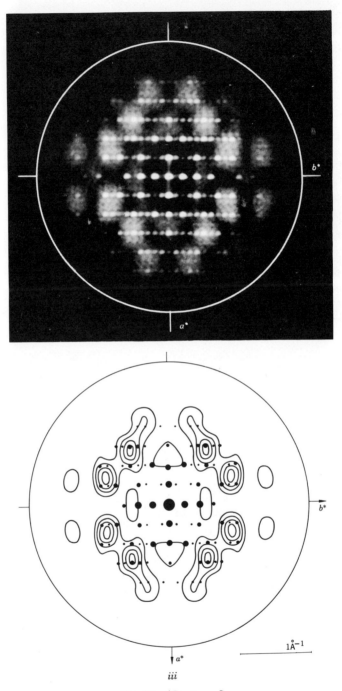

Fig. 20. (*Continued*).

The molecules that do not project identically on the (100) plane are related by a mirror plane along the **b** axis, so the corresponding transforms are related by the same mirror plane:

$$I_1(0kl) = I_3(0k\bar{l}).$$

Figure 20i reproduces the Fraunhofer pattern and the calculated map of the thermally disordered benzene crystal projected on (100). The black circles in the calculated map correspond to the intensity of the unit cell in motion, weighted (areas proportional to the Bragg intensities) at the reciprocal lattice points, and the contour lines correspond to the DFT function. It can easily be seen that the continuous diffuse scattering of the Fraunhofer pattern coincides with the calculated DFT function. Comparing this figure with Fig. 20, Ch. 1, it can be deduced that the DFT of the crystal results from the superimposed contribution of the intensity transforms of the two molecules related by the mirror plane containing the **c** axis. The main difference between the DFT and the intensity molecular transform is the absence of intensity in the DFT near the origin, in agreement with the theory.

On the (010) plane the molecules projected identically are the pairs 1 and 2, and 3 and 4. Since 1 and 4 are related by a mirror plane normal to this plane or along the **c** axis, the corresponding transforms are also related by this symmetry plane. Thus we have

$$I_1(h0l) = I_2(h0l), \qquad I_3(h0l) = I_4(h0l)$$

but

$$I_1(h0l) \neq I_3(\bar{h}0l).$$

The results of the calculations and the Fraunhofer pattern of the structure projected on (010) are reproduced in Fig. 20ii. Here again the observed continuous diffuse scattering corresponds well with the calculated DFT. Again, by comparing this figure with Fig. 20ii, Ch. 1, it can be seen that the DFT results from the overlapping of the intensity transforms of the two molecules symmetrical through the mirror plane that contains the **c** axis, taking account of the absence of intensity in the origin of the DFT map.

On (001), molecule pairs 1 and 3, and 2 and 4 are projected identically, 1 and 2 being related by a symmetry plane along the **a** axis. Accordingly, we have

$$I_1(hk0) = I_3(hk0), \qquad I_2(hk0) = I_4(hk0),$$

but

$$I_1(hk0) \neq I_2(h\bar{k}0).$$

In this case, similar conclusions can be reached by comparing the Fraunhofer pattern and the DFT map of Fig. 20*iii*, and by comparison with Fig. 20*iii*, Ch. 1.

The difference Patterson (rest-motion)

We have already defined the Patterson of the structure at rest $P_0(\mathbf{r})$ in (35) and the Patterson average at the temperature T, $P_T(\mathbf{r})$ in (34). Let us compute the difference

$$\Delta P_{0,T}(\mathbf{r}) = [P_0(\mathbf{r}) - P_T(\mathbf{r})] \cdot s(\mathbf{r}) \tag{74}$$

at any point $\mathbf{r}$ in a unit cell of physical space. This would be identically zero in absence of thermal agitation ($T = 0$), but the difference will increase at increasing temperatures. $\Delta P_{0,T}(\mathbf{r})$ has both positive and negative values, as well as zero lines. Notice that by definition $\Delta P_{0,T}(\mathbf{r})$ is a continuous function, and, being identically zero outside a unit cell, it is not periodic. If no overlap occurs, we can write

$$\Delta P_{0,T}(\mathbf{r}) = Q_{\text{cell}_0}(\mathbf{r}) - \overline{Q}_{\text{cell}_T}(\mathbf{r}) = \Delta Q_{\text{cell}_{0,T}}. \tag{75}$$

The difference Patterson is, of course, centrosymmetric. At the origin it is always positive, its value being given by the difference between the sums of the heights of the self-images of all atoms of the cell at rest and at motion (Canut-Amorós, 1967).

In principle (74) cannot be calculated because it is not possible to know $P_0(\mathbf{r})$, the Patterson of the structure at absolute zero, because the Bragg intensities at absolute zero cannot be obtained experimentally. As a first approximation, however, the Bragg intensities at rest can be calculated from the set $I_T(\mathbf{r}_h^*)$ by dividing by the over-all temperature factor as deduced from Wilson's method (1942), i.e.,

$$I_0(\mathbf{r}_h^*) = \frac{I_T(\mathbf{r}_h^*)}{\exp\left[-2B(\sin^2\theta/\lambda^2)\right]}. \tag{76}$$

With the observed $I_T(\mathbf{r}_h^*)$, and the calculated $I_0(\mathbf{r}_h^*)$, the difference Patterson (74) can be calculated from the Bragg intensities determined experimentally at one temperature only by

$$\Delta P_{0,T}(\mathbf{r}) = v^* \sum_h \left[I_0(\mathbf{r}_h^*) - I_T(\mathbf{r}_h^*)\right] \cdot \exp\left(2\pi i\mathbf{r}\cdot\mathbf{r}_h^*\right), \tag{77}$$

or by the equivalent

$$\Delta P_{0,T}(\mathbf{r}) = v_c^* \sum_h \Delta I_{0,T}(\mathbf{r}_h^*) \cdot \exp(2\pi i \mathbf{r} \cdot \mathbf{r}_h^*). \qquad (78)$$

We can also define a temperature-difference Patterson function as a Patterson function obtained by performing an inverse Fourier synthesis whose coefficients are the differences between two sets of Bragg intensities at two different temperatures:

$$\Delta P_{T_1,T_2}(\mathbf{r}) = v_c^* \sum_h [I_{T_1}(\mathbf{r}_h^*) - I_{T_2}(\mathbf{r}_h^*)] \exp(2\pi i \mathbf{r} \cdot \mathbf{r}_h^*). \qquad (79)$$

If one of the two temperatures is low enough, in relation to the Debye characteristic temperature of the solid, in such a way that the thermal vibrations at that temperature are very small, the corresponding Debye-Waller temperature factors will be almost unity, and the two difference Pattersons given by (78) and (79) will be quite similar, but not identical, because of the change of the atomic coordinates in the structure caused by thermal expansion. Obviously (77) is free from this effect. As an example, let us consider the simple case of the difference two-dimensional Patterson of an hypothetical monoatomic structure of carbon atoms. The functions $Q_0(\mathbf{r})$, $Q_T(\mathbf{r})$, and $Q_{0,T}(\mathbf{r})$ for carbon are represented radially in Fig. 21i. The distribution of $\Delta Q_{0,T}(\mathbf{r})$ is positive near the origin, as is expected, because the electron-density function of a vibrating atom is smeared out at the

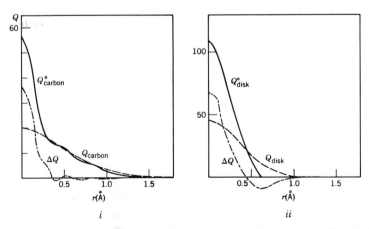

Fig. 21. Two-dimensional linear distribution functions of Q_0, Q_T, and $\Delta Q_{0,T}$. (i) Carbon atom; (ii) disk atom.

center of the atom, and this fact is reflected in its self-image. In this case

$$\Delta P_{0,T}(0) = Q_0(0) - Q_T(0)$$

gives the difference between the heights of the self-images of the densities of the carbon atoms at rest and at motion. The difference-Patterson function is practically zero at distances larger than 1 Å, and between 0.5 and 1.0 Å the function is also nearly zero although minor

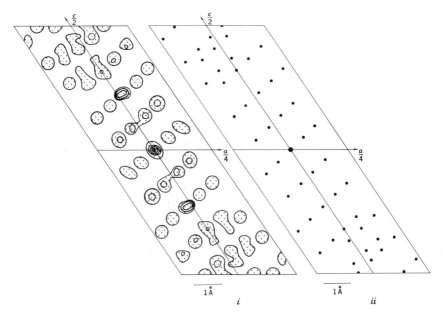

Fig. 22. Anthracene, projection on (010). (*i*) ΔP_{0T}; (*ii*) vector set.

ripples can be seen. The fact that the difference Patterson function for a given atom is zero at small distances of the equilibrium position of the atom has important consequences in the application of the function. The difference-Patterson function behaves at this respect as a sharpened-Patterson function.

In order to be able to analyze the Q functions obtained optically $Q_0(\mathbf{r})$, $Q_T(\mathbf{r})$, and $\Delta Q_{0,T}(\mathbf{r})$ have been also calculated for disks, and are represented radially in Fig. 21*ii*. In this case a clear ripple appears in the difference Patterson with the minimum at about 0.6 Å. Above 1 Å the function is again practically zero. The similarity between Figs. 21*i* and 21*ii* is self evident.

We shall examine now the case of anthracene. As was shown before, anthracene projected on (010) is an example of a unimolecular
crystal. Figure 22i represents the two-dimensional difference
Patterson using the calculated intensities from the known structure
with and without temperature factor. The function $\Delta P_{0,T}(\mathbf{r})$ shows
positive peaks in a background of almost zero value. This is in agreement with what was observed in the difference Patterson of a carbon
atom. All the peaks are very well resolved, and are almost free of
overlapping. We can see that, in this case, $\Delta P_{0,T}$ shows all the peaks

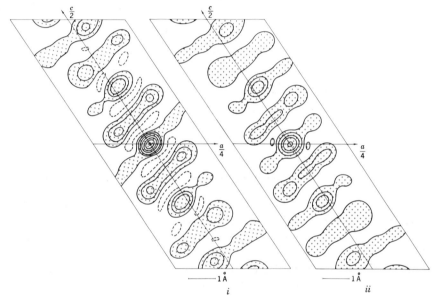

Fig. 23. Anthracene, projection on (010). (i) $\Delta P_{T_1T_2}$; (ii) ΔP_{0T} calculated from the Bragg
intensities with the Debye factor determined by Wilson's method.

that should be expected from the vector set of the structure, represented schematically in Fig. 22ii.

Similar results are obtained when the observed intensity data at
two temperatures are used in computing the difference Patterson, as
shown in Fig. 23i calculated by using (79) with the data of anthracene
of Mason (1964), given at 95°K and 290°K. In this case, the map
shows positive areas with well-marked maxima, and also negative,
small areas. Fig. 23ii shows the difference Patterson calculated from
(76) and (77), and by using the intensities at 290°K reported by
Mason (1964). The similarity of these maps is striking. Most of the
peaks are very well shown but some overlapping is present, due to

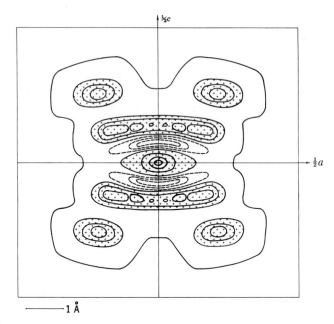

Fig. 24.   Benzene. Projection on (010). $\Delta Q_{0,T}$ corresponding to the model of disk-like atoms.

termination effect resulting from the use of intensities observed with CuKα radiation instead of Mo, used for the map reproduced in Fig. 22i.

In the case of a crystal with more than one molecule per unit cell, the temperature-difference Patterson is given by

$$\Delta P_{0,T}(\mathbf{r}) = \left[\sum_{p=1}^{P} \Delta Q_{P_{0,T}}(\mathbf{r}) + \sum_{p \neq p'}^{P} \sum^{P} \Delta \rho_p(\mathbf{r} - \mathbf{r}_p) \ast \Delta \rho_{p'}(-\mathbf{r} + \mathbf{r}_{p'}) \right] s_{\text{cell}}(\mathbf{r}).$$

(80)

The most interesting part of the temperature-difference Patterson for a polymolecular crystal is the first term of the right side of (80). This term contains the differences of the self-images of the molecules at rest and in motion, and gives the central motif of the difference Patterson. As an example, we reproduce in Fig. 24 this central motif of the temperature-difference Patterson of benzene projected on (010). We can see that the peak at 00 is positive and is surrounded by a negative ripple. All other intramolecular interatomic peaks are positive areas of high value and are very well resolved. They compare very well with the central portion of Fig. 8, corresponding to the self-images of the molecules 1 and 2 of benzene.

The Fourier transform of the difference Patterson (rest-motion)

By applying an inverse Fourier transformation to (58), we have

$$T^{-1}\{I_{DFT}(\mathbf{r}^*)\} = Q_{cell_0}(\mathbf{r}) - Q_{cell_T}(\mathbf{r}) = \Delta Q_{cell_{0,T}}(\mathbf{r}). \qquad (81)$$

This shows that, for a unimolecular crystal, the diffuse scattering as given by the DFT function is merely the Fourier transform of the temperature difference Q function (rest-motion). The Q functions of the unit cell are extended outside the unit cell, and the Patterson functions correspond to the overlap of the Q functions in the different unit cells. If instead of dealing with Q functions, the Patterson functions are considered, we must introduce for a single unit cell the shape function $s_{cell}(\mathbf{r})$. In this case we have, by Fourier inversion,

$$T\{P_0(\mathbf{r}) - P_T(\mathbf{r})\} \cdot s_{cell}(\mathbf{r})\} = T\{\Delta P_{0,T}(\mathbf{r})\} = I_{DFT}(\mathbf{r}^*) * S_{cell}(\mathbf{r}^*). \qquad (82)$$

The property that the DFT function is zero at the origin of Fourier space, (65), is of great importance in convolving the DFT function with the shape amplitude of the unit cell, because the effect of the shape amplitude is small enough so that we can write

$$T\{\Delta P_{0,T}(\mathbf{r})\} \sim I_{DFT}(\mathbf{r}^*). \qquad (83)$$

In the case of a polymolecular crystal, inverse transformation (63) yields

$$T^{-1}\{I_{DFT}(\mathbf{r}^*)\} = \sum_{p=1}^{P} [Q_{p_0}(\mathbf{r}) - Q_{p_T}(\mathbf{r})] = \sum_{p=1}^{P} \Delta Q_{p_{0,T}}(\mathbf{r}), \qquad (84)$$

where $Q_{p_0}(\mathbf{r})$ is the self-image of the molecule p at rest, and $Q_{p_T}(\mathbf{r})$ is the self-image of the "average" molecule p at motion. Equation (84) shows that for a molecular crystal of P molecules per unit cell, the $I_{DFT}(\mathbf{r}^*)$ is the Fourier transform of the sum of the differences between the self-images of the different molecules at rest and at motion.

We are thus led to an interesting result: Since $I_{DFT}(\mathbf{r}^*)$ and $\Delta P_{0,T}(\mathbf{r})$ are basically pairs of Fourier transforms, it will be possible to apply $T\{T^{-1}\}$ transformations to obtain $I_{DFT}(\mathbf{r}^*)$ from a Fourier series whose coefficients are sampled values of the $\Delta P_{0,T}(\mathbf{r}_{h'})$ in a unit-cell content.

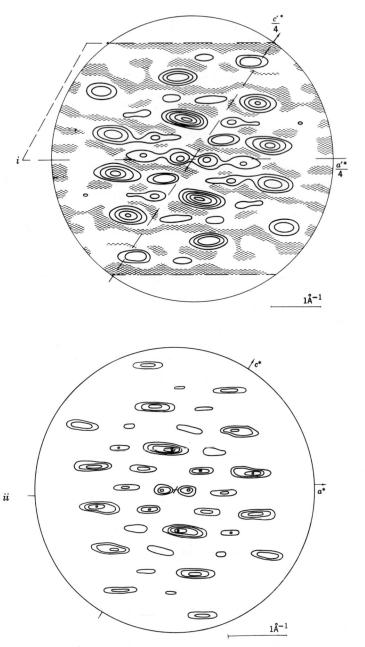

Fig. 25. Anthracene. Section $(010)^*$ of the DFT function (i) calculated as $T^{-1}\{\Delta P_{0,T}\}$; (ii) calculated from the known structure.

As was pointed out, the use of sampled values at $r_{h'}$ introduces repetition of the transform, and the sampling must be fine enough as to avoid overlap of the transforms in Fourier space:

$$T\{\Delta P_{0,T}(r_{h'})\} = I_{\text{DFT}}(r^*) * S_{\text{cell}}(r^*) * z_s(r^*). \qquad (85)$$

If the effect of the shape amplitude is negligible, we can write

$$T\{\Delta P_{0,T}(r_{h'})\} \sim I_{\text{DFT}}(r^*) * z_s(r^*). \qquad (86)$$

With these restrictions taken into account, $I_{\text{DFT}}(r^*)$ can be calculated in terms of the Fourier summation having as coefficients $\Delta P_{0,T}(r_{h'})$,

$$I_{\text{DFT}}(r^*) = \sum_s \Delta P(r_s) \cos 2\pi(hx + ky + lz). \qquad (87)$$

As a simple example, the DFT functions of a carbon atom and of a disk-like atom can be easily obtained by a $T\{T^{-1}\}$ transformation, by using as coefficients of the Fourier series the corresponding sampled values of $\Delta Q_{0,T}$. The curves calculated by these methods coincide with the DFT functions calculated in a direct way (see Fig. 13i).

Anthracene is an example of a unimolecular crystal. The temperature-difference Patterson of Fig. 22i was sampled at $a' = a/50 = 0.17$ Å and $c/50 = 0.22$ Å, $\beta = 137°$. The corresponding DFT function was calculated using (87).

The reciprocal lattice of the sampling lattice has $a'^* = 5.83$ Å^{-1}, $c'^* = 4.54$ Å^{-1}, and the Bragg intensities at rest and in motion were calculated up to 2.8 Å^{-1}; therefore no overlap of limiting spheres will occur with the chosen sampling. The DFT function calculated in this way is shown in Fig. 25i. The circle in the figure corresponds to the limiting sphere of Mo$k\alpha$ x-radiation. The density function inside of the circle corresponds to the DFT function. The shadowed areas in Fig. 25i correspond to very small negative areas arising from ripple effect. It is evident that this effect is of no importance in the DFT function calculated in this way. The good agreement can be seen by comparing Fig. 25i and the DFT given in Fig. 25ii calculated by using (63).

The electron density of an orientationally disordered molecular crystal

Disorder in molecular crystals can also arise from the possibility of the molecule being in different orientations in its site. We shall call this orientational disorder. A nice example is provided by azulene (Robertson, Shearer, Sim, and Watson, 1962). Azulene is an heterocyclic hydrocarbon whose molecule consists of two rings, one of seven carbon atoms and the other of five carbon atoms. Its crystal structure belongs to the same space group as naphthalene, $P2_1/a$, and there are two molecules per unit cell. This situation is incompatible with the noncentrosymmetric structure of the molecule. The explanation of this is that the molecule of azulene occupies two centrosymmetric orientations, and the structure shows the total symmetry of the experimental space group. As the molecule cannot be in both orientations in each site, the experimentally determined crystal structure is the average structure of the statistically disordered crystal. In this case the space group of the average structure has a symmetry operator not contained in any of the actual unit cells that build up the crystal; therefore the space group is a supergroup of that of the ordered structure.

Orientational disorder can also appear when there is a stacking disorder of the molecules that form the crystal. In this case the molecules in the different layers are equivalent through translations that are not proper lattice translations of the ordered structure; α pyridil (Felix, Canut, and Amorós, 1964) is an example.

Since orientational disorder in molecular crystals is more frequent than had been supposed, the picture of the real molecular crystal would be incomplete without paying due consideration to this kind of disorder. Let us consider a disordered unimolecular crystal whose molecules each containing J atoms occupy N different orientations in different cells. Let N be the number of cells of different kinds that build up the disordered crystal. The probability of finding a molecule in a given orientation is $\mu = 1/N$ if random distribution is assumed. We can now imagine an ideal crystal, the average crystal, whose unit cells are identical. The molecules of N different orientations would share, at the same time, each unit cell. The new structure can be described as built up by JN pseudoatoms whose atomic scattering factors are given by f_j/N. Each atom is, in reality, weighted according to the probability μ of finding the molecule in a given position in a given unit cell. The electron density of any unit cell of the average crystal is given by

$$\bar{\rho}(\mathbf{r}) = \sum_{j=1}^{JN} \rho_{j_{\text{pseudo}}}(\mathbf{r} - \mathbf{r}_j). \tag{88}$$

In the real disordered crystal each molecule has only one definite orientation. The orientation of the molecule in a given cell l can be obtained from the average cell by applying to each pseudoatom a displacement $\Delta\mathbf{r}_{jl}$ corresponding to the change in coordinates of the different atoms of the molecule due to the equivalent molecular orientations. It is obvious that $\Delta \mathbf{r}_{jl}$ is zero for the set of J pseudoatoms that are in the selected molecule. The electron density of the cell n is given by

$$\rho_n(\mathbf{r}) = \sum_{j=1}^{JN} \rho_{\text{pseudo}}[\mathbf{r} - (\mathbf{r}_j + \Delta \mathbf{r}_{jl})]. \tag{89}$$

The change in orientation of the molecules introduces small changes in the potential energy of the crystal, as the interatomic interactions between neighboring molecules are different, even though the differences are, in general, small. These differences appear because the number of, and the distances between, the atoms in neighboring molecules depend on the relative orientations of the molecules in the packing forming the crystal. Due to this, random distribution of the molecules is, in general, not attained in short range, and the crystal minimizes its potential energy through nucleation of ordered regions in the crystal. Even if random distribution is assumed, such ordered regions (microdomains) appear (Fig. 26i). When such microdomains are very small, involving only one, or a few, unit cells, the local increase in potential energy is very high, and it is reasonable to assume that they are unstable and that the larger microdomains grow further at the expenses of the small ones. The crystal as a whole has the average structure defined by $\rho(\mathbf{r})$, but the crystal is now formed of microdomains whose unit-cell electron density is equal to $\rho_n(\mathbf{r})$. This fact can be expressed by introducing correlations in the statistics of the disorder.

Let us now consider the case in which some molecules tend to align themselves in an orderly manner along a given crystal direction, namely [001]. The crystal resolves itself in elongated ordered units along the direction [001]. If correlations are imperfect along that direction, the structure along the axis breaks up into units of variable length, called by Canut and Hosemann (1964) *cigarrillos*. A statistical unit built upon the average of n molecules along [001] must be introduced in terms of the shape function of this unit, and the electron density of the corresponding cigarrillo is

$$\rho_{\text{cig}} = \rho_n(\mathbf{r}) \cdot s_{\text{cig}}(\mathbf{r}). \tag{90}$$

The correlations thus maintain the periodicity along [001] inside the volume v defined by the shape function. This can be expressed by one-dimensional peak function along [001] such as

$$z_1(\mathbf{r}) = \sum_{n=-\infty}^{+\infty} L(z - nc). \tag{91}$$

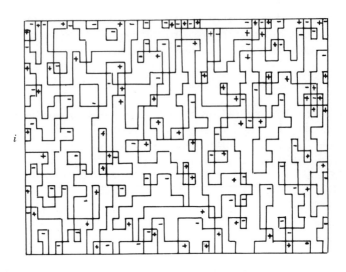

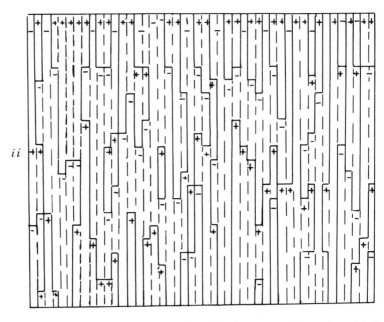

Fig. 26. Statistical microdomains of a disordered structure. (*i*) Random, (*ii*) Correlations along one direction.

The result of having cigarrillos with no correlation in other directions but [001] is given in Fig. 26ii. Here again, sideways intergrowth of such cigarrillos is to be expected from minimum-energy consideration.

The above considerations apply not only to molecular crystals, but also to crystals with rigid groups. To illustrate this part of the chapter we select the very simple case of $NaNO_2$ where the plane angular groups NO_2 are randomly distributed in two centrosymmetric positions in the disordered phase, which is the paraelectric-phase arrangement of the groups NO_2. In our example we shall further simplify the crystal structure by considering an hypothetical two-dimensional crystal built up by only NO_2 groups periodically repeated on a lattice. This coincides with the structure of the ferroelectric crystal of $NaNO_2$ (Fig. 27i), in which the sodium atoms have been suppressed. The ferroelectric structure is taken as the ideal ordered crystal. The disordered phase (paraelectric phase), again without Na atoms, is considered to be built up of NO_2 groups randomly distributed in two antisymmetric positions, designated by + and −, along the [001] axis (Fig. 27ii). A model has also been assumed in which correlations of the NO_2 groups along the polar axis were introduced. The statistical unit consists of a sequence of five + or five −, each sequence comprising a positive or negative cigarrillo (Fig. 27iii). The average structure of both disordered models is the ideal hypothetical crystal represented in Fig. 27iv in which the disks represent pseudoatoms. All the models are built up of disk-like atoms, and correspond to the negatives of the masks used in the optical experiments.

If more than one stable alignment of the molecules is possible in the crystal, two or more systems of correlation appear, each one corresponding to the stable molecular sequence. An extreme case is found in a crystal that has stacking disorder in which infinite correlation is found along any crystal direction contained in the layer, and disorder appears only along the perpendicular to the layers.

A further complication arises when increasing thermal vibrations of the molecules allow the molecule to flip-flop between the possible stable orientations. In this case the disorder is dynamic in nature and the correlation is, in reality, the expression of fluctuation waves of electron density, whose wavelength can be taken as the lengths of the statistical units. The whole problem, however, can also be described in terms of a static configuration of given correlations, with the understanding that now the correlations structure is not fixed at a given position but propagates along the crystal. The orientationally

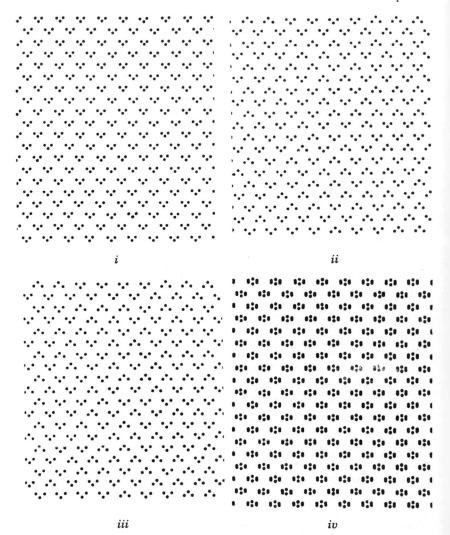

Fig. 27. Nitrite group, projection on (100). Negatives of the models. (*i*) Ordered (ferroelectric) phase; (*ii*) random disordered (paraelectric) phase; (*iii*) disordered phase with [001] correlations (paraelectric); (*iv*) average structure of the paraelectric phase.

disordered crystal with correlations is, therefore, a crystal that has a relatively large short-range order, but long-range disorder. This affects the total electron density, and therefore has important consequences in the Q function and scattering intensity of the crystal.

The Q function of the orientationally random disordered molecular crystal

For simplicity, let us limit to a unimolecular crystal where the molecule (or atomic group) occupies two different orientations in different unit cells, and the disorder is random. This crystal can be described by an ideal average crystal in which the unit cell is built up of pseudoatoms. The Q function of the hypothetical average crystal, obviously periodically ideal, can be described by a solitary function given by

$$\overline{Q}_{\text{dis}}(\mathbf{r}) = \overline{Q}_{\text{cell}}(\mathbf{r}) * z_{\text{cr}}(\mathbf{r}), \tag{92}$$

where

$$\overline{Q}_{\text{cell}}(\mathbf{r}) = \overline{\rho}_{\text{cell}}(\mathbf{r}) * \overline{\rho}_{\text{cell}}(-\mathbf{r}) \tag{93}$$

is the self-image of the electron density of the average cell. For the infinite crystal, it coincides with the Patterson function in current use:

$$P(\mathbf{r}) = \lim_{N \to \infty} \frac{1}{N} \overline{Q}_{\text{dis}}(\mathbf{r}) = v_c^* \sum_h \sum_k \sum_l <F(hkl)>^2 \exp\left[-2\pi i(hx + ky + lz)\right], \tag{94}$$

where $<F(hkl)>$ is the average value of the structure factors of the different cells that build up the disordered structure. If $I_B(hkl)$ are the corrected Bragg intensities, $|<F(hkl)>| = \sqrt{I_B(hkl)}$.

Even though the Patterson function given by (94) is the only one that can be obtained from the experimental Bragg x-ray intensities, it gives a poor image of reality. The average disordered structure does not exist, but rather a given distribution of the molecules in the molecular sites. Therefore it is necessary to use the more powerful Q function of the real disordered crystal. When the self-image of this actual crystal is obtained, terms of two different kinds arise. A series of terms is due to the self-images of each molecule, whose average value is proportional to

$$\overline{\Sigma Q(\mathbf{r})} = \frac{1}{N} \sum_{n=1}^{N} Q_n(\mathbf{r}); \tag{95}$$

this is located at the origin. A second series of terms arises from the image functions of each molecule n in another one n'. The sum of such terms is proportional to

$$\rho_n(\mathbf{r} - \mathbf{r}_n) * \rho_{n'}(-\mathbf{r} + \mathbf{r}_{n'}),$$

whose average value at any lattice point is

$$\overline{Q}(\mathbf{r}) = \frac{1}{N} \sum_{n=1}^{N} \rho_n(\mathbf{r} - \mathbf{r}_n) * \rho_{n'}(-\mathbf{r} + \mathbf{r}_{n'}). \tag{96}$$

Therefore the Q function contains a series of identical motifs given by $\overline{Q}(\mathbf{r}) * z_{cr}(\mathbf{r})$ repeated by the lattice translations. The lattice peak function also includes the point at the origin, $r = 0$, and generates an identical motif at $r = 0$. At the origin of the Q function, however, only the self-images of each molecule appear. Therefore the term $N\overline{Q}(\mathbf{r})$ at the origin must be subtracted. The total expression of the Q function of the orientationally disordered crystal is given by

$$Q_{dis\,cr}(\mathbf{r}) = \{\overline{\Sigma Q(\mathbf{r})}\} - \overline{Q}(\mathbf{r}) + \overline{Q}(\mathbf{r}) * z_{cr}(\mathbf{r}). \qquad (97)$$

We now see that, in the case of a unimolecular disordered crystal, the Q function is quasiperiodic, only the central motif differing from the others, and the Q function corresponds to a pseudosolitary function.

The above discussion can be easily understood if we refer to actual examples. We shall analyze the optical Q functions of the models given in Fig. 27. The optical Q function of the ordered structure, i.e. the one-sided (ferroelectric) structure (Fig. 27i) is given in Fig. 28i. All the motifs are equal and proportional to the self-image of the NO_2 group. The interatomic peaks are all very sharp. In a similar way, the motifs of the Q function of the average paraelectric phase, whose model is represented in Fig. 27iv, are all equal (Fig. 29i) but the interatomic peaks are no longer sharp. They are proportional now to $\overline{Q}_{cell}$. In both cases the Q functions can be defined as solitary functions. However, the Q function of the randomly disordered structure represented in the model of Fig. 27ii is characterized by the fact that the central motif is different of all the others (Fig. 30i) and therefore can be described as a pseudo-solitary function. Comparing Fig. 30i with Figs. 28i and 29i we see that the central motif of the Q function of the randomly disordered structure corresponds to the motif of the Q function of the ordered structure, and that all the other motifs correspond to those of the average structure, in accordance with (97).

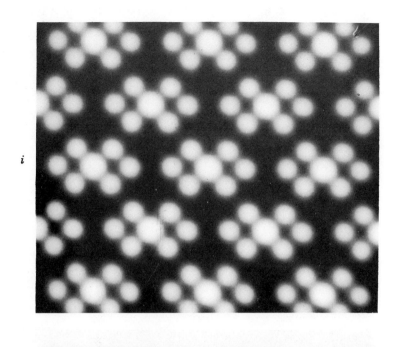

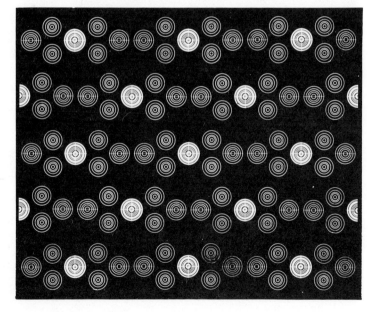

Fig. 28.   Nitrite group, projection on (010). Q function of the model of Fig. 27i (i)
Optical; (ii) calculated.

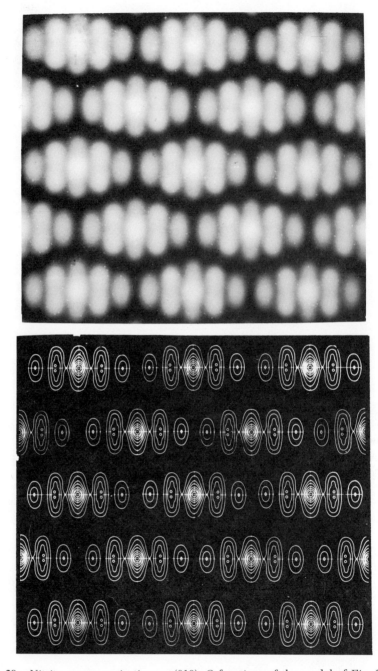

i

ii

Fig. 29. Nitrite group, projection on (010). Q functions of the model of Fig. 27*iv*. (*i*) Optical; (*ii*) calculated.

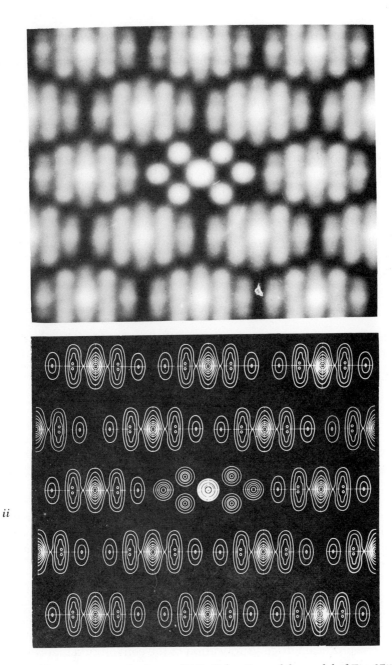

Fig. 30. Nitrite group, projection on (010). Q functions of the model of Fig. 27ii. (i) Optical; (ii) calculated.

185

The intensity diffracted by the randomly disordered crystal

The total intensity diffracted by the disordered crystal can be obtained by Fourier transformation of (97):

$$I_{\mathrm{dis\,cr}}(\mathbf{r}^*) = T\{Q_{\mathrm{dis\,cr}}(\mathbf{r})\}. \tag{98}$$

As the Q function given by (97) has three terms, we shall refer independently to each of them.

The transform of the first term is given by

$$T\left\{\sum_{n=1}^{N} Q(\mathbf{r})\right\} = \sum_{n=1}^{N} |F_n(\mathbf{r}^*)|^2, \tag{99}$$

which is merely the sum of the intensities of all unit-cell contents that have molecules of different kinds. The mean square average of (99) can be expressed by

$$<F_n{}^2(\mathbf{r}^*)> = \frac{1}{N} \sum_{n-1}^{N} |F_n(\mathbf{r}^*)|^2. \tag{100}$$

This function is continuous in Fourier space. Its value at the reciprocal-lattice points is equal to the mean square structure factors of the disordered crystal.

The transform of the second term of (97) is

$$T\{\overline{Q}(\mathbf{r})\} = \left[\sum_{n=1}^{N} F_n(\mathbf{r}^*)\right]^2. \tag{101}$$

Since $F_n(\mathbf{r}^*)$ is a complex number it can be expressed by

$$\left[\sum_{n=1}^{N} A_n(\mathbf{r}^*)\right]^2 + \left[\sum_{n=1}^{N} B_n(\mathbf{r}^*)\right]^2 = [A(\mathbf{r}^*)]^2 + [B(\mathbf{r}^*)]^2. \tag{102}$$

By dividing the summations by N, and performing a Fourier transformation, we have a continuous intensity function, which corresponds to the intensity diffracted by a cell content of the average crystal:

$$\overline{I}_{\mathrm{cell}}(\mathbf{r}^*) = <F(\mathbf{r}^*)>^2. \tag{103}$$

This is again a continuous function in reciprocal space.

Finally, the transform of the last term of (97), which is a periodic function, is a discrete function with nonzero values only at the nodes of the reciprocal lattice. Application of the convolution theorem leads to

$$T\{\overline{Q}(\mathbf{r}) \ast z_{\mathrm{cr}}\} = v_c^* \sum_h <F(\mathbf{r}_h^*)>^2 \cdot L(\mathbf{r}^* - \mathbf{r}_h^*), \tag{104}$$

which corresponds to the Bragg intensities diffracted by the average crystal. $F(r_h^*)$, the structure factors of the disordered structure, can be easily calculated in terms of the pseudoatoms of the average structure. Let the structure factor of the cell l whose origin is at r_l, be

$$F_l(r_h^*) = \sum_{j=1}^{J} f_j \exp\left(2\pi i r_h^* \cdot r_{jl}'\right), \tag{105}$$

where r_{jl}' are the actual coordinates of the atoms j in the cell l. We can express F_l in terms of the coordinates of the JN pseudoatoms of the average crystal as

$$\overline{F_l}(r_h^*) = \sum_{j=1}^{JN} w_j f_j \exp\left(2\pi i r^* \cdot r_j\right) \exp\left(2\pi i r^*\right) \Delta r_j^l, \tag{106}$$

where w_j is the weight of atom j. The structure factor of the disordered structure is given by

$$\langle F(r_h^*) \rangle = \frac{1}{N} \sum_{l=1}^{N} F_l(r_h^*). \tag{107}$$

If the origin of coordinates is chosen such that, for each j, the Δr_{jl} satisfy

$$\sum_{l=1}^{N} \Delta r_{jl} = 0, \tag{108}$$

then

$$\langle F(r_h^*) \rangle = \sum_{j=1}^{JN} w_j f_j \exp\left(2\pi i r^* \cdot r_j\right). \tag{109}$$

Therefore the intensity diffracted by a disordered crystal is built up of two different functions. The first is a discrete function with values only at the reciprocal lattice points that coincide in value with the Bragg intensities of the hypothetical average crystal. The other intensity function is a continuous function that gives rise to a continuous diffuse scattering. This continuous function is given by the difference of the Fourier transform of the first two terms of (97), and can be expressed as

$$I_{DDS}(r^*) = \langle F^2(r^*) \rangle - \langle F(r^*) \rangle^2, \tag{110}$$

according to (100) and (103). We shall call this the intensity-disorder diffuse scattering, or DDS, function. Equation (110) is basically the same as that which Zachariasen (1945) derived for the diffuse scattering by a randomly disordered crystal. The total intensity diffracted by the disordered crystal therefore is given by

$$I_{dis\,cr}(r^*) = \sum_{h}^{\infty} F_n(r_h^*) \cdot L(r^* - r_h^*) + I_{DDS}(r^*). \tag{111}$$

We therefore have a fundamental result: while the Bragg intensities give only information about the hypothetical average crystal, the presence of disorder always implies the appearance of continuous diffuse scattering.

The Q function of a positionally disordered crystal with correlations

The presence of correlations affects the Q function. If the correlations do occur along a given direction, and $s_{cig}(\mathbf{r})$ is the shape function of the cigarrillos, the central motif of the Q function is now given by

$$N \cdot [\rho(\mathbf{r}) * \rho(-\mathbf{r})] * (z \cdot Q_{cig}).$$

This means that the motif at the origin is repeated by lattice translations along the correlation axis inside the volume defined by Q_{cig}. The other motifs lying outside the volume (or area) given by the self-image of the cigarrillo Q_{cig} are proportional to $\overline{Q}$. We finally have

$$Q_{correl}(\mathbf{r}) = (N\overline{\Sigma Q} - N\overline{Q}) * (z_{cr} \cdot \overline{Q}_{cig}) + \frac{1}{v'}\overline{Q} * z_{cr}. \qquad (112)$$

This equation shows that when correlations are present, the Q function is built of motifs of two kinds, as in the case of a unimolecular crystal with random disorder, with the difference that, if correlations are present, the central motif is repeated by the lattice translation along the correlation axis inside the volume defined by the self-image of the shape function of the statistical unit.

The above results can be seen in the optical Q function of the model represented in Fig. 27iii, which corresponds to the paraelectric structure of NO_2 groups with correlations along the c-axis. The corresponding optical Q function is given in Fig. 31. We can see that, where correlations do exist, the motifs along the axis are equal to the motifs of the Q function of the ordered structure (Fig. 28i). All the other motifs are equal among them and are equal to the motif of the average structure (Fig. 29i), in accordance with what we have said.

The intensity diffracted by a disordered crystal with correlations

The total intensity diffracted by the disordered crystal with correlations is simply obtained by Fourier inversion of (112). In this case we have again two terms that can be dealt independently. To perform the transformation of the first term of (112) we need to know the

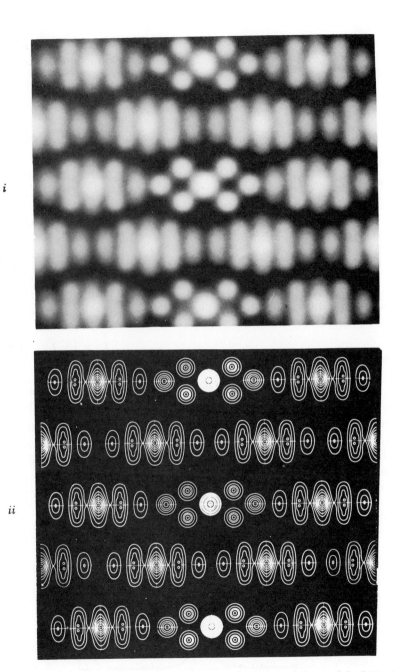

Fig. 31.   Nitrite group, projection on (010). Q functions of the model of Fig. 27*iii*.
(*i*) Optical; (*ii*) calculated.

189

transform of s_{cig}, which can be obtained in terms of the length of the cigarrillo, L_{cig}. The shape factor is given by (Canut and Hosemann, 1964).

$$|S_{cig}|^2 = \left[\frac{\sin \pi c^* L_{cig}}{\pi c^*}\right]^2 \simeq L_{cig}^2 \exp\left(-\frac{\pi^2 c^{*2} L_{cig}^2}{3}\right). \tag{113}$$

Application of the convolution theorem to the first term of the right-hand side of (112) leads to

$$T\{(N\overline{\Sigma Q} - N\overline{Q}) * (z_{cr} \cdot Q_{cig})\} = T\{N\overline{\Sigma Q} - N\overline{Q}\} \cdot \frac{1}{c}(Z_{cr} * |S_{cig}|^2). \tag{114}$$

The last term can then be expressed as a function of the number of cigarrillos:

$$\frac{1}{c}(Z_{cr} * |S_{cig}|^2) = N_{cig}^2 \sum \exp\left[-\frac{\pi^2 L_{cig}^2}{3}\left(c^* - \frac{m}{c}\right)^2\right]. \tag{115}$$

The first term of (114) corresponds to the case in which random distribution of the molecules is present, and its transform is given by (110). Finally, (113) becomes

$$I_{\text{DDS corr}}(\mathbf{r}^*) = [<F^2(\mathbf{r}^*)> - <F(\mathbf{r}^*)>^2]N_{cig}^2 \sum_m \exp\left[-\frac{\pi^2 L_{cig}^2}{3}\left(c^* - \frac{m}{c}\right)^2\right]. \tag{116}$$

The last factor of (116) is represented in Fig. 32. We then see that multiplication of the continuous diffuse scattering, as given in (110) by the function represented in Fig. 32, produces a modulation in the continuous scattering, in the sense that it becomes practically zero except at the planes where $\mathbf{c}^* l =$ integer. Therefore the DDS breaks down in parallel sheets of diffuse-scattering intensity perpendicular

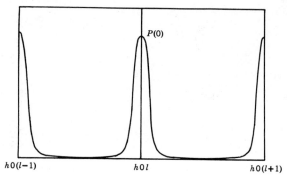

Fig. 32. Correlation function along the axis of correlations.

to the cigarrillo axis, the thickness of the diffuse sheets depending on the finiteness of the length of the cigarrillo in physical space.

If, instead of having cigarrillos, the correlations give rise to planar domains, the Fourier transform of the shape function of the domain consists of lines perpendicular to the layers, and the diffuse scattering is observed along lattice rows. If more than one system of correlation is present in the crystal, the transforms of the corresponding peak functions modulates independently the continuous DDS. Systems of parallel planes or rows are then found in diffraction space, the discontinuities along the rows or planes depending on spatial distribution of the DDS intensity.

Because the last term of the Q function with random distribution and with correlations, represented by (97) and (112), are identical, the intensity maxima are insensible to the kind of statistics of the disorder. The Bragg intensities depend only on the average electron density of the cell, which is the same in both cases.

The Fraunhofer pattern of the orientationally disordered crystal

In order to demonstrate the effect of orientational disorder in the intensity diffracted by a crystal we shall refer to the Fraunhofer patterns of the models of Fig. 27. The ideal cases are represented by the polar (one-sided) ferroelectric crystal (Fig. 27i) and the ideal average paraelectric crystal (Fig. 27iv). As both cases are ideally periodic, the intensity is observed only at the reciprocal-lattice point, i.e., the Bragg intensities. In the first case the intensity maxima of the Fraunhofer pattern (Fig. 33i) correspond to $<F^2(\mathbf{r}^*_h)>$. In the second case (Fig. 33ii), the intensity maxima correspond to $<F(\mathbf{r}^*_h)>^2$. Both Fraunhofer patterns are free of diffuse scattering.

When disorder is present, the model is no longer periodic, but only almost periodic. We have two cases, one (Fig. 27ii) with random disorder, the other one (Fig. 27iii) with correlations. In both cases the Bragg intensities are the ones corresponding to the ideal average crystal, but the Fraunhofer patterns are characterized by the presence of diffuse scattering. In the case of the random disorder, the Fraunhofer pattern (Fig. 34i) shows clearly the continuous diffuse scattering given by the DDS function (110). When correlations are present, the diffuse scattering of the Fraunhofer pattern (Fig. 34ii) is concentrated along the reciprocal-lattice rows perpendicular to the correlation axis. This effect is due to the introduction of the function given in (115). Comparing Figs. 34i and 34ii, it can be seen that the new diffuse

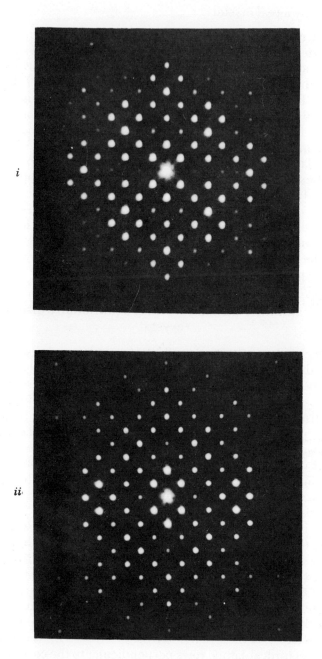

Fig. 33. Nitrite group. Fraunhofer patterns, (100)*: (*i*) of model of Fig. 27*i*; (*ii*) of model of Fig. 27*iv*.

192

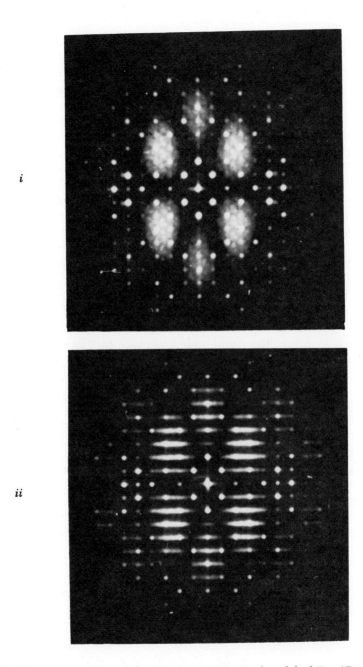

Fig. 34. Nitrite group. Fraunhofer patterns, $(100)_0^*$: (*i*) of model of Fig. 27*ii*; (*ii*) of model of Fig. 27*iii*.

193

scattering is present only in the regions where DDS is strong, showing that (115) is only a modulating function.

The disorder diffuse scattering can be calculated by applying (110). This is equivalent to obtaining the difference between the intensity functions have been computed for the NO_2 model in terms of disk atoms of $R = 0.31$ Å. The intensity transforms of the polar cell and of the average cell are given in Fig. 35i and 35ii, respectively. The two functions are continuous in reciprocal space. The DDS function is just the difference of the two previous functions, and therefore, assuming random disorder, the disorder diffuse scattering can be obtained by subtracting Fig. 35ii from Fig. 35i. It can be easily seen that the maxima along the $\mathbf{b}^*$ axis cancel each other. The DDS function takes the aspect of Fig. 36i. The weighted reciprocal lattice of the average structure has been added to this figure in order to be directly comparable with the Fraunhofer pattern of the randomly disordered structure (Fig. 34i).

By introducing the shape factor of the cigarrillos, the DDS breaks down in elongated domains, as shown in the calculated map represented in Fig. 36ii. Again, the weighted reciprocal lattice of the average structure has been added to make this figure directly comparable with the Fraunhofer pattern of Fig. 34ii.

Computation of Q functions from Patterson syntheses

We can idealize the real disordered structure in two ways. We can suppose, as we indicated earlier, that the crystal has the average structure, in which case the intensity diffracted is proportional to $<F(hkl)>^2$. We can suppose also that the disordered crystal is built up of n different crystals, each one ordered with the molecules in one of the n permissible orientations. The intensity diffracted in this case is proportional to $<F^2(hkl)>$. The two intensities are different. If we use those intensities as coefficients of a Fourier series, we obtain

$$P_A(xyz) = v_c^* \sum_{h=0}^{\infty} \sum_{k=-\infty}^{+\infty} \sum_{l=-\infty}^{+\infty} <F(hkl)>^2 \cdot \cos 2\pi(hx + ky + lz). \quad (117)$$

the average-structure Patterson, which we said corresponds to the Patterson in current use. We also obtain

$$P_D(xyz) = v_c^* \sum_{h=0}^{\infty} \sum_{k=-\infty}^{\infty} \sum_{l=-\infty}^{\infty} <F^2(hkl)> \cdot \cos 2\pi(hx + ky + lz), \quad (118)$$

which we shall call the *disorder Patterson*. This Patterson function cannot be calculated from observed intensity data unless, by chance,

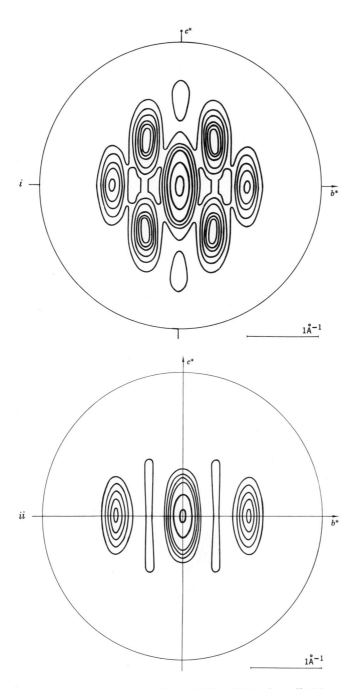

Fig. 35. Nitrite group. Intensity transform, (100)*, of: (*i*) polar cell; (*ii*) average cell.

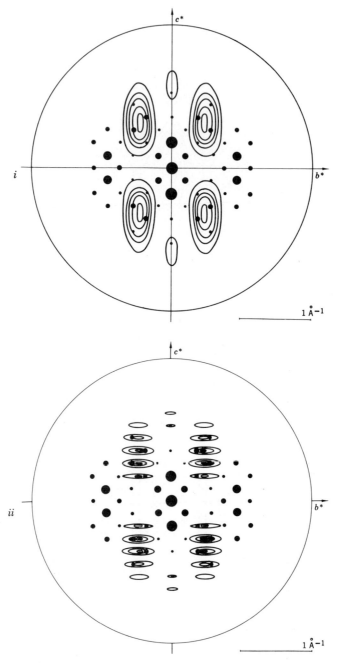

Fig. 36. Nitrite group. Calculated DDS function and weighted reciprocal lattice $(100)_0^*$. (*i*) random disorder; (*ii*) with correlations.

a polymorphic phase does exist corresponding to the one-sided (ordered) configuration of the disordered structure (sodium nitrite is a nice example). As their Fourier coefficients are different, the Patterson functions (117) and (118) also are different (Figs. 29*ii* and 28*ii* respectively). The motifs of (117)and (118) correspond to the two motifs of the pseudosolitary function (97). The Q function can therefore be reconstructed in terms of the two motifs defined by (117) and (118). The convolution operation of $\overline{Q}(\mathbf{r})$ with the lattice-peak function $z(\mathbf{r})$ in (97) can be performed just by repeating the motif of the average-structure Patterson over and over in the framework of the crystal lattice except at the origin, where the motif of the disordered Patterson is placed. The result is shown in Fig. 30*ii*. If correlations are present the motif at the origin is repeated along the axis of correlations, and therefore we can reconstruct the Q function also in this case (Fig. 31*ii*). We see that the calculated Q functions are identical to the corresponding optical Q functions.

The disorder-average difference Patterson and its transform

In a way similar to that for the thermally disordered crystals we can compute the difference

$$\Delta P_{D,A}(\mathbf{r}) = [P_D(\mathbf{r}) - P_A(\mathbf{r})] \cdot s(\mathbf{r}) \tag{119}$$

between the intramolecular motifs of the two Patterson functions (117) and (118). Of course, (119) would be identically zero in absence of positional disorder. $\Delta P_{D,A}(\mathbf{r})$ has both positive and negative values as well as zero lines; it is a continuous function, identically zero outside a unit cell, and therefore is not a periodic function. As (117) and (118) are centrosymmetric, (119) is also a centrosymmetric function. The disorder-order Patterson (119) can be calculated by

$$\Delta P_{D,A}(xyz) = v_c^* \sum_h \left[<F^2(hkl)> - <F(hkl)>^2 \right] \cos 2\pi(hz + ky + lz) \tag{120}$$

When (110) is taken into account, (120) can be written as

$$\Delta P_{D,A}|xyz) = v_c^* \sum_h I_{DDS}(hkl) \cdot \cos 2\pi(hx + ky + lz), \tag{121}$$

and therefore

$$I_{DDS}(\mathbf{r}^*) = T\{\Delta P_{D,A}(\mathbf{r})\}. \tag{122}$$

The disorder-order difference Patterson provides a direct way of calculating the disorder diffuse-scattering function, since $I_{DDS}(\mathbf{r}^*)$ and $\Delta P_{D,A}(\mathbf{r})$ are a pair of Fourier mates. It is then possible to apply the $T\{T^{-1}\}$ transformation to obtain $I_{DDS}(\mathbf{r}^*)$ from an inverse Fourier series whose coefficients are sampled values of $\Delta P_{D,A}$. The sampling must be chosen fine enough as to avoid overlap of the transform, which is built up of $I_{DDS}(\mathbf{r}^*)$ functions repeated by lattice translations (the reciprocal of the sampled lattice).

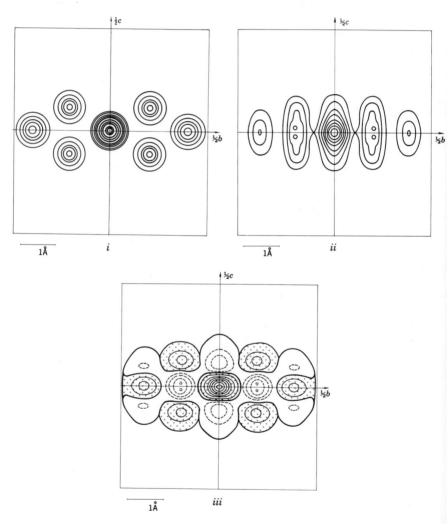

Fig. 37. Nitrite group. Intramolecular Patterson, $(100)_0$. (*i*) Ordered structure; (*ii*) average structures; (*iii*) difference Patterson.

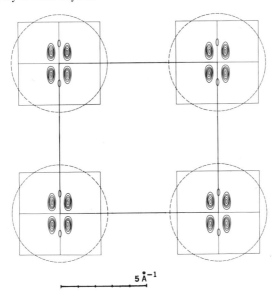

Fig. 38.   Nitrite group. DDS function, $(100)_0^*$ calculated as inverse transform of the
difference Patterson of Fig. 37 *iii*.

We shall apply the above concepts to the case of $NaNO_2$. As the
positional disorder is mostly related to the NO_2 groups, these alone
are considered. The Patterson functions projected on (100) have
been used, and Fig. 37*i* and 37*ii* represent the disorder and average
Patterson, respectively, in a unit cell. The difference between the two
is given in Fig. 37*iii*. To compute these Patterson maps, the calculated
coefficients were used. In order to have a DDS map directly comparable to the Fraunhofer pattern of Fig. 34*i*, the Fourier coefficients
were calculated assuming disk-like atoms of $R = 0.31$ Å. The calculations were extended up to 2.8 Å^{-1}. The $\Delta P_{D,A}(0kl)$ shows areas of
positive value at the origin and at the positions of the peaks of the
P_D. These areas are shaded in the figure. The negative areas have
been bounded, the rest of the map having a practically zero density.

The Fourier transform of $\Delta P_{D,A}$ was calculated by sampling the
difference Patterson at the points of a mesh of 0.15×0.10 Å. The
sampled values were used as coefficients of the corresponding Fourier
series. The resulting periodic DDS function is given in Fig. 38. The
circle corresponds to the limiting sphere of $\lambda(MoK\alpha)$. Comparison
of the DDS function given in Fig. 36*i*, with a single pattern of Fig. 38,
shows the validity of the theory when overlap is not present.

4

The continuous x-ray diffuse scattering of molecular crystals

Of the four types of solid—ionic, metallic, covalent, and molecular —the last, which includes organic crystals, is most numerous. Because this chapter deals with the description of the x-ray diffuse scattering of molecular crystals of different types, it is appropriate to review first the general principles on which the structures of molecular crystals are based.

General characteristics of molecular crystals

The most striking characteristic of molecular crystals is the pronounced difference between the bonding forces linking the atoms of the molecule and the forces that link the molecules to one another. The intramolecular atomic bonds are covalent, whereas the intermolecular are residual forces that are the result of the sum of attractive forces (van der Waals forces of attraction) that act at relatively great distances, and forces of repulsion (van der Waals forces of repulsion) that arise from the overlap of the electron clouds as molecules get too close to one another. These forces differ fundamentally from the covalent forces in that they are not directional, but seem to radiate from the center of the molecule in all directions, so that in the first approximation, they can be considered central forces. The van der Waals forces of attraction follow an r^{-6} law, and therefore the potential energy of the crystal consists mainly of the interaction of closest atoms in neighboring molecules. These forces are much weaker than those of covalent or ionic bonds; the crystals are soft and have relatively low melting points. The normal distances between atoms joined by ionic or covalent bonds are between 1 and 2 Å. In contrast the distances between atoms of different neighboring molecules are of the order of 3 to 5 Å, in accordance with the fact that molecular forces are much weaker than ionic or covalent forces.

Even though molecular crystals are characterized by the presence of van der Waals bonding as the fundamental type of bonding, two types of fundamental structures can be distinguished. In some crystals the only bond between molecules is the classical van der Waals bond, so that the molecules are simply packed according to their shape and size. The bond is then residual. The substances, exemplified by naphthalene, are generally volatile and of low melting point. In other substances the molecules contain strongly negative groups of atoms with replaceable H atoms, such as carboxyl or hydroxyl groups. In this case, due to such groups, strong bonds arise between the two molecules sharing the replaceable H atoms so that the distance between atoms of neighboring molecules is shortened considerably. Because of its strength, bonding by means of shared H plays the decisive role in the structure of the crystal. This kind of bond is known as a hydrogen bond; crystals in which it appears are more brittle and their melting points are generally higher than those of molecular crystals characterized by van der Waals bonds only.

The close-packed nature of the structures of molecular crystals

In the absence of ionic bonding or H bonds, the crystal structure is determined exclusively by the shape of the molecule and by the van der Waals forces. In contrast to the generally simply structures of the other types of solid, molecular crystals tend to have complex structures. The reason for the difference is that in the other types of crystals the structures depend on simple atomic relationships which, in general, are based on the simple rules of atomic coordination. The structures of molecular crystals, on the contrary, depend on the shape of the molecules. In general the crystal structures of molecular compounds are very complicated when described in terms of the atomic coordinates of the different atoms contained in the unit cell.

If we look at the crystal as formed by a packing of equal molecules, each having a definite shape and volume, the whole picture is a much more simple one. In doing so, we consider that the shape of the isolated molecule is the same as in the crystalline field, that is, that the distortion of the intramolecular atomic distances in the molecules forming the crystal is negligible. Accordingly, a crystal of a molecular compound can be considered a system of very closely packed layers, each layer consisting of a closely packed arrangement of molecules in two dimensions, each molecule having coordination numbers of 6 and being so arranged that, in general, no polarities appear perpendicular to the layer. Therefore an organic crystal is described as a packing of bodies of well defined shape such that the projections of one molecule fit into the hollows of a neighboring molecule. This empirical rule has been put forth by Kitajgorodskij (1961b) as the fundamental law of organic chemical crystallography.

The fundamental cell dimensions in molecular crystals are generally greater than in the other types of crystal, and reach extreme values, as in viruses and protein crystals. In addition, since the structural unit is the molecule and not the atom, there is no general correlation between cell dimensions and interatomic distances in the molecule. Thus molecules of widely varying sizes and shapes can be packed into identical cells, so that the dimensions of the molecule are not related strictly to those of the cell.

The packing is apparently consistent with the requirement of minimum free energy, but it is difficult to ascertain this point theoretically because of the complication by factors such as the nature of the atoms constituting the molecule, the dipole moments of the bonds, polarization effects, etc. Nevertheless, despite this apparent complexity, it is the shape of the molecule, that is, its van der Waals envelope, that directly determines the packing and the internal energy of the crystal. This comes from the limited range of molecular interactions. The internal energy is the sum of the elementary interactions of the surface of the molecules.

Symmetry

Because the molecules have, in general, shapes that are not often highly symmetric or symmetric at all, the resulting packing also has low symmetry. This explains the striking differences observed between symmetry of inorganic and organic compounds. This difference is shown in Fig. 1, which is based on the data collected by Donnay and Nowacki (1954) for 3,782 substances. The difference is striking: inorganic compounds (Fig. 1i) have symmetries predominantly (about 60 per cent) cubic, hexagonal, tetragonal and trigonal, reaching 80 per cent for simple structures like elements. Organic compounds (Fig. 1ii), on the contrary, are mostly of monoclinic

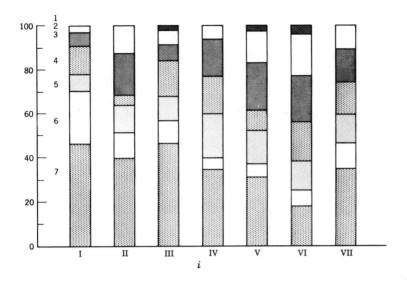

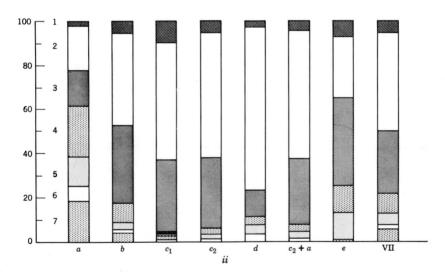

Fig. 1. Frequencies of symmetries among crystals. Spaces between divisions represent: 1, triclinic; 2, monoclinic; 3, orthorhombic; 4, tetragonal; 5, trigonal; 6, hexagonal; 7, cubic. (*i*) Inorganic compounds: I; elements and alloys; II; sulphides; III; oxides; IV; halides; V; bromates, chlorates, iodates, carbonates, nitrates, sulphates and tellurates; VI; all others; VII; total. (*ii*) Organic compounds: *a*, inorganic compounds with organic radicals; *b*, aliphatics; c_1, alicyclics; c_2, aromatics; *d*, heterocyclic; *e*, complex; VII; total.

or orthorhombic symmetry, and only in very special cases displaying higher symmetries.

When a molecule has a center of symmetry it does not interfere with its close packing; therefore centrosymmetric molecules tend to preserve that symmetry operation in the crystal. The case is different when the molecule has a 2-axis or an m-plane. In such a case these elements of symmetry are preserved only if it does not interfere with the close packing. In fact the conservation by the crystal of a major element of symmetry contained in the molecule can be affected, generally speaking, only with a considerable loss of packing density, and results in an increase in energy. The crystal therefore tends to have a lower symmetry than the molecule. For instance, the molecules of anthracene, with mmm symmetry, do not form orthorhombic crystals, but monoclinic.

The existence of a number of independent molecules in a cell increases the free energy, and consequently the crystals tend to have only a single molecule per unit cell. Due to this circumstance a striking difference again appears between inorganic and organic compounds. In inorganic compounds almost every type of cell — primitive, face-centered, or body-centered cell — has equal probability (Fig. 2i). In molecular compounds, however, the primitive Bravais cell is predominant (Fig. 2ii). Even in the cases where the unit cell contains two molecules, the two molecules are symmetry equivalent, not translation equivalent, and the unit cell is still primitive. It is of interest to note that all the Bravais cells but one are represented in molecular compounds (Table 1). The missing one is the face-centered orthorhombic Bravais cell, probably due to the too specialized requirements of such lattice. It is also of interest to note that only globular molecules form crystals with cubic symmetry. In accordance with the above considerations it is found that in molecular crystals the monoclinic and orthorhombic primitive cells are the most common.

Intermolecular distances and packing coefficient

In the case in which intermolecular distances are determined by van der Waals forces we can assume that the distance between neighboring atoms is the sum of van der Waals radii of such atoms. It is found, however, that the intermolecular distances are variable, depending not only on the actual bonding forces between the molecules, but also on the orientation of the molecule itself. It has been observed, for instance, that the radius of a given atom is smaller in directions perpendicular to a covalent bond than in the direction opposite to it. The van der Waals radius therefore is not a physical constant of the atom. For instance, it has been found that the shortest distance between carbons in benzene is about 2.4 Å. The normal

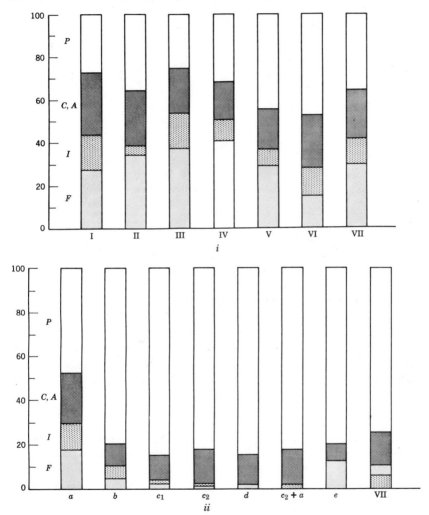

Fig. 2.   Frequencies of Bravais cell types among crystals. Spaces between divisions represent: P, primitive; C, A, base-centered; I, body-centered; F, face centered. (i) Inorganic compounds: I; elements and alloys; II; sulphides; III; oxides; IV; halides; V; bromates, chlorates, iodates, carbonates, nitrates, sulphates and tellurates; VI; all others; VII; total. (ii) Organic compounds: a, inorganic compounds with organic radicals; b, aliphatics; c_1, alicyclics; c_2; aromatics; d, heterocyclic; e, complex; VII; total.

Table 1   Bravais cells of organic compounds

Crystal symmetry	Bravais cells	Examples
Cubic	F	Adamantene, methane
	I	Hexamine
	P	Hexachlorocyclohexane
Tetragonal	I	Pentaerythritol
	P	Pentaerythritol tetranitrate, urea
Hexagonal	H	Urea clathrates (C)
	R	Hydroquinone clathrates, hexabromethyl-benzene
Orthorhombic	P	Thiourea, benzene
	C	Iodine
	F	——
	I	Beryllium dimethyl
Monoclinic	P	Naphthalene, anthracene, adipic and succinic acids
	A	1.5-Dichlorohexane
Triclinic	P	α Succinic acid

radius for carbon, however, is 1.80 Å. Intermolecular distances between two like atoms may change by 15 per cent even in the same crystal. It is useful, however, to assume as a first approximation that the equilibrium distances between atoms in neighboring molecules is constant, so that we can speak about van der Waals radii, and to assume that the volume of the molecule is given by the envelope of spherical surfaces having their centers at the equilibrium position of the atoms in the molecule. With this assumption it is possible, following Kitajgorodskij (1961b), to calculate the relation between the molecular volume and volume of the unit cell, i.e., the packing density,

$$k = Z\frac{v_0}{v},$$

where v is the volume of the unit cell containing Z molecules, and v_0 the molecular volume; k is called the coefficient of molecular packing. It is found that k for aromatic crystals has an average value of 0.7, which compares reasonably well with the packing coefficient 0.74 of the closely packed inorganic structures (Fairbairn, 1943). Therefore we conclude that molecular structures are as closely packed as possible, independently of the shape and size of the molecule involved.

The primary determiner of k is the entire shape of the molecule. The closer the shape is to an ellipsoid, the closer is k to 0.72. As the packing density has a major effect on the energy of the crystal structure, if there are different packing possibilities with almost equal k for a given kind of molecule all such packings are possible structures, and this is one reason for having several polymorphic modifications coexisting at a given temperature. Acridine is a good example. The mode of packing with higher k is the predominant modification. At high temperatures, however, the resulting packing is the one that allows for the increase in thermal vibrations. In this case the vibration volume of the molecule substitutes for the molecular volume, and therefore the high-temperature form has a lower k than the low-temperature form when the calculated molecular volume does not take into account the necessary increase in the volume of the molecule due to thermal vibrations. Examples are succinic acid and suberic urea clathrate.

The energy of a molecular crystal

The stability of a molecular crystal is determined by its free energy. The free energy of an organic crystal, according to Kitajgorodskij (1965), can be expressed by

$$F = \pi(r_i) + E - TS \tag{1}$$

where π is the potential energy of the equilibrium crystal structure, and E the vibration energy of the atoms. E and the entropy S are defined by the values of the vibration terms. Therefore the study of the free energy is determined mainly by the study of the arrangement (structure) and the thermal vibrations of the atoms. In accordance with Ch. 3, we can consider the intermolecular and intramolecular thermal motions independently, and therefore we can consider the contribution to the free energy of a molecular crystal in two parts,

$$F = F_{cr} + F_m, \tag{2}$$

where F_{cr} is the crystal free energy and F_m the molecular free energy. This procedure is legitimate because the vibrational intramolecular states remain practically unchanged when the molecule enters the crystal, and therefore

$$F_m = \psi(r_i) + E_m - TS_m, \tag{3}$$

where $\psi(r_i)$ is the potential energy, E_m the vibrational energy, and S_m the entropy of the free molecule.

The term F_{cr} can be expressed similarly as

$$F_{cr} = \phi(R_i, \phi_i) + E_{cr} - TS_{cr}, \tag{4}$$

where $\phi(R_i, \phi_i)$ is the potential energy of the given crystal structure.

F_{cr} is defined by the intermolecular vibration states and therefore contains the effect of translational and librational vibrations of the molecules. The potential energy of molecular interactions $\phi(R_i, \phi_i)$ at equilibrium depends on the spatial distribution of the molecular loci and the orientation of the molecules. In general, zero-point energy can be disregarded, as normally it is of the order of 0.5 kcal/mol as against about 10 kcal/mol for the heat of formation of a molecule of 10 to 12 atoms (Kitajgorodskij, 1965). Due to this fact, the binding energy for a given structure is the decisive quantity in establishing the stability of the crystal (at absolute zero).

The energy of a van der Waals crystal can be written as intermolecular potential

$$U(r) = -Ar^{-6} + Be^{-r/\rho}, \tag{5}$$

where A and B are parameters depending on the crystal structure, and ρ is a parameter depending on the equilibrium distance of the atoms concerned. We can see from (5) that the interaction between atoms diminishes rapidly with r, and therefore the lattice binding energy is approximately given by

$$\phi = \tfrac{1}{2} \sum \psi_{ik}, \tag{6}$$

the sum of the interactions between the atoms of neighboring molecules. All the interactions follow a similar function. Figure 3 shows the curves corresponding to the interaction of C-C, and H-H as a function of r; r_0 is the empirical equilibrium distance.

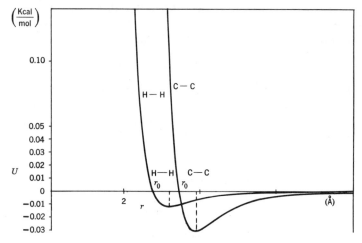

Fig. 3. Atom-atom interaction as a function of mutual distance. $r_0 =$ equilibrium distance.

Crystal-structure types of molecular crystals

Even though the crystal structures of molecular compounds can be very complicated and their classification sometimes is difficult, it is possible to reduce them to a few very simple types. A simple classification proposed by Amorós and Canut (1960), though not totally comprehensive, serves as a good basis for classifying the fundamental patterns of continuous x-ray diffuse scattering observed in molecular crystals. In this scheme molecular crystals are classified according to the predominant bond type and the shape of the molecule, as follows:

Van der Waals forces dominate

Crystals with almost spherical molecules. In this case the crystal symmetry is high. Hexamine, $C_6H_{12}N_4$, is a characteristic example. The molecules in the crystal are almost independent, with 3.72 Å as the minimum distance between CH_2 groups in neighboring molecules. The crystal can be described as built up of almost spherical molecules joined by very weak H bonds. They are arranged at the points of a body-centered cubic lattice. The H bonds are so weak that the molecules can be considered as having a high degree of independence.

Crystals with independent, anisotropic molecules. In this case the structure depends on the type of packing compatible with the shape of the molecules. Naphthalene, $C_{10}H_8$, is one example, the crystal having two molecules per unit cell in two symmetrical orientations.

Hydrogen bonds determine the type of structure

Crystals with chains of molecules. In this case the structure depends on the packing of the chains. In dicarboxylic acids, COOH-$(CH_2)_n$-COOH, the molecules are arranged in parallel chains. Molecules of the same chain are joined by hydrogen bonds, so that they can be considered as forming infinite chains, the different chains being joined by van der Waals bonds.

Crystals whose molecules are joined in layers. Pentaerythritol, $(HOCH_2)_4C$, is a typical example. The unit cell is tetragonal; the molecules are curled and arranged in layers along the c translation. Within the same layer, the molecules are joined by hydrogen bonds in square groups 2.69 Å on a side. The different layers are joined only by van der Waals bonds.

Crystals whose molecules are joined in three-dimensional frameworks. Oxalic acid dihydrate, COOH-COOH, $2H_2O$, is a representative of this type of structure. Each water molecule is joined to two oxygens of different molecules of the same chain, and to an oxygen of an oxalic acid molecule of another chain. The bonding is thus three-dimensional.

Crystals whose molecules join to form a box in whose interior is trapped another molecule.

These are called clathrate molecular compounds or adducts. The urea-suberic acid complex is an example of this type of structure. Joined by hydrogen bonds, the urea molecules form the box in which the suberic acid molecules are trapped. The latter molecules are themselves joined by hydrogen bonds to form infinite chains. The two different kinds of molecules do not have any chemical affinity for each other, being merely joined by van der Waals forces.

Diffuse-scattering domains in molecular crystals

In the following we shall describe the x-ray diffuse scattering as it has been observed for a series of molecular crystals corresponding to the different structural types just described. The diffuse scattering has been recorded using the systematic Laue method, described elsewhere (see Amorós and Canut de Amorós, 1965). The method has been successfully used by the authors to show the existence of the continuous diffuse scattering as given by the DFT function (see Ch. 3) and to show the relation of this continuous diffuse scattering to the shape and orientation of the molecules in the crystal. In this chapter we shall use the descriptions given by Amorós and collaborators in a series of papers. The results are semiquantitative. A more quantitative study will be given in Ch. 5, when the more exact model of thermal waves is adopted.

Crystals with almost spherical molecules joined by van der Waals forces

Hexamine

Hexamine (hexamethylenetetramine), $C_6H_{12}N_4$, crystallizes in a structure having a molecule at each point of a body-centered cubic lattice. The structure (Fig. 4) was solved by trial and error by Dickinson and Raymond (1923) and by Gonell and Mark (1923), and was confirmed later by Wyckoff and Corey (1934). Careful electron-density studies allowed the determination of the hydrogen coordinates by Brill and collaborators (1939). Shaffer (1947) improved the agreement between observed and calculated values by adding independent rotational vibrations to the isotropic temperature factor, as a

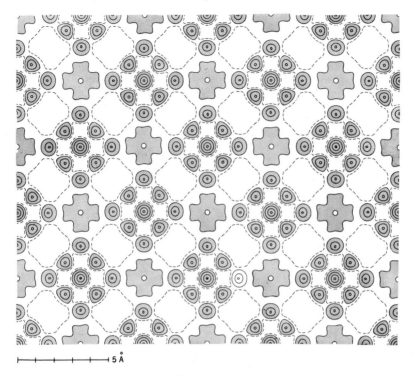

├──┼──┼──┼──┤ 5 Å

Fig. 4. Electron density of hexamine, $C_6H_{12}N_4$, projected on (001).

result of the anomalies discovered in the variation of some of the intensities with temperature. The basic crystal structure was confirmed by Lobatchev (1954) who redetermined all the parameters by electron diffraction. Andresen (1957) refined the structure by neutron diffraction. More recently, Becka and Cruickshank (1963a) studied the crystal structure of hexamine at three temperatures, namely 298°, 100°, and 34°K.

The crystal structure is as follows: The nitrogen atoms are located on the three-fold axis (see Table 2), the carbon atoms on the 4 axis, and the hydrogens on the diagonal [110] of the symmetry planes. The body-centered cubic packing arises because the molecule is exceptionally well suited to it. The hexamine molecule is almost spherical, having six carbons at the corners of an octahedron and four nitrogens protruding from the centers of alternate faces of the octahedron. The packing is achieved by filling the empty face of one octahedron with the protruding nitrogen atom of the neighboring molecule. Each molecule is surrounded by eight others at distances

Table 2   Hexamethylenetetramine, $C_6H_{12}N_4$, crystal-structure data and thermal parameters

Space group $I\bar{4}3m$ Symmetry of molecule: $\begin{cases} \bar{4}3m \text{ if isolated} \\ \bar{4}3m \text{ in crystal} \end{cases}$

Cubic cell: $a(298°K) = 7.021 \pm 9$ Å $Z = 2$

Atomic coordinates

Atom	x	y	z	Equivalent positions
C	0.237_7	0	0	$12e$
N	0.123_5	0.123_5	0.123_5	$8c$
H	0.088_5	0.088_5	-0.327_5	$24g$

Rhombohedral cell: $a(29.8°K) = 6.080 \pm 9$ Å $Z = 1$

Atomic coordinates

Atom	x	y	z	Equivalent positions
C	0	0.237_7	0.237_7	$3b$
	0	-0.237_7	-0.237_7	$3b$
N	0.247_1	0.247_1	0.247_1	$1a$
	-0.247_1	0	0	$3b$
H	-0.416_1	-0.416_1	-0.177_1	$3b$
	-0.238_9	-0.238_9	0.177	$3b$
	0	0.460_7	0.238_9	$6c$

Thermal vibrations at 290°K (referred to the cubic cell)

Atomic tensor components ($Å^2$)

	U_{11}	U_{22}	U_{33}	U_{12}	U_{13}	U_{23}
C	0.0298 ± 32	0.0648 ± 40	0.0648 ± 40	0	0	0
N	0.0490 ± 33	0.0490 ± 33	0.049 ± 33	-0.0105 ± 17	-0.0105 ± 17	-0.0105 ± 17
H	0.1265	0.1265	0.0359	0.0069	0.0105	0.0105

Rigid-body mean square amplitudes
$$t = 0.0271 \pm 26 \text{ Å}^2$$
$$\omega = 43.3 \pm 4.6 \text{ deg}^2$$

of 6.08 Å between centers along [111], and by six others at 7.02 Å along [100], both distances at room temperature. The distances between the centers of the nitrogen and hydrogen atoms are 2.88 Å at 298°K and 2.78 Å at 34°K according to Becka and Cruickshank.

The intermolecular H-H distances are 2.72 Å at 298°K and 2.62 Å at 34°K, about the sum of the van der Waal's radii (1.3 Å) of the hydrogens, and the whole structure can be described as a crystal with pure van der Waals bonds.

The intramolecular N-C distance is 1.476 ± 0.002 Å, which is practically equal to the sum of the covalent radii of C and N, and in satisfactory agreement with the value in the molecule in the gas. The intramolecular angle N-C-N is $113.6 \pm 0.2°$ and the angle C-N-C $= 107.2 \pm 0.1°$, slightly less than the angle of the tetrahedron (109.5°). The intramolecular C-H distance is 1.088 Å and the angle H-C-H $= 108.5 \pm 1.2°$, equivalent to that of methane. The distance reported is equivalent to the 1.09 Å determined by Yagi (1958) by the proton-magnetic-resonance method (p.m.r.).

The atomic-vibration tensor components are given in Table 2. From these values Becka and Cruickshank (1963a) deduced the tensors for the rigid-body translation $\mathbf{T}$ and libration $\boldsymbol{\omega}$, after subtracting the contribution of internal vibrations, estimated at 0.0015 to 0.0024 Å². The values obtained are given also in Table 2. As the molecule occupies a locus of 23 symmetry, the rigid-body translations and librations are isotropic. According to Becka and Cruickshank the zero-point vibrations are appreciable.

Diffuse scattering (Canut and Amorós, 1958). Laue photographs at room temperature show two different kinds of diffuse scattering (Fig. 5). The first kind consists of very intense, more or less ellipsoidal spots that are associated with Bragg reflections. The second kind consists of weak, extended, diffuse clouds that spread continuously through wide areas of reciprocal space, showing clear modulation in intensity, but no discontinuities (zero points) at the forbidden reciprocal-lattice points with $(h + k + l) = $ odd. The existence of systematic extinctions is a consequence of having selected a multiple cell instead of the primitive one, because no systematic extinctions of this class appear when a primitive cell is selected in the description of the crystal structure. The continuous diffuse scattering shows clearly that the proper cell is primitive. In the case of hexamine, instead the body-centered cubic cell, it is necessary to use the corresponding rhombohedral cell. In what follows, however, we shall index the reciprocal-lattice points in terms of the multiple cubic cell, because in this way the symmetry of the reciprocal space is evident.

In order to analyze the large diffuse regions characteristic of hexamine, the experimental maps corresponding to the levels $(001)^*_{1,2,3}$ and the intermediate levels $(001)^*_{1/2,3/2}$ have been plotted in Figs. 6, 7, and 8. The dotted lines correspond to the weak diffuse

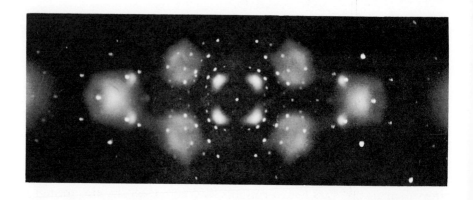

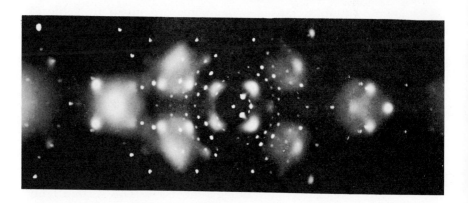

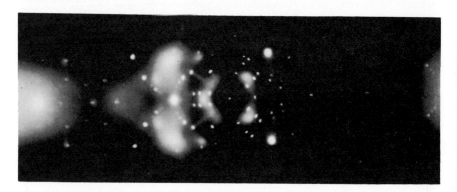

Fig. 5. Hexamine. Laue photographs obtained at room temperature using filtered Cu x-radiation. Crystal mounted along [001]. The continuous diffuse-scattering regions are clearly shown.

214

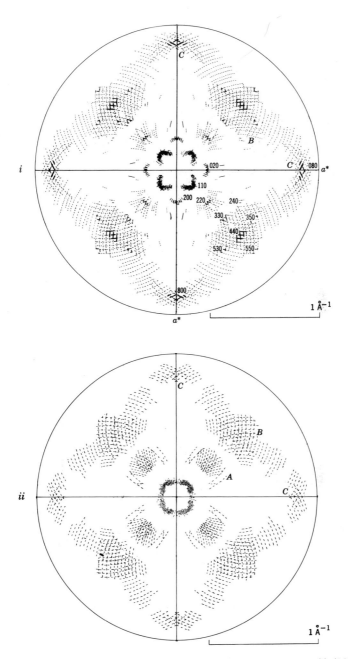

Fig. 6. Hexamine. Experimental continuous diffuse-scattering maps. (i) $(001)_0^*$; (ii) $(001)_{1/2}^*$.

215

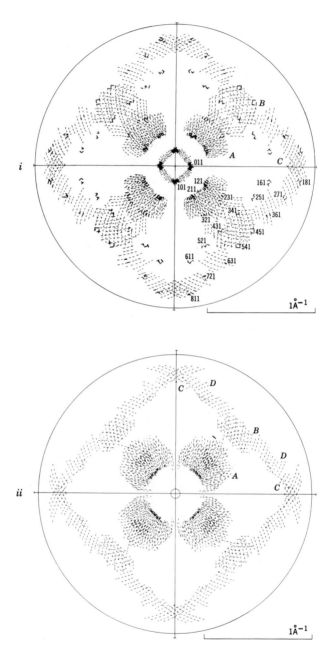

Fig. 7. Hexamine. Experimental continuous diffuse-scattering maps. (*i*) (001)$^*_1$; (*ii*) (001)$^*_{3/2}$.

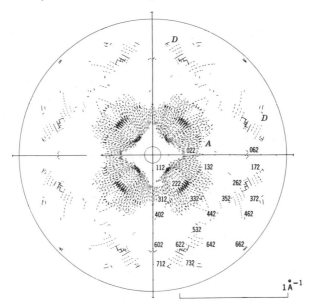

Fig. 8. Hexamine. Experimental continuous diffuse-scattering map, $(001)_2^*$.

scattering observed. In the intermediate levels 1/2 and 3/2, only the diffuse scattering that continuously joins the upper and lower levels has been plotted.

Level $(001)_0^*$, Fig. 6i, shows the diffuse regions at the zero level of hexamine. As can be seen, the most intense diffuse spots are associated with the nonforbidden reciprocal-lattice points 440, 080, and 110. Less intense diffuse spots appear associated with 200, 220, 330, 350, and 550. The diffuse spots are always elongated in the direction of the corresponding planes. A very intense continuous region B surrounds the reciprocal lattice point 440. A second intense continuous region C surrounds 080, and extends so as to join region B. Also, a small, weak, continuous diffuse zone is observed near the reciprocal-lattice point 220.

In level $(001)_{1/2}^*$, Fig. 6ii, the continuous region A, next to 220, which is small at the $(001)_0^*$ level, is more extense in this level. The continuous regions B and C are almost equal in size to the corresponding ones of the zero level. However, these two diffuse regions are no longer bounded in this level. A ring of continuous diffuse scattering also appears near the origin of the diffraction space in this level.

In level $(001)_1^*$, Fig. 7i, the most intense diffuse spots are associated with the reciprocal-lattice points 011, 121, 231, 341, and 451. There are also minor diffuse spots associated with the points 251, 361, 271, 161, and 181. Diffuse scattering associated with the points 011, 101, $10\bar{1}$ and $\bar{1}0\bar{1}$ outlines a square. The important continuous diffuse region A is centered on the forbidden point 221, extending in all directions, up to the lattice points 121, 131 (forbidden), 231, and 331 (forbidden). The second continuous diffuse region, B, is smaller in this level than on the $(001)^*_0$ level, and it is limited by the re-ciprocal-lattice points 341, 351 (forbidden), and 451, with its center at 441. The continuous regions A and B are almost equal in area, and are linked together. The third continuous region C is centered at 081 (forbidden), and extends up to 181, linking up with the region B across the reciprocal-lattice points 271 and 361.

In level $(001)^*_{3/2}$, Fig. 7ii, the first continuous diffuse region, A, is larger here than in the preceding level, while the region B is smaller. The diffuse scattering near the point $22\frac{3}{2}$ is very intense because of the high-intensity, diffuse domain associated with the point 222. The third continuous region C is present with its center at the point $08\frac{3}{2}$. The region near the origin in this level is free from diffuse scattering.

In level $(001)^*_2$, Fig. 8, the continuous diffuse region A is very in-tense. The four symmetry-equivalent regions A overlap so that a continuous ring-like diffuse domain is observed limited by the reciprocal-lattice points 112, 022, 132, and 332 and symmetry equiva-lents. Also, a very intense diffuse-scattering domain is observed inside this continuous region associated with 222 and extending in the direction of the corresponding plane. Analogous features are observed with the high-intensity, diffuse scattering associated to 262.

In summary, the diffuse scattering of hexamine is of two different types:

1. Strong diffuse-scattering spots associated with non-forbidden reciprocal-lattice points; the most intense diffuse spots are at 222, 440, and 800.
2. Continuous diffuse-scattering regions, extending in spheroidal clouds surrounding the more intense spots, and including other (even forbidden) reciprocal-lattice points.

The first type of diffuse scattering is very intense as compared with the second type. The diffuse-scattering spots associated with the reciprocal-lattice points have shapes that can be predicted by Jahn's formula (1942), and coincides with Ahmed's (1952) observations as well as ours. Such diffuse scattering extends in the direction of the crystallographic plane corresponding to the reciprocal-lattice point

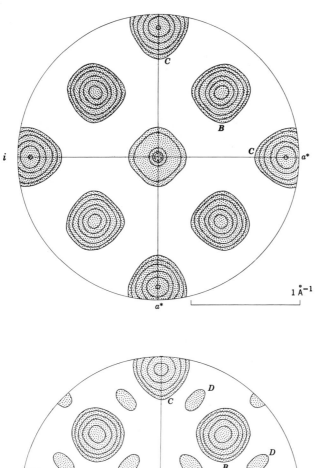

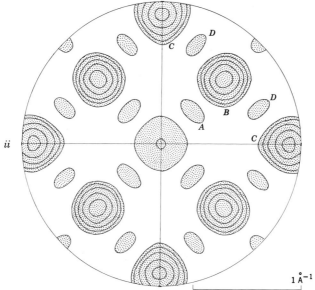

Fig. 9. Hexamine. DFT maps. (i) $(001)^*_0$; (ii) $(001)^*_{1/2}$.

with which it is associated. The second type of scattering is weak and cloud-like. It occurs in spherical regions so wide that Laue diagrams always show such continuous clouds. The intensity in these regions is not uniform, but has fine structure. The diffuse clouds extend over reciprocal-lattice points that should be absent when the multiple cell is used in the description of the crystal.

DFT of hexamine (Amorós, Canut, and de Acha, 1960). We have computed the DFT function for levels $(001)_0^*$, $(001)_{1/2}^*$ (Fig. 9), and $(001)_1^*$ (Fig. 10) by using (63), Ch. 3, and an isotropic temperature coefficient $B = 2.0 \, \text{Å}^2$. The lines of equal intensity are drawn at arbitrary intervals of 25. Comparing the calculated and experimental maps (Figs. 6 to 10), we see clearly that the observed continuous diffuse regions A, B, C coincide in position and size with the computed ones. Region A appears exaggerated in the calculated map. The good agreement between the experimental and computed maps is clear, however, and shows that the DFT function takes account of the observed continuous diffuse scattering. The fact that the diffuse domains are not perfectly spherical is due to the fact that the hexamine molecule is not a perfect sphere but can better be described as an octahedron. In Ch. 5 we shall discuss in greater detail the diffuse scattering of hexamine in the light of the theory of thermal waves.

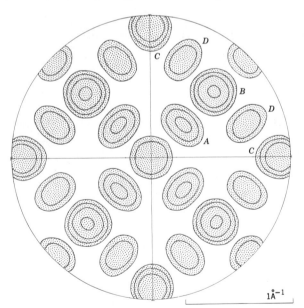

Fig. 10. Hexamine. DFT map $(001)_1^*$.

Crystals with planar molecules joined by van der Waals forces

Naphthalene

The structure of naphthalene was determined by Abrahams, Robertson, and White (1949) and was refined by Ahmed and Cruickshank (1952) and by Cruickshank (1957b). Naphthalene forms monoclinic crystals, space group $P2_1/a$, with two molecules per unit cell (Table 3). The molecules can be considered planar (maximum deviation ± 0.007 Å), with the carbon atoms forming two almost regular benzene rings. The molecule has mmm symmetry and its center of symmetry coincides with that of the cell. Each molecule in the crystal has 12 neighbors within 3 Å. The structure is close-packed (monoclinic), with the molecules inclined at an angle of 61° to the hexagonal packing plane, and at only 7° to the c-axis. The plane of the molecule forms an angle of 26.3° with the b-axis. Figure 11 represents the electron density of naphthalene projected on (010), calculated from the x-ray diffraction data of Abrahams, Robertson, and White (1949). The intermolecular distances are 0.1 Å greater than normal, which indicates that the molecules are joined only by weak van der Waals forces and have a high degree of independence in the crystal. The high volatility of naphthalene is consistent with such a picture. The shortest H-H distance is 2.40 Å, as compared with 2.50 Å in anthracene. However, the next shortest H-H distance in naphthalene is 2.66 Å, considerably larger than the next shortest in anthracene, 2.54 Å, so that the total energies of molecular interactions are roughly comparable.

Table 3 also gives the thermal motion of the molecule of naphthalene in terms of rigid-body vibrations. The rms amplitudes of translational oscillations parallel to the directions of the molecular axes L, M, N are 0.22, 0.20, and 0.19 Å, respectively, and the corresponding rms amplitudes of molecular librations are 4.4°, 3.7°, and 4.2°, respectively. The greatest amplitude of translational vibration is therefore along the long axis of the molecule, as in anthracene. The amplitudes of angular librations determined by x-ray analysis are in agreement with those deduced from the Raman frequencies (Cruickshank, 1956c).

Diffuse scattering (Amorós, Canut, and de Acha, 1960). Figure 12 reproduces some Laue photographs of naphthalene. The photographs show clearly the diffuse scattering characteristic of molecular compounds: very intense, diffuse spots associated to Bragg reflections, and continuous weak diffuse-scattering regions. In order to better relate

Table 3   Naphthalene, $C_{10}H_8$, crystal-structure data and thermal parameters

Space group $P2_1/a$ Symmetry of molecule: $\begin{cases} mmm \text{ if isolated,} \\ \bar{1} \text{ in crystal.} \end{cases}$

Unit cell: $a = 8.235$, $b = 6.003$,
$\quad\quad\quad\quad c = 8.658$ Å, $\beta = 122°55'$ $Z = 2$

Atomic coordinates

Atom	x	y	z	Equivalent positions
C_1	0.0856	0.0186	0.3251	4e
C_2	0.1148	0.1588	0.2200	4e
C_3	0.0472	0.1025	0.0351	4e
C_4	0.0749	0.2471	−0.0784	4e
C_5	0.0116	0.1869	−0.2541	4e
$H_1(C_1)$	0.1375	0.0657	0.4663	4e
$H_2(C_2)$	0.1888	0.3176	0.2752	4e
$H_3(C_4)$	0.1490	0.4056	−0.0233	4e
$H_4(C_5)$	0.0345	0.2999	−0.3394	4e

Thermal vibrations at room temperature

Atomic tensor components (in 10^{-2} Å^2)

	U_{11}	U_{22}	U_{33}	U_{12}	U_{13}	U_{23}
C_1	5.84	6.84	6.34	0.41	0.10	−0.19
C_2	5.48	4.79	5.63	0.82	−0.28	−0.29
C_3	5.47	3.84	3.73	−0.22	0.37	−0.01
C_4	5.98	4.86	4.89	−1.01	0.01	0.10
C_5	5.20	7.57	6.08	−1.51	−0.11	−0.19

Rigid body translational (T) and librational (ω) tensors

$$T = \begin{pmatrix} 5.01 & -0.30 & 0.10 \\ & 4.00 & -0.05 \\ & & 3.44 \end{pmatrix} \quad \omega = \begin{pmatrix} 19.50 & 2.25 & 2.56 \\ & 13.95 & 0.76 \\ & & 17.73 \end{pmatrix}$$

$\quad\quad\quad T_{ij}$ in 10^{-2} Å^2 $\quad\quad\quad\quad\quad\quad \omega_{ij}$ in deg^2

the morphology of these continuous diffuse regions with the molecular orientation of naphthalene, Fig. 13 gives the stereographic projection of the L, M, N and L', M', N' axes of the two molecules of the unit cell.

Figure 14i shows the diffuse scattering plotted in level $(010)_0^*$. It is easy to observe a domain of hexagonal shape, formed by the diffuse scattering joining the reciprocal-lattice points 002, 200, 20$\bar{2}$, and

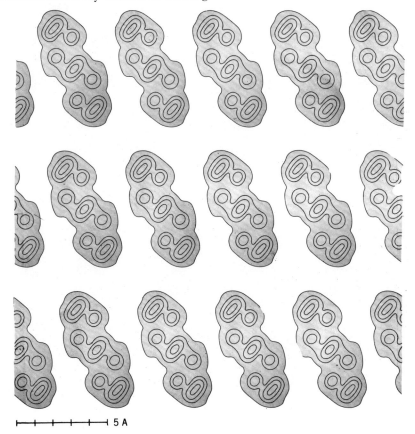

5 A

Fig. 11.   Electron density of naphthalene, $C_{10}H_8$, projected on (010).

symmetrically equivalent. Strong diffuse spots are associated with nonforbidden reciprocal-lattice points of strong Bragg intensity, namely 001, 002, 003, $20\bar{1}$, $20\bar{2}$, 203, 004, $40\bar{7}$, $60\bar{8}$, and $60\bar{4}$, which correspond to values of $|F_0| > 10$. The diffuse spots associated to 003 and 004 spread to join $20\bar{4}$ and 203 and form the continuous diffuse scattering region D. Another continuous diffuse region, G, similar to D, and at about twice the distance from the origin of the reciprocal lattice, is limited by the reciprocal-lattice points $20\bar{7}$, $40\bar{7}$, $60\bar{7}$, and $40\bar{8}$, $60\bar{8}$, and $80\bar{8}$. The two continuous diffuse regions D and G have the aspect of bands, and are normal to $L'L$, the direction of the long axis of the naphthalene molecule. These continuous regions of diffuse scattering do not present zero discontinuities at the reciprocal-lattice points forbidden by space-group requirements.

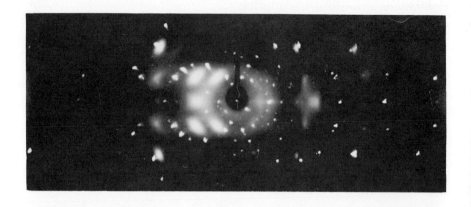

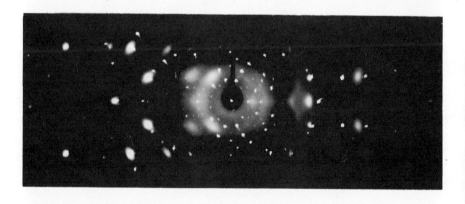

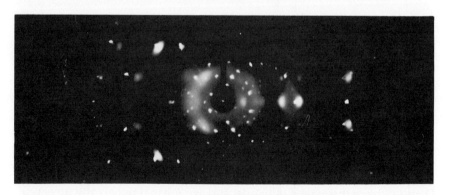

Fig. 12. Naphthalene. Laue photographs obtained at room temperature using filtered Cu x-radiation. Crystal mounted along [010]. The continuous diffuse regions are clearly shown.

224

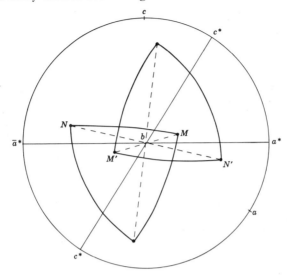

Fig. 13.   Stereographic projection of the molecular axes of naphthalene.

This can be explained as the structure projected on (010), which can be described in terms of a subcell containing only one molecule. The diffuse scattering conforms to this primitive cell and therefore no systematic extinction is shown in the continuous background. Other regions of continuous diffuse scattering can also be observed in the map.

Most of the continuous diffuse-scattering regions that are observed in the zero level of the reciprocal lattice extend through the intermediate level $(010)^*_{1/2}$ to upper levels. The continuous diffuse-scattering regions appear as bands in the Laue photographs. Figure 14*ii* shows the intersections of such zones in this level; these have been labeled in the same way as the corresponding ones of the $(010)^*_0$ level.

In level $(010)^*_1$ (Fig. 15*i*) the diffuse-scattering spots are very blurred except those associated with certain reciprocal-lattice points, among them 110, 210, 21$\bar{1}$, 41$\bar{1}$, 31$\bar{1}$, 111, 31$\bar{4}$, 11$\bar{3}$, 410, 11$\bar{2}$, 11$\bar{4}$, 41$\bar{3}$, and 51$\bar{4}$, whose $|F_0|$ are greater than 10. The two continuous diffuse-scattering regions D and G again are present in this level. The points L, M, N, and L', M', N' in Fig. 15*i* correspond to the intersection with this level of the long (L), middle (M), and normal (N) axes of the molecule. It is seen that both regions D and G are perpendicular to LL''. There is also diffuse scattering about N, forming the region A.

The different continuous diffuse-scattering regions observed in other levels appear crossing intermediate level $(010)^*_{3/2}$ (Fig. 15*ii*). In

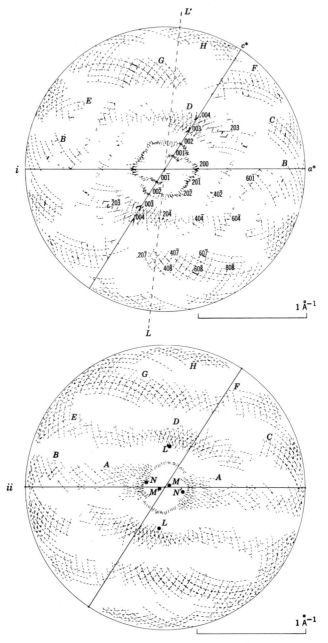

Fig. 14. Naphthalene. Experimental continuous diffuse-scattering maps. (i) $(010)^*_0$; (ii) $(010)^*_{1/2}$.

226

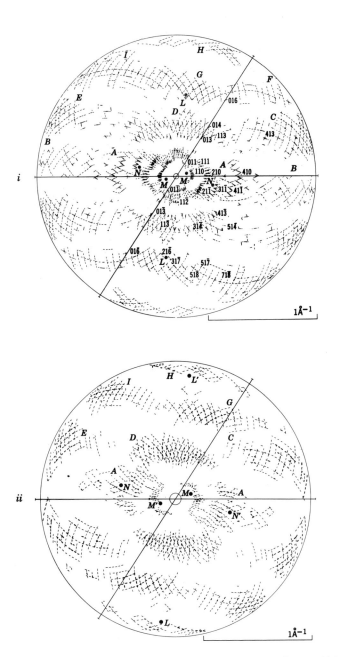

Fig. 15.   Naphthalene. Diffuse-scattering continuous experimental maps. (i) $(010)_1^*$; (ii) $(010)_{3/2}^*$.

level $(010)^*_{1/2}$ as well as here, those zones appear more uniform in intensity since in the intermediate levels there is no overlap of the intense diffuse-scattering spots associated with the nonforbidden reciprocal-lattice points of large $|F_0|$. Another diffuse band H appears to extend parallel to the D and G at a distance from the origin about three times that of the first zone. The continuous diffuse region A associated with the point N can be observed also.

We see again at level $(010)^*_2$ (Fig. 16) that strong diffuse-scattering spots appear associated with the reciprocal lattice points of high $|F_0|$. The most intense spots are associated to the lattice points 021 and 120, and are extended in the direction of the corresponding planes. Other spots are associated to the reciprocal-lattice points $22\bar{3}$, $32\bar{1}$, 320, $52\bar{1}$, $22\bar{4}$, 221, and 023, also with $|F_0| > 10$. The two continuous diffuse-scattering regions D and G appear again in this level. Both regions are again perpendicular to LL'. We also observe diffuse scattering about the point N (continuous region A).

In short, the thermal diffuse scattering of naphthalene is again of two types: highly intense diffuse-scattering spots that are always associated with nonforbidden reciprocal-lattice points, and weak continuous diffuse-scattering regions extended in anisotropic clouds, covering reciprocal-lattice points whose structure factors have high

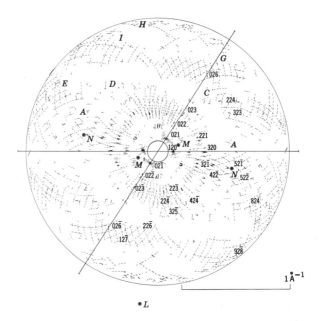

Fig. 16. Naphthalene. Experimental continuous diffuse-scattering maps, $(010)^*_2$.

absolute values. These continuous regions extend through reciprocal-lattice points that are forbidden by the extinction conditions of the static space group. The continuous diffuse-scattering regions can be described as forming columns that produce, by overlap in the different levels, bands of diffuse scattering perpendicular to the axis L of the molecule. The first band is located in reciprocal space at a distance from the origin corresponding to a spacing of 2.4 Å in the direct space, that is, it corresponds to the period of the zig-zag of the carbon atoms in the molecules. The second region of weak diffuse scattering corresponds in position to a spacing of 1.3 Å in direct space. Likewise, the position of the third region of weak diffuse scattering corresponds in direct space to a spacing of 0.83 Å.

The sections at different levels show that the continuous diffuse regions extend in two symmetrical directions that form the same angle with the [010] axis. The angle is related to the symmetrical positions of the two naphthalene molecules in the unit cell as shown by the DFT function.

DFT of naphthalene. The essential features of the DFT of aromatic molecules like naphthalene and anthracene is given by the molecular intensity transform of the benzene ring. We have seen (Ch. 1) that the basic pattern of this transform (Fig. 28, Ch. 1) is given by an hexagonal arrangement of principal maxima P_1 around the origin of the reciprocal lattice, at distances 0.82 Å^{-1}. At distances 0.47 Å^{-1} appear six secondary maxima S_1 at the vertices of another hexagon rotated 30° with respect to the hexagon defined by the P_1 maxima. The DFT of a single molecule of the aromatic hydrocarbons is built up by a set of columns of diffuse-scattering intensity perpendicular to the plane of the molecule and located at the positions of the S and P peaks (Fig. 17i). The location of the DFT peaks in real cases depends on the orientation of the plane of the molecule with respect to the level studied, and corresponds to the intersection of the given level with the DFT function. If the crystal has two molecules with different orientations, the resulting DFT is formed by the sum of the independent DFT functions corresponding to each molecule. We shall apply this to the case of naphthalene.

The projections of the two molecules of the unit cell on (010) are identical, causing the molecular intensity transform of both molecules to be equal. It is therefore sufficient to calculate only the contribution of one molecule and to multiply the result by two to obtain the total DFT for the level (010)$_0^*$. The calculated map (Fig. 17ii) shows the peaks S_1 that correspond to the continuous diffuse regions B, E, and D, and two peaks P_1 corresponding to G, and C. The continuous

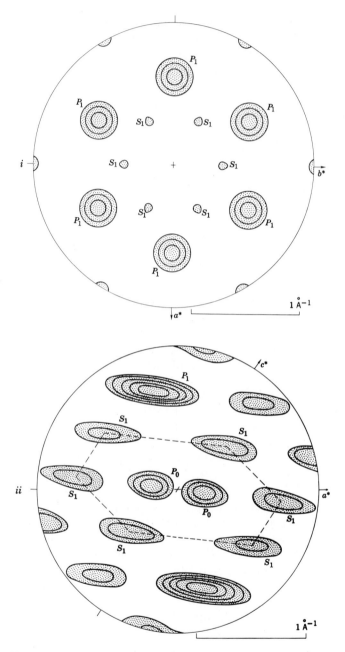

Fig. 17. (*i*) Benzene ring. DFT map showing the principal P_1 and secondary S_1 peaks. (*ii*) Naphthalene. DFT map $(010)_0^*$.

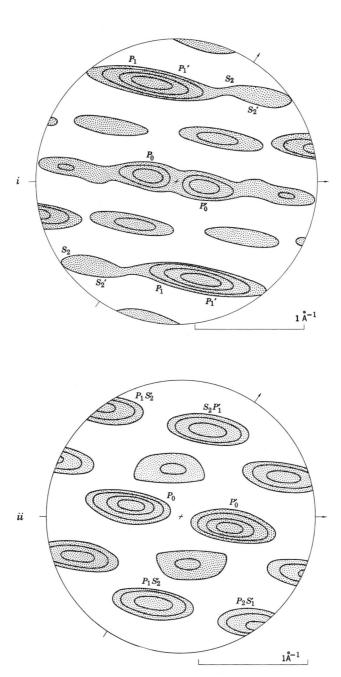

Fig. 18. Naphthalene. DFT maps (i) $(010)^*_{1/2}$; (ii) $(010)^*_{3/2}$.

231

regions F and H correspond to other secondary peaks S. The continuous region A that appears in the calculated map does not correspond to any continuous region of diffuse scattering. It appears in the experimental map as an hexagon of diffuse-scattering spots associated with Bragg peaks.

At higher levels of the reciprocal lattice the intensity transforms of the two molecules are no longer equal, so that the contribution of each molecule to the total DFT function must be calculated. It is clearly shown in the calculated maps (Figs. 18i and 18ii) that the observed continuous diffuse-scattering regions correspond to the intersections at the different levels of the columns S_1 and P_1 that are split into two families because of the different (symmetric) orientations of the two molecules of the unit cell. The region A corresponds to the P_0 column passing through the origin of reciprocal space. This column is perpendicular to the molecular plane, and therefore its location coincides with the intercept of the axis N of the molecule by the different levels of the reciprocal lattice.

From the results obtained for naphthalene it is clear that the difference Fourier transform explains not only the shape, but also the location, orientation, and intensity of the continuous diffuse regions, columns in this case.

Anthracene

The molecular structure of anthracene, $C_6H_4:(CH)_2:C_6H_4$, is very similar to that of naphthalene, the difference being that the molecule is formed by three, rather than two, benzene rings. The crystal structure was determined by Sinclair, Robertson, and Mathieson (1950) and refined by Cruickshank (1956b). The crystallography of anthracene at two temperatures has been recently studied by Mason (1964). Figure 19 represents the electron-density map of anthracene projected on (010). The crystal-structure data are summarized in Table 4. Within experimental error the molecule of anthracene can be considered as planar and having mmm symmetry. It seems, however, that the deviation from planarity, although small—0.007 Å—is real. In the packing of the molecules this causes a shortening of the intermolecular distances to 2.67 Å between certain atoms. Each molecule has six neighbors in its packing plane, and a total of twelve in the first coordination sphere, just as in naphthalene. The nature of the bonding is also similar to that of naphthalene. Table 4 includes also the anisotropic vibrations of the molecules of anthracene as a function of rigid-body translational and librational oscillations. The rms amplitudes of the translational vibrations are 0.20, 0.16, and 0.16 Å at

Table 4 Anthracene, $C_{14}10_{10}$ crystal-structure data and thermal parameters

Space group $P2_1/a$ Symmetry of molecule: $\begin{cases} mmm \text{ if isolated,} \\ \bar{1} \text{ in crystal.} \end{cases}$

Unit cell: $a = 8.561$, $b = 6.036$,
$c = 11.163$ Å, $\beta = 124°42'$ $Z = 2$

Atomic coordinates

Atom	x	y	z	Equivalent positions
C_1	0.08754	0.02906	0.36585	$4e$
C_2	0.11887	0.15548	0.28059	$4e$
C_3	0.05902	0.08212	0.13816	$4e$
C_4	0.08743	0.20847	0.04728	$4e$
C_5	0.03014	0.13086	−0.08984	$4e$
C_6	0.06061	0.25865	−0.18236	$4e$
C_7	0.00406	0.17922	−0.31611	$4e$
$H_1(C_1)$	0.1327	0.0910	0.4726	$4e$
$H_2(C_2)$	0.1887	0.3168	0.3185	$4e$
$H_3(C_4)$	0.1554	0.3703	0.0841	$4e$
$H_4(C_6)$	0.1307	0.4172	−0.1432	$4e$
$H_5(C_7)$	0.0278	0.2790	−0.3852	$4e$

Thermal vibrations at room temperature

Atomic-tensor components (in 10^{-2} Å^2)

	U_{11}	U_{22}	U_{33}	U_{12}	U_{13}	U_{23}
C_1	3.86	6.81	5.14	0.60	−0.20	0.58
C_2	4.62	4.20	5.04	0.92	0.01	−0.24
C_3	3.90	3.79	2.66	0.04	0.01	0.03
C_4	4.37	2.63	3.67	−0.03	−0.13	0.28
C_5	3.95	3.13	2.95	−0.33	0.03	−0.10
C_6	4.58	3.84	3.78	−0.89	−0.06	0.32
C_7	4.14	6.77	5.32	−1.14	0.20	0.24

Rigid body translational (**T**) and librational ($\boldsymbol{\omega}$) tensors

$$\mathbf{T} = \begin{pmatrix} 3.87 & -0.12 & 0.01 \\ & 2.70 & 0.06 \\ & & 2.66 \end{pmatrix} \quad \boldsymbol{\omega} = \begin{pmatrix} 14.56 & 1.57 & 0.87 \\ & 5.03 & -0.57 \\ & & 9.64 \end{pmatrix}$$

T_{ij} in 10^{-2} Å^2 ω_{ij} in deg^2

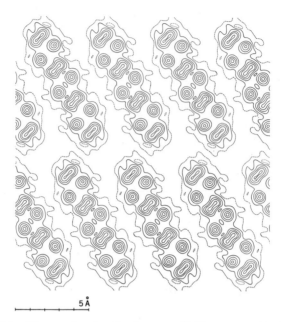

5 Å

Fig. 19.   Electron density of anthracene, $C_{14}H_{10}$, projected on (010).

room temperature, along the axes L, M, and N of the molecule. The librational oscillations are 3.8, 2.2, and 3.1°, respectively. (Cruickshank, 1957a). The general picture of the thermal vibrations of the anthracene molecule is therefore very similar to that of naphthalene. Figure 20 represents the axes of the molecules in stereographic projection.

Diffuse scattering (Annaka and Amorós, 1960).   The diffuse scattering of anthracene is also similar to that of naphthalene. Figure 21 reproduces three Laue photographs of anthracene, in which appear the diffuse-scattering characteristic of a molecular crystal, consisting of diffuse spots associated with Bragg reflections, and continuous regions of diffuse scattering covering large areas. The regions of continuous diffuse scattering are represented in Figs. 22, 23, and 24, which correspond to the levels $(010)_0^*$, $(010)_1^*$, $(010)_2^*$, $(010)_{1/2}^*$, and $(010)_{3/2}^*$. In these maps it is seen that the continuous regions of diffuse scattering A, B, C, ... extend in the direction of $\mathbf{a}^*$ and through different reciprocal-lattice levels. The continuous diffuse regions are bands that appear at spacings of about 0.81 and 0.4 Å^{-1}. The maps of the preceding figures were plotted from Laue photographs. In order to show with more detail the fine structure of the diffuse scattering, a

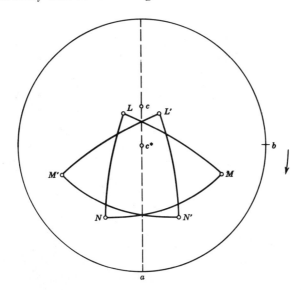

Fig. 20. Stereographic projection of the molecular axes of anthracene.

region of the diffraction space was surveyed carefully with x-ray diffractometer. The result is shown in Fig. 25. In addition to the continuous diffuse scattering, there can be observed the presence of fine lines and planes of diffuse scattering between certain reciprocal-lattice points. These lines and planes are considered to be due to the low acoustic frequencies of vibrations of the molecules, while the regions of continuous diffuse scattering are supposed to be due to the optical and higher-frequency acoustic vibrations. The experimental conclusions are of the same sort as in the case of naphthalene, so that it does not seem necessary to discuss them in greater detail.

DFT of anthracene (Annaka and Amorós, 1960). The DFT function has been computed for levels $(010)_0^*$, $(010)_{1/2}^*$ and $(010)_{3/2}^*$ of anthracene. Figures 26 and 27 show the results obtained. In $(010)_0^*$ the DFT shows clearly the hexagon formed by the secondary S_1 peaks of the molecular intensity transform of the benzene ring. As in the case of naphthalene, only two centrosymmetric primary P_1 peaks are also present. By comparing Fig. 26i with 22i we can identify the regions B, E, and D as S_1 peaks and the region G as a P_1 peak. The region C corresponds to another P_1 peak that lies almost on the limiting sphere.

The diffuse bands perpendicular to the plane of the molecule are more extended at a direction almost parallel to $\mathbf{a}^*$ than in the case of

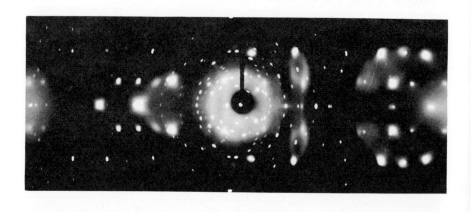

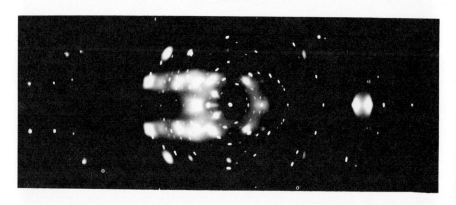

Fig. 21. Anthracene. Laue photographs obtained at room temperature using filtered Cu x-radiation. Crystal mounted along [010]. The continuous diffuse regions are clearly shown.

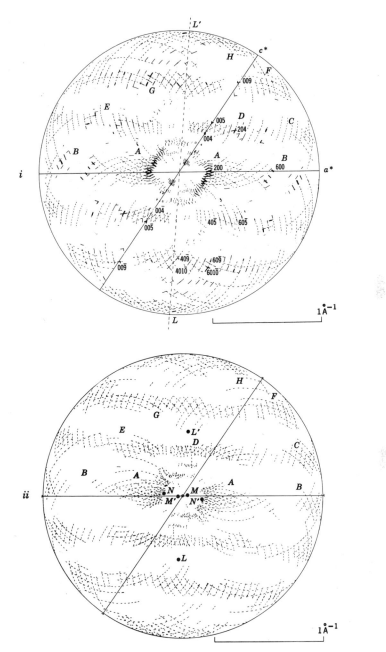

Fig. 22. Anthracene. Experimental continuous diffuse-scattering maps. (*i*) $(010)_0^*$; (*ii*) $(010)_{1/2}^*$.

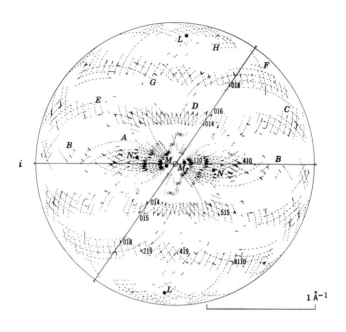

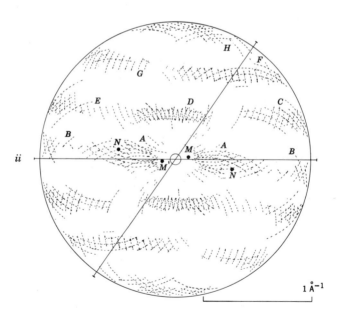

Fig. 23. Anthracene. Experimental continuous diffuse-scattering maps. (*i*) $(010)^*_1$; (*ii*) $(010)^*_{3/2}$.

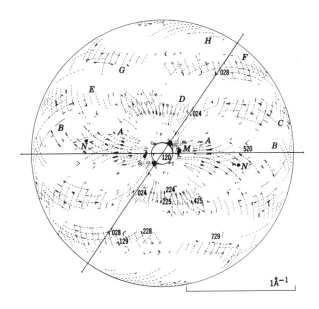

Fig. 24.   Anthracene. Experimental continuous diffuse-scattering map, $(010)_2^*$.

naphthalene. This effect can be explained by taking into account the difference in length of the two molecules, and it is clearly seen in comparing Figs. 26i and 17ii. In the level $(010)_{1/2}^*$ the two peaks P_1 of the two molecules overlap, giving rise to a single, extended, diffuse region which, by overlapping with the S_2 peaks, gives rise to a continuous band of variable intensity (Fig. 26ii and Fig. 22ii). In the level $(010)_{3/2}^*$, however, the P_1 peaks of the two molecules are resolved (Fig. 27), and the corresponding diffuse scattering is no longer a continuous diffuse band (Fig. 23ii). This is due to an exact overlapping of the S_2 peaks with the P_1. The intercept of the columns P_0 is clearly seen in the computed DFT and corresponds to the diffuse region A in the experimental maps. It is clear again that the DFT function takes account of the continuous diffuse scattering in this case.

The effect of including small librations of the molecules in the DFT was studied by Annaka and Amorós (1960). The results were applied to a small region of diffraction space, represented in Fig. 28iv. The contributions of small independent librations (Fig. 28ii) show that when this effect, even though small, is added to the normal DFT function (Fig. 28i) it gives better agreement (Fig. 28iii) with the experimental map than the DFT alone.

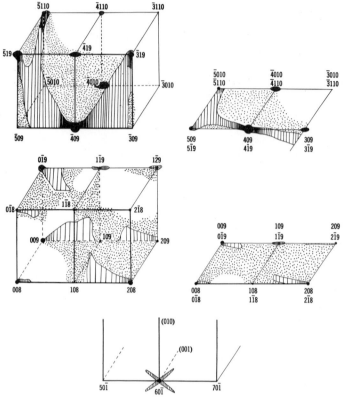

Fig. 25. Region of the diffraction space of anthracene, in which the continuous diffuse-scattering and its fine structure are shown with greater detail.

Acridine III

The crystal structure of acridine III at 20°C was determined by Phillips (1956). The crystal is monoclinic, space group $P2_1/n$, with four molecules per unit cell. The electron density of the structure projected on (010) is given in Fig. 29. The acridine molecule is heterocyclic, and can be derived from the anthracene molecule by replacing a central CH group by a nitrogen. The molecule is therefore not centrosymmetric, and not perfectly planar. Table 5 gives the structural data for acridine III. The crystal structure of acridine III is related to those of naphthalene and anthracene. However, while in the latter two crystals the centers of the molecules coincide with the centers of symmetry of the crystal, in acridine III the polar, imperfectly planar molecules are arranged in antiparallel pairs about the centers of symmetry of the crystal. The two molecules of the pair are

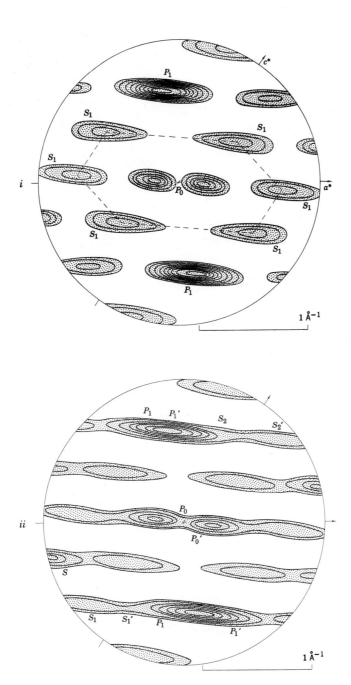

Fig. 26. Anthracene. DFT maps (i) $(010)^*_0$; (ii) $(010)^*_{1/2}$.

241

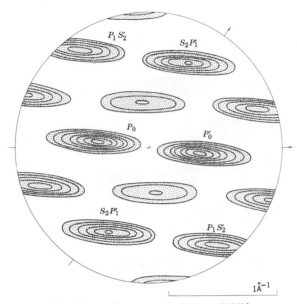

Fig. 27. Anthracene. DFT map $(010)^*_{3/2}$.

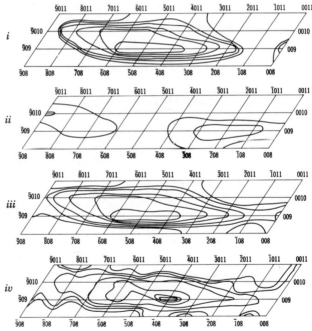

Fig. 28. Anthracene. Detail of the G region in $(010)^*_0$. (*i*) DFT map; (*ii*) map of independent librations; (*iii*) sum of (*i*) and (*ii*); (*iv*) experimental continuous diffuse scattering.

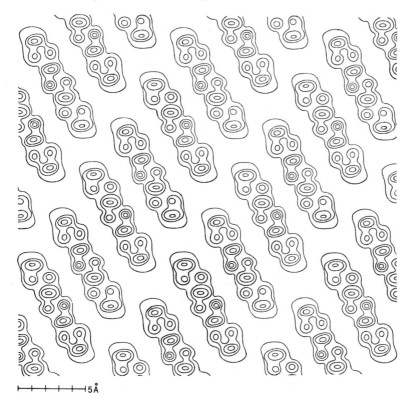

Fig. 29.   Electron density of acridine III, $C_{13}NH_{10}$, projected on (010).

not strictly opposed, but are displaced such that the atoms of one molecule fit into the depressions of the other. The packing of the molecule pairs is determined by intermolecular contacts similar to those found in the structure of benzene. The distances between the molecules of different pairs are greater than 3.6 Å, while the distance between the molecules of the same pair is 3.47 Å. All the intermolecular distances are shorter than in anthracene, indicating that the bonding forces in acridine III are stronger, perhaps due to the fact that the bonding is not simply of the van der Waals type. The molecules are subject to rigid body librational and translational vibration, with a mean amplitude of translational vibration $\bar{u} = 0.37$ Å (see Table 5). In order to visualize the relations existing between the continuous diffuse scattering regions with the crystal structure, the stereographic projection of the axes L, M, N, L', M', N' of the pairs of molecules 1, 2, and 3, 4 has been plotted in Fig. 30.

Table 5   Acridine III, $C_{13}H_9$, crystal-structure
data and thermal parameters

Space group $P2_1/n$ Symmetry of molecule: $\begin{cases} mm \text{ if isolated} \\ \bar{1} \text{ in crystal} \end{cases}$

Unit cell: $a = 11.375$, $b = 5.988$,
$c = 13.647$ Å, $\beta = 98°58'$ $Z = 4$

Atomic coordinates

Atom	x	y	z	Equivalent positions
C_1	0.1385	0.2917	0.9571	4e
C_2	0.2027	0.2255	0.8853	4e
C_3	0.2631	0.0183	0.8907	4e
C_4	0.2553	0.8757	0.9686	4e
C_5	0.1801	0.7987	0.1261	4e
C_6	0.1073	0.7450	0.2848	4e
C_7	0.0473	0.8269	0.3561	4e
C_8	0.9932	0.0410	0.3455	4e
C_9	0.9997	0.1706	0.2633	4e
N	0.0700	0.2249	0.1095	4e
C_{11}	0.1321	0.1498	0.0402	4e
C_{12}	0.1896	0.9352	0.0447	4e
C_{13}	0.1178	0.8757	0.1985	4e
C_{14}	0.0637	0.0908	0.1877	4e
H_1	0.096	0.448	0.953	4e
H_2	0.207	0.336	0.825	4e
H_3	0.311	0.963	0.834	4e
H_4	0.297	0.717	0.974	4e
H_5	0.223	0.636	0.133	4e
H_6	0.151	0.584	0.292	4e
H_7	0.041	0.724	0.419	4e
H_8	0.946	0.105	0.401	4e
H_9	0.957	0.332	0.256	4e

Thermal vibrations at room temperature

The molecules are subject to rigid-body vibrations and librations with $(\bar{u}_i{}^2)^{1/2}$ due to vibrations alone of about 0.37 Å.

Diffuse scattering (Amorós, de Acha, and Canut, 1961). The Laue photographs of acridine III reproduced in Fig. 31 show very intense diffuse spots and large anisotropic continuous diffuse regions. These large, continuous regions extend between levels. The thermal diffuse

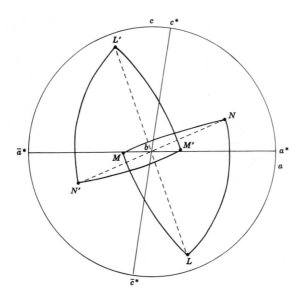

Fig. 30.   Stereographic projection of the molecular axes of acridine III.

scattering of acridine III is again typical of molecular crystals: there
are very intense diffuse-scattering spots near nonforbidden reciprocal-
lattice points, and weak, continuous diffuse regions that appear as
anisotropic clouds extending through reciprocal-lattice points of
large $|F_o|$, and with no discontinuities at the forbidden points of the
static space group (Figs. 32 to 34). In acridine III, as in naphthalene
and anthracene, the continuous diffuse regions occur in bands perpendicular to the line LL', that is, the long axis of the molecule. The
periodicity of the bands along LL'' is reciprocal to the spacing of the
carbon-carbon zig-zag in the molecule. Again, we observe that the
continuous regions, built up by the overlapping of the different bands,
are displaced from one level to the next along a direction perpendicular to the axis LL'. The displacement is identical for areas within
the same band, but is in opposite directions for adjacent bands. In the
band passing through the origin displacements in both directions are
present. The displacement of the columns reflect the two orientations
of the pairs of molecules in the crystal. The cross section of the
columns is elongated, its largest dimension corresponding to the
smallest dimension of the molecule. As can be seen, the pattern of the
diffuse scattering of acridine III is very similar to those of naphthalene and anthracene.

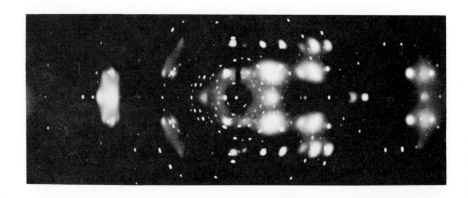

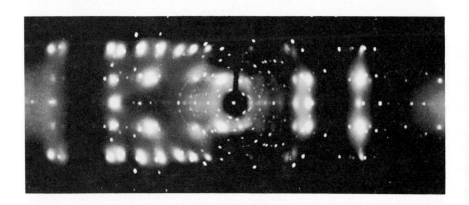

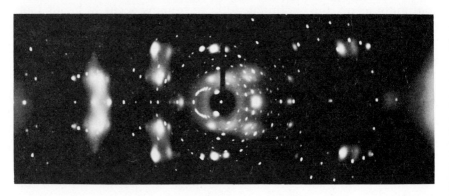

Fig. 31. Acridine III. Laue photographs obtained at room temperature using filtered Cu x-radiation. Crystal mounted along [010]. The continuous diffuse regions are clearly shown.

246

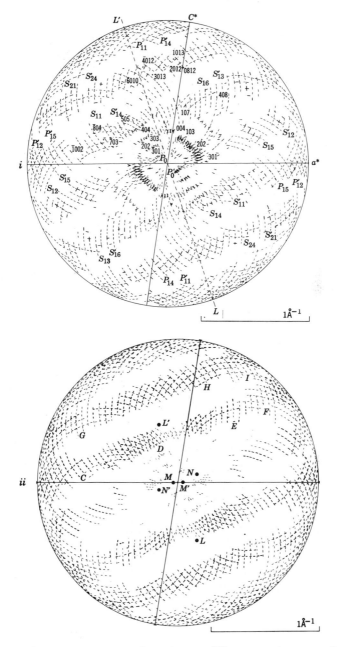

Fig. 32. Acridine III. Experimental continuous diffuse-scattering maps. (*i*) $(010)_0^*$; (*ii*) $(010)_{1/2}^*$.

247

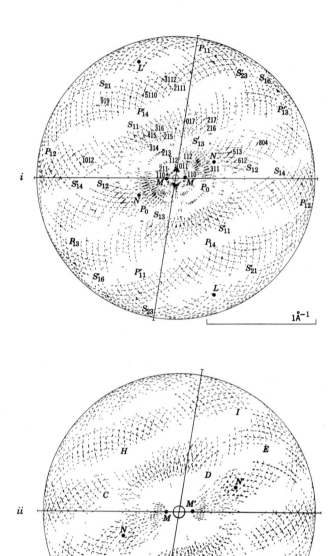

Fig. 33. Acridine III. Experimental continuous diffuse-scattering maps. (*i*) $(010)^*_1$; (*ii*) $(010)^*_{3/2}$.

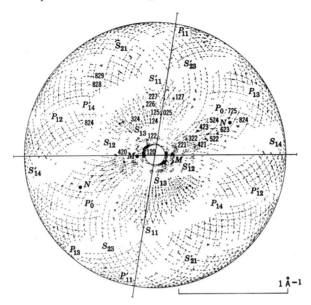

Fig. 34.   Acridine III. Experimental continuous diffuse-scattering maps, $(010)_2^*$.

DFT of acridine III.   The four molecules of acridine III project equally on (010). Therefore the transforms of the four molecules are equal in absolute value for the zero level $(010)_0^*$, and the total DFT function can be obtained just by calculating the contribution of a single molecule. Figure 35 shows the map of the total DFT, in which the essential features of the benzene-ring DFT are again clear. The central peak P_0 is separated into two parts at the origin since the DFT function vanishes at the origin. P_0 is surrounded by a hexagon of secondary maxima S_1. The orientation of the hexagon and its shape tell us the orientation of the plane of the molecule and the orientation of the molecule in its plane. It is noted that the maxima are located in bands normal to LL'. The maxima P_1, which appear at this level, have much greater intensity than the secondary maxima S_1. The location of the computed maxima coincide with the corresponding experimental regions.

In order to show the contribution to the DFT of a single molecule (Fig. 36i) and the total DFT (Fig. 36ii) both functions have been plotted on level $(010)_1^*$. It can be seen that the central maximum, or region N, is displaced from the origin, and an equal displacement of the S_1 hexagon is easily seen. N is the intersection of the normal axis of the molecule with this level of reciprocal space, and we see that

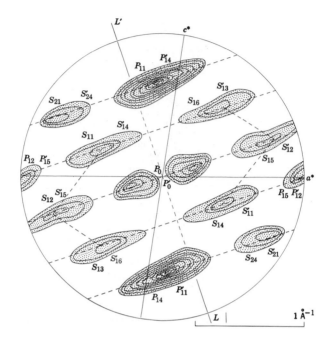

Fig. 35. Acridine III. DFT map $(010)_0^*$. The S_{ij} and P_{ij} peaks are shown.

it coincides with the maximum of region P_0. In the map of the total DFT we see the relative displacements of two hexagons S_1 and S'_1, corresponding to the two symmetrical orientations of the pairs of molecules in the unit cell. The agreement between the experimental map (Fig. 33i) and computed DFT (Fig. 36ii) is clear.

For level $(010)_2^*$ we have also plotted the map of the DFT for a single molecule and the map of the total DFT (Figs. 37i and 37ii). The results are very similar to those of the lower level, although the displacements are more marked. At this level, the calculated maxima S_{13} and S'_{11} clearly overlap, coinciding with the observed map of Fig. 34, in which only a single diffuse region is seen. It is clear that the DFT function takes account of the continuous diffuse-scattering regions in acridine III.

Crystals with chain-like molecules joined by hydrogen bonds

Dicarboxylic acids

The series of the dicarboxylic acids, $COOH-(CH_2)_n-COOH$, is a typical example of structures with long molecules joined in chains

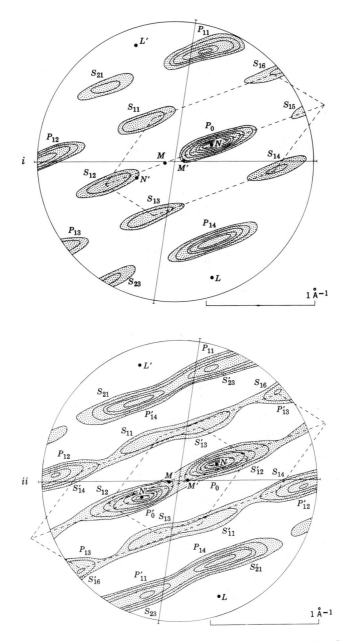

Fig. 36. Acridine III. DFT map $(010)_1^*$: (i) calculated with only one molecule; (ii) with two molecules. S_{ij} = secondary peaks of molecule 1, S'_{ij} = secondary peaks of molecule 2. Similar nomenclature for other peaks.

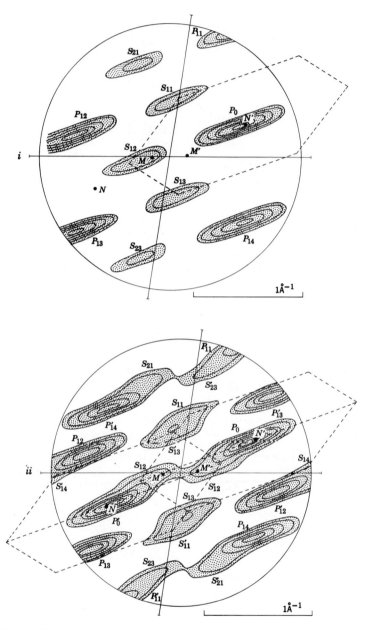

Fig. 37. Acridine III. DFT map $(010)_2^*$: (*i*) calculated with only one molecule; (*ii*) with two molecules. S_{1j} = secondary peaks of molecule 1, S'_{1j} = secondary peaks of molecule 2. Similar nomenclature for other peaks.

by hydrogen bonds, with the chains oriented in a single direction (the c-axis). These acids show a clear alternation of physical and chemical properties that can be explained in terms of the odd or even number of carbon atoms in the molecule. The packing of the carboxyl groups in any layer parallel to (001) is practically the same for both even and odd acids. In acids with an even number of carbon atoms in the molecule, the COOH groups of adjacent molecules are parallel, a situation not compatible with the planarity of the molecule. In this case there is a rotation about the single carbon bonds, altering both the molecular symmetry and the space group. Steric hindrance in the molecule is minimal when we have a planar zig-zag configuration; therefore, the rotation requires energy. Thus the internal energies of the odd members are higher than those of the even members, explaining the alternation of physical properties between the two series. As a result of their configuration, the molecules of the even acids have a center of symmetry, while the molecules of the odd acids have a 2-fold axis normal to their plane. When referred to similar cells, the morphotrophism of the series is clear and is revealed in all the crystallographic properties of the substances. Table 6 shows the crystallographic constants as a function of the number of carbon atoms and as a function of the number of carbons. We can see that the length of a and b remain approximately constant for acids of the same series, as should be expected since these directions do not contain the long

Table 6   Crystallographic constants of dicarboxylic acids

Acid	$n(CH_2)$	a_0	b_0	c_0	$a:b:c$	β	Δc	$\Delta\beta$
				Even acids				
Succinic	2	5.10	8.88	7.61	0.574:1:0.856	133.6		
							2.32	+3.5°
Adipic	4	10.07	5.17	10.03	1.947:1:1.940	137.1		
							2.45	−2.1°
Suberic	6	10.12	5.06	12.58	1.800:1:2.486	135.0		
							2.52	−1.2
Sebacic	8	10.10	5.00	15.10	2.020:1:3.020	133.8		
				Odd acids				
Glutaric	3	10.05	4.87	17.40	2.063:1:3.572	132.6		
							5.03(2×2.51)	−2.2
Pimelic	5	9.84	4.89	22.43	2.012:1:4.586	130.4		
							4.71(2×2.36)	−0.9
Azelaic	7	9.72	4.83	27.14	2.012:1:5.639	129.5		

dimensions of the chains. The direction of the chains is along [001], and the addition of carbon atoms is manifested in the value of c, which increases about 2.5 Å per pair of additional carbons. The angle β appears to decrease by a constant amount of about 2° per additional pair of carbons. Succinic acid (first member of the even series) is an exception in the series. Malonic acid (first member of the odd series) has not been considered here, since it does not have a clear chain structure.

Diffuse scattering of β-succinic and α-adipic acids (Canut and Amorós, 1957). The room-temperature form or β form of succinic acid, $COOH-(CH_2)_2-COOH$, was first studied by Miss Yardley (1924), redetermined by Verwell and MacGillavry (1940), refined by Morrison and Robertson (1949a), and finally by Broadley, Cruick- shank, Morrison, Robertson, and Shearer (1959). β succinic acid cry- stals are monoclinic, space group $P2_1/a$. There are two molecules per unit cell. The dimensions of the cell and the atomic coordinates are given in Table 7. All the carbon atoms of the molecule are coplanar

Table 7　β-succinic acid, $COOH \cdot (CH_2)_2 \cdot COOH$, crystal-structure data and thermal parameters

Space group $P2_1/a$.　Symmetry of molecule: $\begin{cases} 2/m \text{ if isolated} \\ \bar{1} \text{ in crystal} \end{cases}$

Unit cell: $a = 5.126$, 　$b = 8.880$,
$c = 7.619$Å,　$\beta = 133°36'$　$Z = 2$

Atomic coordinates

Atom	x	y	z	Equivalent positions
C_1	0.05352	0.06651	0.08258	$4e$
C_2	0.02642	0.03450	0.26070	$4e$
O_1	−0.12482	−0.07780	0.25386	$4e$
O_2	0.16813	0.14041	0.42508	$4e$
$H_1(C_1)$	−0.12310	0.16104	−0.03006	$4e$
$H_2(C_2)$	0.33125	0.09685	0.18152	$4e$
$H_3(O_2)$	0.15099	0.11577	0.55165	$4e$

Thermal vibrations at room temperature

Atomic tensor components (in 10^{-2} Å²)

	U_{11}	U_{22}	U_{33}	U_{12}	U_{13}	U_{23}
C_1	4.8	2.7	0.5	−0.2	0.2	−0.3
C_2	2.6	3.2	1.5	1.0	−0.3	0.0
O_1	4.9	3.0	0.9	−0.7	−0.1	0.2
O_2	5.7	3.3	0.9	−1.2	0.0	−0.3

and lie in the same plane as the center of symmetry of the molecule. The plane of the carboxyl group contains another center of symmetry, which is situated between the ends of adjacent molecules in the direction of the c axis. Hence the carboxyl groups of adjacent molecules that are joined by hydrogen bonds are coplanar. Figure 38 shows the electron density of β succinic acid projected on (010). The structure is notable for a number of rather short lateral intermolecular distances, resulting in a compact overall crystal structure. For instance, the distance between carbons of adjacent molecules along [100] is 3.58 Å, and 3.34 Å between oxygens of adjacent molecules along the same direction. No H-H distances are reported, the positions of the hydrogen atoms being only assumed.

The rms amplitudes of vibration for the structure as a whole are 0.21, 0.18, and 0.10 Å along a^*, b and c, respectively. The angular vibrations of the succinic acid molecule around its inertia axis are interesting. The angular rms amplitudes about the axes perpendicular to the chain are small, on the order of 0° and 2° respectively. However, the torsional vibration about an axis almost parallel to the chain direction is of about 9°. The rigid-body translation vibrations of the molecules gives a minimum vibration of rms amplitude of about 0.1 Å along the chain direction and of about 0.17 and 0.15 Å at right angles of the chain. The translational vibration along the direction of the hydrogen-bonded molecular chains is therefore much less than in other directions in the crystal. This result is in agreement with the emphasis given by Canut and Amorós (1957) and Amorós and Canut

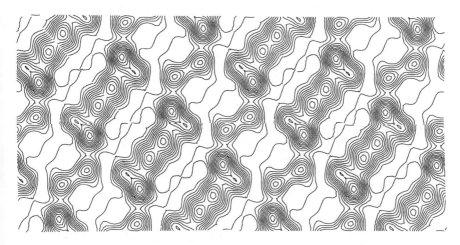

Fig. 38. Electron density of β succinic acid, COOH-$(CH_2)_2$-COOH, projected on (010).

(1958) to the intercolumn vibrations in the interpretation of the x-ray diffuse scattering.

The structure of α adipic acid, stable at room temperature, was studied by MacGillavry (1941), Morrison and Robertson (1949*b*), Hirokawa (1950), and finally by Housty and Hospital (1965). α adipic acid belongs also to the monoclinic space group $P2_1/a$. The dimensions of the unit cell and the atomic coordinates reported by Housty and Hospital are given in Table 8. The carbon atoms of the molecule

Table 8 α-adipic acid, $COOH(CH_2)_4COOH$, crystal-structure data and thermal parameters

Space group $P2_1/c$.   Symmetry of molecule: $\begin{cases} 2/m \text{ if isolated} \\ \overline{1} \text{ in crystal} \end{cases}$

Unit cell: $a = 10.01$, $b = 5.15$,
$c = 10.06$Å, $\beta = 136°45'$ $Z = 2$

Atomic coordinates

Atom	x	y	z	Equivalent positions
C_1	0.0520	0.0392	−0.0252	4e
C_2	0.2056	−0.1624	0.0493	4e
C_3	0.3310	−0.0907	0.0236	4e
O_1	0.2961	0.1013	−0.0707	4e
O_2	0.4746	−0.2450	0.1023	4e
$H_1(C_1)$	0.090	0.210	0.010	4e
$H_2(C_1)$	−0.055	0.080	−0.175	4e
$H_3(C_2)$	0.140	−0.325	−0.030	4e
$H_4(C_2)$	0.300	−0.200	0.195	4e
$H_5(O)$	0.580	−0.150	0.100	4e

Thermal parameters

No data of anisotropic vibrations are available.

are coplanar with a center of symmetry, as in succinic acid. The carboxyl group is inclined about 6° to the plane containing the carbons. The plane of the carboxyl group has another center of symmetry, between the adjacent molecules along [001], and also contains the carboxyl group of the neighboring molecule. The most important bonds are hydrogen bonds, of length 2.64 Å, which connect the carboxyl groups of molecules along c. These bonds have the same length as those of succinic acid. Unfortunately no data on anisotropic vibrations of the atoms are available for this substance. Amorós, Belgrano, and Canut (1957), however, reported an rms amplitude of

0.21 Å perpendicular to the chain direction. Figure 39 shows the projection (010) of the electron density of α adipic acid.

The Laue photographs of β succinic (Fig. 40) and α adipic acid (Fig. 41) show again the two types of diffuse scattering characteristic of molecular cystals. There are diffuse spots, more or less oblong, associated with certain Bragg reflections of high intensity, and there are continuous regions of diffuse scattering, that appear in the Laue photographs as streaks. Those streaks are characteristic of chain molecules (Lonsdale, 1942). When these streaks are plotted in reciprocal space it can be seen that they correspond to the intersection in the Laue photographs of continuous diffuse sheets. The streaks do not obey the extinction condition, otherwise there would show discontinuities when passing through reciprocal-lattice points with $h =$ odd in the $(010)_0^*$ level.

The $(010)_0^*$ and $(010)_1^*$ maps of diffuse scattering of β succinic acid are given in Fig. 42. The continuous sheets are perpendicular to the c (chain) axis and therefore only line sections appear in the maps. The most intense sheets correspond to the reciprocal layers hkl with $l = 3$, 6, 9. The most intense diffuse spot corresponds to 110, the plane that contains the molecule.

Fig. 39.   Electron density of α adipic acid, $COOH\text{-}(CH_2)_4\text{-}COOH$, projected on (010).

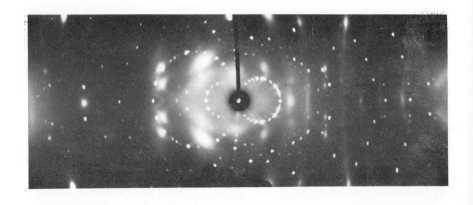

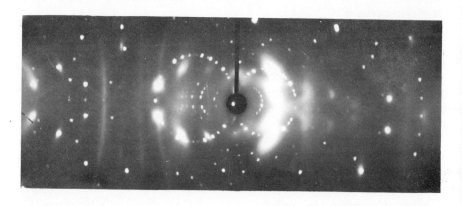

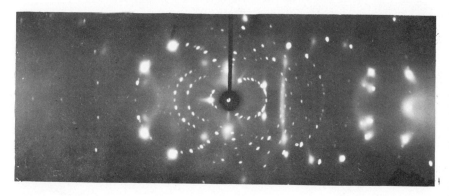

Fig. 40. β succinic acid. Laue photographs obtained at room temperature using filtered Cu x-radiation. Crystal mounted along [010]. The continuous diffuse regions are clearly shown.

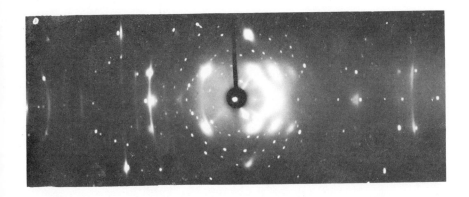

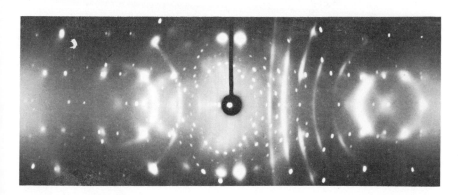

Fig. 41. α adipic acid. Laue photographs obtained at room temperature using filtered Cu x-radiation. Crystal mounted along [010]. The continuous diffuse regions are clearly shown.

259

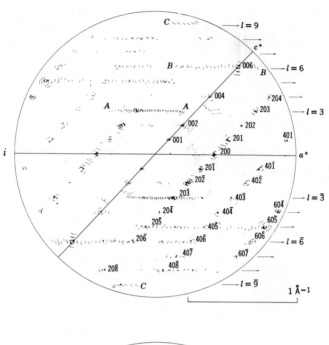

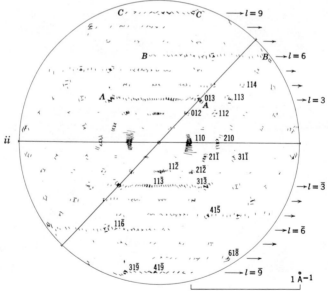

Fig. 42. β succinic acid. Experimental continuous diffuse-scattering maps. (i) $(010)^*_0$; (ii) $(010)^*_1$.

The diffuse scattering maps of α adipic acid are very similar to those just described. In Fig. 43 the maps $(010)_0^*$ and $(010)_1^*$ are plotted. The continuous sheets of α adipic acid are better shown than in β succinic acid because the structure of α adipic acid is more chain-like. The continuous sheets are again perpendicular to the c (chain) axis, but the most intense are, in this case, those corresponding to the layers hkl with $l = 4$, 8, 9, which correspond to almost the same spacings as in the sequence of prominent layers of β succinic acid. Those spacings are directly related to the C-C spacing in the molecular chain. The most intense diffuse spot of α adipic acid is associated with (200), the more densely packed plane of the crystal.

The diffuse sheets are continuous, but their intensity is far from constant. This was shown in the early work of Velasco, Canut, and Amorós (1954) on α adipic acid, in which it was shown that bands of high intensity are found along a pair of symmetry-related directions in the sheets.

Patterns of diffuse scattering very similar to those of α adipic and β succinic acids have been found in the closely related molecular crystals of suberic, α succinic, glutaric, pimelic, and azelaic acids (Amorós and Canut de Amorós, 1965). The systematic study of diffuse scattering from dicarboxylic acids leads to the following general description of the phenomenon:

Even acids. Extense anisotropic diffuse scattering sheets appear perpendicular to [001]. Such sheets of diffuse scattering are always recorded in the photographs in the form of streaks. The first sheet of significant intensity for β succinic acid is at $l = 3$, for α adipic acid at $l = 4$, and for suberic acid at $l = 5$, which corresponds to a spacing in the chain of about 2.5 Å. Further sheets occur for $l = nN$, where $n = 1$, 2, 3, ... and $N = 3$, 4, or 5, depending on the kind of acid. Figure 44 shows a schematic drawing of the phenomenon. Another characteristic of the diffuse-scattering sheets is that their extent is determined by the angle between the vectors of the reciprocal-lattice points through which they pass, and the direction of the chains in the structure. Therefore, although the streaks are in planes of the reciprocal lattice perpendicular to the direction of the chains, the reciprocal-lattice points through which the streaks pass correspond to planes in the crystal that are not necessarily perpendicular but may be at angles as small as 45° to the chains. The sheets of diffuse scattering are continuous and do not obey the extinction conditions $h = 2n + 1$ of the space group to which the crystal belongs. In addition to the streaks, there are small but more intense spots of diffuse scattering associated with reciprocal-lattice points that obey the space-group absences.

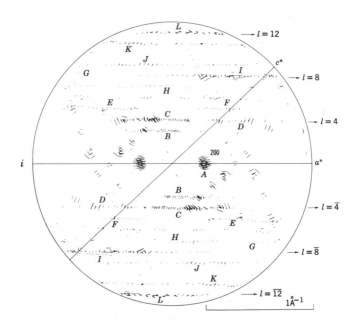

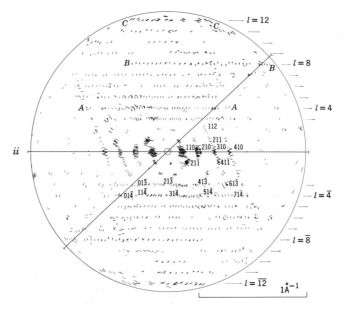

Fig. 43. α adipic acid. Experimental continuous diffuse-scattering maps. (*i*) (010)$_0^*$; (*ii*) (010)$_1^*$.

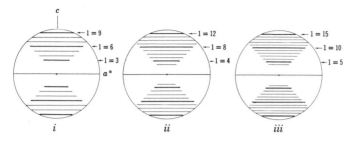

Fig. 44.   Scheme of the intercepts of the continuous diffuse-scattering sheets in the equator $(010)_0^*$ of the even dicarboxylic acids: (i) succinic; (ii) adipic, and (iii) suberic acids.

The most intense diffuse spots are associated with the planes containing the chains of molecules, and that therefore have the largest structure factors of a given crystal.

Odd acids. The strongest diffuse scattering is connected with the reciprocal-lattice point 200, corresponding to the plane containing the layers of chains. The round diffuse spots occur only at the reciprocal-lattice points that are not forbidden by space-group considerations. Thus, at the zero level we find them where $h = 2n$ and $k = 2n$, and at the first level when $h + k = 2n$. The acids of the odd series show again sheets of diffuse scattering perpendicular to the chain direction, but these sheets are less extense and clear than those of the even acids. In the high levels, the streaks become also more blurred in the odd acids than in the even acids. This can be related to the different shape of the molecular chains in both kinds of acids.

DFT of dicarboxylic acids.   The great uniformity observed in the diffuse-scattering pattern of chain-like molecular crystals makes it sufficient to calculate the DFT function for only a couple of examples. Figure 45i shows the $(010)_0^*$ DFT map of β succinic acid. This figure is in good agreement with the experimental map given in Fig. 42i. The different streaks are very well explained in terms of the DFT function. Similar features occur for α adipic acid whose $(010)_0^*$ DFT is shown in Fig. 45ii. The good agreement with the experimental map (Fig. 43i) is evident and is specially good for the regions A, B, C, D, F, H, I, J, K, and L. Despite the good agreement, there are still two important discrepancies in the two cases. First, the sharpness of the diffuse areas is lost in the DFT, and second, in the area centered at a^* there are no zones of continuous diffuse scattering in the experimental map, but they are present in the DFT map. The explanation for both discrepancies is clear if we take into account the anisotropy

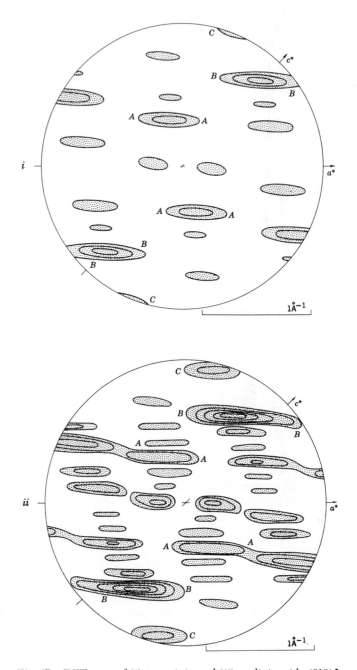

Fig. 45. DFT maps of (*i*) β succinic, and (*ii*) α adipic acids. (010) $^*_0$.

of the bonding forces joining the molecules in the crystal. The molecules are joined by strong hydrogen bonds along the chains (along the c axis of the crystal), but only weak van der Waals forces join the chains (that is, perpendicular to the c axis). The nature of the bonding forces suggests that the vibrations between different chains should be almost out of phase (almost independent motion of one chain with respect to the others), but that there should be strong interaction in the motion of the molecules along the same chain. This fact can be taken into account by introducing along the chain an infinite correlation function, which modulates the DFT and reduces the diffuse scattering to thin sheets perpendicular to the chain axis. Both discrepancies—the widening of the computed contours contrasted with the sharpness of the observed diffuse zones, and the appearance of maxima of diffuse scattering in the calculated maps in regions where such diffuse scattering has not been observed—can also be explained by using the more exact theory of thermal waves that will be discussed in Ch. 5.

Notwithstanding these discrepancies, the DFT function is very useful in interpreting the continuous diffuse scattering of the sheets, specially when considered as a function of the molecular transform of an aliphatic chain (see Ch. 1). We have selected the sheets appearing at $(001)^*_3$ and $(001)^*_4$ of β succinic and α adipic acids, respectively (Figs. 46 and 47). The intensity in such sheets is modulated according to what is expected from our knowledge of the molecular transform of the chain. We see that in both cases (Figs. 46i and 47i) the DFT is not a continuous sheet of uniform intensity, but some bands of intensity can be recognized, namely AA and $A'A'$. These bands form an angle complementary to the angle between the planes of the two molecules in the respective unit cells. In fact, the whole DFT sheet is the result of the sum of the symmetric systems of parallel bands corresponding to each of the molecules in the unit cell. In Figs. 46ii and 47ii the system of bands of a single molecule of β succinic and α adipic acids, respectively, are represented. The whole DFT sheet can be reconstructed just by summing up such figures with their mirror images along a plane containing c^* and a^*. This picture of the DFT sheet is in agreement with the high anisotropy of the diffuse sheets observed in the early description of the continuous diffuse scattering of the two acids (Velasco, Canut, and Amorós, 1954).

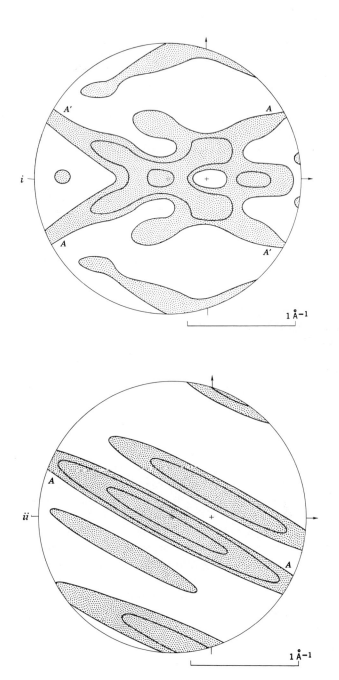

Fig. 46. DFT map of β succinic acid. $(010)_3^*$. (i) Total; (ii) one molecule.

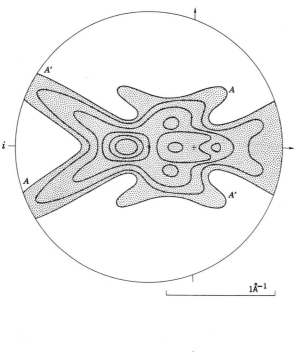

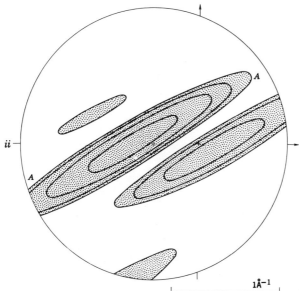

Fig. 47. DFT map of α adipic acid. $(001)_4^*$. (*i*) Total; (*ii*) one molecule.

Crystals of planar molecules joined in layers by hydrogen bonds

Pentaerythritol

The crystal structure of pentaerythritol, $C(CH_2OH)_4$, was determined by Llewellyn, Cox, and Goodwin (1937), and by Nitta and Watanabé (1937). A refinement of the structure by x-ray diffraction was carried out by Shiono, Cruickshank, and Cox (1958). Hvoslef (1958) found the positions of the hydrogen atoms by neutron diffraction. According with such studies the pentaerythritol crystal is tetragonal, space group $I\bar{4}$, with two molecules per unit cell. The cell dimensions and atomic coordinates are given in Table 9. The molecules are warped, and lie in layers at 0 and $\frac{1}{2}$ along the [001] axis.

Table 9   Pentaerythritol, $C(CH_2OH)_4$, crystal-structure
data and thermal parameters

Space group $I\bar{4}$.   Symmetry of molecule: $\begin{cases} \bar{4} \text{ if isolated} \\ \bar{4} \text{ in crystal} \end{cases}$

Unit cell: $a = 6.083, c = 8.726$ Å, $Z = 2$

	Atomic coordinates			
Atom	x	y	z	Equivalent positions
C_1	0	0	0	$2a$
C_2	0.1621	0.1242	0.1059	$8g$
O	0.3172	0.2476	0.0188	$8g$
H_1	0.240	0.013	0.164	$8g$
H_2	0.066	0.252	0.177	$8g$
$H_3(OH)$	0.229	0.108	0.003	$8g$

Thermal parameters

No analysis of the thermal vibrations is available.

Within a layer, the molecules are joined to each other by hydrogen bonds of length 2.69 Å. The length of the C-C bond in the molecule is 1.548 Å, and the length of the C-O bond is 1.425 Å. Within the limits of error, the valence angles are tetrahedral, that is 109°30'. The spacing between molecular layers is greater than 3.5 Å, which explains the good (001) cleavage. There are two hydrogen bonds parallel to (001) connecting hydroxyl group of adjacent molecules. The hydrogen bonds form angles of 137° and 115° with the C-O bond. All other intermolecular distances are greater than 2.7 Å. Each one of the molecules touches four others in its layer through hydrogen bonds. The coordination number of the molecules is 12. The greatest amplitude of vibration of the atoms of the molecules is along the [001] axis, but the vibrations of the central carbon is approximately isotropic. Figure 48 gives the map of the electron density projected on (001).

Diffuse scattering (Alonso, Canut, and Amorós, 1958*b*). The Laue photographs of pentaerythritol at room temperature (Fig. 49) show again the two types of diffuse scattering. There are intense round spots at nonforbidden reciprocal-lattice points, and weak continuous regions of diffuse scattering joining the spots and crossing different levels. The weak regions of diffuse scattering have different lengths; some cross only one level, while others extend through two or three

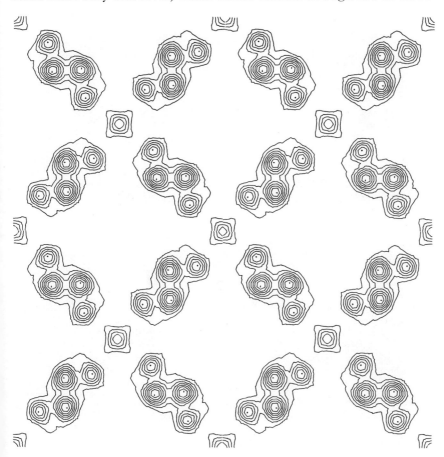

Fig. 48.   Electron density of pentaerythritol, C(CH$_2$OH)$_4$, projected on (001).

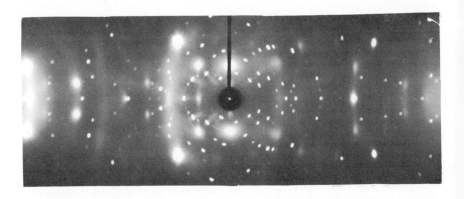

Fig. 49. Pentaerythritol. Laue photographs obtained at room temperature using filtered Cu x-radiation. Crystal mounted along [001]. The continuous diffuse regions are clearly shown.

270

levels. In all the Laue photographs taken with the [001] axis of the crystal vertical only the outer part of the spot at 002 can be seen because of the blind area in recorded reciprocal space due to the normal-incidence technique used in the experiment.

In level $(001)_0^*$, Fig. 50i we can see clearly the presence of a 4-fold axis, and the lack of planes of symmetry at (100), (010), and (110). The most intense diffuse-scattering spot is associated with the reciprocal-lattice point 200. Those associated with 220, 110, 710 follow in intensity. The diffuse-scattering spots clearly extend in the direction of the corresponding planes. There is a weak, but quite extense, diffuse-scattering region near the forbidden reciprocal-lattice points 120, 250, and 340. Such regions are the sections of certain diffuse bands extending normal to the equator.

At level $(001)_1^*$, Fig. 50ii, the 4-fold symmetry is again clear, with the most intense diffuse spots being connected with the reciprocal lattice points 121, 341, 101, and 321, listed in descending order of intensity. There are also extended diffuse-scattering regions through forbidden points that again are due to the intersection at this level of the previously mentioned columns of diffuse scattering.

The characteristic feature of level $(001)_2^*$, Fig. 51i, is the perfectly circular spot of diffuse scattering about the origin of this level. The center of this diffuse spot, of course, also has diffuse scattering that is still more intense but was not recorded on the Laue photographs because it occurs in the blind area due to the normal-incidence technique used in the experiment. This spot is associated with 002, which is the strongest and most characteristic of the structure, and corresponds to the plane that contains the molecules. Very intense diffuse-scattering spots also occur at the reciprocal-lattice points 202, 222, 532, all such spots extending along the direction of the corresponding planes. The continuous region near the forbidden point 122 arises from the intersection of a diffuse band perpendicular to the equator.

In level $(001)_3^*$, Fig. 51ii, the 4-fold symmetry is again obvious. The most intense diffuse-scattering spots are associated with the recip-rocal-lattice points 123, 343, 033, 523, listed in descending order of intensity. Near the point 213 there is a very weak, but very large, area of continuous diffuse scattering.

The most important feature of the continuous diffuse scattering of this crystal is the presence of diffuse bands which, as seen with the Laue photographs, intersect the equator of the reciprocal lattice perpendicularly, and in some cases reach the second or third level. The continuous bands not only pass through nonforbidden reciprocal-

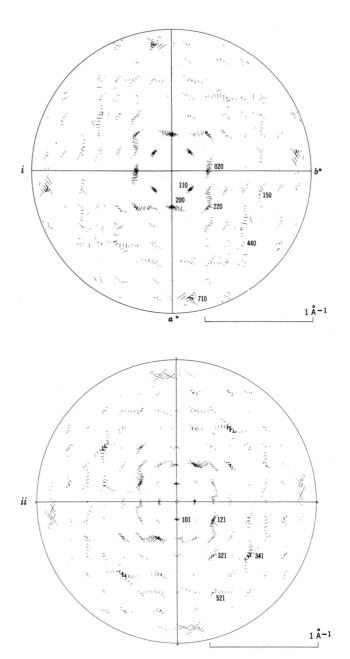

Fig. 50. Pentaerythritol. Experimental continuous diffuse-scattering maps. (*i*) (001)$_0^*$; (*ii*) (001)$_1^*$.

272

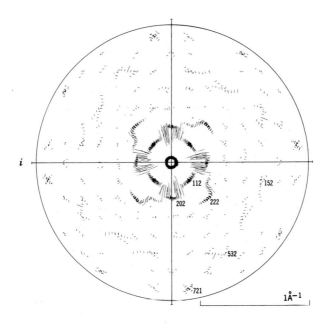

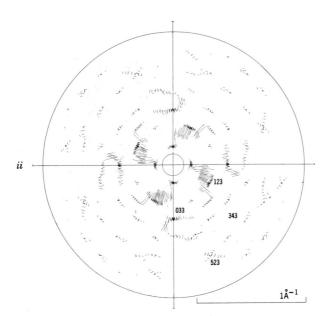

Fig. 51. Pentaerythritol. Experimental continuous diffuse-scattering maps. (i) $(001)_2^*$; (ii) $(001)_3^*$.

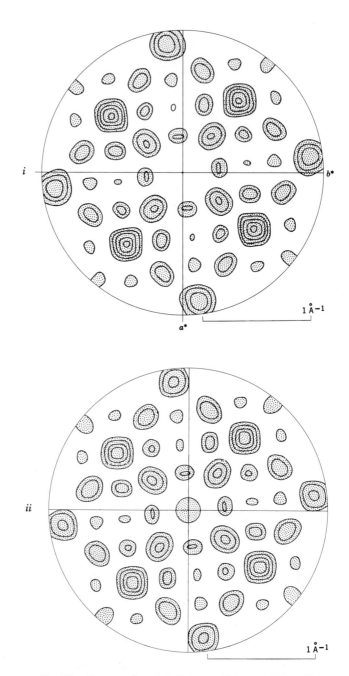

Fig. 52. Pentaerythritol. DFT maps (i) $(001)^{*}_{0}$; (ii) $(001)^{*}_{1}$.

274

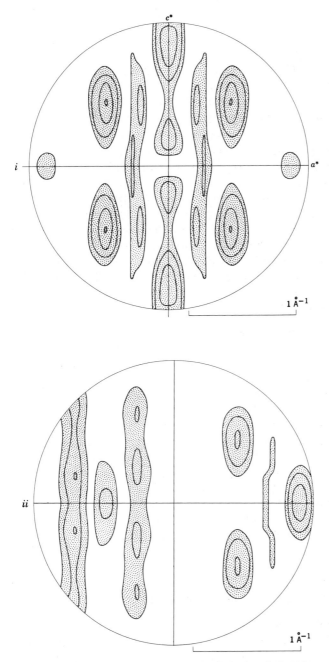

Fig. 53. Pentaerythritol. DFT maps (i) $(010)^*_0$; (ii) $(010)^*_1$.

275

lattice points with intense diffuse scattering spots, but also pass through reciprocal-lattice points forbidden by the space-group symmetry. The diffuse bands have different cross sections, as can be seen in the maps. The most significant diffuse bands are as follows:

One band joins 220 and 222 with very intense diffuse scattering, passing through the forbidden point 221, and extending up to the third level. The same column is joined to another diffuse band that expands through 121 and 123, passing through the forbidden points 120 and 122. Another diffuse band, passing through 340 and 341, crosses the equator through the forbidden point 340, and extends up to the second level of the reciprocal lattice. A diffuse band of high intensity can be seen extending through the reciprocal-lattice points 710 and 712 across the forbidden point 711. Another diffuse band joins the reciprocal-lattice points 200 and 202, passing through the forbidden point 201. Another diffuse band can be observed crossing the reciprocal-lattice points 523 and 52$\bar{3}$, and through the forbidden reciprocal-lattice points 520 and 522. A diffuse band is also observed joining the reciprocal-lattice points 150 and 152 and passing through the forbidden point 151.

DFT of pentaerythritol. In order to test whether the observed diffuse-scattering bands can be taken into account by the DFT function two kinds of maps were calculated. The maps $(001)_0^*$ and $(001)_1^*$, Fig. 52, show that the DFT is built up of discrete patches of intensity, these patches being just the intersections of columns of DFT intensity along [001], shown in the DFT maps $(010)_0^*$ and $(010)_1^*$, Fig. 53. Therefore the DFT function again takes care of the main morphology of the continuous diffuse scattering as observed in pentaerythritol. The reduction in thickness of the DFT columns to give the observed bands can be accounted for by the introduction of suitable correlations. A qualitative explanation of such bands will be given also in Ch. 5 taking into account the point of view of thermal-wave propagation in the crystal. However, it is interesting to note that in this case the DFT function also explains the location of the continuous diffuse scattering.

Crystals with molecules forming a three-dimensional framework

Oxalic acid dihydrate

The crystal structure of oxalic acid dihydrate was first determined by Robertson and Woodward (1937), and refined by Ahmed and Cruickshank (1953), whose lattice parameters and atomic coordinates

Table 10   Oxalic acid dihydrate, COOH · COOHH · 2H$_2$O,
crystal-structure data and thermal parameters

Space group $P2_1/n$ Symmetry of molecule: $\begin{cases} mmm \text{ if isolated} \\ \bar{1} \text{ in crystal} \end{cases}$

Unit cell: $a = 6.119$, $b = 3.604$,
$c = 12.051$ Å, $\beta = 106°16'$ $Z = 2$

Atomic coordinates

Atom	x	y	z	Equivalent positions
C	−0.0455	0.0543	0.0507	4e
O$_1$	0.0854	−0.0523	0.1485	4e
O$_2$	−0.2204	0.2156	0.0364	4e
(H$_2$)O	−0.4527	−0.3972	0.1796	4e
H$_1$	0.010	—	0.210	4e
H$_2$	−0.1255	—	0.3355	4e
H$_3$	0.048	—	0.383	4e

Thermal parameters

No analysis of the thermal vibrations is available.

are given in Table 10. Figure 54 shows the electron density of the crystal projected on (010). The molecule of oxalic acid is planar, and is inclined 29° to the (010) plane, in two symmetric orientations with respect to that plane. The crystal structure contains strong hydrogen

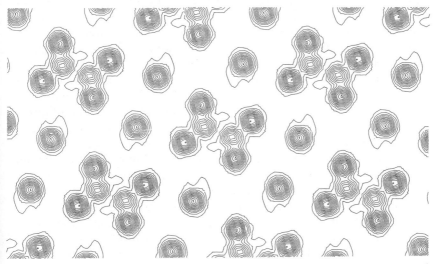

Fig. 54.   Electron density of oxalic acid dihydrate, COOH-COOH, 2H$_2$O, projected on (010).

bonds between the carboxyl-group oxygen atoms and the water molecules, with bond lengths: $H_2O-O_1 = 2.49$, $H_2O-O_2 = 2.88$ and $2.89\,\text{Å}$. The hydrogen bonds form closed quadrilaterals, with sides 2.88 and $2.89\,\text{Å}$, resulting in infinite spiral chains of the form $HOOC-COOH-H_2O-HOOC-COOH-H_2O-\cdots$ along the (102) and (10$\bar{1}$) axes. The system of hydrogen bonds results in a three-dimensional structure, with its peculiar properties.

Diffuse scattering (Canut and Amorós, 1960). The very intense round, diffuse spots and weak, diffuse sheets of the Laue photographs (Fig. 55) are typical of a molecular crystal: The intersections of these sheets in the photographs form streaks inclined to the equator of the photograph, while others appear as diffuse bands almost normal to the level zero.

Figure 56i is a map of the diffuse scattering at level $(010)_0^*$. Strong diffuse spots are connected to reciprocal-lattice points with large $|F_0|$, Fig. 56ii. The three sets of reciprocal-lattice points, $\bar{1}0\bar{7}$, $00\bar{6}$, $10\bar{5}$, $20\bar{4}$, $30\bar{3}$, $40\bar{2}$; $10\bar{1}\bar{1}$, $30\bar{9}$, $50\bar{7}$; $30\bar{1}5$, $40\bar{1}4$, $50\bar{1}3$, $60\bar{1}2$, mark three bands of continuous diffuse scattering placed at constant intervals along the line LL', the long axis of the molecule, and perpendicular to that line. The line LL' is also the direction of the chains of molecules joined by H bonds through the water molecules. The most intense diffuse spot is located at the reciprocal-lattice point 204, and the spot extends in the direction of the plane. Large areas of continuous, weak, diffuse scattering are observed at $(010)_{1/2}^*$, Fig. 57i, and do not appear to be associated with any particular reciprocal-lattice point. This intermediate level is similar to that of naphthalene. In this level there are again three bands normal to the line LL', with the first coinciding with the intercept of the L-axis with this level of reciprocal space. Near the intercept N of the axis perpendicular to the plane of the molecule there also appears a weak line of diffuse scattering. Also, there are rows that are the result of plotting the inclined streaks of the Laue photographs. The most important sheets of continuous diffuse scattering are normal to a single direction, namely [211], which does not coincide with any of the principal axes. This direction corresponds to the molecular chains in the crystal.

The characteristic feature of the level $(010)_1^*$, Fig. 57ii is the presence of continuous rows of diffuse scattering for values of $h = 1, 2, 3, \ldots$ These rows are again the result of plotting in reciprocal space the streaks that, in the Laue photographs, appear inclined to the level zero.

In short, there are three types of diffuse scattering for oxalic acid

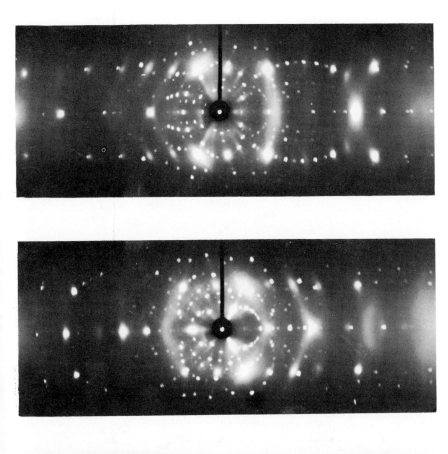

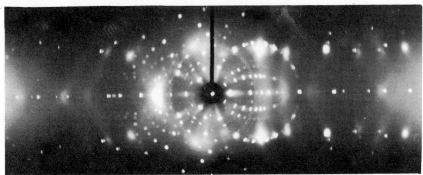

Fig. 55. Oxalic acid dihydrate. Laue photographs obtained at room temperature using filtered Cu x-radiation. Crystal mounted along [010]. The continuous diffuse regions are clearly shown.

279

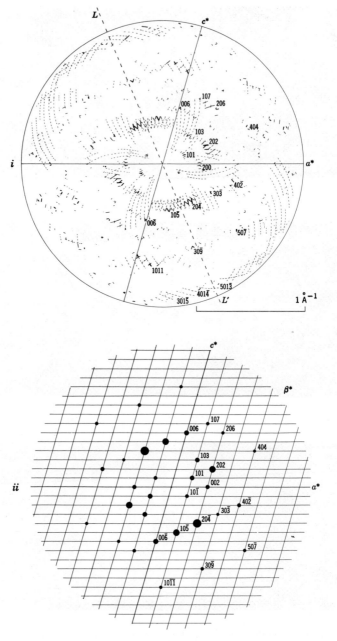

Fig. 56. Oxalic acid dihydrate. (*i*) Continuous diffuse scattering experimental map. (010)$^*_0$; (*ii*) weighted reciprocal lattice.

280

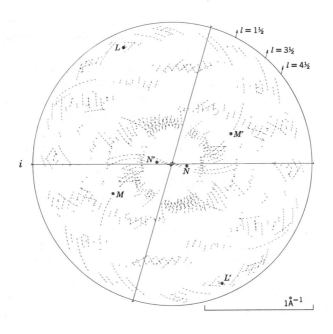

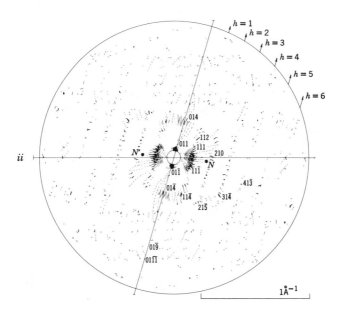

Fig. 57. Oxalic acid dihydrate. Continuous diffuse scattering experimental maps. (i)
$(010)^*_{1/2}$; (ii) $(010)^*_1$.

dihydrate: intense diffuse spots associated to nonforbidden reciprocal-lattice points, regions of continuous diffuse scattering, and
sheets of diffuse scattering that form a grid of diffuse streaks in reciprocal space. The diffuse scattering of oxalic acid dihydrate is intermediate between that of a structure with independent, well-defined
molecules and that of a structure with chains of molecules. The
presence of diffuse sheets normal to a given direction shows the existence of chains in that direction. The sheets are oriented in two
different directions, corresponding to the two main molecular chains
in the structure.

DFT of the oxalic acid dihydrate. The DFT maps of oxalic acid
dihydrate are shown in Fig. 58. The $(010)_0^*$ map adequately accounts
for the continuous diffuse-scattering regions observed, but it does not
account for the sharpening of the streaks. This effect can be easily
explained by introducing correlations along the axes $[10\bar{1}]$ and $[102]$,
which cut the DFT continuous regions in the observed lines as given
in Fig. 58, lower part. In the case of oxalic acid dihydrate, therefore,
the DFT alone does not take into account all the observed facts, but
the calculation shows that the diffuse scattering is observed where the

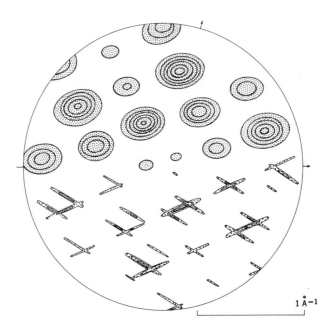

$1\,\overset{\circ}{\text{A}}{}^{-1}$

Fig. 58.   Oxalic acid dihydrate. DFT map $(010)_0^*$. Upper part, without correlations;
lower part, with correlations.

DFT is intense. Therefore the DFT plus correlations allow the calculation of the observed diffuse scattering in cases like oxalic acid dihydrate where the structure is of intermediate type.

Crystals of clathrate compounds

Urea + suberic acid

The crystals of this compound are hexagonal prismatic. The structure of the form stable at room temperature corresponds to the one determined by Smith (1952) for urea-hexadecane, isomorphic with urea-suberic acid. The crystal belongs to space group $P6_12$; the lattice constants and atomic coordinates are given in Table 11.

Table 11   Urea-suberic acid, crystal-structure data and thermal parameters

Space group $P6_122$
Unit cell: $a = 8.230$ Å, $c = 11.005$ Å, $Z = 6$

Atomic coordinates

Atom	x	y	z	Equivalent positions
N	0.4415	0.5225	0.1035	$12c$
O	0.3193	−0.3193	0.0833	$6b$
C	0.4094	−0.4094	0.0833	$6b$

Thermal parameters

No analysis of the thermal vibrations is available.

The urea molecules are joined by hydrogen bonds, and form infinite spiral chains along [0001]. The chains form the walls of a honeycomb structure in which channels the suberic acid molecules are located in statistical positions. The normal hydrogen bonds between carboxyl groups of adjacent suberic acid molecules are retained. Figure 59 represents the electron density projected on (0001). The period of the trapped acid molecule chain is 12.2 Å, while the c dimension of the box (urea molecules) containing it is 11.004 Å, explaining the disorder of the captured molecules. At low temperature, the captured molecules have too little energy to maintain their random orientation (or vibration), so that the structure collapses and the crystal becomes monoclinic (Amorós and Abásolo 1961).

Diffuse scattering. The statistical orientation of the trapped molecules contrasts with the regular hexagonal structure of the container.

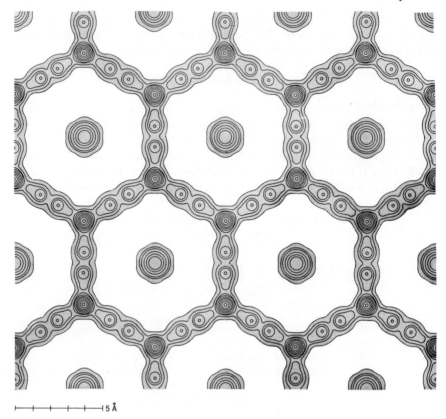

$\vdash\!\!-\!\!+\!\!-\!\!+\!\!-\!\!+\!\!-\!\!+\!\!-\!\!\dashv 5\,\text{Å}$

Fig. 59. Electron density of suberic acid clathrate projected on (0001).

These two different structural units give distinct components of the
diffuse scattering. The Laue photographs of this clathrate compound
(Fig. 60) have therefore an appearance entirely different from that
found in other molecular compounds. There are very clear horizontal
diffuse streaks (intersections of diffuse sheets), whose periodicity
does not correspond to the periodicity along the c-axis of the crystal.
There are also diffuse spots associated with the nonforbidden points
of the reciprocal lattice of the crystal. The two types of diffuse scattering are easily distinguished in the Laue photographs. When the
diffuse scattering spots are plotted in reciprocal space, the maps of
Figs. 61 and 62 are obtained. At levels $(0001)^*_{0,1,2}$ of the reciprocal
lattice of urea, we find mostly intense diffuse spots, associated with
the nonforbidden reciprocal-lattice points. However, the spots are
extended perpendicular to the direction $[10\bar{1}0]$ and the hexagonal

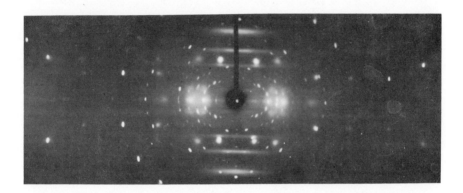

Fig. 60. Urea suberic acid clathrate. Laue photographs at room temperature using filtered Cu x-radiation. Crystal mounted along [0001]. The continuous diffuse streaks are clearly shown.

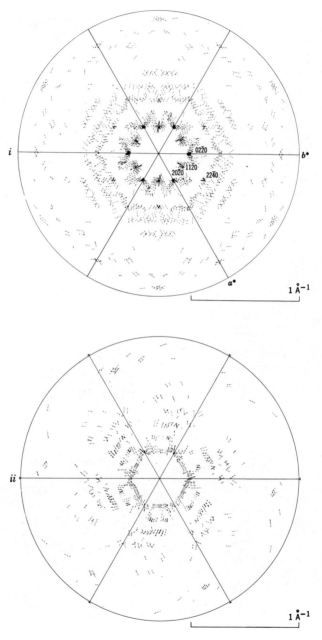

Fig. 61. Urea suberic acid clathrate. Experimental continuous diffuse-scattering maps. (*i*) (0001)$^*_0$; (*ii*) (0001)$^*_1$.

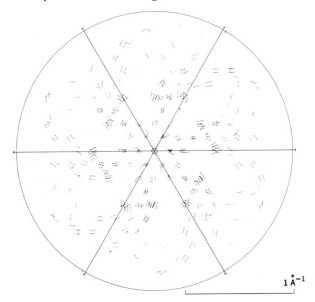

Fig. 62. Urea suberic acid clathrate. Experimental continuous diffuse-scattering maps $(0001)^*_2$.

symmetry is clearly shown in the maps. The continuous sheets appear at levels that correspond to reciprocal spacings of 0.7, 1.2, and 2.5 Å^{-1}. These reciprocal spacings correspond to those of the diffuse sheets observed for suberic acid along the chain direction. Therefore we can associate the streaks observed in this crystal with the presence of chains of suberic acid molecules, parallel to the threefold axis. The chains have high thermal or statistical disorder and they do not produce Bragg reflections, but only diffuse scattering. A similar situation was observed by Smith with urea-hexadecane (1952).

The DFT maps of this compound have not been calculated, but it is obvious from what was said in relation to succinic and adipic acid that the continuous sheets of diffuse scattering perpendicular to the chain of long molecules trapped in the channels of the clathrate compound correspond to the DFT of such molecules plus infinite correlations.

Summary of experimental data

The experimental survey of the diffuse scattering of molecular crystals leads us to the conclusion that what we have called continuous diffuse scattering is closely related to the shape and position

of the molecule in the crystal. Continuous diffuse-scattering regions
are weak and spread over large areas between reciprocal-lattice
points even through lattice points forbidden by the space group. We
shall summarize here the findings for different types of structure.

1. Spherical molecules joined by van der Waals forces. Hexamine
   is an example. In this crystal we have found continuous diffuse
   regions of spheroidal shape. It is evident that the transform of a
   sphere in direct space is another sphere of different radius in
   reciprocal space.
2. Planar molecules joined by van der Waals forces. Examples:
   naphthalene, anthracene, and acridine III. In reciprocal space
   we find intense, but limited, regions of continuous diffuse
   scattering. The anisotropy and finite dimensions of the molecules are reflected in the anisotropic and well defined finite
   regions of continuous diffuse scattering. We also find that the
   two orientations of the molecules in the unit cell are shown
   in the two symmetric orientations of the corresponding diffuse
   regions.
3. Elongated molecules joined in chains by hydrogen bonds. Examples: dicarboxylic acids. In these acids we observe well
   defined continuous diffuse sheets normal to the molecular
   chains. The sheets are practically two-dimensional sheets of
   continuous diffuse scattering. The transform of a cylinder, which
   schematically represents the chain, is a series of planes normal
   to the axis of the cylinder. Therefore, the shape of the regions of
   scattering once again coincides with the transform of the molecule. Since the chain has infinite length, the regions of continuous scattering have practically zero thickness.
4. Molecules joined in layers by hydrogen bonding. Example:
   pentaerythritol. In the case of pentaerythritol, the diffuse
   scattering observed consists of continuous bands normal to the
   plane of the molecules. The transform of a plane in direct space
   are lines perpendicular to it in reciprocal space. The structure
   within the plane is manifested in the spacing of the bands of
   scattering, since their spacing is related to the intramolecular
   interatomic distances.
5. Molecules joined in a three-dimensional framework. Example:
   oxalic acid dihydrate. In oxalic acid, the molecules have two
   symmetric orientations, and form clear spiral chains within
   the structure. The diffuse continuous regions observed are
   sheets normal to the two directions of the chains and with two
   different orientations related to the orientations of the molecules

in the cell, but there also appear wider regions of diffuse scattering, and the whole phenomenon is of an intermediate type.
6. Clathrate compounds. Example: urea suberic acid. In this case
   we have independent diffuse scattering corresponding to each
   of the two constituents of the structure: the molecules forming
   boxes, and the molecules trapped within. Thus the reciprocal
   spacing of the continuous diffuse sheets that correspond to the
   trapped molecules is independent of the reciprocal spacing of
   the cage.

The mutual relation between the shape of the molecule and the
shape of the continuous diffuse-scattering regions is clear. It is evident that we are dealing with a form factor of the molecule. This
molecular-form factor is completely different from the form factor
of the crystal, for the latter is reflected in each and every one of the
reciprocal-lattice points. The molecular form factor is similar to the
form factor of the atom, in the sense that is reflected in a unique form
in the whole reciprocal space.

The relationship between the shape and orientation of the molecules and the regions of continuous diffuse scattering of molecular
crystals is described in a simple way by the DFT function developed
in Ch. 3.

Continuous diffuse scattering as a tool in crystal structure determination

The close relationship existing between continuous diffuse scattering and the shape and orientation of the molecules building up the
crystal enables us to use such information in the early stages of a crystal structure determination of a molecular crystal. This relationship is
further emphasized by the fact that, in the case where more than one
orientation or kind of molecule is present in the crystal, the continuous diffuse scattering is the sum of the incoherent intensities
scattered by each molecule, that is, without the phases of the diffracted amplitudes of different molecules. Therefore continuous
diffuse scattering can be advantageously used in crystal-structure
determination.

One of the earliest uses of the dependence of diffuse scattering
and crystal-structure type of molecular crystals in crystal-structure
determination was given by Lonsdale, Robertson, and Woodward
(1941) in their study of sorbic acid. Lonsdale herself (1942–1943)
was the first to show that certain features of the x-ray diffuse scattering
were due to the shape of the molecules and, therefore, that it was

possible to determine the orientation of the molecule in the unit cell from diffuse-scattering analysis alone. Our systematic work described early in this chapter shows clearly the close relationship existing between shape and orientation of the molecule and the continuous diffuse scattering. The use of diffuse scattering in the early stages of the determination of the crystal structure of molecular crystals was illustrated by Hoppe (1956a) by using what he calls the pseudoacoustic approximation, based on the concept that the Fourier transform of the molecule enters in the diffuse-scattering function. Using this method he was able to determine the orientation of the molecules in the unit cell of anthraquinone (Hoppe, 1956b), cyanid acid trichloride (Hoppe, Lenné, and Morandi, 1957, 1,5,NN^1-dipyrrolidylpentamethin perchlorate (Hoppe and Baumgartner, 1957), phyllochlorine ester (Hoppe, 1957) and other substances.

The main difficulties of the method are the small intensity of the continuous diffuse scattering and the lack of sharpness of the diffuse maxima. To overcome the first difficulty the time of exposure must be increased. The identification of the continuous diffuse scattering is also sometimes disturbed by the superimposed Bragg or Laue spots. Although this problem is never a severe one, a way to eliminate it is by recording the continuous diffuse scattering at intermediate levels of the diffraction space. By doing this, however, another problem arises, namely the overlapping of the diffuse scattering due to symmetry-related molecules. If the overlapping is severe, the identification of the maxima corresponding to the different symmetrically equivalent molecules can be a problem.

In spite of the inherent limitations of the method diffuse scattering, when studied in detail, can give valuable information about the orientation of the molecules in the crystal. A straightforward case, for instance, occurs when the molecules array themselves as chains. In this case the presence of sheets of diffuse scattering indicates the direction of such chains in a very direct way.

Moreover, as the crystallographers who are concerned with the determination of crystal structures are accustomed to use Bragg intensities alone, the identification and plotting of the continuous diffuse scattering may cause another problem. In view of the direct relation between the continuous diffuse scattering and the DFT function, it seems more appropriate to use a method of computing this function directly from Bragg intensities alone. This method is discussed in the following section.

Crystal-structure analysis through the direct DFT method

As the continuous diffuse scattering contains the mean features of the molecular intensity Fourier transform through the DFT function, the possibility of using the information of continuous diffuse scattering in crystal structure determination is an extension of the molecular Fourier transform method used in crystal-structure determination (see, for instance, Lipson and Cochran, 1957, 1966; Buerger, 1960; Taylor and Lipson, 1965). It is only reasonable, then, that the DFT function itself can be used in crystal-structure determination (Amorós and Canut-Amorós, 1967). We have shown that the DFT function can be calculated as the Fourier transform of the difference Patterson (rest-motion), and that the intensity DFT function can be given by (83), Ch. 3. The practical method of calculating the DFT function in this case is in terms of the Fourier summation [(87), Ch. 3] having as coefficients the sampled values of the difference Patterson. With this method the DFT function can be calculated directly from Bragg-intensity data without any knowledge of the crystal structure itself. The main advantage of the method over the molecular-transform method is that it gives the actual orientation of the molecular-transform function, and therefore it is a direct method for crystal-structure determination. In order to show the potentiality of the method we shall select the simple case of molecules built up of benzene rings. The essential features of the DFT of benzene (Fig. 63) is the presence of primary P_1 and secondary maxima S_1, equivalent to those of the molecular transforms, studied in Ch. 1. The location of such maxima depends on the orientation of the molecule with respect to the reciprocal-lattice plane under study. From the location of such maxima in the reciprocal-lattice plane $(100)_0^*$, $(010)_0^*$ or $(001)_0^*$, the orientation of the molecule can be determined. The method is based on the study of the intersections of the P_1 and S_1 columns by a given reciprocal-lattice plane. An elegant method, based on the fact that the intersections of the P_1 and S_1 columns by the reciprocal-lattice plane are always ellipses, has been developed by Mackay (1962) as a tool for the interpretation of the weighted reciprocal lattice via the molecular-transform method. The method, however, is general and can be directly applied to the study of the DFT function of molecules containing benzene rings.

Let us define two reference axes in the benzene molecule: the L-axis, determined by a pair of opposite atoms, and the N-axis perpendicular to the plane of the molecule. The P_1 columns parallel to N are located at the vertices of a regular hexagon rotated $30°$ from the L-

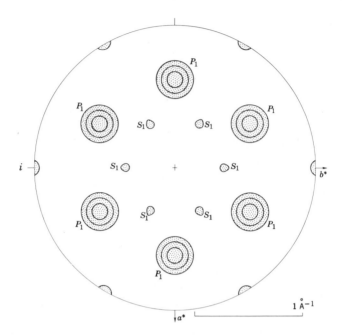

Fig. 63. Principal section of the DFT of benzene.

axis. In general, a given reciprocal-lattice plane forms an angle ϕ with the N-axis of the benzene molecule, and the intercept of the plane of the molecule with such a plane is a line forming an angle ω with the LL-axis. The axes of the six columns P_1 are on the surface of a cylinder perpendicular to the plane of the molecule. Therefore their intercepts by the given reciprocal-lattice plane lie on an ellipse whose small axis will be equal to $0.820\,\text{Å}^{-1}$, the diameter of the cylinder, and whose long axis is equal to $0.820\cos\phi$. Analogously, the intercepts of the S_1 columns by the same plane are an ellipse whose small axis is $0.472\,\text{Å}^{-1}$ and whose long axis $0.472\cos\phi\,\text{Å}^{-1}$. A set of ellipses can be drawn for each case giving values to ϕ (Fig. 64). The drawing on a transparent paper can be superimposed on the map of the DFT function in such a way that the S_1 or P_1 peaks are on a given ellipse. From this setting, the angles ω and ϕ can be directly read as explained in Fig. 65. In order to have the orientation of the benzene ring fully determined it is necessary to obtain the angle ψ between the small axis of the ellipse and a given direction in reciprocal space, for instance $\mathbf{a}^*$ (see Fig. 65). Once the angles ϕ and ω have been determined, the coordinates of the carbon atoms that form the benzene

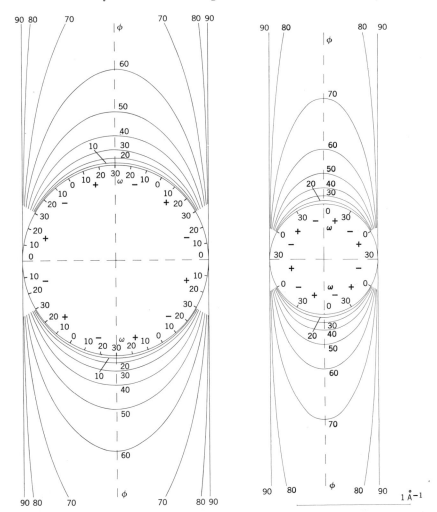

Fig. 64. Set of ellipses corresponding to the P_1 and S_1 peaks of the molecular Fourier transform of the benzene ring. (After Mackay, 1962, modified.)

ring can be calculated by using the set of equations given in Table 12, where D is the distance carbon-carbon in the benzene ring. These coordinates can be further refined through normal crystal-structure procedure.

Let us apply the previous information to the case of anthracene. We shall use the projection (010), where the two molecules project identically, and the crystal can be described in terms of a lattice

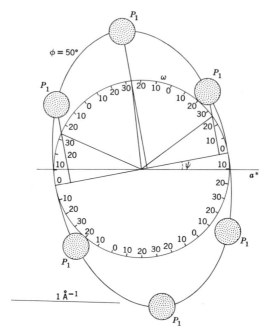

Fig. 65. Graphical determination of the angles ω and ϕ. (After Mackay, 1962, modified.)

whose cell contains one molecule. From the intensity data reported by Mason (1964) at 95° and 295°K, the two dimensional $\Delta P_{95°,295°}(\mathbf{r})$ was calculated by using

$$\Delta P_{95°,295°}(x0z) = A^* \sum_h \sum_l [I_{95°}(h01) - I_{295°}(h01)] \cos 2\pi(hx+lz), \quad (7)$$

where A^* is the area of the reciprocal mesh of the $(h0l)$ reciprocal-lattice plane, and $I_{95°}(h0l)$, $I_{295°}(h0l)$ are the Bragg intensities of the reflections $h0l$ at 95°K and 295°K respectively. The sampling lattice was the same as described in Ch. 3. The sampled values of this tem-

Table 12   Coordinates of the vertices of the regular hexagon

	x	y	z
A	$D \sin \omega$	$D \cos \omega \cos \psi$	$\pm D \cos \omega \sin \psi$
B	$D \cos (30°-\omega)$	$D \sin (30°-\omega) \cos \psi$	$\pm D \sin (30-\omega) \sin \psi$
C	$D \cos (30°+\omega)$	$-D \sin (30°+\omega) \cos \psi$	$\pm D \sin (30+\omega) \sin \psi$

perature difference Patterson, given in Fig. 66i, were used as coefficients in the series

$$I_{DFT}(h'0l') = A' \sum_{h'} \sum_{k'} \Delta P_{95°,295°}(x0z) \cos 2\pi(h'X^* + l'Z^*), \qquad (8)$$

where A' is the area of the sampling mesh in physical space, $h'0l'$ are the indices of the sampled points [see (77), Ch. 2], and X^*, Z^* are the fractional coordinates of the points in a unit cell reciprocal to that of the sampling lattice. The calculation was carried out only up to $X^* = Z^* = 0.25$ at fractional intervals of $\Delta X^* = \Delta Z^* = 0.01$. The area calculated covers practically the limiting sphere of reflection for $CuK\alpha$ x-radiation. The resulting DFT function is given in Figs. 66ii and 67i. The Eller photosummator (von Eller, 1951) has been used to obtain Fig. 66ii.

A similar DFT function can be calculated from the intensities at room temperature and those corrected by the over-all temperature factor, as outlined in Ch. 3. In this case the $\Delta P_{0°,295°}(x0z)$ was calculated by using

$$\Delta P_{0°,295°}(x0z) = A^* \sum_{h} \sum_{l} [I_0(h0l)] - I_{295°}(h0l)] \cos 2\pi(hx + lz), \qquad (9)$$

and, using the sampled values of this function in a similar way,

$$I_{DFT}(h'0l') = A' \sum_{h'} \sum_{l'} \Delta P_{0°,295°}(x0z) \cos 2\pi(h'X' + l'Z'). \qquad (10)$$

The resulting DFT function is given in Fig. 67ii. The two DFT functions are quite similar.

The maxima of the DFT function can be now interpreted directly from our knowledge of the Fourier transform of a benzene ring. The six S_1 maxima are readily recognizable, but only two P_1 maxima are shown inside the limiting sphere. The S_1 maxima allow the determination of the apparent obliquity ϕ and the angle ψ between the axis of tilt and a principal direction in reciprocal space. We have selected ψ as the angle with $\mathbf{a}^*$. The positions of the maxima S_1 also allow us to determine the angle ω between the axis of tilt and a symmetry axis of the benzene ring. The determined values are $\phi = 62°$, $\omega = -8°$, $\psi = -82°$. From these values the coordinates of the vertices of the regular benzene ring were determined. Figure 68 shows the atomic positions of the central benzene ring deduced from the DFT function by using the equations of Table 12. The figure also shows the corresponding atomic positions of the known structure. It is obvious that the whole crystal structure could be refined directly from the set

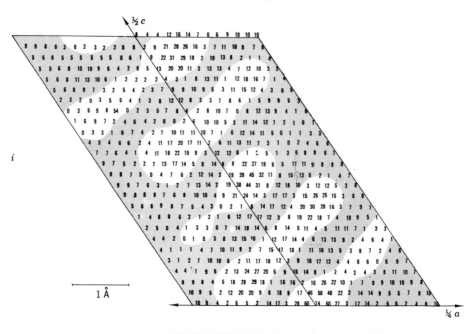

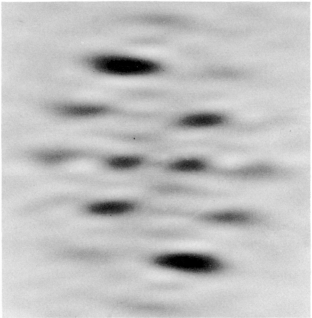

Fig. 66. (*i*) Sampled values of $\Delta P_{90°, 293°}(h0l)$ of anthracene. (*ii*) DFT function obtained with the Eller photosummator. (Courtesy of Jarrel-Ash Co.)

296

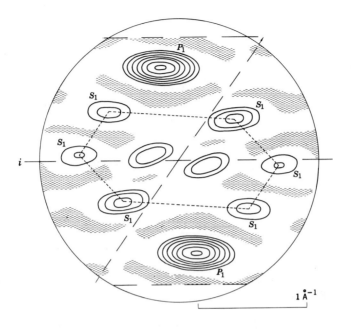

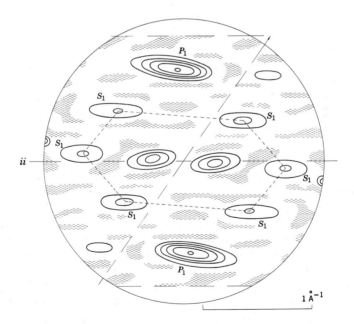

Fig. 67. Anthracene. $(010)_0^*$. DFT maps calculated from $\Delta P_{0°,293°}$ and $\Delta P_{90°,293°}$ $(h0l)$.

297

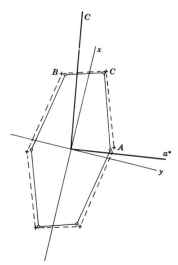

Fig. 68. Atomic coordinates of the basic benzene ring of anthracene deduced from DFT, compared with that reported by Mason (1964).

of the coordinates deduced from the analysis of the DFT function alone.

Another example of the usefulness of the DFT computed in a direct way is given by anthraquinone, whose structure was determined by Hoppe (1956b) using the information derived from continuous diffuse scattering. The crystals of anthraquinone are pseudo-orthorhombic, but the space group is monoclinic $P2_1/a$, with two centrosymmetrical molecules per unit cell. The molecules are almost parallel to (010), and this projection has been selected here in order to show the power of the direct DFT method.

The $\Delta P_{0°,295°}(\mathbf{r})$ was calculated by using the room-temperature intensities $I(h0l)$ as given by Lonsdale, Milledge, and El Sayed (1966) and $I_0(h0l)$ obtained by correcting those intensities by a B temperature coefficient equal to 4 Å². The values $\Delta X = 0.01$ and $\Delta Z = 0.02$ define a sampling lattice of $a' = 0.16$ Å, $c' = 0.16$ Å, $\beta = 102.5°$ whose reciprocal lattice is given by $a'^* = 6.47$ Å⁻¹, $c'^* = 6.49$ Å⁻¹, $\beta = 77.5°$. As in the previous case, the sampled values of the difference Patterson, Fig. 69i, were used as coefficients in the cosine Fourier series (10). The calculation was carried out in the same way as in the case of anthracene. Figure 69ii gives the direct DFT function, which shows clearly all the S_1 and P_1 peaks. From the positions of such peaks, the orientation of the benzene ring can be easily deduced using the procedure already outlined.

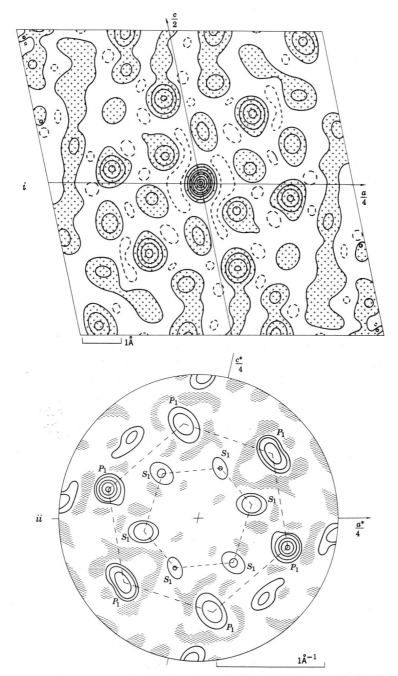

Fig. 69. Anthraquinone. $(010)_0^*$. (i) $\Delta P_{0°,293°}$ $(h0l)$; (ii) DFT map calculated from $\Delta P_{0°,293°}(h0l)$.

5

Diffuse scattering by thermal waves

In the preceding chapter we have pointed out the fact that in molecular crystals there are two types of diffuse scattering: the first, which is weak, continuous, and may spread even through the forbidden points of the reciprocal lattice; and the second, which is strong and is associated with the nonforbidden points. The DFT gives us a simple way of computing the continuous part of the diffuse scattering. That function, however, cannot be used in computing the part of the scattering associated with the reciprocal-lattice points. The Born-Laval theory does allow such a computation, and it is based on the consideration that the thermal vibration of the atoms in a crystal is resolved into thermal waves which are propagated through the crystal, and these waves selectively reflect x-rays. The theory that describes the thermal-vibration waves was developed about 50 years ago by Born and von Karman (1912) for the case of a one-dimensional atomic chain, and the same authors extended the theory to the three-dimensional case. They considered nearest and next-nearest neighbor interactions. The original ideas were contained in the book of Max Born, "Dynamik der Kristallgitter" (1915). The theory has been the basis for the studies of lattice dynamics to date. However, a new development was given by Begbie and Born (1947) by introducing the notion that the vibrational properties of a crystal depend, in particular, on the second derivatives of the potential energy between the atomic nuclei, whose positions are assumed to be any arbitrary function of their displacements. The current reference book in the field is Born and Huang's (1956). A good reference is also to be found in the work of Maradudin, Montroll, and Weiss

300

(1963), that expanded the harmonic approximation of the theory of crystal structure to the effect of defects and disorder on vibrations of crystal structures. In the following, as an introduction to the effect on the x-ray diffraction by elastic waves in crystals, we shall explain briefly the theory of crystal dynamics as developed from the original ideas of Born.

The potential energy of the thermally agitated crystal

Following Born, we shall assume the existence of a conservative field inside the crystal. This is equivalent to assuming that the force applied to each atom makes the work null at the end of a cycle, that is, during the displacement from which the atom returns to its equilibrium position in relation to all the other atoms of the crystal. We can derive such a field from a potential.

The potential energy of an atom lj in the force field created by the atom $l'j'$ (Begbie and Born, 1947) is represented by

$$\phi\left(\begin{matrix} l-l' \\ jj' \end{matrix}\right).$$

Similarly

$$\phi\left(\begin{matrix} l'-l \\ j'j \end{matrix}\right)$$

represents the potential energy of the atom $l'j'$ in the field created by the atom lj. These two energies are equal and negatives

$$\phi\left(\begin{matrix} l-l' \\ jj' \end{matrix}\right) = \phi\left(\begin{matrix} l'-l \\ j'j \end{matrix}\right). \tag{1}$$

This energy obviously depends on the nature of the two atoms involved, and is a function of the interatomic distance of the two atoms concerned. It does not depend, therefore, on the actual position of the respective atoms in the crystal. The absolute distance between the two atoms lj and $l'j'$ is given by

$$R = |\mathbf{r}_l - \mathbf{r}_{l'} + \mathbf{r}_j - \mathbf{r}_{j'}|. \tag{2}$$

The atom lj in the field produced, not only by atom $l'j'$, but by all other atoms in the crystal has a potential energy given by

$$\phi\left(\begin{matrix} l \\ j \end{matrix}\right) = \sum_{l'j'}{}' \, \phi\left(\begin{matrix} l-l' \\ jj' \end{matrix}\right) \tag{3}$$

where the symbol (') in the summation indicates that the term for which $l' = l$ and $j' = j$ [i.e., $\phi\left(\begin{smallmatrix} l-l \\ jj \end{smallmatrix}\right)$] should be omitted. When the interatomic potentials $\phi\left(\begin{smallmatrix} l-l' \\ jj \end{smallmatrix}\right)$ are classified and ordered according to increasing R, (3) forms a rapidly convergent series. The summation over j extends over all J atoms of the cell. Since, in theory, the summation over l extends to the n cells of the given crystal, it is a triple summation over l, m, n ($lmn = -2, -1, 0, 1, 2, \ldots$). In fact, only a few terms of (3) are needed, the remaining terms being negligible.

The potential energy of the whole crystal is given by

$$\phi_0 = \tfrac{1}{2} \sum_{lj} \phi'\binom{l}{j},\tag{4}$$

where the summation over j is extended up to J and the summation over l to all n cells.

We can also represent (4) by

$$\phi_0 = \tfrac{1}{2} \sum_{lj} \sum_{l'j'} \phi\binom{l-l'}{jj'}.\tag{5}$$

The mutual potential energy between the two atoms lj and $l'j'$ appears twice in the summation, and therefore the total result must be divided by 2.

The potential energy of the crystal, as given by (5), is the sum of pairwise interactions between all the atoms in the crystal, each pair of atoms interacting through a potential function that depends on the magnitude of the separation of the atoms involved and on their kind. In the preceding we have considered a perfect periodic crystal. Perfect periodicity, as is assumed in the lattice theory of the crystal, implies that the atoms should be motionless. However, atoms vibrate in a crystal at all temperatures, even at absolute zero, if it could be attained. That vibration is peculiar in that it takes place without the atoms receiving any outside impulse, and the amplitude of vibration increases with temperature. We can understand these vibrations qualitatively by recalling the potential-energy curve of two atoms (Fig. 1). We merely assume that the atoms are equal and that each two exert mutual forces on each other, independent of the presence of other atoms, and that at great distances the attracting forces are dominant, but at very small distances, smaller than the equilibrium distance, the repeling forces are dominant. In the absence of kinetic energy the two atoms form a molecule, their centers being at a distance r_e, for which the ensemble has the minimum potential energy

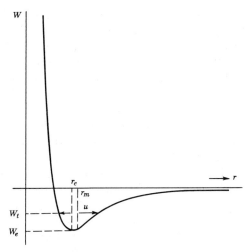

Fig. 1. Potential energy of two atoms as a function of the interatomic distance r. W_e = potential energy at the equilibrium position; W_T = energy at the temperature T; r_e = equilibrium distance; r_m = mean position at the temperature T; u = vibration amplitude at the temperature T.

W_e. If they possess relative kinetic energy less than W_e they execute vibrations about a given mean position, the amplitude being represented by u. The potential-energy curve, in general, is not a parabola, and therefore these vibrations are neither isochronous nor simply harmonic. For simplicity, however, we can assume that, at a given temperature, the atomic vibrations are harmonic. Due to the presence of such vibrations the positions of the atoms as they are described in studies of crystal structure are only mean positions, not instantaneous positions. At any given instant the crystal ceases to be a strictly periodic medium; there appears a disorder given by the difference between instantaneous positions and mean positions, the disorder increasing with temperature. The position of the atom j in the cell l, at a given moment during the thermal fluctuation, is given by

$$\mathbf{r}\binom{l}{j} = \bar{\mathbf{r}}\binom{l}{j} + \mathbf{u}\binom{l}{j}, \tag{6}$$

where $\mathbf{u}\binom{l}{j}$ is the displacement vector, a vector from the mean position $\bar{\mathbf{r}}\binom{l}{j}$ of the atom jl to its instantaneous position at time t. Vectors $\mathbf{r}\binom{l}{j}$ are, in general, functions of time, as well as of $\mathbf{u}$. Due to the cohesive field of the crystal such displacements are equivalent to vibrations. Thermal vibrations alter the periodicity of the crystalline medium only very slightly, and, although the forces of interaction which they develop are not perfectly linear functions of the relative displacements, they cannot differ very greatly from the linear case. If, in addition to varying in intensity only with distance, the forces act along the straight line joining the centers of the atoms, they are central forces. Born adopted the concept of central forces in his study of the dynamics of crystal structures. Although the central-force model is useful in the first approximation, it does not describe a true structure. The electrons contribute to the forces of interaction, and only a spherically symmetrical electron-density distribution, as in the case of ionic crystals, can produce purely central forces. Therefore the vibrations in real crystals can be of a very complex nature, although always with a very small amplitude. In most crystals, and at moderate temperatures (near room temperature), the amplitude of the vibrations is of the order of 0.2 Å, that is, a small fraction of the distance between neighbouring atoms whose separation is of the order of 1.5 to 2Å. Even though the electron density of the atom fluctuates during the vibration of the atom in a manner not necessarily in phase with the motion of the atomic nucleus, it is assumed that the vibrations of atoms in crystal propagate from atom to atom, but not inside the atom. This is to say that the atoms behave as rigid bodies. This approximation is known as the adiabatic approximation.

The potential energy of the thermally agitated crystal is also a function of the interatomic potentials and, therefore, a function of the relative positions of the atoms that form the crystal. We can calculate the potential energy of the thermally agitated crystal by assuming that there is a function $\Phi(\mathbf{u}_{jl})$ which expresses the potential energy of the whole crystal in terms of the instantaneous positions of all the atoms, that is, in terms of their instantaneous displacements. We may expand ϕ as a Taylor's series in powers of the orthogonal components $u_\alpha\binom{l}{j}$ of $\mathbf{u}\binom{l}{j}$ around this point:

$$\phi = \phi_0 + \sum_{lj\alpha} \phi_\alpha\binom{l}{j} u_\alpha\binom{l}{j} + \frac{1}{2} \sum_{\substack{ll',jj' \\ \alpha\beta}} \phi_{\alpha\beta}\binom{l-l'}{jj'} u_\alpha\binom{l}{j} u_\beta\binom{l'}{j'}$$

$$+ \frac{1}{3!} \sum_{\substack{ll'l'',jj'j'' \\ \alpha\beta\gamma}} \phi_{\alpha\beta\gamma}\binom{l-l'}{jj'} u_\alpha\binom{l}{j} u_\beta\binom{l'}{j'} u_\gamma\binom{l''}{j''} + \cdots. \tag{7}$$

Here each of the subscripts α, β, γ take three values corresponding to orthogonal x, y, and z components. In (7), ϕ_0 is the potential energy of the crystal structure with the atoms in their equilibrium position, as given by (5).

The terms

$$\phi_\alpha\binom{l}{j} = \left[\frac{\partial\phi}{\partial u_\alpha(\substack{l\\j})}\right]_0 \tag{8}$$

correspond to the component along the direction α of the force that acts on the atom lj in its equilibrium position. In a stable crystal the sum of these forces must be zero. The third summands of (7) are

$$\phi_{\alpha\beta}\binom{l-l'}{jj'} = \left[\frac{\partial^2\phi}{\partial u_\alpha(\substack{l\\j})\partial u_\beta(\substack{l'\\j'})}\right]_0, \tag{9}$$

where the subscript 0 indicates that the derivatives are calculated in the equilibrium configuration at absolute zero and in the absence of zero point energy. The coefficients $\phi_{\alpha\beta}(\substack{l-l'\\jj'})$ are the components in the direction α of the force acting on the atom lj when the atom $l'j'$ is displaced a unit distance in the β direction.

For a crystal of N atoms, there are $9N^2$ coefficients. However, the actual number is much smaller, (1) because of the symmetry properties of the coefficients (due to the relation between j, l and j', l' with α and β), (2) because of the symmetry of the crystal, and (3) because of the periodicity of the crystal.

In the harmonic approximation no terms higher than the second order are considered. As we have seen that the vibrations of the atoms in the crystal are very small in relation to the interatomic distances, the harmonic approximation is currently used. Further terms can be taken indirectly when the coefficients (9) are calculated at the mean positions of the atoms in the crystal structure at the temperature T. This is the pseudoharmonic approximation (Leibfried and Ludwig, 1961).

In short, the potential energy of a thermally agitated crystal can be given as the sum of two contributions

$$\phi = \phi_0 + \phi_T, \tag{10}$$

the potential energy of the crystal structure at rest, and the potential energy of the thermal agitation. ϕ_0 is always negative; contrarywise ϕ_T is always positive. If the temperature is raised and the crystal is kept at constant volume, the potential energy of the crystal ϕ is increased only by the increase of the energy ϕ_T of the thermal agitation. If the crystal is kept at constant pressure there is thermal expansion. In this case, work has been done against the cohesive forces and ϕ_0 increases accordingly. The potential energy of the crystal ϕ increases then in a 2-fold way due to the increase in ϕ_0 and the presence of ϕ_T. However, ϕ_T is always small compared with ϕ, even at the melting point.

The equations of motion

The atoms of a crystal have a great deal of rigidity and are in contact with each other, so that any one atom cannot be displaced without displacing at least its immediate neighbors. The crystal may then be described as a mechanical system of JN particles, where J is the number of atoms per unit cell and N the number of unit cells contained in the whole crystal. Accordingly, the vibrations of the different atoms are coherent, and can be described as forming trains of elastic waves. For simplicity, we shall decompose thermal vibrations into trains of plane waves, where $\mathbf{g}$ is the wave vector of modulus $1/\Lambda$, perpendicular to the plane of the thermal-vibration waves, and Λ the wavelength. To resolve the vibrations of the crystal structure into waves we must first obtain the equations of motion of the atoms in the crystal. Let us impose the condition that each of the three displacement-vector components $u_\alpha\binom{l}{j}$ is a linear combination of the three vector components of the $u_\beta\binom{l'}{j'}$ of all other atoms in the crystal. We have

$$F_\alpha\binom{l}{j} = \sum_{l'j'\beta} \phi_{\alpha\beta}\binom{l-l'}{jj'} u_\beta\binom{l'}{j'}, \tag{11}$$

where $F_\alpha\binom{l}{j}$ is the α component of force acting on the lj atom. Newton's second law for the motion of the atoms can now be written as

$$F_\alpha\binom{l}{j} = m_j \frac{\partial^2 u_\alpha\binom{l}{j}}{\partial t^2} = -\sum_{l'j'\beta} \phi_{\alpha\beta}\binom{l-l'}{jj'} u_\beta\binom{l'}{j'}, \tag{12}$$

where m_j is the mass of atom j, and t is the time. The equations of motion (12) form an infinite set of simultaneous linear differential equations. The solution of these equations is simplified if one takes into account the periodicity of the crystal.

With the assumption that the displacements can be represented as a superposition of waves, one can try to satisfy (12) by assuming that the solution is an elastic wave in which the displacements are given by

$$u_\alpha\binom{l}{j} = \frac{1}{\sqrt{m_j}} U_\alpha\binom{\mathbf{g}}{j} \cdot \exp\left[2\pi i \mathbf{r}\binom{l}{j} . \mathbf{g}\right] \cdot \exp\left[-i\omega(\mathbf{g})t\right], \tag{13}$$

where $U_\alpha\binom{\mathbf{g}}{j}$ does not depend on l, and both $U_\alpha\binom{\mathbf{g}}{j}$ and $\omega(\mathbf{g})$, the circular frequency (2π times the frequency ν), are functions of the wave vector g; the mass has been eliminated as a factor in the equations of motion. It is seen that (13) is a set of functions of the time t describing $u\begin{pmatrix} l \\ j \end{pmatrix}$ for each value of l. Substitution of this expression in (12) yields

$$\omega^2(\mathbf{g})\, U_\alpha\begin{pmatrix} \mathbf{g} \\ j \end{pmatrix} = \sum_{j'\beta} D_{\alpha\beta}\begin{pmatrix} \mathbf{g} \\ jj' \end{pmatrix} U_\beta\begin{pmatrix} \mathbf{g} \\ j' \end{pmatrix}, \tag{14}$$

where

$$D_{\alpha\beta}\begin{pmatrix} \mathbf{g} \\ jj' \end{pmatrix} = \frac{1}{\sqrt{m_j m_{j'}}} \sum_{l} \phi_{\alpha\beta}\begin{pmatrix} l-l' \\ jj' \end{pmatrix} \exp\left[-2\pi i \mathbf{g} \cdot \mathbf{r}(l)\right]. \tag{15}$$

The solution can be obtained by summing the right-hand side over all allowed values of the wave vector g. In (15), $\mathbf{r}\begin{pmatrix} l \\ j \end{pmatrix}$ of (13) has been replaced by $\mathbf{r}(l)$, since this merely redefines the phase of $U_\alpha\begin{pmatrix} \mathbf{g} \\ j \end{pmatrix}$.

Equation (14) represents $3J$ simultaneous equations for the $3J$ displacements of the J atoms in the unit cell. Thus the problem of solving the $3JN$ infinite set of equations of motion (12) has been reduced to the problem of solving $3J$ linear homogeneous equations (14) in the $3J$ unknown $U_\alpha\begin{pmatrix} \mathbf{g} \\ j \end{pmatrix}$. This simplification follows from the periodic nature of the crystal, and to calculate its dynamics we only need information about the structure of a single unit-cell content.

We know that (14) has a nonvanishing solution only if the determinant of the coefficients vanishes. This is an equation of $3J$th degree determining ω^2, in terms of g. It is a secular equation of finite order and, if the $D_{\alpha\beta}(\mathbf{g})$ are known, it can be solved exactly (Slater, 1958).

The quantities (15) are called the elements of the *Born dynamical matrix*. In matrix notation (14) can be written as

$$\omega^2 \mathbf{dU} = \mathbf{DU}, \tag{16}$$

where d is a diagonal matrix, U(g) a column matrix, and D(g) a square matrix of the order $3n \times 3n$. The nonvanishing solution of (16) is imposed by

$$\det(\mathbf{D} - \mathbf{d}\,\omega^2) = 0. \tag{17}$$

The Born dynamic matrix can be represented in reciprocal space by means of a Fourier transform, and their elements play the role of the Fourier transforms of the force tensor represented by $\phi_{\alpha\beta}\begin{pmatrix} l \\ jj' \end{pmatrix}$.

The $3J$ solutions for each value of $\mathbf{g}$ are denoted by $\omega_\gamma^2(\mathbf{g})$, where $\gamma = 1, 2, \ldots, 3J$. The matrix is obtained from the coefficients $D_{\alpha\beta}\begin{pmatrix} \mathbf{g} \\ jj' \end{pmatrix}$ by pairing the indices (α, j) and (β, j'). Three of the $3J$ solutions for each value of $\mathbf{g}$ go to zero as $\mathbf{g}$ goes to zero, implying the existence of vibrations whose frequencies, in the limit of large wavelengths, cannot be distinguished from those of sound waves that can be induced mechanically in the crystal. Those frequencies form what is called the *acoustical branch* of the vibrational spectrum. The remaining $3J-3$ are called *optical modes*, and do not go to zero with the wave vector. The $3J-3$ optical-branch frequencies corresponding to $g = 0$ are very important and constitute the fundamental modes of vibration, whose properties can be enumerated from a consideration of only the unit cell instead of the entire crystal. They correspond to modes of vibration in which equivalent atoms move identically in phase, and can be studied by infrared absorption and the Raman scattering.

Suppose we know the value of a particular frequency $\omega_\gamma(\mathbf{g})$, and that we substitute this value into (14). One obtains a set of values $U_{\alpha\gamma}\begin{pmatrix} \mathbf{g} \\ j \end{pmatrix}$, the elements of a column matrix $\mathbf{U}_\gamma(\mathbf{g})$. Those values specify in which way the different atoms move in this mode of vibration. The wave amplitude introduced by (13) becomes

$$U_\alpha\begin{pmatrix} \mathbf{g} \\ j \end{pmatrix} = \sum_\gamma U_{\alpha\gamma}\begin{pmatrix} \mathbf{g} \\ j \end{pmatrix}. \tag{18}$$

Cochran (1963) introduced $\hat{\mathbf{U}}_\gamma\begin{pmatrix} \mathbf{g} \\ j \end{pmatrix}$ as normalized wave amplitudes (polarization vectors) in terms of

$$\sum_j m_j \left| \hat{\mathbf{U}}_\gamma\begin{pmatrix} \mathbf{g} \\ j \end{pmatrix} \right|^2 = \sum_{j=1}^J m_j = m_c, \tag{19}$$

where m_c is the mass of the unit-cell content. In order to fix the phases of the $\hat{\mathbf{U}}_{\alpha\gamma}\begin{pmatrix} \mathbf{g} \\ j \end{pmatrix}$ one can require that, for a given value of $\mathbf{g}$, one of the $\hat{\mathbf{U}}_{\alpha\gamma}\begin{pmatrix} \mathbf{g} \\ j \end{pmatrix}$ be entirely real. Now we can introduce a normal-coordinate mode of vibration $A_\gamma(\mathbf{g})$ that characterizes the actual phase and extent of excitation of the mode. We have

$$U_{\alpha\gamma}\begin{pmatrix} \mathbf{g} \\ j \end{pmatrix} = A_\gamma(\mathbf{g}) \hat{U}_{\alpha\gamma}\begin{pmatrix} \mathbf{g} \\ j \end{pmatrix}. \tag{20}$$

The atomic displacement of the atom l_j resulting from a single mode of vibration is given by

$$\mathbf{u}\binom{l}{j} = A_\gamma(\mathbf{g})\hat{\mathbf{U}}_\gamma\binom{\mathbf{g}}{j}\exp\left[2\pi i\mathbf{g}\cdot\mathbf{r}\binom{l}{j}\right]\exp\left[-\omega_\gamma(\mathbf{g})t\right], \qquad (21)$$

and the atomic displacement resulting from the simultaneous excitation of all possible modes of vibration can be written as

$$\mathbf{u}\binom{l}{j} = \sum_{\mathbf{g},\gamma} A_\gamma(\mathbf{g})\hat{\mathbf{U}}_\gamma\binom{\mathbf{g}}{j}\exp\left[2\pi i\mathbf{g}\cdot\mathbf{r}\binom{l}{j}\right]\exp\left[-\omega_\gamma(\mathbf{g})t\right]. \qquad (22)$$

The total energy associated with one mode of vibration is

$$E_\gamma(\mathbf{g}) = mN|A_\gamma(\mathbf{g})|^2\omega_\gamma^2(\mathbf{g}). \qquad (23)$$

The equations of motion of a unimolecular crystal

The preceding sections deal with the vibrations of the atoms in the crystal. The molecular crystals are formed by molecules consisting of numerous atoms, and the problem is, in general, insoluble if no simplifications are introduced. One way to simplify the problem is by analyzing the potential energy of the molecular crystal. Let us assume the sublimation of a molecular crystal that gives rise to a rarified molecular vapour. This sublimation will absorb definite amounts of energy that will be evolved when the crystal is again formed. We shall call the potential energy of the molecular crystal an equal energy but of negative sign, if we do not take into account the zero-point energy. It is commonly assumed that the potential of two molecules is the sum of the interactions of the atoms of one molecule with the atoms of the other and that this interaction is additive, i.e. is independent of the presence of any atom other than the pair in which interaction is considered. The potential energy of the molecular crystal then takes a form similar to (5), modified in the sense that the summation takes place now over all interatomic vectors connecting atoms of one molecule with all the atoms of the remaining molecules (Kitajgorodskij, 1965). Accordingly, the symbolism used in (5) has now a special meaning, i.e. the atom lj belongs to the molecule l and the atom $l'j'$ belongs to the l' molecule, in the case of a unimolecular crystal.

The potential energy of a molecular crystal can be given in a very suitable form by

$$\phi(r) = -AR^{-6} + Be^{(-R/\rho)}, \qquad (24)$$

in which A, B, and ρ are constants depending on the crystal geometry. The first term corresponds to the attracting van der Waals energy, the second term is the repelling van der Waals energy. Both depend on the interatomic distance R between atoms of different molecules. Both terms decrease rapidly with the increase of R, and therefore the contribution to the potential energy of a pair of atoms in a molecular crystal tends to zero rapidly for distances higher than a few angstroms apart. This means that long-range forces are practically nonexistent in a molecular crystal, and that the motion of a molecule affects only the very nearest neighbors. The vibrations of the atoms in the molecule have high frequencies, of the order of 1,000 cm^{-1}, and these vibrations are almost identical whether the molecule is free or bound in the crystal. In this case the internal vibrations of the molecules are practically independent. However, the vibration of the molecules as a whole affect slightly the motion of the neighboring molecules, and there appear characteristic vibrations of the whole structure due to the actual packing of the molecules in the crystal. The frequencies of these new modes of vibration are one order of magnitude smaller than the internal modes. It is then reasonable to treat the thermal motion of the molecules considered as rigid bodies, as given in Ch. 3. Taking into account that the vibrations of the rigid-body molecules can be described in terms of translations and librations, the potential energy of the thermal agitation ϕ_T of an unimolecular cubic crystal (Cochran, 1963) includes terms of the form

$$\tfrac{1}{2} \sum_{ll'\alpha\beta} [\phi_{\alpha\beta}{}^{(1)}(l-l')u_\alpha(l)u_\beta(l') + a\phi_{\alpha\beta}{}^{(2)}(l-l')u_\alpha(l)\theta_\beta(l')$$
$$+ a\phi_{\beta\alpha}{}^{(2)}(l'-l)\theta_\alpha(l)u_\beta(l') + a^2\phi_{\alpha\beta}{}^{(3)}(l-l')\theta_\alpha(l)\theta_\beta(l')]$$

In this expression the quantities $u_\alpha(l)$ and $\theta_\alpha(l)$ correspond to the orthogonal components of the translational and librational displacements of the molecule l. The displacement of an individual atom is given by

$$\mathbf{u}\binom{l}{j} = \mathbf{u}(l) + \boldsymbol{\theta}(l) \times \mathbf{r}'(j), \tag{25}$$

where $\mathbf{r}'(j)$ gives the position of the atom relative to the center of mass of the molecule. The coefficients $\phi_{\alpha\beta}^{(i)}(l-l')$ correspond to intermolecular force constants that can be related to the force constants between the individual atoms. For instance,

$$\phi_{\alpha\beta}{}^{(1)}(l-l') = \sum_{jj'} \phi_{\alpha\beta}\binom{l-l'}{jj'}. \tag{26}$$

The length a is introduced to give the various intermolecular force constants $\phi_{\alpha\beta}^{(i)}(l-l')$ the same dimensions. In the expression of the thermal agitation ϕ_T the internal vibrations are disregarded and the positions of the atoms in the molecule are averaged over the displacements produced by the internal modes of vibration of the molecule.

For a unimolecular crystal with rigid-body molecules, the equations of motion (Cochran and Pawley, 1964) are

$$F_\alpha(l) = m\frac{\partial^2}{\partial t^2}[u_\alpha(l)] = -\sum_{l'\beta L'} \{\phi_{\alpha\beta}^{(1)}(l-l')u_\beta(l') + \phi_{\alpha L'}^{(2)}(l-l')\theta_{L'}(l')\}$$

$$C_L(l) = I\frac{\partial^2}{\partial t^2}[\theta_L(l)] = -\sum_{l'\beta L'} \{\phi_{L\beta}^{(2)}(l'-l)u_\beta(l') + \phi_{LL'}^{(3)}(l-l')\theta_{L'}(l')\},$$

$$\text{(27)}$$

where $I = mK^2$ is the moment of inertia, with K the radius of gyration of the molecule. In (27), L and L' ($L, L' = 1, 2, 3$) give the orientation of the libration axes of the molecules l and l', respectively. The system (27) can be solved by assuming solutions in terms of waves of the type

$$u_\alpha(l) = U_\alpha(g) \cdot \exp\{2\pi i[g \cdot r(l)]\} \cdot \exp[-i\omega(g)t]$$

$$\theta_L(l) = \Theta_L(g) \cdot \exp\{2\pi i[g \cdot r(l)]\} \cdot \exp[-i\omega(g)t] \qquad \text{(28)}$$

Substitution of (27) in (26) yields

$$m\omega^2(g)U_\alpha(g) = \sum_\beta D_{\alpha\beta}^{(1)}(g)U_\beta(g) + \sum_{L'} D_{\alpha L'}^{(2)}(g)\Theta_{L'}(g)]$$

$$IK^2\omega^2(g)\Theta_L(g) = \sum_\beta D_{L\beta}^{(2)^*}(g)U_\beta(g) + \sum_{L'} D_{LL'}^{(3)}(g)\Theta_{L'}(g), \qquad \text{(29)}$$

where, in a manner similar to (15),

$$D_{\alpha\beta}^{(1)}(g) = \sum_{l'} \Phi_{\alpha\beta}^{(1)}(l-l') \exp\{2\pi ig \cdot [r(l') - r(l)]\}. \qquad \text{(30)}$$

If there are P molecules per unit cell, there will be 6P branches of dispersion relation $\omega_\gamma(g)$, three corresponding to acoustical modes, and 6P-3 to optical modes. Due to the presence of librations in molecular crystals the optical modes are always present, even in a crystal with a single molecule per unit cell. These modes correspond to vibrations in which the molecules in the cell are (almost) out of phase.

In a molecular crystal in which rigid-body molecular motion is assumed and the motion can be described in terms of translational and librational components, the normalized wave amplitudes are given by

$$\hat{U}_\gamma(g) + \hat{\Theta}_\gamma(g) \times r'(j).$$

These satisfy the conditions

$$|U_\gamma(g)|^2 + K^2|\Theta_\gamma(g)|^2 = \hat{1}. \tag{31}$$

In a molecular crystal the displacement of an atom ljp by one particular mode of vibration is given (Cochran and Pawley, 1964) by

$$u\binom{l}{jp} = A_\gamma(g)\left[\hat{U}_\gamma\binom{g}{j} + \Theta_\gamma\binom{g}{j} \times r'\right)(j)\right]$$

$$\exp\left[2\pi i\, g \cdot r\binom{l}{j}\right] \cdot \exp\left[-\omega_\gamma(g)t\right]. \tag{32}$$

ljp identifies the jth type of atom in the pth molecule belonging to the lth unit cell of the crystal.

The normalizing condition (19) in a molecular crystal becomes

$$\sum_{j=1}^{J} m_j\left|\hat{U}_\gamma\binom{g}{j}\right|^2 + I_j\left|\Theta_\gamma\binom{g}{j}\right|^2 = \sum_{j=1}^{j} m_j = m_c, \tag{33}$$

where I is the inertia moment which, in terms of the mean axes LMN of the molecule, can be written as

$$I|\Theta|^2 = I_L|\theta_L|^2 + I_M|\theta_M|^2 + I_N|\theta_N|^2. \tag{34}$$

The correct picture is obtained when the distribution of frequencies in each of these branches is calculated. This is a formidable task, but can be done in a reasonable manner if other approximations are used.

Boundary conditions and Brillouin zones

The theory described in the preceding sections is based on an infinite crystal. However, real crystals are finite. This finiteness imposes boundary conditions on the propagation of waves in the crystal. In all problems of elasticity these conditions are generally very inconvenient, and this is specially true in crystals, since the waves reaching the faces of the crystal do not merely reflect, but rather decompose into different types of waves that propagate backward into the crystal along different directions. The problem is further complicated by the fact that the crystal field is truncated at the surface and, as a consequence, the spacings of the lattice planes near the free surface are distorted. Fortunately this distortion is small compared with the usual size of the crystal, and we can neglect, as a first approximation, the effect of the distortion of the crystal border. However, the effect of the boundary is still to be considered. If the calculations of the waves propagating in the crystal were critically dependent on the particular choice of the boundary conditions, we could not develop any theory with enough generality. We can intuitively see that the effect of the boundary conditions cannot affect the dynamics of the crystal in a fundamental manner. For instance, if we have a crystal block sufficiently large (Fig. 2), we can easily transform it by slicing a layer from the right side of the crystal block and adding it to the left side of the crystal. We can do this because the crystal is periodic. Obviously the dynamic properties of the crystal block will not be seriously affected by the operation. Therefore we can always identify the $(l+L)$th layer with lth layer of the crystal. The greater the number of atoms in the crystal block (and therefore the bigger the crystal is), the smaller is the error.

A suitable boundary condition was developed by Born and von Karman (1912, 1913) which they called the periodic boundary conditions, that is equivalent to what Born and Huang (1956) later called the cyclic boundary conditions. In the cyclic boundary conditions the crystal is assumed divided in macrocrystals, all of them of $N \times N \times N = N^3$ unit cells. Such macrocrystals are formed by parallelepipeds defined by translation vectors $N\mathbf{a}$, $N\mathbf{b}$, $N\mathbf{c}$. These macrocrystals are called kinetic cells. It is assumed that the vibrations of one kinetic cell are repeated identically in each of the other kinetic cells. This

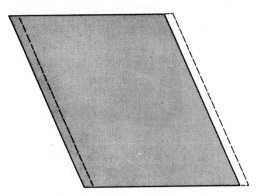

Fig. 2. Scheme to illustrate the cyclic conditions. The limits of the crystal have been moved by an amount a_1 to the right; this does not affect the dynamics of most of the crystal. (After Knox and Gold, 1964.)

is equivalent to saying that the vibrations of the atoms are periodic with the periodicity of the kinetic cell, i.e. that the atoms at corresponding points on opposite faces of the macrocrystal move exactly in the same way. This can be readily understood by assuming a one-dimensional crystal closed on itself forming a ring, a two-dimensional crystal rolled into a two-dimensional torus, or a three-dimensional crystal wrapped into an n-dimensional torus. The real finite crystal can also be considered as built up of one kinetic cell. The cyclic boundary conditions postulate that

$$\mathbf{u}\binom{l+L}{j} = \mathbf{u}\binom{l}{j}. \tag{35}$$

This mathematical assumption simplifies the calculations of crystal dynamics that do not depend explicitly on the crystal's surface, and provides a convenient way of normalizing the potential and kinetic energies of a crystal to a given, finite volume.

The translations $N\mathbf{a} = \mathbf{A}$, $N\mathbf{b} = \mathbf{B}$, $N\mathbf{c} = \mathbf{C}$ of the kinetic cell generate a lattice of the crystal with a multiple cell. We shall call this lattice the kinetic lattice. The kinetic lattice has a reciprocal lattice defined by the translation vectors

$$\mathbf{A}^* = \frac{1}{N}\mathbf{a}^*, \qquad \mathbf{B}^* = \frac{1}{N}\mathbf{b}^*, \qquad \mathbf{C}^* = \frac{1}{N}\mathbf{c}^* \tag{36}$$

that evidently defines a submultiple cell of the ordinary reciprocal lattice of the crystal. This lattice is known as the Gibbs lattice. Any Gibbs lattice point $\mathbf{G}_H^*$ is defined by a Gibbs vector given by

$$\mathbf{G}_H^* = H\mathbf{A}^* + K\mathbf{B}^* + L\mathbf{C}^*, \qquad H, K, L = 1, 2 \cdots \tag{37}$$

and the Gibbs lattice peak function is given by

$$Z_G(\mathbf{r}^*) = v_G^* \sum_{H=-\infty}^{+\infty} \sum_{K=-\infty}^{+\infty} \sum_{L=-\infty}^{+\infty} L(\mathbf{r}^* - H\mathbf{A}^* - K\mathbf{B}^* - L\mathbf{C}^*)$$
$$= v_G^* \sum_H L(\mathbf{r}^* - \mathbf{G}_H^*) \tag{38}$$

The mesh of the Gibbs lattice is always very small in comparison with the mesh of the reciprocal lattice. The density of points of the Gibbs lattice is therefore very high, and we can assume, without great error, that any reciprocal vector $\mathbf{r}^*$ can be identified with a Gibbs vector $\mathbf{G}_H^*$. Therefore

$$\mathbf{r}^* = \mathbf{G}_H^* + \boldsymbol{\epsilon}^* \sim \mathbf{G}_H^*. \tag{39}$$

The physical dimensions of the kinetic cell and the periodicity of the crystal define all possible wavelengths of the plane waves propagating in the macrocrystal. Let us assume in a monoatomic structure plane waves parallell to (100). The thermal wave with minimum wavelength compatible with the periodicity of the crystal has $\Lambda_{min} = 2d_{100}$, and also, $g_{max} = \frac{1}{2}a^*$. The maximum wavelength for a thermal wave propagating along the same direction is obviously $\Lambda_{max} = Na$, whose wave vector is $g_{min} = \frac{1}{N}a^*$. It is easy to see that all permitted wave vectors of the kinetic cell are given by

$$g_H = HA^* + KB^* + LC^*, \quad \left(H, K, L = \pm1, \pm2, \ldots \pm\frac{N}{2}\right). \quad (40)$$

According to the definition of the first Brillouin zone (see Ch. 2), it is clear that the set of points given by (40) are the points of the Gibbs lattice contained in and on the first Brillouin zone at the origin of the reciprocal lattice. Inside that volume there are N^3 Gibbs lattice points, and therefore N^3 values of g.

Let us introduce in Fourier space the shape function of the Brillouin zone

$$S_{Br}(\mathbf{r}^*) = \begin{cases} 1 & \text{inside the first Brillouin zone} \\ 0 & \text{everywhere else} \end{cases}$$

Multiplication of the Gibbs lattice peak function by this shape function obviously restricts the infinite discrete set of vectors $\mathbf{G}_H^*$ to a finite discrete set g_H having nonzero values only inside the first Brillouin zone

$$Z_G^*(\mathbf{r}^*) \cdot S_{Br}(\mathbf{r}^*) = v_G^* \sum_{H=-N/2}^{+N/2} \sum_{K=-N/2}^{+N/2} \sum_{L=-N/2}^{+N/2} (\mathbf{r}^* - HA^* - KB^* - LC^*)$$

$$= v_G^* \sum_H L(\mathbf{r}^* - \mathbf{g}_H^*) \quad (41)$$

Only the Gibbs lattice points defined by (41) have real physical meaning. Any other Gibbs $\mathbf{G}_H^*$ vector whose tip is outside the first Brillouin zone at the origin of the reciprocal space, can be expressed by

$$\mathbf{r}^* = \mathbf{G}_H^* = \mathbf{r}_h^* + \mathbf{g}, \quad (42)$$

where $\mathbf{r}_h^*$ is the reciprocal-lattice vector of the reciprocal-lattice point P_h nearest to G (Fig. 3), and g is a vector identical to a wave vector of the first Brillouin zone at the origin, but whose origin is now at P_h. A wave having $\mathbf{G}_H^*$ as its wave vector produces in the crystal the same displacement as the wave defined by g. It can be easily seen

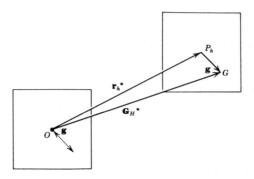

Fig. 3.   Equivalence of reciprocal vectors in different Brillouin zones.

that the motion caused by both waves is identical. A wave propagating in the crystal can be represented by

$$\psi = A \exp\left\{2\pi i \left[-\nu t - (\mathbf{g} \cdot \mathbf{r}_l)\right]\right\}$$

By using (42) we can write

$$A \exp\left\{2\pi i \left[\nu t - (\mathbf{G}_H^* \cdot \mathbf{r}_l)\right]\right\} = A \exp\left[2\pi i \left\{\nu t - \left[(\mathbf{r}_H^* + \mathbf{g})\mathbf{r}_l\right]\right\}\right]$$

$$= A \exp\left[2\pi i (\nu t - \mathbf{g} \cdot \mathbf{r}_l)\right] \tag{43}$$

since the product $\mathbf{r}_H^* \cdot \mathbf{r}$ is a whole number.

The first Brillouin zone repeats itself around each point of the reciprocal lattice. All the points of the Gibbs lattice around any reciprocal-lattice point, and contained on and in the first Brillouin zone associated to such reciprocal lattice point, correspond to all the wave vectors of the kinetic cell of the crystal. The tips of a wave vector $\mathbf{g}$ repeated in every Brillouin zone of the reciprocal lattice form a lattice identical to the reciprocal lattice, but displaced by a translation $\mathbf{g}$. Reciprocal space now represents a periodic elastic space.

We have seen that every wave vector $\mathbf{g}$ is associated to $3J$ frequencies if the unit cell contains J atoms. In a way analogous to the way the wave vectors are periodically repeated in reciprocal space the frequencies are associated to $\mathbf{g}$:

$$\omega^2(\mathbf{g}) = \omega^2(\mathbf{r}_h^* \pm \mathbf{g}). \tag{44}$$

Therefore each point of the Gibbs lattice is associated to $3J$ frequencies. However, if there is only one atom per unit cell, only translational vibrations are possible, and the wave vector is associated to three acoustic modes, two transverse and one longitudinal. Along only certain principal directions of the crystal, either transverse or longitudinal waves are propagating, and therefore, the corresponding points of the Gibbs lattice are associated with only one frequency. This is why it is necessary to reduce the multiple cell to the primitive one when studying the elastic behavior of the crystal structure. In order to simplify the study of vibrations of the structure it is necessary also to consider that only one particle (in molecular crystals, one molecule) is contained in the primitive cell.

Along any radius vector from the center of the first Brillouin zone, the frequency is a function of the distance only, and if the corresponding equation is solved along this particular line, we can find out the distance from the origin to the point at which the frequency has an assigned value. If the secular equation can be solved along a large number of such lines, the sum of the resulting distribution will be the desired frequency distribution. It almost goes without saying that the closer the lines are taken, the more accurate will be the result. If the complete point symmetry of the reciprocal lattice is taken into account, it is sufficient to consider values of $\mathbf{g}$ along lines contained in a small region, the irreducible element of the complete Brillouin zone. This irreducible element corresponds to the fundamental domain, a concept used in classical crystallography. As is known, the number of homologous fundamental domains is a function of the point symmetry. Thus, in cubic crystals with high symmetry the assymmetrical part is $\frac{1}{48}$ of the volume of the Brillouin zone.

By means of this concept of the elasticity reciprocal lattice the frequency ω can be represented as a periodic function in $\mathbf{g}$ space, for example, along certain special directions such as the axes [100], [110], and [111]. In this manner, for each direction we obtain three different $\omega(\mathbf{g})$ dispersion curves or branches. In each branch the mode frequency depends upon the wave vector, which can assume all values in and on the Brillouin zone.

The linear chain

A simple way to understand the dynamic behavior of a crystal is to analyze the behavior of a discontinuous string, called the linear chain. In the linear chain a one-dimensional crystal with cyclic boundary conditions is assumed. The dynamics of such a linear chain is very simple, and it is not only worth study for the sake of simplicity, but also because the three-dimensional crystal can be assumed to be built up of linear chains. In fact every two atoms in the dynamical crystal define a wave vector. If the atoms selected are translation equivalent in different unit cells, they not only define a wave vector, but also a definite lattice direction. In a crystal with only one atom per unit cell every pair of atoms is translation-equivalent, and therefore defines both things. The crystal is built up of the sum of linear chains.

The simplest example of a linear chain is obtained by considering a monoatomic one-dimensional crystal. The atoms have a mass m and the lattice translation is a. We can assume that the atoms are bound to each other by elastic forces α that act only between first neighbors (Fig. 4i). The unit cell of the lattice corresponding to such a linear chain contains only one atom and has translation a. The atoms of such a linear chain have three degrees of freedom, but we shall consider only longitudinal vibrations. The potential energy of the monoatomic one-dimensional crystal can be expressed as a function of the displacements of the atoms from their equilibrium positions, and is of the form

$$\phi_T = \tfrac{1}{2} \sum_l \alpha(u_l - u_{l+1}) \tag{45}$$

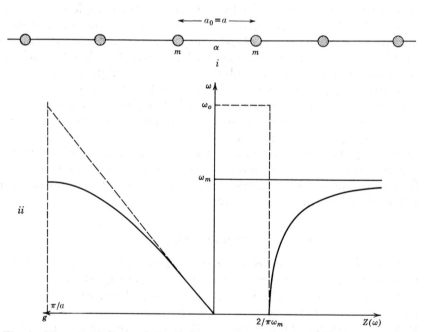

Fig. 4. Monoatomic linear chain. (i) Arrangement: m = mass of the atom; α = elastic restoring force; a = interatomic distance; a_0 = lattice translation; (ii) Dispersion relation between ν and g, and frequency-distribution function. (After Ludwig, 1966, modified.)

where u_l and u_{l+1} are longitudinal displacements of the lth and $(l+1)$th atoms. The equations of motion (12) for an atom l now become:

$$m\frac{\partial^2 u_l}{\partial t^2} = -\alpha(u_l - u_{l-1}) - \alpha(u_l - u_{l+1}) = \alpha(u_{l+1} + u_{l-1} - 2u_l). \quad (46)$$

This equation can be solved by a plane wave of the type

$$u_l = U(g) \exp(2\pi i gl) \exp[\pm i\omega(g)t]. \quad (47)$$

Substituting this solution into (46), we obtain

$$m\frac{\partial^2 u(g)}{\partial t^2} = U(g)(\alpha \exp[2\pi iga] + \alpha \exp[-2\pi iga] - 2\alpha)$$

$$= U(g)4\alpha \sin^2 \pi ga. \quad (48)$$

Equation (48) is the equation of a simple harmonic oscillator with frequency

$$\omega(g) = \omega_{max} \sin \pi ga \quad \text{or} \quad \nu(g) = \sqrt{\frac{\alpha}{m}} 2 \sin \pi ga. \quad (49)$$

It is easily seen that all possible vibrations are given by values of g in the range

$$-\frac{1}{2a} \leqslant g \leqslant \frac{1}{2a} \quad (50)$$

because any value of g lying outside this range simply repeats precisely the same vibration, and therefore only the wave vectors inside the first Brillouin zone have to be considered. In fact the frequency ν is a periodic function with period $1/a$, and maxima at $N/2a$ with N odd and either positive or negative. The variation of ν with g therefore needs to be represented only in the range (50); this is illustrated in Fig. 4ii. The positive g values correspond to waves propagated in one direction, while waves going in the opposite direction are represented by negative g values. From this figure, we can see that for small values of g, that is for $ga \ll 1$,

$$\nu(g) = \sqrt{\frac{\alpha}{m}} 2\pi ga, \quad (51)$$

and the frequency is proportional to the wave vector corresponding to the well known property of the continuum. This merely says that for large wavelengths the linear monoatomic chain behaves as a heavy elastic string in classical mechanics. For large values of g, however, the proportionality is lost and this fact is known as dispersion. It is interesting to note that there exists a maximum frequency ν_{max} that can be propagated through the chain. This does not occur in a continuous string, for which no frequency limit exists. This is equivalent to saying that for sufficiently short waves the atomicity of the chain becomes important.

A quantity of interest is the number Z of frequencies between ν and $\nu + d\nu$. The distribution $Z(\nu) \, d\nu$ of frequencies is known as the frequency spectrum, and it is represented in Fig. 4ii. For the monoatomic one-dimensional crystal this is an increasing function, approaching infinity as ν_{max} is approached.

A more complicated case is a diatomic one-dimensional crystal consisting of alternating atoms of different mass M and m. The interatomic distance is a and the unit cell translation is $2a$ (Fig. 5i). We now consider only interactions between nearest neighbors that can be represented by a single force constant α, and we limit ourselves to longitudinal vibrations. If the atoms are numbered in such

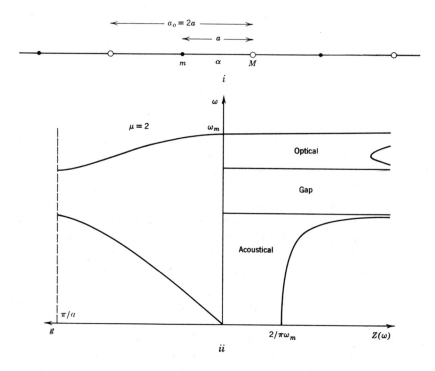

Fig. 5. Diatomic linear chain. (i) Scheme, m, M = masses of the atoms; α = elastic restoring force; a = interatomic distance; a_0 = lattice translation; (ii) dispersion relation between ν and g, frequency-distribution function (After Ludwig, 1966, modified.)

a way that the even numbers correspond to mass M and the odd ones to m, the equations of motion (12) take the form

$$M\frac{\partial^2 u_{2l}}{\partial t^2} = \alpha(u_{2l+1} + u_{2l-1} - 2u_{2l}),$$

$$m\frac{\partial^2 u_{2l+1}}{\partial t^2} = \alpha(u_{2l+2} + u_{2l} - 2u_{2l+1}). \tag{52}$$

Equations (52) cannot be satisfied by a single plane wave because, due to the difference of masses M and m, the amplitudes of the vibrations of the atoms l and $l+1$ are different. Therefore we may try to solve these equations by two plane waves of the type

$$u_{2l} = U\left(\frac{g}{l}\right)\exp\left[i\omega(g)t\right]\exp\left(2\pi i 2lga\right)$$

$$u_{2l+1} = U\left(\frac{g}{2l+1}\right)\exp\left[i\omega(g)t\right]\exp\left[2\pi i(2l+1)ga\right], \tag{53}$$

where $U\left(\frac{g}{2l}\right)$ and $U\left(\frac{g}{2l+1}\right)$ are the amplitudes corresponding to atoms of mass M and m respectively.

Substituting the solution into differential equations (52) yields the following system:

$$[2\alpha - M\omega^2(g)]U\left(\frac{g}{2l}\right) - 2\alpha\cos 2\pi ga U\left(\frac{g}{2l+1}\right) = 0$$

$$-2\alpha\cos 2\pi ga U\left(\frac{g}{2l}\right) - [2\alpha - m\omega^2(g)]U\left(\frac{g}{2l+1}\right) = 0. \tag{54}$$

The solution is obtained by imposing the condition that the determinant of the coefficients of $U\left(\frac{g}{2l}\right)$ and $U\left(\frac{g}{2l+1}\right)$ vanishes;

$$\begin{vmatrix} 2\alpha - M\omega^2(g) & -2\alpha\cos 2\pi ga \\ -2\alpha\cos 2\pi ga & 2\alpha - m\omega^2(g) \end{vmatrix} = 0. \tag{55}$$

For the square of the frequency this yields

$$\omega^2(g) = \frac{\alpha}{\mu} \pm 4\pi^2\alpha\left(\frac{1}{\mu^2} - \frac{4\sin^2 2\pi ga}{Mm}\right)^{1/2}$$

or

$$\nu^2(g) = \frac{1}{4\pi^2}\frac{\alpha}{\mu} \pm \left(\frac{\alpha^2}{\mu^2} - \frac{4\alpha^2\sin^2 2\pi ga}{Mm}\right)^{1/2}, \tag{56}$$

where μ is the reduced mass of the unit cell. Here again the possible values of g are in the range defined by (50). There is no proportionality between ω and g, and therefore there is dispersion.

Since ν should be positive, each value of ν^2 leads to a single value of ν. According to (56) there are now two frequencies ν_+ and ν_- corresponding to a single value of the wave vector g. One of the frequencies namely ν_-, behaves similarly to ν in the case of a monoatomic chain, while the other frequencies ν_+ do not tend to zero for small values of g. In a plot of ν_- versus g (Fig. 5ii) the two solutions are separated in two "branches." The ν_- branch corresponds to so-called acoustic modes, while the ν_+ branch is known as the optical branch. The two branches are separated by a frequency gap that increases its width with increasing mass ratio M/m. The two branches tend to approach each other in frequency when g increases. The frequency spectrum of the one-dimensional diatomic crystal is represented in Fig. 5ii. The frequencies are distributed now in two bands, the acoustical and optical bands, separated by a gap. The acoustical spectrum is very similar to that of the monoatomic linear crystal (Fig. 4ii). The optical spectrum is a band with definite lower and upper frequencies. The band becomes narrower with increasing M/m ratio. A diatomic linear chain can always be reduced to a monoatomic case when the masses of the chemically different particles have a mass ratio near 1. In this case it is necessary to define a pseudocell whose fundamental translation $a' = \frac{1}{2}a$. The particle in each unit cell may be chemically different, but mechanically they are equal. Using this simplification, all the vibrations can be described as belonging to the acoustical branch.

Let us analyze now the vibrations of a molecular linear chain. The simplest case is a linear arrangement of diatomic molecules. In this case the linear chain consists of atoms of the same kind, but now we must consider two force constants α_1 and α_2 that correspond to the forces developed by the intramolecular and intermolecular displacements respectively. For such diatomic molecular chains the frequency of vibration (Zhdanov, 1965) is given by

$$\omega^2(g) = \frac{1}{m}[2(\alpha_1 + \alpha_2) \pm \sqrt{4(\alpha_1 + \alpha_2)^2 - 16\alpha_1\alpha_2 \sin^2 \pi ga}, \qquad (57)$$

where m is the mass of the atom. The vibrations of this diatomic unimolecular linear chain have both optical and acoustical frequencies. However, the frequency spectrum is of a special kind because the intramolecular force constant α_1 is stronger than the intermolecular force constant α_2. If we assume $\alpha_1 \gg \alpha_2$, which is the normal situation when dealing with molecules with strong covalent intramolecular bonds and weak intermolecular van der Waals bonds, then the optical branch has a constant frequency

$$\omega_{\text{op}} = 2\sqrt{\frac{\alpha_1}{2m}}. \tag{58}$$

This is the frequency of the characteristic intramolecular vibrations. The frequencies of the acoustical branch are given by

$$\omega_{\text{ac}}(g) = 2\sqrt{\frac{\alpha_2}{2m}} \sin \pi g a. \tag{59}$$

These frequencies correspond to vibrations of the linear chain built up of particles of mass $2m$, the mass of the molecule. Therefore they correspond to rigid-body vibrations. In actual molecular crystals the vibrations are somewhat different. The molecule has a complex structure, and the linear chain is formed by arrays of molecules equivalent by translation, provided that the crystal has only one molecule per unit cell, or by a sequence of symmetry-equivalent molecules in cases where there is more than a molecule per unit cell. If we consider the molecules as rigid bodies, that is, if we disregard intramolecular vibrations, the vibrations of the molecules will be of two types: translational and librational. In the case of translational motion the vibrations of all the atoms of a molecule have the same amplitude and phase. We can therefore simplify the linear chain just by referring the vibration of the whole molecule to a point that represents the position of the molecule in the chain. We shall call this point, for simplicity, the center of the molecule. With this assumption, the chain of translation-equivalent molecules is equivalent to the monoatomic linear chain, and the translational vibrations will give rise only to the acoustical branch. In this case, instead of a single wave, we shall have a train of identical parallel waves, one wave for each atom of the molecule. This will just cause the frequency density to be multiplied by the number of atoms in the molecule.

Librations, however, produce a more complex vibration. This arises because the amplitude of movement of the different atoms in the molecule depends on the distance of the given atom from the center of libration of the molecule. The train of waves is no longer homogeneous, so the vibrations split into translational and librational (optical) branches.

In the case of a chain of two symmetry-equivalent molecules the relative orientations of the molecules makes them distinguishable, and therefore we have a situation similar to a diatomic linear chain, in which, however, the masses of the particles are identical, but not the orientations. If we disregard the orientational effect, we can always define a pseudocell with $a' = a/2$ to describe the translational motion of the new chain. It is easily understood that the librations of the molecules will produce a train of waves of high complexity, and again there will appear the two branches of acoustical and optical vibrations.

The vibrations of a molecular chain can be derived, in this case, by using Sándor's (1962) modified version of the Born-Karman method. Let us consider a monomolecular chain in which the molecules are translation equivalent. We shall further assume that the chain is infinite, linear and close packed, and that the molecules are plane rings of six close-packed spherical atoms. The molecular mass is m, its moments of inertia I, and the fundamental translation of the chain is a. Also we assume that, at equilibrium, all the molecules lie in the same plane (Fig. 6i). We shall further assume that the interaction between neighboring molecules is represented by two harmonic restoring forces. One force, with force constant α_1, corresponds to the interaction between neighboring molecules; it has the character of a

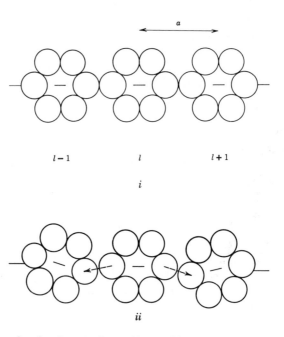

Fig. 6. Monomolecular linear chain. (*i*) Equilibrium position; (*ii*) with angular displacements. a = chain translation.

central force radiating from the center of the molecule. The other force, with force constant α_2, corresponds to the interaction between the nearest atoms of neighboring molecules and has the character of a noncentral force. In this scheme, the central force depends only on the linear displacement of the neighboring molecules, but the non-central force depends also on the angular displacements of the molecules relative to its equilibrium position (Fig. 6ii).

We can allow the motion to have two degrees of freedom: a transverse translational vibration in the equilibrium plane of the chain, and a rotational vibration of the molecules around an axis perpendicular to the plane of the chain. The equation of motion for the transverse translational vibration of lth molecule, in this case, is given by

$$m\frac{\partial^2 u_l}{\partial t^2} = (\alpha_1 + \alpha_2)(u_{l+1} + u_{l-1} - 2u_l) - \alpha_2 R(\theta_{l+1} - \theta_{l-1}), \quad (60)$$

where u_l and θ_l are the instantaneous transverse and angular displacements of the lth molecule, and R is the distance of each atomic center from the center of its molecule. Similarly, the equation of motion for the rotational vibration of the lth mlecule is given by

$$I\frac{\partial^2 \theta_l}{\partial t^2} = \alpha_2 R(u_{l+1} - u_{l-1}) - \alpha_2 R^2(\theta_{l+1} + \theta_{l-1} + 4\theta_l), \quad (61)$$

where the right-hand side is the total instantaneous moment acting on the lth molecule.

Equation (60) may be solved by a plane wave representing transverse translational vibrations, of the type

$$u_l = u \cdot \exp(i\omega(g)t)\exp(2\pi igr_l). \quad (62)$$

Similarly, (61) may be solved by a plane wave representing rotational vibrations of the type

$$\theta_l = \theta \cdot \exp(i\omega(g)t)\exp(2\pi igr_l). \quad (63)$$

In these equations u and θ are the respective amplitudes, while r_l is the position vector of the lth molecule in equilibrium.

The two simultaneous homogeneous equations for the amplitudes u and θ, namely

$$[m\omega^2(g) - 4(\alpha_1 + \alpha_2)\sin^2 \pi ga]u + (2i\alpha_2 R \sin 2\pi ga)\theta = 0,$$

and $\qquad\qquad\qquad\qquad\qquad\qquad\qquad\qquad\qquad\qquad\qquad\qquad (64)$

$$(-2i\alpha_2 R \sin 2\pi ga)u + [I\omega^2 - 4\alpha_2 R^2(\cos^2 \pi ga + \tfrac{1}{2})]\theta = 0,$$

are compatible only if the determinant of their coefficients vanishes:

$$\begin{vmatrix} m\omega^2(g) - 4(\alpha_1 + \alpha_2)\sin^2 \pi ga & 2i\alpha_2 R \sin 2\pi ga \\ -2i\alpha_2 R \sin 2\pi ga & I\omega^2 - 4\alpha_2 R^2(\cos^2 \pi ga + \tfrac{1}{2}) \end{vmatrix} = 0 \qquad (65)$$

This equation, quadratic in ω^2, is the secular equation and yields two real roots of ω^2 for every value of g; therefore we have, for a monomolecular chain with two degrees of freedom, two branches in the dispersion curve of ω versus g. The corresponding dispersion curves for a given value of $\alpha_1/\alpha_2 = F$ and $I/mR^2 = \beta$ are given in Fig. 7. The β factor can be considered a molecular form factor, that, in the case illustrated, is equal to 1. The general transverse normal modes of the monomolecular chain represent, in general, mixed vibrations, derived from the superposition of translational and rotational vibrations of the same frequency because, in general, the roots depend on both the masses and moments of inertia of the molecules.

The situation is slightly different for longitudinal vibrations. If we again restrict the vibrations to only two degrees of freedom, allowing translational displacement along the chain direction and angular

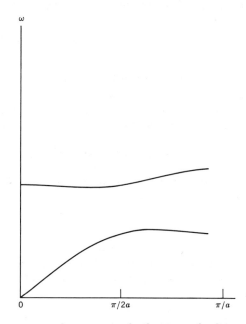

Fig. 7. Dispersion curves for transversal vibrations of a linear chain of identical ring-shaped molecules for a force constant $\alpha = 1$ and a given form factor $\beta = 1$. (After Sándor, 1962.)

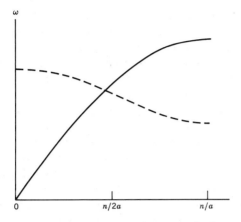

Fig. 8. Dispersion curves for longitudinal vibrations of a linear chain of identical ring-shaped molecules. Solid line: translation branch; broken line: librational branch. (After Sándor, 1962.)

displacements about the same axis, as before, we find that the two types of vibrations are uncoupled. The equations of motion are given by

$$m\frac{\partial^2 u_l}{\partial t^2} = (\alpha_1 + \alpha_2)(u_{l-1} + u_{l+1} - 2u_l),$$

and

$$I\frac{\partial^2 \theta_l}{\partial t^2} = -\alpha_2 R^2(\theta_{l+1} + \theta_{l-1} + 4\theta_l), \tag{66}$$

while the possible frequencies are given by

$$\omega_t^2(g) = \frac{4(\alpha_1 + \alpha_2)}{m} \sin^2 \pi g a$$

$$\omega_r^2(g) = \frac{4\alpha_2 R^2}{I}(\cos^2 \pi g a + \tfrac{1}{2}). \tag{67}$$

The vibrations are pure translational or rotational. The two dispersion curves are separated (Fig. 8).

The effect of thermal waves on the scattering of x-rays by crystals

Thermal vibrations of the atoms modulate the electron density of the crystal, and, as has been shown in Ch. 3, any fluctuation in the electron density gives rise to diffuse scattering. The thermal vibrations of the atoms in the crystal have frequencies lower than that of the x-rays. Therefore, the modulation of the electron density by thermal vibrations of the atoms is a function of time, and we can speak of the instantaneous configuration of the crystal structure, defined by the actual positions of the atoms at a given moment. All the instantaneous configurations have, however, the same Q-function because they contain all possible interatomic vectors. As a consequence the total intensity diffracted by the different instantaneous configurations is constant and cannot be distinguished from the total intensity observed experimentally. In the preceding parts of this chapter we have seen that the vibrations of the atoms in the crystal can be described as caused by the superposition of displacement waves propagating in the crystal. If the displacements of the atoms are small, the principle of superposition applies and each wave travels through the crystal structure independently of any other. Therefore we can consider that the thermal waves scatter the x-ray incoherently and we can analyze the thermal diffuse scattering observed by deducing the intensity scattered by a crystal whose structure is modulated by the propagation of thermal waves of given wavelength, wave vector, frequency, and amplitude.

Let us consider the effect of a single plane thermal wave in the crystal. The atom in the position $\mathbf{r}_j$ is displaced from its equilibrium position by a distance according to (6). All the atoms that are at distances $\mathbf{r}_j - \mathbf{r}_{j'} = \Lambda$ are in phase. As the wave is of the running type, at two different times the actual displacement $\mathbf{u}_j$ of the atom j are different, but at a given time the displacements $\mathbf{u}_j$ and $\mathbf{u}_{j'}$ of the atoms j and j' are equal. Therefore from the point of view of diffraction, the periodicity of the structure is determined by the wavelength Λ of the thermal wave involved (Fig. 9). The actual displacement of

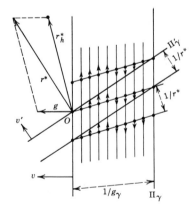

Fig. 9. Diagram of the planes of the elastic waves π_α and π'_α and of their wave vectors $\mathbf{g}_\alpha$ (fundamental) and $\mathbf{g}_\alpha + \mathbf{r}_h^*$.

the atom at a given instant is a function of the position of the atom in the crystal structure and of the wavelength Λ of the thermal wave. The thermal waves present in the crystal are running waves; however their velocities are so small in comparison with the frequency of the x-rays that for practical purposes the waves can be considered at rest. By eliminating the time dependence in (13), we obtain that the instantaneous displacement of the atom lj is given by

$$\mathbf{u}\binom{l}{j} = \mathbf{U}_\gamma\binom{\mathbf{g}}{j} \exp\left(2\pi i \mathbf{g} \cdot [\mathbf{r}(l) + \mathbf{r}(j)]\right) \tag{68}$$

The instantaneous configuration of the crystal structure diffracts the incident x-ray radiation giving rise to a diffracted wave of amplitude

$$F(\mathbf{r}^*) = \sum_{l=1}^{N} \sum_{j=1}^{J} f_j(\mathbf{r}^*) \exp\left(2\pi i \mathbf{r}^* \cdot [\mathbf{r}(l) + \mathbf{r}(j) + \mathbf{u}\binom{l}{j}]\right) \tag{69}$$

If (69) is expanded in terms of the displacement vectors and only the first term involving $\mathbf{u}\binom{l}{j}$ is considered one obtains

$$F(\mathbf{r}^*) = \sum_{l=1}^{N} \sum_{j=1}^{J} f_j(\mathbf{r}^*) \left[2\pi \mathbf{r}^* \cdot \mathbf{u}\binom{l}{j}\right] \exp\left(2\pi i \mathbf{r}^* [\mathbf{r}(l) + \mathbf{r}(j)]\right) \tag{70}$$

By substituting (68) in (70) we obtain

$$\begin{aligned}
F_{g_a}(\mathbf{r}^*) &= \sum_{lj} \left[2\pi \mathbf{r}^* \cdot \mathbf{U}_\gamma\binom{\mathbf{g}}{j}\right] f_j(\mathbf{r}^*) \exp\left\{2\pi i (\mathbf{r}^* + \mathbf{g})[\mathbf{r}(l) + \mathbf{r}(j)]\right\} \\
&= \sum_{j=1}^{J} \left[2\pi \mathbf{r}^* \cdot \mathbf{U}_\gamma\binom{\mathbf{g}}{j}\right] f_j(\mathbf{r}^*) \exp\left\{2\pi i [(\mathbf{r}^* + \mathbf{g}) \cdot \mathbf{r}(j)]\right\} \\
&\qquad\qquad\qquad \sum_{l=1}^{N} \exp\left\{2\pi i [\mathbf{r}^* + \mathbf{g}] \cdot \mathbf{r}_l\right\} \tag{71}
\end{aligned}$$

For N large enough, the last factor in (71) has the characteristics of a reciprocal-lattice peak function in Fourier space. We shall call this function the wave-vector lattice-peak function. It defines a set of lattice points shifted with respect to the ordinary reciprocal lattice points by the vector $\mathbf{g}$,

$$Z_g(\mathbf{r}^* - \mathbf{g}) = v_c^* \sum_h L[\mathbf{r}^* + \mathbf{g} - \mathbf{r}_h^*]. \tag{72}$$

This wave vector-lattice-peak function is concentrated at the points of reciprocal space given by $\mathbf{r}_h^* - \mathbf{g}$, that is, this function is zero everywhere except at one point in each Brillouin zone defined by the wave vector **g** from each reciprocal-lattice point r_h^*, i.e.

$$Z_g(\mathbf{r}^*) = 0 \qquad \text{for} \qquad \mathbf{r}^* \neq \mathbf{r}_h^* - \mathbf{g}$$

$$= 1 \qquad\qquad\qquad \mathbf{r}^* = \mathbf{r}_h^* - \mathbf{g}. \qquad (73)$$

Now the whole Fourier space is filled, and the Brillouin zone has a motif formed by all the possible **g** vectors which are the fundamental wave vectors. Every wave-vector lattice-peak function is a solitary function of the continuous Fourier space.

The intensity diffracted by the mode of vibration γ of wave vector **g** at a point defined by $\mathbf{r}^*$ is then given by

$$I(\mathbf{r}^* - \mathbf{g}) = N v_c^* \sum_h L[\mathbf{r}^* - (\mathbf{r}_h^* - \mathbf{g})] \cdot \left| \sum_{j=1}^{J} \left[2\pi \mathbf{r}^* \cdot \mathbf{U}_\gamma \binom{\mathbf{g}}{j} \right] f_j(\mathbf{r}^*) \right.$$

$$\left. \exp\{2\pi i[(\mathbf{r}^* + \mathbf{g}) \cdot \mathbf{r}(j)]\} \right|^2. \quad (74)$$

It follows that the intensity diffracted by a single wave is entirely concentrated at a distance -**g** from each reciprocal lattice point r_h^*. The same wave can propagate along opposite directions. There-fore the two wave vectors **g** and -**g** of each plane wave give rise to two optical ghosts at symmetric points of each reciprocal-lattice point. Because the density of points of the Gibbs lattice is very high, the whole assemble of the intensity scattered by the thermal waves in the crystal forms a diffuse cloud around each reciprocal-lattice point. By using (20) one can write

$$\left| \sum_{j=1}^{J} \left[2\pi \mathbf{r}^* \cdot \mathbf{U}_\gamma \binom{\mathbf{g}}{j} \right] f_j(\mathbf{r}^*) \exp\{2\pi i(\mathbf{r}^* + \mathbf{g}) \cdot \mathbf{r}(j)]\} \right|^2 =$$

$$\left| [2\pi \mathbf{r}^* \cdot \mathbf{A}_\gamma(\mathbf{g})] \sum_{j=1}^{J} \hat{\mathbf{U}}_\gamma \binom{\mathbf{g}}{j} f_j(\mathbf{r}^*) \exp\{2\pi i[\mathbf{r}_h^* \cdot \mathbf{r}(j)]\} \right|^2.$$

The quantity

$$|\mathbf{r}^*| G_\gamma(\mathbf{r}^*) = \mathbf{r}^* \sum_{j=1}^{J} \mathbf{U}_\gamma \binom{\mathbf{g}}{j} f_j(\mathbf{r}^*) \exp\{2\pi i[\mathbf{r}_h^* \cdot \mathbf{r}(j)]\} \qquad (75)$$

is dependent on the crystal structure and is called the structure factor of the first-order diffuse scattering. For practical purposes it is equal to the structure factor at the point of reciprocal space under consideration.

The mode of vibration γ has an energy $E_\gamma(\mathbf{g})$ given by (23). In terms of the energy of the mode γ, we can write (74) as

$$I^{(\gamma)}_{TDS_1}(\mathbf{r}^*) = \frac{4\pi^2 v_c^* E_\gamma(\mathbf{g})|\mathbf{r}^*|^2}{m\omega_\gamma^2(\mathbf{g})} \sum_h |G_\gamma(\mathbf{r}^*)|^2 \cdot L(\mathbf{r}^* + \mathbf{g} - \mathbf{r}_h^*). \quad (76)$$

Associated with a wave vector $\mathbf{g}$ there are $3J$ modes of vibration. The contribution of all modes $3J$ to the diffuse-scattering intensity at $\mathbf{r}^* + \mathbf{g} = \mathbf{r}_h^*$ is given by

$$I_{TDS_1}(\mathbf{r}^*) = \frac{4\pi^2 N|\mathbf{r}^*|^2}{m} \sum_{\gamma=1}^{3J} \frac{E_\gamma(\mathbf{g})}{\omega_\gamma^2(\mathbf{g})} |G_\gamma(\mathbf{r}^*)|^2 \cdot L(\mathbf{r}^* + \mathbf{g} - \mathbf{r}_h^*). \quad (77)$$

We then see that this diffuse intensity is made up of independent contributions from states of polarization γ of each wave ψ_γ. Accordingly, the intensity of the first-order diffuse scattering is inversely proportional to the frequency of the thermal wave defined by $\mathbf{g}$. The frequencies of the acoustic waves go to zero when $\mathbf{g} \to 0$ and, therefore, the first-order diffuse scattering is a decreasing function with $\mathbf{g}$, whose maxima are superimposed on the sharp maxima of the Bragg reflections, the diffuse scattering extending itself as a cloud of diminishing intensity around the reciprocal lattice points. The frequency is a function of the velocity of propagation of the thermal wave, and this velocity is an anisotropic function. Because of this, the cloud of diffuse scattering is normally very anisotropic, as can clearly be observed in the Laue photographs reproduced in Ch. 4. We can define a surface of equal diffusion that corresponds to the surface for which different values of $\mathbf{g}$ give the same diffuse scattering (Jahn, 1942). These surfaces are very anisotropic even for cubic crystals and, as a first approximation, they are centrosymmetric.

Since we are dealing with running elastic waves, the selective reflections are produced with a change in frequency. This fact is interpreted as a Doppler effect, since the reflection is from a collection of running waves instead of from standing waves of electron density. According to whether the diffraction vector and the velocity V of the elastic wave are in the same or in opposite directions (Fig. 10), the scattered radiation is of a slightly greater frequency $\nu + \nu_\alpha$, or a slightly lower frequency $\nu - \nu_\alpha$ than that of the incident x-radiation. In x-ray diffraction the wavelength of the radiation used is normally of less than 2 Å. In our experiments with molecular crystals we have used CuKα radiation with $\lambda = 1.54$ Å. Under these conditions, the relative difference $|(\nu - \nu')/\nu|$ between the frequency ν of the incident

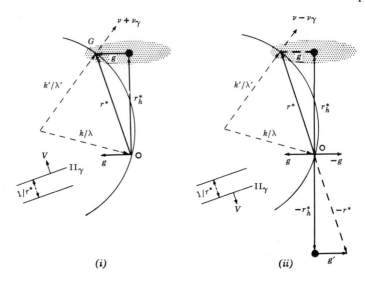

Fig. 10. TDS_1 scattering conditions for the point G. (i) Diffraction vector $\mathbf{r}^*$ coinciding
with $\mathbf{r}_h^* + \mathbf{g}$; (ii) diffraction vector $\mathbf{r}^*$ coinciding with $\mathbf{r}_h^* - \mathbf{g}'$.

rays and the frequency ν' of any scattered rays of detectable intensity
is of the order of 10^{-5}. Therefore the change in frequency is very
small and, in practice, the condition for selective reflection can be
represented geometrically by means of an Ewald sphere of radius $k/\lambda =
k'/\lambda'$. Figure 10 illustrates this extreme. Because both types of wave
are determined by equal and opposite vectors, the vibrations are
conjugate by pairs, with equal frequencies, and the structure factors
G_g and $G_{g'}$ are also equal in pairs.

The total first-order diffuse-scattering intensity referred to that of
a free electron is

$$I_{TDS_1}(\mathbf{g}) = \frac{|\mathbf{r}^*|^2}{Zm} \cdot \sum_{\gamma=1}^{3J} \frac{E_{\nu_\gamma}(\mathbf{g})}{\nu_\gamma^2(\mathbf{g})} |G_{g_\gamma}|^2 \cdot L(\mathbf{r}^* + \mathbf{g} - \mathbf{r}_h^*). \tag{78}$$

The energy E_γ of the thermal wave is given by

$$E_\gamma = h\nu_\gamma \left(\frac{1}{\exp\left(\dfrac{h\nu}{kT}\right) - 1} + \frac{1}{2} \right). \tag{79}$$

At temperatures higher than the characteristic temperature Θ_D of
the crystal, the law of equipartition can be applied, and we can write

$$E_\gamma = E = kT, \qquad (T > \Theta_D). \tag{80}$$

For molecular crystals room temperature is usually greater than the Debye temperature, so that the first-order diffuse scattering can be written

$$I_{TDS_1}(\mathbf{g}) = \frac{|\mathbf{r}^*|^2 kT}{Zm} \sum_{\gamma=1}^{3J} \frac{1}{\nu_\gamma^2} |G_{\mathbf{g}_\gamma}|^2. \tag{81}$$

Second-order diffuse scattering

In the first-order diffuse scattering we have considered the intensity diffracted by a single thermal wave at a time. Isolated thermal waves, however, do not exist in the crystal. Several thermal waves occur at the same time, and therefore we must expect diffraction by two, three, or more thermal waves at the same time. These are two-, three-, or n-phonon processes.

In the second-order diffuse scattering the geometrical condition for scattering to $\mathbf{r}_H^* - \mathbf{g}$ is

$$\mathbf{k} - \mathbf{k}_0 = \mathbf{r}^* = \mathbf{r}_H^* - (\mathbf{g}_\gamma - \mathbf{g}_\delta), \tag{82}$$

where $\mathbf{g}_\gamma$ and $\mathbf{g}_\delta$ are the wave vectors of the two thermal waves of modes of vibration γ and δ, involved in the process. Both $\mathbf{g}_\gamma$ and $\mathbf{g}_\delta$ are fundamental wave vectors (Fig. 11). In order to calculate the diffuse intensity caused by second-order scattering at a point given by $\mathbf{r}^* = G_H$ we must first determine all possible pairs of fundamental wave vectors that can contribute to the intensity in such a point. The wave vectors are determined by all the Gibbs lattice points in and on a first Brillouin zone centered at G_H. The Gibbs lattice point G_H is, in general, near to eight reciprocal-lattice points $B_H(i)$, $(i = 1, 2, \ldots)$. The wave vectors $\mathbf{g}_\delta$ are then defined by

$$\mathbf{g}_\gamma - \mathbf{g}_\delta = \mathbf{R}(i), \tag{83}$$

where $\mathbf{R}(i)$ is the distance vector between G_H and $B_H(i)$.

Centered at each lattice point $B_H(i)$ there is a first Brillouin zone $G(i)$. The polyhedron G_H overlaps with them. G_H is accordingly divided into eight parts. Each of these parts contains all the Gibbs lattice points of G_H that are near to one of the eight reciprocal lattice points $B_H(i)$. We can substitute in (82) $\mathbf{g}_\delta$ by its value in (83), so that the condition for scattering to $\mathbf{r}^*$ is given by

$$\mathbf{k} - \mathbf{k}_0 = \mathbf{r}^* = \mathbf{r}_H^* - [\mathbf{g}_\gamma + \mathbf{R}(i) - \mathbf{g}_\gamma]. \tag{84}$$

Expression (84) is more convenient than (82) since all the vectors involved can readily be determined.

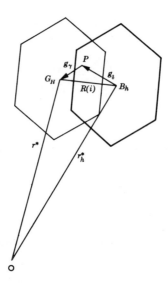

Fig. 11. Diagram of the contribution to TDS_2 at G from the pair of elastic waves of wave vectors $g_\gamma g_\delta$.

The intensity diffracted by a two-phonon process is given by

$$I_2(\mathbf{g}_\gamma, \mathbf{g}_\delta) = \frac{N}{4m^2} \sum_{\gamma,\delta} \sum_{g} \frac{E(\mathbf{g}_\gamma)E(\mathbf{g}_\delta)}{\omega^2(\mathbf{g}_\gamma)\omega^2(\mathbf{g}_\delta)} \cdot |G_{\gamma,\delta}(\mathbf{r}^*)|^2, \qquad (85)$$

where $G_{\gamma,\delta}$ is the structure factor of the crystal structure modulated by the two plane waves $\mathbf{g}_\gamma$ and $\mathbf{g}_\delta$ and is given by

$$|G_{\gamma,\delta}(\mathbf{r}^*)|^2 = \left| \sum_j f_j(\mathbf{r}^*) \exp(2\pi i \mathbf{r}^* \mathbf{r}_j) \left[2\pi \mathbf{r}^* \cdot \hat{\mathbf{U}} \binom{\mathbf{g}_\gamma}{j} \right] \left[2\pi \mathbf{r}^* \cdot \hat{\mathbf{U}} \binom{\mathbf{g}_\delta}{j} \right] \right|^2$$

$$(86)$$

Because the atomic vibrations due to the thermal waves $\pm \mathbf{g}_\gamma$ and $\pm \mathbf{g}_\delta$ are conjugated by pairs, it holds that

$$G_{\mathbf{g}_\gamma \mathbf{g}_\delta} = G_{\mathbf{g}'_\gamma \mathbf{g}_\delta} = G_{\mathbf{g}_\gamma \mathbf{g}'_\delta} = G_{\mathbf{g}'_\gamma \mathbf{g}'_\delta} \qquad (87)$$

where the prime indicates the effect due to the thermal wave propagating in the negative sense.

The total second-order diffuse scattering can be simply expressed by

$$I_{TDS_2}(\mathbf{r}^*) = \frac{|\mathbf{r}^*|^4}{m^2} I_2(\mathbf{g}_\gamma, \mathbf{g}_\delta), \qquad (88)$$

where $I_2(\mathbf{g}_\gamma, \mathbf{g}_\delta)$ are given in (85). Because the kind of atomic vibration is not changed with the order in which the wave vectors $\mathbf{g}_\gamma$ and $\mathbf{g}_\delta$ are taken, the factors $I_2(\mathbf{g}_\gamma, \mathbf{g}_\delta)$ and $I_2(\mathbf{g}_\delta, \mathbf{g}_\gamma)$ are the same and are taken into account only once. As in the case of first-order diffuse scattering, in the second-order diffuse scattering it also occurs that the x-rays are diffracted with change in frequency. As in this case two thermal waves are involved, there are four possible frequencies for each interaction

$$\nu_1 = \nu + \nu_\gamma + \nu_\delta, \qquad \nu_3 = \nu - \nu'_\gamma + \nu_\delta,$$
$$\nu_2 = \nu + \nu_\gamma - \nu'_\delta, \qquad \nu_4 = \nu - \nu'_\gamma - \nu'_\delta. \tag{89}$$

The change in frequency, however, is very small and is negligible for practical purposes.

The problem becomes more and more complex for higher orders of diffuse scattering. The total intensity due to an nth-order diffuse scattering can be given by

$$I_n(\mathbf{g}_\gamma, \mathbf{g}_\delta, \cdots, \mathbf{g}_\omega) = \sum_{\gamma,\ldots,\omega} \frac{E_\gamma}{\nu_{\mathbf{g}_\gamma}{}^2} \frac{E_\delta}{\nu_{\mathbf{g}_\delta}{}^2} \cdots \frac{E_\omega}{\nu_{\mathbf{g}_\omega}{}^2} |G_{\mathbf{g}_\gamma \mathbf{g}_\delta \cdots \mathbf{g}_\omega} \tag{90}$$

$$(\gamma, \cdots, \omega = 1, 2, \cdots, 3J),$$

where $\mathbf{g}_\gamma \cdots \mathbf{g}_\omega$ are the thermal waves of frequencies $\nu_{\mathbf{g}_\gamma} \cdots \nu_{\mathbf{g}_\omega}$ and energies $E_\gamma \cdots E_\omega$ involved in the process. The factor $G_{\mathbf{g}_\gamma \mathbf{g}_\delta \cdots \mathbf{g}_\omega}$ has the significance of a structure factor given by

$$|G_{\mathbf{g}_\gamma \cdots \mathbf{g}_\omega}|^2 = \left| \sum_{j=1}^{J} f_j(\mathbf{r}^*) \exp(2\pi i \mathbf{r}^* \cdot \mathbf{r}_j) \left(2\pi \mathbf{r}^* \cdot \hat{\mathbf{U}}_\gamma\right)\left(2\pi \mathbf{r}^* \cdot \hat{\mathbf{U}}_\delta\right) \right.$$
$$\left. \cdots \left(2\pi \mathbf{r}^* \cdot \hat{\mathbf{U}}_\omega\right) \right|^2. \tag{91}$$

The total intensity diffracted by a thermally agitated crystal is then given by

$$I_{\text{total}}(\mathbf{r}^*) = I_0(\mathbf{r}^*) + I_{TDS_1}(\mathbf{r}^*) + I_{TDS_2}(\mathbf{r}^*) + \cdots + I_{TDS_n}(\mathbf{r}^*). \tag{92}$$

The value of the diffracted intensity diminishes considerably with the order of the process involved. For practical purposes the diffuse scattering of order higher than two is negligible and need not be considered.

Physical quantities deducible from diffuse-intensity measurements

Of the $6J$ harmonic vibrations of the atoms that contribute to the diffuse intensity, 6 are of the acoustic type and $6J-6$ of the optical type, with directions given by the same wave vectors. The six acoustic vibrations have equal frequencies in pairs and their directions are given by two equal and opposite wave vectors, $\mathbf{g}$ and $-\mathbf{g}$. The directions of vibration of these vibrations are along a set of three orthogonal axes.

The frequencies are low, and decrease for small values of $\mathbf{g}$ almost linearly with $|\mathbf{g}|$. The diffuse intensity produced by the acoustic waves is given by

$$I_{TDS_1}(\mathbf{g}_{ac}) = \frac{|\mathbf{r}^*|^2}{Zm} \sum_{\gamma=1}^{3} \frac{E_\gamma}{\nu^2_{\mathbf{g}_\gamma(ac)}} |G_{\mathbf{g}\gamma}|^2, \tag{93}$$

where

$$G_\gamma(\mathbf{r}^*) = \cos(\mathbf{r}^* \cdot \mathbf{e}_\gamma) \cdot F(\mathbf{r}^*), \tag{94}$$

Here $\mathbf{e}_\gamma$ are unit vectors in the direction of the polarization of the lattice wave $U_\gamma(\mathbf{g})$.

On the other hand, the diffuse intensity produced by the $6J$-6 atomic vibrations of high frequency is given by

$$I_{TDS_1}(\mathbf{g}_{op}) = \frac{|\mathbf{r}^*|^2}{Zm} \sum_{\gamma=1}^{3J-3} \frac{E_\gamma}{\nu^2_{\gamma(op)}} |G_{\mathbf{g}\gamma}|^2. \tag{95}$$

The summation here extends over the $3J$-3 vibrations.

Even when there are many atoms in the unit cell, the contribution of these high-frequency vibrations is negligible compared with the acoustic contribution, a fact that is important because the frequencies are low. Near the Bragg reflections the contribution of the acoustic waves can then be considered alone without introducing a large error.

For a monoatomic crystal the problem is greatly simplified. There exist only acoustic waves, so that only three thermal waves are associated with each wave vector $\mathbf{g}$. In this special case the first-order diffuse scattering intensity in electronic units per electron is reduced to

$$I_{TDS_1}(\mathbf{g}) = \frac{|\mathbf{r}^*|^2 f^2 e^{-2M}}{Zm} \sum_{\gamma=1}^{3} \frac{E_\gamma \cos^2(\mathbf{r}^*, \mathbf{e}_\gamma)}{\nu_{\mathbf{g}_\gamma}^2}. \tag{96}$$

The sum over γ extends over the three independent elastic waves which have the same wave vector $\mathbf{g}$ but different directions of vibration. In (96) $(\mathbf{r}^*, \mathbf{e}_\gamma)$ is the angle between r^* and the direction of polarization of the lattice wave U_γ; ν_γ is the frequency of the wave whose wave vector is $\mathbf{g}$.

Taking into account that the velocity V of a running wave and its frequency ν are related by

$$|\mathbf{V}| \cdot |\mathbf{g}| = \nu, \qquad (97)$$

expression (96) becomes

$$I_{TDS_1}(\mathbf{g}) = \frac{|\mathbf{r}^*|^2 f^2 e^{-2M}}{Zm} \frac{1}{|\mathbf{g}|^2} \sum_{\gamma=1}^{3} \frac{E_\alpha \cos^2 (\mathbf{r}^*, \mathbf{e}_\gamma)}{|V_\gamma|^2} \qquad (98)$$

since three waves are associated with the same wave vector $\mathbf{g}$.

When the wave vector coincides with an axis of symmetry of the crystal and is parallel to the diffraction vector, we have the special condition that only the longitudinal acoustic wave contributes to the diffuse-scattering intensity, since the others are transverse and their vibrations are normal to the diffraction vector, so that $\cos^2 (\mathbf{r}^*, \mathbf{e}_\gamma) = 0$. It can then be shown

$$I_{TDS_1}(\mathbf{g}) = \frac{|\mathbf{r}^*|^2 f^2 e^{-2M} kT}{Zm} \frac{1}{\nu_l^2}. \qquad (99)$$

Therefore, starting from absolute measurements of the diffuse scattering at different points at distances $\mathbf{g}$ from the center of the first Brillouin zone, we can obtain the frequencies of the longitudinal acoustic waves of different wave vectors. That is, we can obtain the dispersion law of those frequencies $\nu = \nu(\mathbf{g})$.

In an analogous way we have, for longitudinal waves of velocity V_l,

$$I_{TDS_1}(\mathbf{g}) = \frac{|\mathbf{r}^*|^2 f^2 e^{-2M}}{Zm} \frac{1}{|\mathbf{g}|^2} \frac{1}{V_l^2}. \qquad (100)$$

This expression allows us to determine the velocity of propagation of longitudinal acoustic waves for different wave vectors $\mathbf{g}$.

Since in the limit of large wavelengths, that is, small $\mathbf{g}$'s, the velocities of propagation are directly related to the elastic constants of the crystal, extrapolation of the velocity-dispersion curve, determined through [100] from diffuse intensity measurements, allows us to determine the elastic constants of the crystal through $V_{g \to 0}$. In addition the dispersion curves of the transverse acoustic waves can be obtained through measurements of the diffuse scattering along appropriate lines in reciprocal space that form right angles with the symmetry axes.

It has been seen that the Fourier matrix determines all the harmonic vibrations that the atoms of the crystal can experience, and therefore the matrix at the same time determines all the harmonic components of thermal vibration and allows the calculation of the diffuse-scattering intensity of the crystal. Conversely, the Fourier matrix can be deduced from masurements of diffuse scattering. The values of the independent frequencies of waves whose directions are given by maximal vectors and along symmetry axes, are used to obtain the interatomic forces. Likewise we can obtain the spectrum of frequencies by considering a large number of wave vectors distributed uniformly throughout the fundamental domain of the first Brillouin zone.

Thus we determine, at least approximately, the Born dynamic matrix and with it the field of forces present in the crystal. These concepts will be applied in this chapter to the unimolecular hexamine crystal.

Through the detailed study of thermal diffuse scattering it has been possible to determine elastic constants, force constants, and elastic spectra of a certain number of substances. These studies have been carried out for the most part in three countries; in France by collaborators of Laval, in England by Wooster and collaborators, and in the United States by collaborators of Warren. Thus at the school in Paris potassium chloride (Laval, 1939), aluminum (Olmer, 1948), alpha-iron (Curien, 1952b), and lithium (Champier, 1959) have been studied. At Cambridge potassium bromide, potassium chloride, and galena (Ramachandran and Wooster, 1951a,b), sphalerite (Prince and Wooster, 1951), diamond (Prince and Wooster, 1953), silicon and germanium (Prasad and Wooster, 1955a,b), white tin (Prasad and Wooster, 1955c), lead (Prasad and Wooster, 1956a), pyrite (Prasad and Wooster, 1956b), and vanadium (Sándor and Wooster, 1959) have been studied. In the United States the following have been studied: beta-bronze (Cole and Warren, 1952), silver chloride (Cole, 1953), zinc (Joynson, 1954), copper (Jacobson, 1955), aluminum (Walker, 1956), and β-AuZn (Schwartz, 1957; Schwartz and Muldawer, 1958). In Japan, Annaka determined the elastic constants of silver (1956).

As for molecular crystals, only the elastic constants of hexamine have been determined (Ramachandran and Wooster, 1951b). Our group in Madrid has carried out a complete study of the dynamics of that substance (Carbonell and Canut, 1964). Because it was the first time that the theory was applied in detail to a molecular crystal, in this chapter we shall describe the investigation in detail.

Qualitative effect of the propagation of thermal waves through molecular crystals

We have seen that the morphology of the domains of diffuse scattering associated with nonforbidden reciprocal-lattice points depends on the velocities (and frequencies) of the waves whose wavefronts are normal to the direction under consideration. For a given substance, for example, if the waves that propagate in a certain direction have a velocity lower than that of waves propagating in another direction, the diffuse domain will be oblong with the direction of elongation parallel to the direction of lower velocity. These qualitative concepts can be applied directly to the analysis of diffuse scattering in molecular crystals of special types.

Chain structures; adipic and succinic acids

As we have described in Ch. 4, the structure of these organic acids is one of parallel chains. In this case we can apply the concepts developed by Lonsdale (1942), based on Müller's conclusions (1930) concerning hydrocarbons in chains. In such structures the following types of waves are possible:

1. Transverse waves propagating in directions normal to the chains. They affect the relative positions of the chains, but not the positions of the atoms within a given chain.
2. Transverse waves propagating along the chains. They affect the relative positions of the atoms within a chain.
3. Longitudinal waves propagating normal to the chains. They affect the spacing between chains.
4. Longitudinal waves along the chains are virtually impossible.

Theory tells us that the regions of diffuse scattering always extend in reciprocal space in the direction of propagation of the wave, be it longitudinal or transverse. Accordingly, the effect of transverse waves, propagating in a direction normal to the chains, will be as in Fig. 12i; that is, extensive zones of diffuse scattering for values of $l =$ constant, and not only in planes normal to the chains, but also throughout a certain angle. Figure 12ii shows the effect of transverse waves propagating along the same chains. The normal planes are not affected, but a zone of diffuse scattering elongated along c is produced.

Propagation of longitudinal waves along the direction of the chains should produce a spreading along that direction of the lattice points corresponding to planes normal to the chains. That effect was not

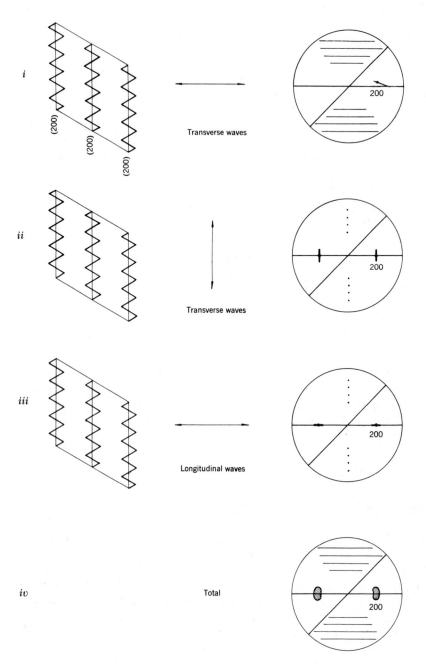

Fig. 12. Diagram of the effect of the propagation of thermal waves in dicarboxylic acids on the diffuse scattering on the $(010)_0^*$ level.

observed to any appreciable extent with any of the dicarboxylic acids studied. However, the existence of longitudinal waves propagating in directions normal to the chains is quite evident. The effect is represented schematically in Fig. 12*iii*. Comparing the configuration of Fig. 12*iv* with Fig. 43, Ch. 4, we see the fruitfulness of our model.

With these ideas we can analyze the propagation of waves in a chain structure: In adipic and succinic acids the chains are parallel to [001]; therefore, the streaks we have described are the manifestation of transverse waves propagating along [001]. This motion, because it does not affect the relative positions of the atoms within a chain, does not seem to be detectable by the structural method. The diffuse scattering zone associated with 200 is elongated in a direction parallel to [001] and widened in the direction normal to [001]. These two phenomena correspond to longitudinal and transverse waves perpendicular to [001], respectively.

Lonsdale suggested in 1942 that the consequence of structures in chains is the appearance of disks of diffuse scattering at the reciprocal-lattice points normal to the chain direction. We have consistently found zones of continuous diffuse scattering along planes of the reciprocal lattice. We believe that this characteristic is much more general than just the appearance of disks. The zones can be formed by the coalescence of disks, but we do not believe such must necessarily be the case. The zones cover extensive regions of planes of the reciprocal lattice where $l = $ const; they are anisotropic, and the intensity within them is modulated by the squares of the structure factors of the reciprocal lattice points where they cover.

Layers structures; pentaerythritol

In a layered structure such as pentaerythritol the maximum amplitude of atomic vibration is in the direction normal to the planes containing the layers, that is, along [001], and such has been the observation by structural methods (Shiono, Cruickshank, and Cox, 1958).

Associated with the reciprocal lattice point 002 is an intense spot of diffuse scattering, characteristic of this structural type. For atomic vibrations normal to the planes of the layers, there are transverse waves parallel to the planes of the layers (waves contained in the planes) and longitudinal waves that propagate in a direction normal to the layers. Since the diffuse zones extend in the direction of propagation of the waves, the effect of longitudinal waves normal to the layers is a spreading of the reciprocal lattice point in the direction of the reciprocal vector associated with the reciprocal lattice point 002. On the other hand, the effect of transverse waves propagating in the planes of the layers is a spreading normal to the previous one. The fact that the spreading due to the latter effect is completely circular and equal in intensity in all directions on the plane (002) indicates that the transverse waves propagate with the same velocity in all directions in the planes (002). The joint result of the two types of waves is the presence of a zone of diffuse scattering associated with the reciprocal lattice point 002, which is consistent with the vibration ellipsoid of a crystal with a fourfold axis. The diffuse zone is very intense near the reciprocal lattice point, and indicates that the acoustic branch of the vibration spectrum makes the preponderant contribution to the phenomenon, so that the vibrations take place in such a way that there is little, if any, difference in phase between neighboring atoms.

In contrast, transverse waves normal to the layers of the molecules imply vibrations in the planes of these layers. If we suppose that the molecules vibrate as rigid bodies, and if these vibrations take place in such a way that neighboring molecules vibrate with opposite phases in different layers, then the frequencies of the optical branch of the vibrational spectrum of the crystal will predominate, in which case diffuse scattering will extend between reciprocal lattice points. The consequence of these vibrations is diffuse scattering extending between reciprocal lattice points parallel to [001]. This effect is observed clearly in the case of pentaerythritol. In the Laue photographs there can be observed diffuse bands extending parallel to [001], and if the diffuse zones are plotted in reciprocal space there appear diffuse bands extending normal to the different levels $(001)^*_{0,1,2,3}$. This is the demonstration that the movements of a molecule against neighboring molecules of adjacent layers are characteristic of this type of layered molecular crystal structure.

The phenomenon is similar to that mentioned in dealing with dicarboxylic acids. We could say that one is the reciprocal case of the other since, when there exist chains of great electron density parallel to a single crystallographic direction [the [001] axis], there appear in reciprocal space continuous sheets of diffuse scattering located in planes of the reciprocal lattice normal to the direction of the chains in the structure. The periodicity of the sheets of maximum intensity corresponds in direct space to the most important spacing in the chain. Similarly, in the case of pentaerythritol we have sheets of great electron density, and in reciprocal space there appear bands of large scattering intensity, since, evidently, this type of molecular vibration must produce a certain disorder (thermal) in the layers of molecules, and the anisotropy of the sections of the columns reveals the complexity of the motion, probably torsional.

The effect we have observed in dicarboxylic acids (chains) and in pentaerythritol (layers) is, in some ways, similar to that which Guinier describes (1956) with respect to linear or planar statistical disorders, but in the present case is of thermal origin.

Application of the theory to anthracene

The general morphology of the diffuse scattering of anthracene has been described in Ch. 4, as well as its crystal structure. In this case the elementary cell contains two molecules that are not equivalent by simple translation. Therefore, in order to obey the criterion of one molecule per unit cell, it is necessary to define a pseudocell that contains a single molecule (Annaka and Amorós, 1960b). Figure 13 shows the pseudocell chosen. The parallelepiped $OAEB\text{-}CDGF$ corresponds to the unit cell of anthracene, so that $OABE$ is the plane (001) of the cell and the points A and P represent the pseudoequivalent points of the molecules, that is, the centers of equilibrium of the two molecules of the unit cell. With this cell it is clear that the most important alignment of the molecules in the crystal is that formed by the points $APB \cdots$. The pseudocell $APOP'Q'CQD$ contains a single molecule, and therefore the extension of Laval's theory can be applied to it directly.

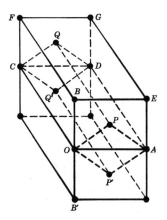

Fig. 13.   Anthracene. Primitive pseudocell $OP'AP\text{-}CQ'DQ$ and primitive cell $OAEB\text{-}CDGF$.

In studying the diffuse scattering of anthracene, one area, corresponding to Fig. 14, was measured with extreme care. In that map we can see a direction of intense diffuse scattering that forms and angle of 17° with the line joining the point $(\overline{4}09)$ and $(\overline{5}09)$. It is reasonable to suppose that this intense line is due to transverse waves of the acoustic branch. The basis for this conclusion is the intensity and definition of the line of scattering, as well as the configuration of the primitive cell of Fig. 13. With this assumption, the intensity was measured along a line in the plane defined by the aforementioned line of scattering. The line measured forms an angle of 35° with the plane (010). The dispersion curve of transverse waves whose direction of vibration is approximately parallel to the plane (010) has been calculated using the following formula

$$I_{TDS_1}(\mathbf{r^*}) = |\mathbf{r^*}|^2 \frac{kT}{m} \cdot |F_m|^2 \exp{(-2M)} \frac{1}{v_\gamma^2} \cos^2{(\mathbf{r^*}, \mathbf{e}_\gamma)}, \qquad (101)$$

where m is the mass of the molecule, and $(\mathbf{r^*}, \mathbf{e}_\gamma)$ is the angle between the diffraction vector and the direction of vibration of the transverse waves. In addition the molecular structure factor F_m was taken to be the mean value of the structure factors of the two molecules, without correction by second-order diffuse scattering.

We assume that this dispersion curve corresponds to the transverse waves produced by the chain of molecules $(APB \cdots)$ of Fig. 13 because the line chosen is approximately parallel to that chain. If we assume such a chain, formed by equal particles, the frequency is given (Kittel, 1956) by

$$2\pi v = \pm \left(\frac{4\beta}{m}\right)^{1/2} \sin{\pi g a_j}, \qquad (102)$$

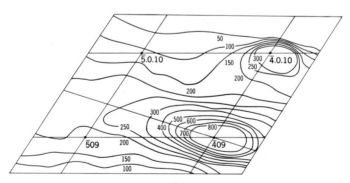

Fig. 14. Anthracene. Experimental isodiffraction lines in a special zone of diffraction space. Arbitrary values.

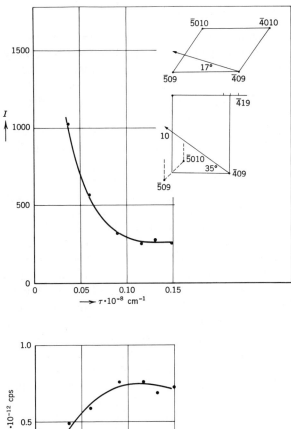

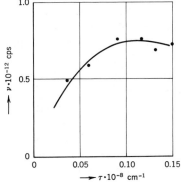

Fig. 15. Anthracene. Intensity and frequency dispersion curves.

where m is the mass, g the wave vector, a_j the distance between particles. From this simple formula and from the dispersion curve of Fig. 15, the value of the force constant of the chain can be obtained, which in this case is $\beta = 1.6 \times 10^3$ dynes/cm. Although the method used is only approximate, a reasonable value for the force constant β is obtained.

Study of the lattice dynamics of hexamine

The crystal structure of hexamine was described in Ch. 4 as being formed by almost-spherical molecules arranged in a body-centered cubic cell. The crystal lattice can then be described by a primitive rhombohedral cell whose dimensions are given in Table 2, Ch. 4. This primitive cell is appropriate for the study of the lattice dynamics and diffuse scattering, since in this way the theory is simplified by suppressing, in the equations, the index j describing the atoms within the cell. With the primitive rhombohedral cell, the extinction conditions of the centered cell disappear. Figure 16 shows two index fields of different principal sections of the reciprocal lattice of hexamine with the indices corresponding to the primitive cell (large numbers) and the multiple cubic cell (small numbers).

In a molecular compound such as hexamine there are strong covalent bonding forces between atoms of the same molecule, and weak van der Waals forces between neighboring molecules. Keeping in mind those forces, we shall use the simple dynamic model according to which the molecules move as rigid bodies, that is, ignoring intramolecular vibrations. It is evident that the vibrations of a rigid molecule will be not only translational, but also librational about the inertial axes of the molecule. Nevertheless, for the sake of simplicity we shall consider only translational motion, for the results obtained with anthracene showed that molecular librations contributed very little to the diffuse intensity. In addition we shall consider a molecule to be subject only to the action of its first, second, and third neighbors, with the action of more distant molecules assumed negligible. This simplification is based on the fact that van der Waals forces decrease with the sixth power of the distance, that is, so rapidly that the interaction rapidly becomes negligible.

According to this model, we shall have only an acoustic branch, and therefore, to each wave vector $\mathbf{g}$ there will be associated three thermal waves, one longitudinal and the other two transverse.

Born's secular equation

$$\begin{vmatrix} D_{11}(\mathbf{g}) - \omega^2 & D_{12}(\mathbf{g}) & D_{13}(\mathbf{g}) \\ D_{21}(\mathbf{g}) & D_{22}(\mathbf{g}) - \omega^2 & D_{23}(\mathbf{g}) \\ D_{31}(\mathbf{g}) & D_{32}(\mathbf{g}) & D_{33}(\mathbf{g}) - \omega^2 \end{vmatrix} = 0 \qquad (103)$$

will be of third degree, where for each $\mathbf{g}$ we shall have only three frequencies.

In solving the secular equation, substitution of the values of the three frequencies associated with each wave vector in equations (103)

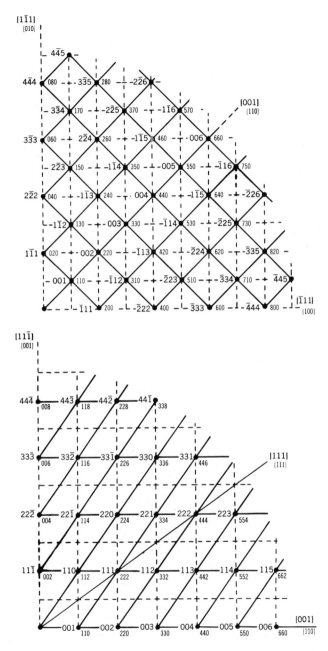

Fig. 16. Hexamine. Levels $(001)_0^*$ and $(110)_0^*$. Arrays of indices for the rhombohedral (large numerals) and cubic (small numerals) lattices.

permits us to obtain the direction vibration corresponding to each frequency.

Since the interaction between molecules is a function of the distances between them, it is necessary to be able to calculate these distances. The computation is much simplified if an orthogonal coordinate system is used. Therefore, it is convenient to use the system of reference given by the body-centered cubic cell. In this case we shall call the fundamental translation $2a$, instead of a.

Figure 17 is a schematic representation of the structure of hexamine, where the molecules have been represented by spheres. An arbitrary molecule, taken at (000) for reference, is surrounded by a first coordination sphere consisting of its eight first neighbors located on the 3-fold axes at a distance of $a\sqrt{3}$. These molecules have been numbered from 1 to 8. The second coordination sphere consists of six molecules, second neighbors, which are located on the 4-fold axes, and have been numbered from 1' to 6'. Finally, the third coordination sphere consists of 12 third neighbors, at a distance of $2a\sqrt{2}$ on the 2-fold-symmetry axes, and numbered from 1" to 12". Table 1 gives the coordinates of the molecules that are first, second, and third neighbors of the reference molecule located at (000).

The dynamic matrix of a primitive lattice has in principle nine force constants for each value of $(l-l')$, but we shall see that in the case of a body-centered cubic lattice the number is reduced to seven on application of the symmetry operators corresponding to rotations,

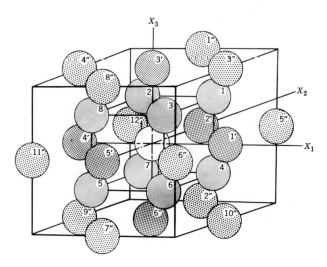

Fig. 17. Hexamine. Diagram of first, second, and third neighbors.

Table 1 Positions of the centers of the molecules in the first three coordination spheres

		First neighbors						
	x	y	z			x	y	z
1	1	1	1		5	−1	−1	−1
2	−1	1	1		6	1	−1	−1
3	1	−1	1		7	−1	1	−1
4	1	1	−1		8	−1	−1	1

		Second neighbors						
	x	y	z			x	y	z
1′	2	0	0		4′	−2	0	2
2′	0	2	0		5′	2	−2	0
3′	0	0	2		6′	2	0	−2

		Third neighbors						
	x	y	z			x	y	z
1″	0	2	2		7″	0	−2	−2
2″	0	2	−2		8″	0	−2	2
3″	2	0	2		9″	−2	0	−2
4″	−2	0	2		10″	2	0	−2
5″	2	2	0		11″	−2	−2	0
6″	2	−2	0		12″	−2	2	0

translations, and symmetry planes. The multiple translations of the base vectors have been taken into account in assuming that the dynamic matrix $D(l-l')$ depends on the combination $(l-l')$ and not on l or l' separately.

Let us consider a reference system in which a point is determined by the orthogonal coordinates $r_\alpha(\alpha = 1, 2, 3)$. Let T be the operator that operates on the orthogonal axes to give them a new position, so that r_A ($A = 1, 2, 3$) is the point in the new system. It is then seen that

$$r_\alpha = \Sigma_A T_{\alpha A} r_A. \tag{104}$$

The coefficients $T_{\alpha A}$ depend on the particular transformation that is applied. If the point r_α is a lattice point, it is verified that

$$r_\alpha\binom{l}{j} = \Sigma_A \ T_{\alpha A} r_A\binom{l}{j}. \tag{105}$$

If T is a symmetry operator of the lattice, it will be possible to find a point $\binom{l}{j}$ of the lattice such that

$$r_\alpha\binom{l}{j} = r_B\binom{L}{J} \qquad \text{for } \alpha, B = 1,2,3. \tag{106}$$

Combining (105) and (106),

$$r_B\binom{L}{J} = \sum_A T_{\alpha A} r_A\binom{l}{j}. \tag{107}$$

If the symbol T names the matrix of quantities $T_{\alpha A}$, $T \equiv (T_{\alpha A})$ and if r is considered to be a matrix of one column, then (107) can be written in the matrix form

$$r\binom{L}{J} = Tr\binom{l}{j}. \tag{108}$$

The elements of the dynamic matrix $D_{\alpha\beta}\binom{l-l'}{jj}$ behave with respect to the indexes α and β as a second-order covariant tensor. The transformation relation is:

$$D_{\alpha\beta}\binom{l-l'}{jj'} = \sum_{A,B} T_{\alpha A} T_{\beta B} D_{AB}\binom{l-l'}{jj'}, \qquad (A, B = 1, 2, 3). \tag{109}$$

Points $\binom{L}{J}$ and $\binom{L'}{J'}$ can be found such that

$$D_{\alpha\beta}\binom{l-l'}{jj'} = D_{MN}\binom{L-L'}{JJ'}, \qquad (\alpha, \beta, M, N = 1, 2, 3). \tag{110}$$

Therefore,

$$D_{MN}\binom{L-L'}{JJ'} = \sum_{A,B} T_{\alpha A} T_{\beta B} D_{AB}\binom{l-l'}{jj'}, \tag{111}$$

and in matrix notation,

$$D\binom{L-L'}{JJ'} = TD\binom{l-l'}{jj'}\widetilde{T}, \tag{112}$$

where $\widetilde{T}$ is the transpose of matrix T, and the change of $\binom{l}{j}$ to $\binom{L}{J}$ and and $\binom{l'}{j'}$ to $\binom{L'}{J'}$ is obtained from equations (107) or (108).

The space group of a given lattice has a basis from which all the elements of the group can be obtained by composition. If we call $T_1, T_2, \cdots$ the matrices representing that basis, and if we substitute the matrices in equation (112), we obtain a collection of matrix equations, from which we can in turn, obtain the elements of the dynamic matrix. We shall apply these ideas, due to Begbie and Born (1947), to the structure of hexamine, in a way similar to Curien's (1952) in the case of iron.

The complete symmetry operations of the lattice can be generated by applying the following symmetry operations A, B, C.

A. A threefold axis $x = y = z$, to which is associated the following matrix

$$T_t = \begin{vmatrix} 0 & 1 & 0 \\ 0 & 0 & 1 \\ 1 & 0 & 0 \end{vmatrix}. \tag{113}$$

To apply formula (112) the changes of indices $l \to L$ must be specified, which can be obtained from Table 1 using the substitution group notation. Thus

$$(2,3,4)\,(6,7,8)\,(1)\,(5),$$
$$(1',2',3')\,(4',5',6'),$$
$$(1'',3'',5'')\,(7'',9'',11'')\,(2'',4'',6'')\,(8'',10'',12''),$$

which indicates that a matrix with index l is obtained from the matrix whose index is the next number of the cycle by applying to it the operation $T \cdots \tilde{T}$, for example,

$$D^2 = T_t D^3 \tilde{T}_t \tag{114}$$

B. A symmetry plane in the position $z = 0$, with the matrix and change of notation in which we have omitted the cycles with one element

$$T_m = \begin{vmatrix} 1 & 0 & 0 \\ 0 & 1 & 0 \\ 0 & 0 & -1 \end{vmatrix}. \tag{115}$$

Thus

$$(1,4)\,(2,7)\,(3,6)\,(5,8),$$
$$(1')\,(2')\,(4')\,(5')\,(3',6'),$$
$$(1'',2'')\,(3'',10'')\,(4'',9'')\,(7'',8'')\,(5'')\,(6'')\,(11'')\,(12'').$$

C. A diagonal symmetry plane $x = y$ with matrix and change of indexes as follows:

$$T_d = \begin{vmatrix} 0 & 1 & 0 \\ 1 & 0 & 0 \\ 0 & 0 & 1 \end{vmatrix}. \tag{116}$$

Thus

$$(2,3)\,(6,7)\,(1)\,(4)\,(5)\,(8),$$
$$(1',2')\,(4',5')\,(3')\,(6'),$$
$$(1'',3'')\,(2'',10'')\,(4'',8'')\,(6'',12'')\,(7'',9'')\,(5'')\,(11'').$$

If we apply this operation first to the cycles with only one index, we obtain, for example, for T_t applied to D^l, the identity

$$\begin{vmatrix} D_{11}{}^1 & D_{12}{}^1 & D_{13}{}^1 \\ D_{21}{}^1 & D_{22}{}^1 & D_{23}{}^1 \\ D_{31}{}^1 & D_{32}{}^1 & D_{33}{}^1 \end{vmatrix} = \begin{vmatrix} D_{22}{}^1 & D_{23}{}^1 & D_{21}{}^1 \\ D_{32}{}^1 & D_{33}{}^1 & D_{31}{}^1 \\ D_{12}{}^1 & D_{13}{}^1 & D_{11}{}^1 \end{vmatrix}, \tag{117}$$

hence

$$D_{11}{}^1 = D_{22}{}^1 = D_{33}{}^1, D_{12}{}^1 = D_{23}{}^1 = D_{31}{}^1, D_{13}{}^1 = D_{21}{}^1 = D_{32}{}^1. \quad (118)$$

And repeating these operations, we obtain the matrices as a function of the molecular force constants given in Table 2. The last expression,

Table 2   Elements of the dynamic matrix

$$\left.\begin{matrix}D^1\\D^5\end{matrix}\right\} = -\frac{1}{m}\begin{vmatrix}\alpha & \beta & \beta\\ \beta & \alpha & \beta\\ \beta & \beta & \alpha\end{vmatrix}\qquad\qquad \left.\begin{matrix}D^2\\D^6\end{matrix}\right\} = -\frac{1}{m}\begin{vmatrix}\alpha & -\beta & -\beta\\ -\beta & \alpha & \beta\\ -\beta & \beta & \alpha\end{vmatrix}$$

$$\left.\begin{matrix}D^3\\D^7\end{matrix}\right\} = -\frac{1}{m}\begin{vmatrix}\alpha & -\beta & \beta\\ -\beta & \alpha & -\beta\\ \beta & -\beta & \alpha\end{vmatrix}\qquad\qquad \left.\begin{matrix}D^4\\D^8\end{matrix}\right\} = -\frac{1}{m}\begin{vmatrix}\alpha & \beta & -\beta\\ \beta & \alpha & -\beta\\ -\beta & -\beta & \alpha\end{vmatrix}$$

$$\left.\begin{matrix}D^{1'}\\D^{4'}\end{matrix}\right\} = -\frac{1}{m}\begin{vmatrix}\alpha' & 0 & 0\\ 0 & \beta' & 0\\ 0 & 0 & \beta'\end{vmatrix}\qquad\qquad \left.\begin{matrix}D^{2'}\\D^{5'}\end{matrix}\right\} = -\frac{1}{m}\begin{vmatrix}\beta' & 0 & 0\\ 0 & \alpha' & 0\\ 0 & 0 & \beta'\end{vmatrix}$$

$$\left.\begin{matrix}D^{3'}\\D^{6'}\end{matrix}\right\} = -\frac{1}{m}\begin{vmatrix}\beta' & 0 & 0\\ 0 & \beta' & 0\\ 0 & 0 & \alpha'\end{vmatrix}$$

$$\left.\begin{matrix}D^{1''}\\D^{7''}\end{matrix}\right\} = -\frac{1}{m}\begin{vmatrix}\alpha'' & 0 & 0\\ 0 & \beta'' & \gamma''\\ 0 & \gamma'' & \beta''\end{vmatrix}\qquad\qquad \left.\begin{matrix}D^{2''}\\D^{8''}\end{matrix}\right\} = -\frac{1}{m}\begin{vmatrix}\alpha'' & 0 & 0\\ 0 & \beta'' & -\gamma''\\ 0 & -\gamma'' & \beta''\end{vmatrix}$$

$$\left.\begin{matrix}D^{3''}\\D^{9''}\end{matrix}\right\} = -\frac{1}{m}\begin{vmatrix}\beta'' & 0 & \gamma''\\ 0 & \alpha'' & 0\\ \gamma'' & 0 & \beta''\end{vmatrix}\qquad\qquad \left.\begin{matrix}D^{4''}\\D^{10''}\end{matrix}\right\} = -\frac{1}{m}\begin{vmatrix}\beta'' & 0 & -\gamma''\\ 0 & \alpha'' & 0\\ -\gamma'' & 0 & \beta''\end{vmatrix}$$

$$\left.\begin{matrix}D^{5''}\\D^{11''}\end{matrix}\right\} = -\frac{1}{m}\begin{vmatrix}\beta'' & \gamma'' & 0\\ \gamma'' & \beta'' & 0\\ 0 & 0 & \alpha''\end{vmatrix}\qquad\qquad \left.\begin{matrix}D^{16''}\\D^{12''}\end{matrix}\right\} = -\frac{1}{m}\begin{vmatrix}\beta'' & -\gamma'' & 0\\ -\gamma'' & \beta'' & 0\\ 0 & 0 & \alpha''\end{vmatrix}$$

$$D^0 = -(4\alpha+\alpha'+2\beta'+2\alpha''+4\beta'')\begin{vmatrix}1 & 0 & 0\\ 0 & 1 & 0\\ 0 & 0 & 1\end{vmatrix}$$

D^0, is obtained by subtraction from equation (7) where the summation extends only to third neighbors. Therefore, because of the particular symmetry of this type of lattice, there are only seven independent molecular coefficients, which are the second derivatives of the lattice energy with respect to the different displacements of the 26 molecules considered (8, 6, and 12, first, second, and third neighbors, respectively), with respect to the reference molecule.

The coefficients α, β refer to the first neighbors; α', β' to the second neighbors; and α'', β'', γ'' to the third neighbors.

We shall now calculate the Fourier matrix that will permit us to write the secular equation (103) as a function of the molecular coefficients. Applying the equation

$$D_{\alpha\beta}(\mathbf{g}) = \sum_l D_{\alpha\beta}^l \exp(-2\pi i \mathbf{g}\mathbf{r}_l) \tag{119}$$

in which we substitute the values of the matrices in Table 2, we obtain:

$$D_{11}(\mathbf{g}) = \frac{8\alpha}{m}(1 - \cos u_1 \cos u_2 \cos u_3) + \frac{4}{m}[\alpha' \sin^2 u_1$$

$$+ \beta' (\sin^2 u_2 + \sin^2 u_3)] + \frac{4}{m}[\alpha'' (1 - \cos 2u_2 \cos 2u_3)$$

$$+ \beta'' (2 - \cos 2u_1 \cos 2u_2 - \cos 2u_1 \cos 2u_3)]$$

$$D_{23}(\mathbf{g}) = \frac{8}{m} \sin u_2 \sin u_3 (\beta \cos u_1 + 2\gamma'' \cos u_2 \cos u_3), \tag{120}$$

where

$$u_1 = 2\pi g_1 a$$

$$u_2 = 2\pi g_2 a \tag{121}$$

$$u_3 = 2\pi g_3 a,$$

and g_1, g_2, g_3 are the components of the wave vector along the axes and a is half the lattice parameter of the cubic cell.

The other elements can be obtained by cyclic permutations of the indices u_1, u_2, u_3. The domain of variation of u_1, u_2, u_3 is obtained by restricting the wave vector inside of some first Brillouin zone.

Long waves: limiting velocities and elastic constants

When the wave vector tends to zero, the wavelengths become very large compared with the distances between molecules. If the elements of the Fourier matrix are expanded in a series in powers of $\mathbf{g}$, and terms of order higher than one are neglected, the secular equation becomes

$$\begin{vmatrix} \frac{16\pi^2 a^2}{m}[\alpha(g_1{}^2 + g_2{}^2 + g_3{}^2) + \alpha' g_1{}^2 + \beta' (g_2{}^2 + g_3{}^2) + 2\alpha''(g_2{}^2 + g_3{}^2) \\ \qquad + 2\beta''(2g_1{}^2 + g_2{}^2 + g_3{}^2)] - \omega^2 & \cdot\ \cdot \\ \frac{16\pi^2 a^2}{m}(2\beta g_2 g_3 + 4\gamma'' g_2 g_3) & \cdot\ \cdot \\ \qquad \cdot & \cdot\ \cdot \end{vmatrix} = 0. \tag{122}$$

For these large wavelengths the vibrations are similar to the acoustic vibrations that can be induced in the crystal by mechanical means. Therefore, from the study of these waves we can define the coefficients of elasticity that are deduced from measurements of propagation velocities, as defined by the classical theory of elasticity in the equation

$$\begin{vmatrix} c_{11}p_1{}^2 + c_{44}(p_2{}^2 + p_3{}^2) - \rho V^2 & (c_{12}+c_{44})p_1p_2 & \cdot \\ & \cdot & \cdot \\ & \cdot & \cdot \end{vmatrix} = 0$$

$$(123)$$

The three velocities V_i and the three polarization vectors e_i of the three elastic waves whose wave vector g has direction cosines p_1, p_2, p_3 with respect to the cubic axes are given by the three solutions of the system (Jahn, 1942)

$$[c_{11}p_1{}^2 + c_{44}(p_2{}^2 + p_3{}^2) - \rho V_i{}^2]\xi_{i1} + (c_{12}+c_{44})(p_1p_2\xi_{i2} + p_1p_3\xi_{i3}) = 0,$$
$$[c_{11}p_2{}^2 + c_{44}(p_1{}^2 + p_3{}^2) - \rho V_i{}^2]\xi_{i2} + (c_{12}+c_{44})(p_1p_2\xi_{i1} + p_2p_3\xi_{i3}) = 0,$$
$$[c_{11}p_3{}^2 + c_{44}(p_1{}^2 + p_2{}^2) - \rho V_i{}^2]\xi_{i3} + (c_{12}+c_{44})(p_1p_3\xi_{i1} + p_2p_3\xi_{i2}) = 0,$$

$$(124)$$

where c_{11}, c_{12}, c_{44} are the elastic constants and ρ the density of the crystal. ξ_{i1}, ξ_{i2}, ξ_{i3} are the direction cosines of the unit polarization vectors e_i. The solution of the system is obtained by imposing the condition that the determinant of the coefficients, called the Christoffel determinant, is identically zero:

$$\begin{vmatrix} c_{11}p_1{}^2 + c_{44}(p_2{}^2 + p_3{}^2) - \rho V_i{}^2 & (c_{12}+c_{44})p_1p_2 & (c_2+c_{44})p_1p_3 \\ (c_{12}+c_{44})p_1p_2 & c_{11}p_2{}^2 + c_{44}(p_1{}^2 + p_3{}^2) - \rho V_i{}^2 & (c_{12}+c_{44})p_2p_3 \\ (c_{12}+c_{44})p_1p_3 & (c_{12}+c_{44})p_2p_3 & c_{11}p_3{}^2 + c_{44}(p_1{}^2 + p_2{}^2) - \rho V_i{}^2 \end{vmatrix} = 0.$$

$$(125)$$

Equation (124) is of third degree in V, and its solution gives three velocities V_i associated with the same wave vector g. The polarization vectors are mutually orthogonal, but need not be perpendicular or parallel to g. Nevertheless, the polarization vector corresponding to the longitudinal wave is nearly parallel to g, while the other two, corresponding to the transverse vibrations, are nearly normal to g. Equations (124) can turn out to be three independent equations for waves that propagate in special directions of the crystal; for example, along [100], [110], and [111], since in these directions the waves become purely longitudinal and purely transverse.

When the elastic waves propagate along the 4-fold axis [100], it can be shown that $p_1 = 1$, $p_2 = p_3 = 0$, and equations (124) reduce to

$$(c_{11} - \rho V_i^2)\xi_{i1} = 0,$$
$$(c_{44} - \rho V_i^2)\xi_{i2} = 0, \tag{126}$$
$$(c_{44} - \rho V_i^2)\xi_{i3} = 0,$$

giving the solutions

$$\begin{array}{llll}
\rho V_1^2 = c_{11}, & \xi_{11} = 1, & \xi_{12} = 0, & \xi_{13} = 0, \\
\rho V_2^2 = c_{44}, & \xi_{21} = 0, & \xi_{22} = 1, & \xi_{23} = 0, \\
\rho V_3^2 = c_{44}, & \xi_{31} = 0, & \xi_{32} = 0, & \xi_{33} = 1,
\end{array} \tag{127}$$

which correspond to one longitudinal wave and two transverse waves whose modes are degenerate and have the same velocity:

$$V_{l[001]} = \left(\frac{c_{11}}{\rho}\right)^{1/2},$$
$$V_{t[001]} = \left(\frac{c_{44}}{\rho}\right)^{1/2}. \tag{128}$$

For elastic waves propagating along the 2-fold axis, we have $p_1 = p_2 = 1/\sqrt{2}$, $p_3 = 0$, and equations (124) become

$$[\tfrac{1}{2}(c_{11} + c_{44}) - \rho V_i^2]\xi_{i1} + \tfrac{1}{2}(c_{12} + c_{44})\xi_{i2} = 0,$$
$$[\tfrac{1}{2}(c_{11} + c_{44}) - \rho V_i^2]\xi_{i2} + \tfrac{1}{2}(c_{12} + c_{44})\xi_{i1} = 0, \tag{129}$$
$$(c_{44} - \rho V_i^2)\xi_{i3} = 0.$$

Combining the first two, we obtain the three solutions:

$$\begin{array}{llll}
\rho V_1^2 = \tfrac{1}{2}(c_{11} + c_{12} + 2c_{44}), & \xi_{11} = \xi_{12} = \dfrac{1}{\sqrt{2}}, & \xi_{13} = 0, \\
\rho V_2^2 = \tfrac{1}{2}(c_{11} - c_{12}), & \xi_{21} = -\xi_{22} = \dfrac{1}{\sqrt{2}}, & \xi_{23} = 0, \\
\rho V_3^2 = c_{44}, & \xi_{31} = \xi_{32} = 0, & \xi_{33} = 1,
\end{array} \tag{130}$$

the first being purely longitudinal and the other two transverse waves. The velocities are

$$V_{l[001]} = \left[\frac{c_{11}+c_{12}+2c_{44}}{2\rho}\right]^{1/2},$$

$$V_{t_2[001]} = \left[\frac{c_{11}-c_{12}}{2\rho}\right]^{1/2}, \tag{131}$$

$$V_{t_1[001]} = \left[\frac{c_{44}}{\rho}\right]^{1/2}.$$

Finally, when the elastic waves propagate along the 3-fold axis [111], $p_1 = p_2 = p_3 = 1/\sqrt{3}$, and equations (124) reduce to

$$[\tfrac{1}{3}(c_{11}+2c_{44}) - \rho V_i^2]\xi_{i1} + \tfrac{1}{3}(c_{12}+c_{44})(\xi_{i2}+\xi_{i3}) = 0,$$

$$[\tfrac{1}{3}(c_{11}+2c_{44}) - \rho V_i^2]\xi_{i2} + \tfrac{1}{3}(c_{12}+c_{44})(\xi_{i1}+\xi_{i3}) = 0, \tag{132}$$

$$[\tfrac{1}{3}(c_{11}+2c_{44}) - \rho V_i^2]\xi_{i3} + \tfrac{1}{3}(c_{12}+c_{44})(\xi_{i1}+\xi_{i2}) = 0,$$

from which we obtain the solutions

$$\rho V_1^2 = \tfrac{1}{3}(c_{11}+2c_{12}+4c_{44}), \qquad \xi_{11} = \xi_{12} = \xi_{13} = \frac{1}{\sqrt{3}},$$

$$\rho V_2^2 = \tfrac{1}{3}(c_{11}-c_{12}+c_{44}), \qquad \xi_{21} = -\xi_{22} = \frac{1}{\sqrt{2}}, \qquad \xi_{23} = 0, \tag{133}$$

$$\rho V_3^2 = \tfrac{1}{3}(c_{11}-c_{12}+c_{44}), \qquad \xi_{31} = \xi_{32} = -\tfrac{1}{2}, \qquad \xi_{33} = \frac{1}{\sqrt{6}}.$$

The transverse modes are degenerate, that is, they have the same frequency. In this case the velocities are given by

$$V_{l[111]} = \left[\frac{c_{11}+2c_{12}+4c_{44}}{3\rho}\right]^{1/2}$$

$$V_{t[111]} = \left[\frac{c_{11}-c_{12}+c_{44}}{3\rho}\right]^{1/2} \tag{134}$$

The elastic constants c_{11}, c_{44}, c_{12} can thus be determined experimentally from measurements of the velocities of propagation.

Force constants and elastic constants

These constants are related to the atomic coefficients by setting equations (122) and (123) identically equal, taking into account that the components of **g** are $g_1 = p_1/\Lambda$, $g_2 = p_2/\Lambda$, $g_3 = p_3/\Lambda$, and that

$$V = \frac{\omega\Lambda}{2\pi}, \qquad \rho = \frac{m}{8a^3}. \tag{135}$$

We obtain the following relations

$$ac_{11} = \alpha + \alpha' + 4\beta'',$$
$$ac_{44} = \alpha + \beta' + 2\alpha'' + 2\beta'', \tag{136}$$
$$a(c_{12} + c_{44}) = 2\beta + 4\gamma''$$

among the seven molecular coefficients.

The radial displacements of the first, second, and third neighbors can be expressed for a body-centered cubic lattice as a function of force constants through the following expressions:

$$F = (\alpha + 2\beta)\, dr,$$
$$F' = \alpha'\, dr, \tag{137}$$
$$F'' = (\beta'' + \gamma'')\, dr.$$

From the secular equation it is now easy to write the dispersion curves along the axes of symmetry [100], [110], and [111]; and these equations give the variation of the frequency with the wave vector for longitudinal and transverse waves propagating along the 2-fold, 3-fold, and 4-fold axes.

We have seen that in order to study thermal vibration it is sufficient to consider wave vectors only within a single Brillouin zone. The Brillouin zones for a body-centered cubic cell are rhombododecahedra (Fig. 18), whose assymmetric part is bounded by the planes $z = 0$, $x = y$, $y = z$. The Fourier dynamic matrix is simplified considerably for special positions of the wave vector. We shall consider the different cases.

g in the direction of the fourfold axis [100]. If we take into account relations (120) and (122), the elements of the Fourier matrix reduce to

$$D_{11} = \frac{16}{m}\left[\alpha + (\alpha' + 4\beta'')\cos^2\frac{u_1}{2}\right]\sin^2\frac{u_1}{2},$$

$$D_{22} = D_{33} = \frac{16}{m}\left[\alpha + (\beta' + 2\alpha'' + 2\beta'')\cos^2\frac{u_1}{2}\right]\sin^2\frac{u_1}{2}, \tag{138}$$

$$D_{12} = D_{13} = D_{23} = 0.$$

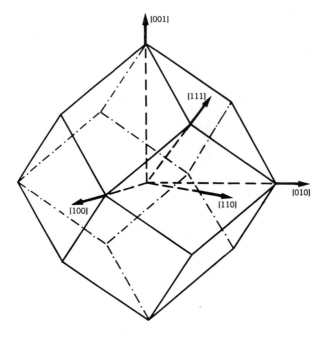

Fig. 18.   Hexamine. First Brillouin zone.

One of the waves associated with **g** is longitudinal, with frequency $\omega_1/2\pi$, and the other two are transverse waves with a common frequency equal to $\omega_t/2\pi$ and with direction of vibration in the plane (100). We can show that

$$\omega_l^2 = D_{11},$$
$$\omega_t^2 = D_{22} \qquad (139)$$

if $0 < u_1 < \pi$.

At the boundary of the Brillouin zone ($u_1 = \pi$) we have

$$\left.\begin{array}{l} D_{11} = \omega_l^2 \\[1mm] D_{22} = \omega_t^2 \end{array}\right\} = \frac{16\alpha}{m}. \qquad (140)$$

With the vector **g** of modulus $\tfrac{1}{2}a$ there are associated three thermal waves, whose directions are a set of mutually orthogonal axes that has an arbitrary orientation. If we consider the body-centered cubic lattice to be made up of two simple cubic lattices of cell edge $2a$, one translated with respect to the other by (a, a, a), the waves of the propagation vector $(\tfrac{1}{2}a, 0, 0)$ are such that they propagate without deforming the two simple lattices, but simply cause one to vibrate with respect to the other, where the only molecular force constant entering in this vibration is α.

g in the direction of the twofold axis [110]. In this case the elements of the Fourier matrix satisfy

$$D_{11} = D_{22}, \qquad D_{13} = D_{23} = 0,$$

$$D_{11} = \frac{4}{m} \left[2\alpha + \alpha' + \beta' + 2\alpha'' + 2\beta'' \left(1 + 2 \cos^2 u_1 \right) \right] \sin^2 u_1.$$
(141)

$$D_{33} = \frac{8}{m} \left(\alpha + \beta' + 2\beta'' + 2\alpha'' \cos^2 u_1 \right) \sin^2 u_1,$$

$$D_{12} = \frac{8}{m} \left[\beta + 2\gamma'' \cos^2 u_1 \right] \sin^2 u_1,$$

with $u_1 = u_2 < \pi/2$, $u_3 = 0$.

One of the waves along [110] is strictly longitudinal and its frequency is given by

$$\omega_l^2 = D_{11} + D_{12} = \frac{4}{m} \left[2\alpha + 2\beta + \alpha' + \beta' + 2\alpha'' + 2\beta'' \right.$$

$$\left. + 4(\beta'' + \gamma'') \cos^2 u_1 \right] \sin^2 u_1. \quad (142)$$

The other two waves are strictly transverse waves, one along [1$\bar{1}$0], with frequency

$$\omega_{t_1}^2 = D_{11} - D_{12} = \frac{4}{m} \left[2\alpha - 2\beta + \alpha' + \beta' + 2\alpha'' + 2\beta'' \right.$$

$$\left. + 4(\beta'' - \gamma'') \cos^2 u_1 \right] \sin^2 u_1, \quad (143)$$

and the other along [001] with frequency

$$\omega_{t_2}^2 = D_{33} = \frac{8}{m} \left(\alpha + \beta' + 2\beta'' + 2\alpha'' \cos^2 u_1 \right) \sin^2 u_1. \quad (144)$$

If in the preceding expressions we introduce the relations (136) between the force constants and the elastic constants, we obtain:

$$D_{11} + D_{12} = \omega_l^2 = \frac{4}{m} \left[a(c_{11} + 2c_{44} + c_{12}) - 4(\beta'' + \gamma'') \sin^2 u_1 \right] \sin^2 u_1,$$

$$D_{11} - D_{12} = \omega_{t_1}^2 = \frac{8}{m} \left[\frac{a}{2} (c_{11} - c_{12}) - 2(\beta'' - \gamma'') \sin^2 u_1 \right] \sin^2 u_1,$$

$$D_{33} = \omega_{t_2}^2 = \frac{8}{m} \left[ac_{44} - 2\alpha'' \sin^2 u_1 \right] \sin^2 u_1. \quad (145)$$

g in the direction of the threefold axis [111]. In this case we see that $u_1 = u_2 = u_3$, with $0 < u_1 < \pi/2$, and the values of the elements of the matrix are

$$D_{11} = D_{22} = D_{33} = \frac{8}{m} \alpha(1 - \cos^3 u_1) + \frac{4}{m}(\alpha' + 2\beta') \sin^2 u_1$$

$$+ \frac{4}{m}(\alpha'' + 2\beta'') \sin^2 2u_1, \qquad (146)$$

$$D_{12} = D_{13} = D_{23} = \frac{8}{m} \sin^2 u_1 \cos u_1 (\beta + 2\gamma'') \cos u_1.$$

From the secular equation (103) we obtain, for longitudinal waves,

$$\omega_l^2 = D_{11} + 2D_{12}, \qquad (147)$$

while the transverse modes are degenerate, the two transverse vibrations are normal to each other, but the two together can have any orientation in the plane (111), and their common angular frequency is given by

$$\omega_t^2 = D_{11} - D_{12}. \qquad (148)$$

When the vector g is at the boundary of the Brillouin zone, we have

$$|g| = \frac{\sqrt{3}}{4a}, \qquad u_1 = u_2 = u_3 = \frac{\pi}{2}, \qquad (149)$$

in which case the secular equation has a triple root. The mutually orthogonal directions of the three vibrations have an indeterminate orientation for this wave vector. The common angular frequency of these three vibrations satisfies

$$\omega^2 = \frac{4}{m}(2\alpha + \alpha' + 2\beta') \qquad (150)$$

Extension of Laval's theory to the hexamine monomolecular structure

As we have seen, Laval postulates that the atoms vibrate almost entirely as if they were rigid bodies, and consequently the vibrations are not propagated within the atoms, but only from atom to atom. Therefore, the expression for the diffuse intensity due to thermal waves is a function of the Fourier transform of the electron density of the atom. For a monoatomic structure, the intensity is simply proportional to f^2 (Laval, 1954).

Similarly, if in a unimolecular structure it is postulated that the intramolecular vibrations are negligible, the diffuse intensity due to thermal waves in such a crystal will be expressed as a function of the square of the Fourier transform of the molecular electron density $|F_0(r^*)|^2$. This function is continuous, and the diffuse intensity due to thermal waves is conditioned by that function at each point of diffraction space.

First-order diffuse scattering

According to these ideas, I_{TDS_1} in hexamine is expressed by

$$I_{TDS_1}(g) = \frac{kT}{Zm}|r^*|^2 I_T(r^*) \sum_{\gamma=1}^{3} \frac{\cos^2(r^*, e_\gamma)}{\nu_\gamma^2}, \tag{151}$$

where the summation extends over the three acoustic thermal waves of wave vector g, m is the mass of the molecule, and Z its number of electrons. $I_T(r^*)$ is the intensity scattered by the molecule, corrected by the Debye-Waller temperature factor.

Since the study of the dynamics has been made at room temperature, the energy of the thermal waves, applying equipartition, is given for $T = 300°K$ by

$$E = kT = 404.4836 \times 10^{-16} \text{ erg} \tag{152}$$

where $k = $ Boltzmann constant $= 1.3850 \times 10^{-16} \text{ erg}(°C)^{-1}$.

The mass of the hexamine $C_6H_{12}N_4$ molecule is $m = 232.7816 \times 10^{-24}$g and its number of electrons $Z = 76$, so that

$$\frac{kT}{Zm} = 2.286 \times 10^6 \text{ erg} \cdot \text{g}^{-1}.$$

The first-order expression for hexamine is thus reduced to

$$I_{TDS_1}(r^*) = 2.286 \times 10^6 \times |r^*|^2 I_T(r^*) \sum_{\gamma=1}^{3} \frac{\cos^2(r^*, e_\gamma)}{\nu_\gamma^2}, \tag{153}$$

where $|r^*|$ is expressed in cm^{-1} and ν in s^{-1}. The dimensional formula for the right-hand side of the equality, except for $I_T(r^*)$, is

$$\frac{(L^2MT^{-2}\Theta^{-1})\Theta L^{-2}}{MT^{-2}}.$$

Therefore $I_{TDS_1}(r^*)$ will be expressed in electron units per electron (e.u./e) if $I_T(r^*)$ is expressed in electron units per primitive cell.

The analysis of the dynamics of hexamine is simplified when the diffuse scattering is analyzed along the directions of higher symmetry [100], [110], and [111]. For the study of longitudinal waves the wave vector $\mathbf{g}$ is parallel to the diffraction vector $\mathbf{r}^*$, and expression (153) reduces to

$$I_{TDS_1}(\mathbf{g}_1) = 2.286 \times 10^6 \times |\mathbf{r}^*|^2 I_T(\mathbf{r}^*) \frac{1}{\nu_l^2} \qquad (154)$$

In order to study the transverse waves the diffuse intensity is measured along the appropriate lines in reciprocal space that are at right angles to given symmetry axes. In this case $\mathbf{r}^*$ forms an angle Φ with the original direction.

When the wave vector $\mathbf{g}$ is parallel to a 3-fold or 4-fold axis of symmetry, the two corresponding transverse waves are equivalent and their vibrational-amplitude vectors, perpendicular to each other, have an arbitrary orientation within the plane normal to the axis of symmetry. Calling Φ the angle which $\mathbf{r}^*$ forms with the original longitudinal direction, equation (153) for hexamine becomes

$$I_{TDS_1}(\mathbf{r}^*) = 2.286 \times 10^6 \times |\mathbf{r}^*|^2 I_T(\mathbf{r}^*) \left(\frac{\sin^2\Phi}{\nu_t^2} + \frac{\cos^2\Phi}{\nu_l^2} \right). \qquad (155)$$

The vibrational-amplitude vector of the third wave is perpendicular to the vector $\mathbf{r}^*$, thus eliminating the contribution of one of the transverse waves. Expression (155) permits us to determine, for each vector $\mathbf{g}$, the value of ν_t when I_{TDS_1} has been determined experimentally and ν_l has been obtained from a previous experiment through expression (154).

When the wave vector $\mathbf{g}$ is parallel to a 2-fold axis, the two transverse waves are not equivalent; one of them, t_1, has its vibration vector in the principal plane $(001)_0^*$, and the other, t_2, in the diagonal plane $(1\bar{1}0)_0^*$. To study the amplitude vector parallel to [100], the vector $\mathbf{r}^*$ is chosen in the reciprocal plane $(1\bar{1}0)_0^*$, so that the transverse vibration t_1 is eliminated. To study the vibration of the amplitude vector parallel to [1$\bar{1}$0], the vector $\mathbf{r}^*$ is chosen in the reciprocal plane $(010)_0^*$, so that the vibration of t_2 is eliminated.

From the point of view of elasticity, all the Brillouin zones are equivalent. From the point of view of diffuse scattering, however, the intensity scattered by a molecule has large values in some Brillouin zones and small values in others. Since diffuse scattering is always relatively weak, the most appropriate Brillouin zones must be chosen carefully. In Ch. 4 it was seen how the DFT function accounts well for the continuous diffuse scattering. Figure 19 gives the Brillouin zones with the contour lines of the DFT superimposed for levels $(001)_0^*$ and $(110)_0^*$. It is clear that the appropriate Brillouin zones are 222, 440, and 800. Figure 20 shows the directions chosen in those

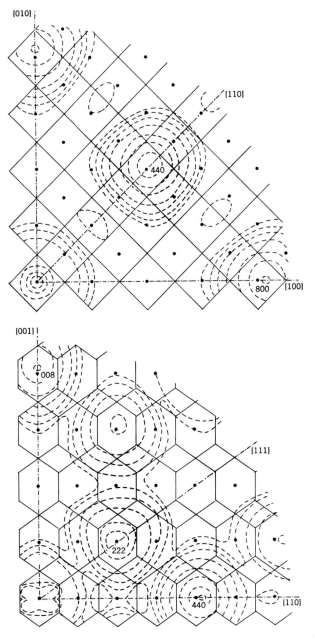

Fig. 19. Hexamine. Levels $(001)_0^*$ and $(110)_0^*$. Sections of the first Brillouin zones and the DFT function.

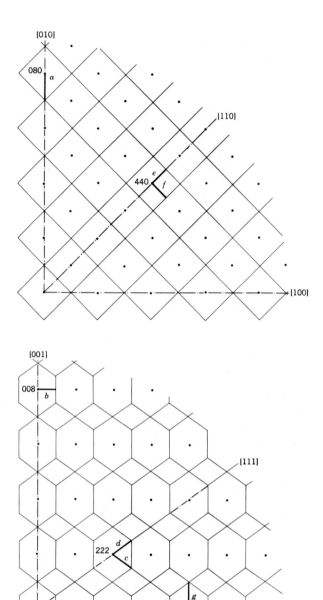

Fig. 20. Hexamine. Intersection of planes $(001)^*_0$ and $(110)^*_0$ with the first Brillouin zones, showing the lines $a, b, c, d, e, f,$ and g, along which experimental measurements were made.

364

Brillouin zones for measurements of the diffuse intensity, and Fig. 21 gives the variation of the function $I_0(\mathbf{r}^*)$ in the seven directions chosen.

Correction for second-order diffuse scattering

The experimental diffuse intensity contains not only the diffuse scattering of one phonon, but also that of two phonons, which may not be negligible, and the Compton scattering. In order to obtain the dispersion curves by means of I_{TDS_1}, we must subtract the other contributions from the observed diffuse scattering reduced to an absolute scale.

Laval's expression (90), corresponding to I_{TDS_2}, is simplified in the case of the hexamine unimolecular structure for the dynamic model that we apply. Considering only the acoustic waves, the summation over $\mathbf{g}_\gamma$, $\mathbf{g}_\delta$, extends only to 3. Also, because we are dealing with a unimolecular crystal and measurements at room temperature, it can be shown that

$$E_\gamma = E_{\delta'} = kT. \tag{156}$$

On the other hand, in our case we have

$$G_{\mathbf{g}_\gamma \mathbf{g}_\delta} = \cos(\mathbf{r}^*, \mathbf{e}_\gamma)\cos(\mathbf{r}^*, \mathbf{e}_\delta)\cdot F_T(\mathbf{r}^*). \tag{157}$$

The three waves of a given propagation vector are mutually orthogonal. Therefore

$$\cos^2(\mathbf{r}^*, \mathbf{e}_\gamma)\cdot\cos^2(\mathbf{r}^*, \mathbf{e}_\delta) = 1, \tag{158}$$

so that

$$|G_{\mathbf{g}_\gamma \mathbf{g}_\delta}|^2 = I_T(\mathbf{r}^*). \tag{159}$$

Since a priori we have no information on the different frequencies of wave vectors $\mathbf{g}_\gamma$ and $\mathbf{g}_\delta$, it is necessary to introduce a mean velocity of the acoustic thermal waves, defined by

$$\frac{1}{V_m^2} = \frac{1}{3}\left(\frac{1}{V_l^2} + \frac{2}{V_t^2}\right), \tag{160}$$

where V_l and V_t represent the velocities of the longitudinal and transverse waves, respectively. Likewise, V_l and V_t can be considered equal to the mean values of the velocities along some given directions, directly obtainable from the elastic constants of the crystal. Thus

$$V_{lm} = \tfrac{1}{3}(V_{l[010]} + V_{l[110]} + V_{l[111]})$$

$$V_{tm} = \tfrac{1}{6}(2V_{t[001]} + 2V_{t[11\bar{1}]} + V_{t_1[1\bar{1}0]} + V_{t_2[110]}) \tag{161}$$

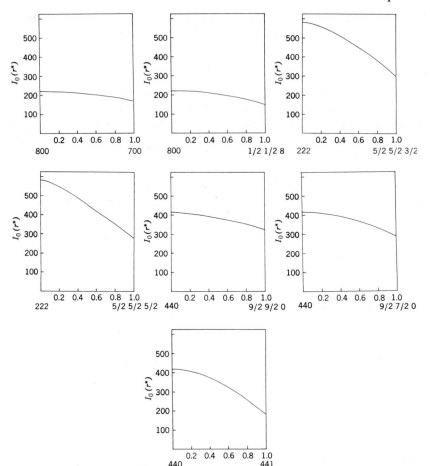

Fig. 21. Hexamine. Variation of the function $I_o(\mathbf{r}^*)$ along the seven lines measured.

These velocities have been calculated by means of expressions (128), (131), and (134), using the values of the elastic constants of hexamine obtained by Haussühl (1958) by ultrasonic method.

The intensity scattered by the pairs of acoustic waves characterized by the point P (Fig. 11) is given by

$$dI_p = \frac{k^2 T^2}{2 m^2 V_m^{\,4}} |\mathbf{r}^*|^4 I_T(\mathbf{r}^*) \sum_{\gamma, \delta = 1}^{3} \frac{1}{|\mathbf{g}_\gamma|^2 |\mathbf{g}_\delta|^2}, \tag{162}$$

where the 2 in the denominator arises from the fact that we must consider the symmetric arrangement of the vectors $\mathbf{g}_\gamma$ and $\mathbf{g}_\delta$ which correspond to the same physical phenomenon. The points P in a volume $v_{B_{h(i)G}}$ must be points of the Gibbs lattice. If $\sigma = N/v_r*$ is the density of the Gibbs lattice points, and $dv_{B(i)G}$ is a volume element, the total number of lattice points in that element of volume is

$$N' = \sigma \cdot dv_{B(i)G} . \tag{163}$$

All the points P contribute to the total intensity, and since the density of the lattice points is high, the sum of dI_p extending over all the points P can be replaced by an integral without introducing errors. For each common volume we have

$$I_{v_{B(i)}} = \int_{v_{B(i)}} \sigma \cdot dI_p \, dv_{B(i)G}. \tag{164}$$

Taking into account that in the most general case there are eight common volumes, the total second-order intensity is given by

$$I_2 = \sum_{i=1}^{8} \int_{v_{B(i)}} \sigma \cdot dI_p \, dv_{B(i)G} . \tag{165}$$

Figure 22 shows the hypothetical Brillouin zone centered at G with its neighboring zones superimposed. For this example, the summation extends only over six zones.

Substituting dI_p for its value (162) we obtain the following expression for the second order diffuse scattering in electron units,

$$I_{TDS_2} = \frac{k^2 T^2}{2 Z m^2 v_r * V_m^4} |r^*|^4 \, I_T(r^*) \sum_{i=1}^{8} \int_{v_{B(i)}} \sum_{\gamma,\delta}^{3} \frac{1}{|g_\gamma|^2 |g_\delta|^2} \, dv_{B(i)}. \tag{166}$$

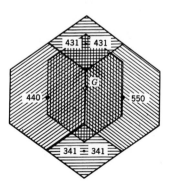

Fig. 22. Diagram of the volumes of superposition of first Brillouin zones of hexamine with a hypothetical zone G [(section $(110)_0^*$)].

To simplify computation, the Brillouin zones, with the shape of rhombododecahedra, can be replaced by tangent spheres that have volume $v_r{}^*$ equal to that of a zone. Thus we see

$$\tfrac{4}{3}\pi R^3 = v_r{}^* \tag{167}$$

where R is the radius of the spheres. In hexamine $v_r{}^* = 231.25 \times 10^{20}$ cm^{-3}.

Thus at the point G there is centered a sphere, which in the most general case intersects eight spheres centered at $B_h(i)$, $(i = 1, 2, 3, \ldots)$. It is evident that the distance g between the centers of the spheres is not exactly equal to the distance between the centers of the Brillouin zones; for example $g_{max} \neq R$, so that it is necessary to apply the pertinent correction. Let us call $g_c = yR$ the distance between the center of the sphere G and the center of the sphere at $B_h(i)$ (Fig. 23) which gives the corrected g. When these two spheres are tangent y becomes two, and when they coincide y becomes zero. The correction can be made so that the volume of intersection of the Brillouin zones will be equal to those of the hypothetical spheres.

The ratios between the volumes of intersection of the Brillouin zones and the volume of each reciprocal cell can be easily calculated for certain special direction. Figure 24 is a schematic representation

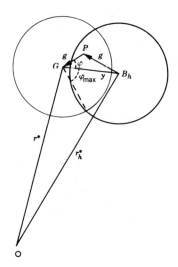

Fig. 23. Hypothetical spheres substituted for the first Brillouin zones in the approximate calculation of I_{TDS_2}.

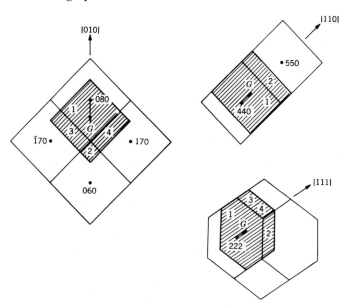

Fig. 24. Regions of superposition of the Brillouin zones investigated in hexamine and zone G centered at a point on the axes [010], [110], and [111].

of the common regions of the Brillouin zones when the point G is displaced along each of the three directions [010], [110], and [111]. We can see that for [010]

$$\frac{v(1)}{v_{r^\bullet}} = \left(1 - \frac{g}{2g_m}\right)^2,$$

$$\frac{v(2)}{v_{r^\bullet}} = \frac{1}{4}\left(\frac{g}{g_m}\right)^2, \tag{168}$$

$$\frac{v(3)}{v_{r^\bullet}} = \frac{1}{2}\left[\frac{g}{g_m} - \frac{1}{2}\left(\frac{g}{g_m}\right)^2\right];$$

for [110]

$$\frac{v(1)}{v_{r^\bullet}} = 1 - \frac{g}{2g_m}, \tag{169}$$

$$\frac{v(2)}{v_{r^\bullet}} = \frac{g}{2g_m};$$

for [111]

$$\frac{v(1)}{v_{r^\bullet}} = \left(1 - \frac{g}{2g_m}\right)^3$$

$$\frac{v(2)}{v_{r^\bullet}} = \frac{1}{8}\left(\frac{g}{g_m}\right)^3,$$

$$\frac{v(3)}{v_{r^\bullet}} = \frac{1}{4}\left(\frac{g}{g_m}\right)^2\left(v - \frac{g}{2g_m}\right) \quad \text{(triply degenerate)},$$

$$\frac{v(4)}{v_{r^\bullet}} = \frac{1}{2}\left(\frac{g}{g_m}\right)\left(1 - \frac{g}{2g_m}\right)^2 \quad \text{(triply degenerate)}.$$

(170)

The preceding expressions were derived by Schwartz (1957) for cubic Brillouin zones.

We can express the ratio between the volume of intersection of two spheres and the volume of a single sphere by

$$f(y) = \frac{\int_{v_{s(i)}} dv}{v_r^*}.$$

(171)

Figure 25 shows $v(i)/v_{r^\bullet}$ as a function of $|\mathbf{g}|/|\mathbf{g}_m|$, when the point G is displaced along [010], [110], and [111], respectively. For different values of y, $f(y)$ is plotted on the same graph. Thus we can determine graphically the values of y that correspond to given $|\mathbf{g}|/|\mathbf{g}_m|$.

The integral

$$\int \frac{dv}{|\mathbf{g}_\gamma|^2|\mathbf{g}_\delta|^2}$$

was also calculated by Schwartz (1957). By making a change to cylindrical coordinates, he obtained

$$\int \frac{dv}{|\mathbf{g}_\gamma|^2|\mathbf{g}_\delta|^2} = \frac{\pi^3}{R}Y(y),$$

(172)

where

$$Y(y) = \frac{1}{\pi^2 y}\left[\frac{\pi}{2}\psi_{max} - \psi_{max}^2 + \int_0^{\psi_{max}} \tan^{-1}\left(\frac{1 - y\cos\psi}{y\sin\psi}\right)d\psi\right],$$

(173)

and ψ and ψ_{max} are shown in Fig. 23. Figure 26 is the graph of $Y(y)$.

Combining (166) and (173) we obtain, finally,

$$I_{TDS_2} = \frac{k^2 T^2 \pi^3}{2Zm^2 Rv_{r^\bullet}V_m^4}|\mathbf{r}^*|^4 I_T(\mathbf{r}^*)\sum_{i=1}^{8} Y(y)$$

(174)

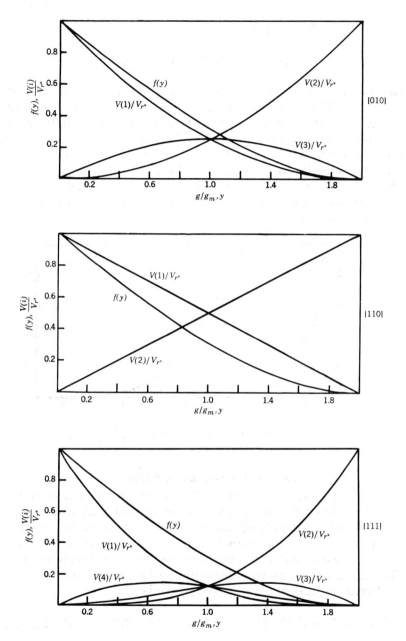

Fig. 25. Graph of the ratios between the common volumes of two Brillouin zones $(v(i)/v_{r^*})$ and that of the spheres $f(y)$ as G moves along the length of [010], [110], and [111].

371

For hexamine the preceding expression reduces to

$$I_{TDS_2} = 1.89 \times 10^{-36} |\mathbf{r}^*|^4 I_T(\mathbf{r}^*) \sum_{i=1}^{8} Y(y) \tag{175}$$

The above expression was applied at certain points of diffraction space. Specifically, the 080 Brillouin zone along [010] was studied (Fig. 24), and the values of TDS_2 at the points 0.2, 0.5, and 0.9 are 0.67, 0.16, and 0.11, respectively. In the Brillouin zone centered at 222 along [111] the values of TDS_2 at the points 0.2 and 1.0 are 0.10 and 0.01 respectively. In the zone 440 along [110] in the points 0.2 and 0.8 are 0.45 and 0.13, respectively. Finally, in zone 440 along [010], at the points 0.2, 0.6, and 1.0, the values of TDS_2 are 0.45, 0.32, and 0.10, respectively.

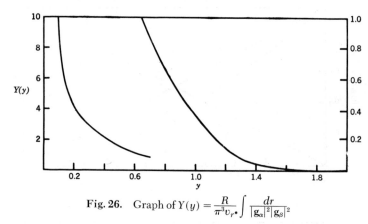

Fig. 26.   Graph of $Y(y) = \dfrac{R}{\pi^3 v_{r^*}} \displaystyle\int \dfrac{dr}{|g_\alpha|^2 |g_\beta|^2}$

Incoherent or Compton scattering in hexamine

We know that, in addition to the coherent x-rays scattered by a crystal, there exists the Compton or incoherent scattering which is a function only of the atomic numbers of the atoms of the crystal, and is independent of the crystal structure. This type of scattering is relatively weak and varies continuously with the reciprocal vector. This incoherent scattering intensity function for a hexamine crystal, in electron units per electron, is expressed by

$$I_{C_6H_{12}N_4}(\mathbf{r}^*) = Z^{-1}B^{-2}[12(Z - \Sigma f_e^2)_H + 6(Z - \Sigma f_e^2)_C + 4(Z - \Sigma f_e^2)_N]. \tag{176}$$

In this expression $B^{-2}(Z - \Sigma f_e^2)$ is the incoherent-intensity function for each atom according to Wentzel (1927). Z is the atomic number, and B^{-2} is the Breit-Dirac factor. It is interesting to note that the polarization of the Compton radiation is the same as for Thompson scattering.

Figure 27 shows the variation of the Compton intensity in hexamine as computed by (176). As can be seen, the intensity of Compton scattering is very weak. In this calculation the atomic scattering factors of carbon, nitrogen, and hydrogen are from the data of McWeeny (1951). The Compton effect for carbon is from data of Keating and Vineyard (1956), and the Compton effect for the nitrogen and hydrogen atoms were computed from data of Compton and Allison (1954), modifying the curves slightly in the direction of those for carbon given by Keating and Vineyard.

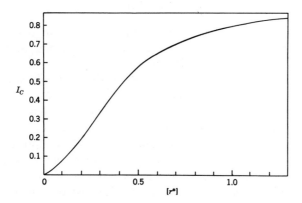

Fig. 27.   Hexamine. Theoretical intensity curve for the incoherent or Compton scattering.

Conversion of diffuse intensity to absolute units

The diffuse-intensity measurements were carried out with a diffractometer. Although the x-ray beam incident on the crystal had already been monochromatised by an LiF crystal, the harmonics of the characteristic wavelength had not been eliminated, and its was necessary to make a $\lambda/2$ correction. For that correction an Ni-Al filter was used. For each point studied, the counts per second were measured, interposing successively the nickel and aluminum. The difference in counts C_{Ni}-C_{Al} automatically eliminates the effects of cosmic rays and half-wavelength radiation, but not the effect of scattering by the air and the Compton scattering.

The scattering of the air is corrected graphically with a curve constructed previously with measurements for different values of $|\mathbf{r}^*|$

with the diffractometer under the same conditions as the experiment, but without the crystal. On the other hand, the number of counts registered by the counter tube per unit time is proportional to the scattered intensity

$$\text{Counts} = K \cdot (PF) \cdot \frac{N_0}{2\mu} \cdot I, \tag{177}$$

where K is a constant that depends on the geometry of the experiment (divergence of the beam, etc.), N_0 the number of molecules per unit volume, μ the coefficient of linear absorption; PF is the double polarization factor given by Azaroff (1955):

$$PF = \frac{1 + \cos^2 2\theta_n \cos^2 2\theta}{1 + \cos^2 2\theta_n}, \tag{178}$$

where θ_n is the glancing angle of the monochromator used. In our example, we used LiF for a monochromator. The Bragg angle θ_{LiF} of the selective reflection 200 for LiF is $22°32'$.

The resulting corrected counts must be reduced to absolute units. When we are dealing with metals, alloys, etc., the correction is made from a previous experiment, in which the counts are measured from a sample of an amorphous organic substance, such as lucite, paraffin, etc., at large θ angles. Since these substances are amorphous and there are no selective reflections, the observed intensity corresponds only to the incoherent scattering, which can be calculated theoretically in electron units per electron by means of the expression, which for lucite ($C_5O_2H_8$) (Schwartz, 1957) is:

$$I_L = [5(f_C{}^2 + B^{-2}(Z - f_e{}^2)_C) + 2(f_O{}^2 + B^{-2}(Z - f_e{}^2)_O)$$
$$+ 8(f_H{}^2 + B^{-2}(Z - f_e)_H)] \cdot (Z)^{-1}. \tag{179}$$

These calculated values are used to scale the observed intensity for a large value of θ, for example, $\theta = 60°$.

For an organic crystal such as hexamine, the reduction to an absolute scale can, in principle, be carried out by comparing the incoherent intensity scattered by the same crystal with that of the amorphous substance, for the same large angles θ, and at special points where $I_0(\mathbf{r}^*)$ is zero. For instance, in hexamine there are some first Brillouin zones associated with reciprocal-lattice points such as 037, of very small structure factor. In the equator $(001)^*{}_0$ the molecular transform has only a real part, and it changes in sign along a line on the boundary of the zone at 370, defined by the reciprocal-lattice points 360 and 470. Therefore $I_0(\mathbf{r}^*)$ vanishes along that line. At these points of large $|\mathbf{r}^*|$ the scattering detected by the counter tube can be expressed theoretically as a function of the incoherent scattering of a hexamine molecule, so that the counts can be reduced to an absolute scale without resorting to an auxiliary amorphous substance.

Comparison of the counts obtained for the Compton effect with hexamine, and the corresponding theoretical values from (179) showed that the observed Compton effect was greater than that observed, an observation similar to that of Laval (1941) for crystals of sylvite and aluminum. Therefore the scaling was finally carried out by means of a sample of lucite of shape and size approximately equal to that of the hexamine crystal used. Calling μ_m the mass absorption coefficient, and M the molecular mass, the conversion to absolute scale in e.u/e. was made through the following expression:

$$I_H(\mathbf{r}^*) = \frac{(\mu_m M)_H}{(\mu_m M)_L} \frac{I_L(\mathbf{r}_l^*)}{C_L(\mathbf{r}_l^*)/(PF)_L} \cdot \frac{C_H(\mathbf{r}^*)}{(PF)_H}, \qquad (180)$$

where the subindices H and L refer to hexamine or lucite, respectively.

Once the counts $C_H(\mathbf{r}^*)$ are reduced to absolute intensities by means of (180), we must subtract the theoretical Compton intensity for each point, determined from the graph of Fig. 27, as well as I_{TDS_2}. The final intensity thus obtained is the one-phonon thermal diffuse scattering expressed in e.u./e.

Figure 28 shows the mean intensities along the seven lines indicated in Fig. 20, reduced to absolute units. The experimental points are plotted in Fig. 28.

Frequency and velocity dispersion curves; molecular force constants

The absolute diffuse intensities represented in Fig. 28 allow us to calculate the vibrational frequencies by means of equations (154) and (155). Solving equation (154) for the frequency ν_l, one obtains

$$\nu_l = \left[\frac{2.285 \times 10^5 |\mathbf{r}^*|^2 I_T(\mathbf{r}^*)}{I_{TDS_1}(\mathbf{g})} \right]^{1/2} s^{-1}, \qquad (181)$$

which allows us to calculate the frequency of the longitudinal waves for different wave vectors. Similarly, solving for ν_t in equation (155) we can obtain the corresponding values for the transverse waves. The values of the frequencies thus obtained for both types of waves have been plotted in Figs. 29–35. Using these values we can draw experimental frequency-dispersion curves as a function of the wave vector. However, the latter curves are not given.

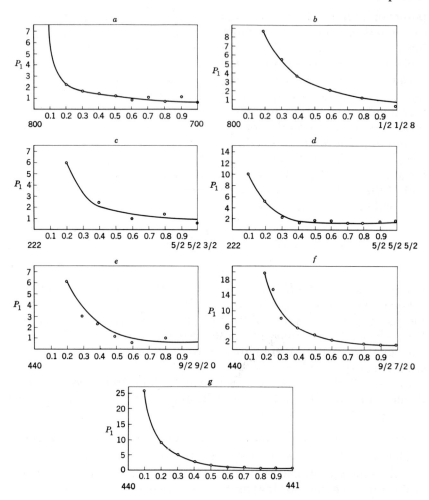

Fig. 28. Hexamine. I_{TDS_1} in electron units per electron. The circles correspond to the experimental values measured on lines $a, b, \ldots g$ of Fig. 20.

The expressions for calculating the molecular force constants are simplified for wave vectors whose tips are located at the boundary of the Brillouin zone. The value of the frequency at those points is related to the molecular force constants through equations (140), (144), and (150) which, together with the three equations (136), form a system of eight equations in seven unknowns.

The coefficient α was obtained by introducing in expression (140),

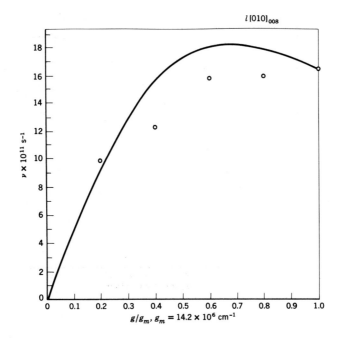

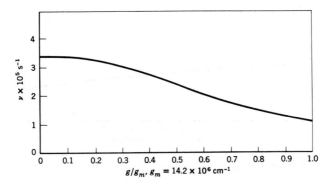

Fig. 29. Frequency and velocity dispersion curves: l [010].

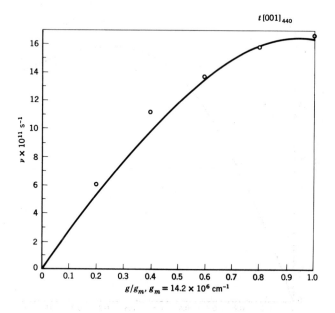

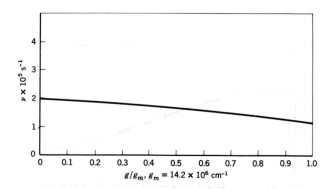

Fig. 30. Frequency and velocity dispersion curves: t [001].

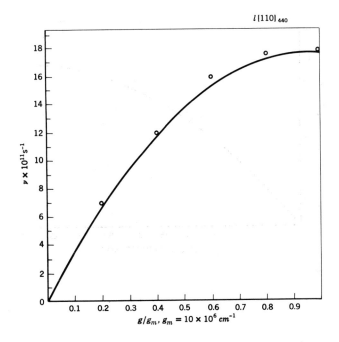

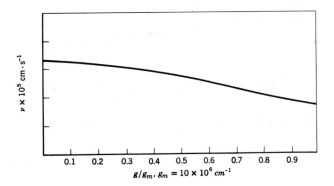

Fig. 31. Frequency and velocity dispersion curves: l [110].

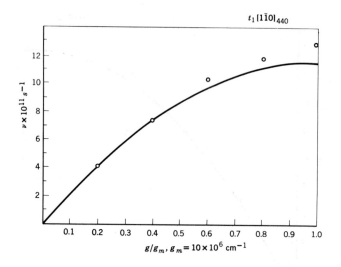

t_1 [1$\bar{1}$0]$_{440}$

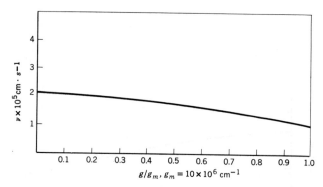

Fig. 32. Frequency and velocity dispersion curves: t_1 [1$\bar{1}$0].

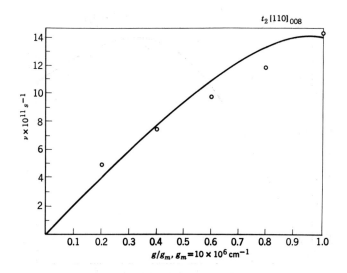

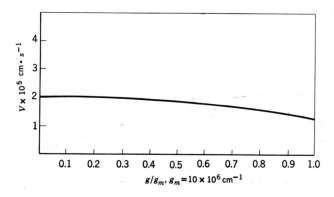

Fig. 33. Frequency and velocity dispersion curves: t_2 [110].

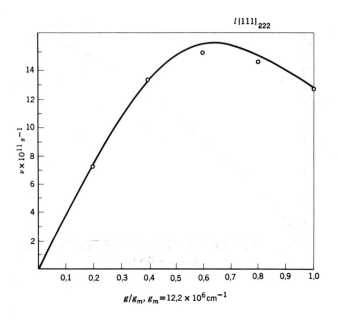

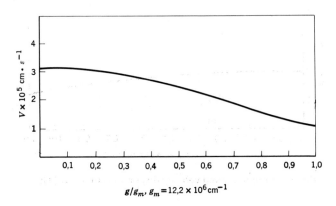

Fig. 34. Frequency and velocity dispersion curves: l [111].

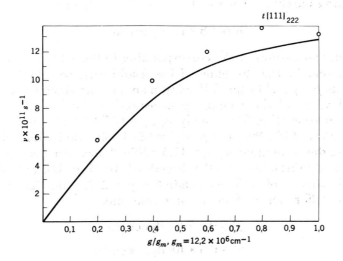

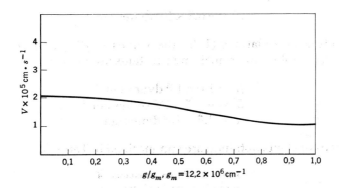

Fig. 35. Frequency and velocity dispersion curves: t [111].

$v = 16.6 \times 10^{11} s^{-1}$, the experimental value at the boundary of the 440 Brillouin zone (Fig. 30) in the direction [010], obtaining

$$\alpha = 1.6 \times 10^3 \text{ dynes cm}^{-1}.$$

From expressions (145), corresponding to the vibrations of waves propagating in the direction of the 2-fold axis, we obtain the coefficients β'', γ'', α'' in the following manner: introducing the experimental value of the frequency measured at the boundary of the Brillouin zone (Fig. 31), namely $v_{l[110]} = 17.7 \times 10^{11} s^{-1}$, in the first of expressions (145), the sum $\beta'' + \gamma'' = 933$ is obtained. Similarly, substituting the frequency $v_{t_1[1\bar{1}0]} = 11.5 \times 10^{11} s^{-1}$, measured at the boundary of Brillouin zone 440 in the direction $[1\bar{1}0]$ (Fig. 32), and using the second equation of (145), we obtain $\beta'' - \gamma'' = 293$. From the preceding sum and difference we find the force constants

$$\beta'' = 0.6 \times 10^3 \text{ dynes cm}^{-1},$$

$$\gamma'' = 0.3 \times 10^3 \text{ dynes cm}^{-1}.$$

Introducing the experimental value of the frequency measured at the boundary of Brillouin zone 008 in the direction [110] (Fig. 33), namely $v = 14.2 \times 10^{11} s^{-1}$, in the third expression of (145), we obtain

$$\alpha'' = -0.3 \times 10^3 \text{ dynes cm}^{-1}.$$

Substituting in equations (136), the values of β'', γ'', and α'' already obtained, the following remaining constants are found;

$$\beta = 1.0 \times 10^3 \text{ dynes cm}^{-1},$$
$$\beta' = -0.5 \times 10^3 \text{ dynes cm}^{-1},$$
$$\alpha' = 1.7 \times 10^3 \text{ dynes cm}^{-1}.$$

The force constants obtained are summarized in Table 3.

Table 3 Force constants of hexamine obtained from x-ray diffuse scattering intensity

α	=	1.6×10^{-3} dynes cm^{-1}.
α'	=	1.7
α''	=	−0.3
β	=	1.0
β'	=	−0.5
β''	=	0.6
γ''	=	0.3

The mean value observed at the boundary of the Brillouin zone for the frequency of the longitudinal and transverse waves which propagate in the direction of the threefold axis (Figs. 34 and 35) is $\gamma = 12.9 \times 10^{11}\text{s}^{-1}$. Substituting in expression (150) the values for α, α', and β' previously obtained, we obtain for the frequency at the boundary of the Brillouin zone the value $13.0 \times 10^{11}\text{s}^{-1}$. This value is in agreement with that obtained from the experimental dispersion curve.

The smooth lines of Figs. 29 and 30 represent the frequencies and velocities as functions of $\mathbf{g}$ for the longitudinal waves $l[001]$ and transverse waves $t[010]$ which propagate in the direction of the 4-fold axis, the curves being computed from equations (138) and (139), where the previously obtained values of the force constants α, α', β', α'', and β'' in Table 3 are used.

The smooth lines of Figs. 31, 32, and 33 correspond to the theoretical curves of the frequencies and velocities of the longitudinal waves $l[110]$ and the transverse waves $t_1[1\bar{1}0]$ and $t_2[110]$ which propagate in the direction of the 2-fold axis, the curves being calculated from expressions (145). The theoretical curves of Figs. 34 and 35 are computed from expressions (147) and (148) for the longitudinal waves $l[111]$ and transverse waves $t[11\bar{1}]$ which propagate along the 3-fold axis. We can see that the theoretical curves thus obtained fit the experimental data quite well. The velocity dispersion curves are obtained from the frequencies by means of the expression $\nu = |\mathbf{g}| \cdot |\mathbf{V}|$.

The relative error with which the force constant has been calculated is 9 per cent, the error for α'' is 11 per cent; for the constants β'' and γ'', in the calculation of which the measured diffuse intensity enters twice, the error is 20 per cent. The constants α', β, β' have errors of 29, 20, and 30 per cent, respectively.

From the velocity-dispersion curves (Figs. 29 to 35) we have obtained the extrapolated values for velocities as $|\mathbf{g}| \to 0$. In Table 4 the values thus obtained are compared with those calculated from the elastic constants given by Haussühl. The agreement obtained shows the precision of the diffractometer measurements and the validity of Laval's theory in reference to the acoustic modes for large wavelengths in this molecular crystal.

Table 5 compares the values for the elastic constants as obtained in our experiments with those obtained by Ramachandran and Wooster (1951b) and the precise values given by Haussühl (1958).

Table 4   Limiting velocities of the acoustic waves
of hexamine (in 10^5 cm sec^{-1})

$V_{\lambda\to\infty}$	Haussühl (1958)	Carbonell and Canut (1964)
$V_{l[010]}$	3.50	3.40
$V_{t[100]}$	1.96	1.96
$V_{l[110]}$	3.40	3.40
$V_{t_1[110]}$	2.12	2.12
$V_{t_2[110]}$	1.96	1.96
$V_{l[111]}$	3.37	3.17
$V_{t[111]}$	2.07	2.07
V_{lm}	3.40	3.32
V_{tm}	2.00	2.02
V_{av}	2.99	2.29

Table 5   Elastic constants of hexamine according to different authors

c_{ij}	Ramachandran and Wooster (1951b)	Haussühl (1958)	Carbonell and Canut (1964)
c_{11}	1.5×10^{-11} dyne cm^{-2}	1.643×10^{-11} dyne cm^{-2}	1.55×10^{-11} dyne cm^{-2}
c_{12}	0.3	0.433	0.35
c_{44}	0.7	0.515	0.52

Hexamine frequency spectrum

The elements of the Fourier matrix for any value of the wave vector
g are obtained by solving the third-degree equation (103). The approximate frequency spectrum of the hexamine lattice is calculated by
taking a collection of vectors **g** whose tips cover the first Brillouin
zone with uniform density; the symmetry of the cubic lattice allows
us to restrict our study to 1/48 of its volume. That volume is defined
by the planes (001), (110), (011) and by the face of the rhombododeca-
hedron perpendicular to the direction (110).

The values of **g** chosen are defined by a simple Gibbs lattice of
edge $a^*/40$, which is equivalent to considering 506 different wave
vectors in the fundamental domain of the first Brillouin zone. Each
point in a general position has a multiplicity of 48 which is reduced
to 24, 12, 8, or 6 when the tip of the vector **g** is located on some symmetry element of the fundamental domain thus, the secular equation

is solved for 17,240 wave vectors regularly distributed in the first Brillouin zone. To these wave vectors there correspond 51,720 frequencies. The computation of the elements of the 506 matrices was done with an IBM 1620 computer, and then the corresponding multiplicities were applied.

The components of the wave vector are multiples of $a^*/40$, $g_i = an_i/40$, $(i = 1, 2, 3)$. The integers n_i satisfy the following conditions:

$$0 \leqslant n_3 \leqslant 10$$
$$n_3 \leqslant n_2 \leqslant 10,$$
$$n_2 \leqslant n_1 \leqslant 20 - n_2$$

The frequencies obtained are between 0 and 17×10^{11} s^{-1}; this range has been broken down into intervals and the corresponding histogram has been drawn (Fig. 36). The function $N(\nu)$ represents the frequency spectrum of the lattice, its value being the number of frequencies in the interval between ν and $\nu + d\nu$.

Figure 36i shows in increasing order the breakdown of the frequencies of hexamine into longitudinal and transverse branches, according to the solutions of the secular equation (103) corresponding to the 506 matrices using the force constants of Table 3. The function $N(\nu)$ (Fig. 36ii), sums of the preceding three branches, represents the approximate acoustic spectrum of vibrational frequencies. The function exhibits two maxima, at $\omega = 87 \times 10^{11}$ s^{-1} and $\omega = 111 \times 10^{11}$ s^{-1}. As was to be expected, the frequency spectrum obtained differs from the spectrum calculated by the Debye theory. Blackman (1955) already called attention to the fact that even in a monoatomic cubic crystal there would exist several maxima of the function $N(\nu)$ instead of the single maximum corresponding to the highest frequency according to the theory of continuous solids.

Comparison of the constants obtained from hexamine with those of other body-centered cubic structures

The results obtained by Curien (1952b) and Champier (1959b) in their study of iron and lithium crystals by diffuse scattering, respectively, applying Laval's theory, are compared in Table 6 with the constants obtained by us for hexamine. We observe in the table that the values for the force constants, radial displacements, Debye characteristic temperature, and thermal expansion coefficients at room temperature for iron are higher than the corresponding values for lithium and hexamine. For lithium the values of the elastic constants (except c_{11}), the Debye characteristic temperature, and coefficient of thermal expansion are intermediate between the values for

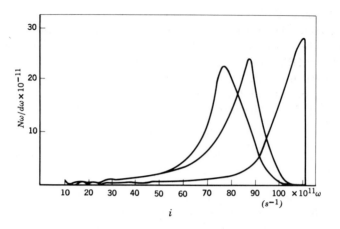

i

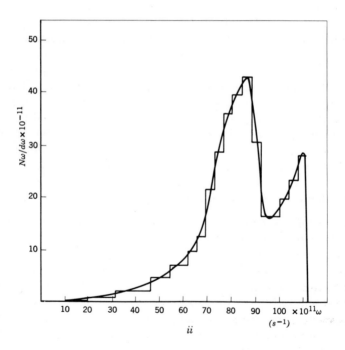

ii

Fig. 36. Hexamine. (*i*) Decomposition of the approximate frequency spectrum into the longitudinal and transverse branches; (*ii*) approximate frequency spectrum of the elastic waves of hexamine.

388

Table 6   Elastic constants, force constants, and radial displacements of three substances with body-centered crystal structure

	Fe	Li	HMT
$a(\text{Å})$	1.43	1.75	3.51
$c_{11}(10^{-11}\text{dynes cm}^{-2})$	23.2	1.0	1.63
c_{12}	13.0	0.76	0.33
c_{44}	11.1	0.70	0.57
$\alpha(10^{-3}\text{ dynes cm}^{-1})$	11.7	1.06	1.6
α'	11.6	0.80	1.7
α'	0.8	–	−0.3
β	11.9	1.33	1.0
β'	−2.5	0.21	−0.5
β''	2.6	−0.025	0.6
γ''	2.6	–	0.3
$F_1(10^{-3}(\text{dr})^{-1}\text{ dynes}\cdot\text{cm})$	35.3	3.69	3.6
F_2	11.6	0.80	1.7
F_3	5.2	−0.05	0.9
$\Theta_D(^{10}\text{K})$	420	342	115
Thermal expansion coefficient $A10^6$	12 †	45 †	62 ‡

† (Pearson, 1954)
‡ (Lonsdale, 1959)

the other substances. Computing the radial displacements with expression (137), we observe that hexamine and lithium have similar values for $F_1\, dr$ and $F_2\, dr$, which are very low compared with the corresponding values for iron. The difference in values agrees with the fact that iron has a high cohesion. If we assume radial displacements of the Ar^{-6} type, we obtain for hexamine 1.3 and 0.2 dyne.cm for radial displacements of second and third neighbors, respectively; for the first neighbors, we obtain $F_1 = 3.5$ dyne. cm, which are values of the same order of magnitude as those determined through the aforementioned experiments. Similarly, for iron we obtain for $F_2 dr$ and $F_3 dr$, 14.0 and 1.8 dyne.cm, respectively. There is thus a good agreement with the experimental values obtained by Curien. Nevertheless, in the case of lithium, the values obtained for $F_2\, dr$ and $F_3\, dr$ are too low (the expected values would be 1.54 and 0.2 dyne.cm), indicating that Champier's data may perhaps need revision. It is interesting to note that F_3 is higher for iron and hexamine than the value obtained by applying the Ar^{-6} law, showing that the forces between iron atoms and between hexamine molecules are stronger than van der Waals forces, since in hexamine we must consider hydrogen bonds, and in iron, metallic bonds.

Linear dispersion and DFT

In a recent study by Becka and Cruickshank (1963a,b) of the structure of hexamine at different temperatures these authors utilized a dynamic model based on the following hypotheses: the vibrational spectrum is composed of six branches of intermolecular frequencies and sixty of intramolecular frequencies. The three acoustic branches are due to pure translational vibrations of the molecule considered as a rigid body, and they have a distribution of the Debye type, that is, it is considered that the dispersion of the frequencies is linear throughout the Brillouin zone, as is observed for small $|g|$, considering the solid a continuum. The three exterior optical branches are due to pure librations of the molecules.

In our dynamic model we have neglected, as has been mentioned, the molecular librations, based on the results obtained with anthracene, where it was shown that the contribution of the librations to the diffuse scattering was small.

To extrapolate to the entire Brillouin zone a linear dispersion of the frequencies is to accept the Debye model, which, from the strictly dynamic point of view, is preferable to the independent vibration model of Einstein. Nevertheless we shall see that from the point of view of the interpretation of continuous diffuse scattering, the Becka and Cruickshank model is not satisfactory. Figures 37 and 38 show the dispersion curves obtained by diffuse scattering (smooth line) and the straight lines (broken lines) that correspond to a linear frequency-dispersion law. For their computation it has simply been assumed that the velocities of the waves obtained from the elastic constants (for $g = 0$) do not vary with $|g|$. As can be seen, whereas for small values of $|g|$ this approximation is good, it is far from being good in the whole of the Brillouin zone. Figure 39 shows the frequency spectrum of hexamine for the Debye approximate model, which differs greatly from that obtained from the absolute diffuse intensities (Fig. 36ii).

In order to test whether the hypothesis of a linear frequency dispersion accounts for the continuous diffuse regions the diffuse intensities have been calculated along the seven lines measured (Fig. 40). The solid lines correspond to the observed intensities, and the broken lines show the first-order intensities obtained by introducing a linear dispersion of ν. Near the center of the Brillouin zone the calculated diffuse intensity in this case is greater than that observed, but as the distance from the center of the zone increases, the intensity decreases rapidly, becoming practically zero in certain directions. Such an intensity distribution is in disagreement with the observed

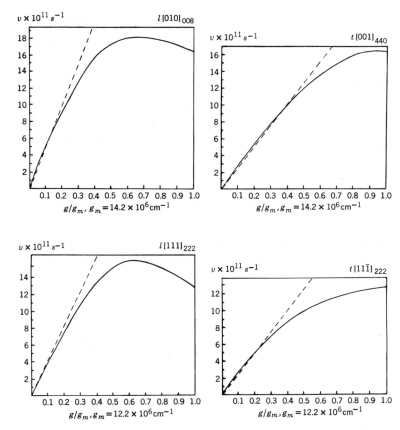

Fig. 37. Hexamine. Frequency dispersion for the 3-fold and 4-fold axes. Solid line: curve calculated from the observed diffuse scattering. Straight broken line: curve calculated with constant velocity assumed.

continuous diffuse scattering. On the other hand, the diffuse scattering calculated with this model is concentrated near the reciprocal lattice point.

Figure 41 shows the isointensity lines in Brillouin zones 800 and 440. The lines calculated with the hypothesis of linear dispersion are shown in (*i*), where the hatched area has an intensity of practically zero. The first contour line (broken) which corresponds to 0.5 e.u.e.$^{-1}$ is within the Brillouin zone. In contrast, the intensity calculated from our model (*ii*) is the same in appearance as that observed (*iii*), as was to be expected. In (*ii*) and (*iii*) the line of 0.5 e.u.e.$^{-1}$ has not been drawn, since it lies outside the zone. The zones are thus covered by continuous diffuse scattering.

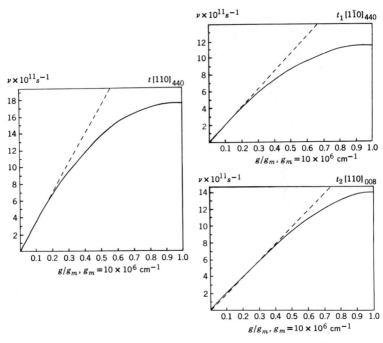

Fig. 38. Hexamine. Frequency dispersion for the 2-fold axis. Solid line: curve calculated from observed diffuse scattering. Straight broken line: curve calculated with constant velocity.

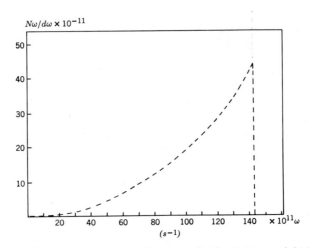

Fig. 39. Frequency spectrum of hexamine for the Debye model ($\nu^2 d\nu$).

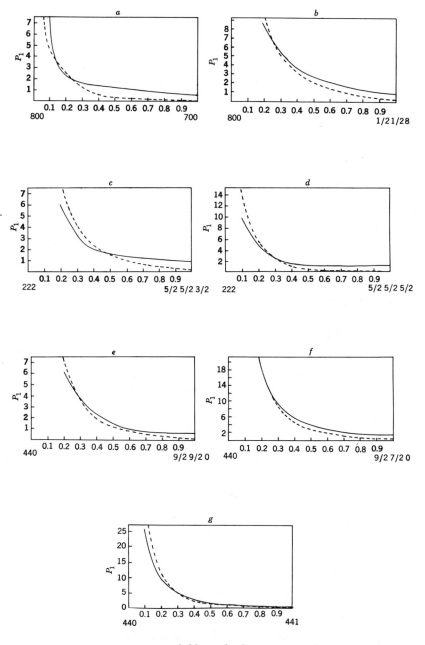

Fig. 40. Hexamine. I_{TDS_1} curves. Solid line: absolute intensity observed. Broken line: intensity calculated with the hypothesis of linear dispersion.

393

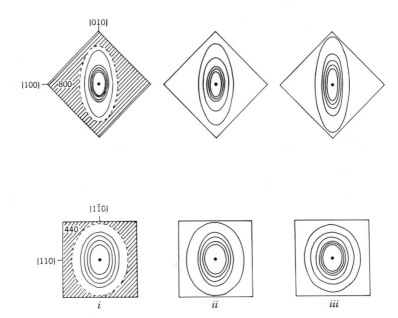

Fig. 41. Hexamine. I_{TDS_1} contours in the sections of the 800 and 440 Brillouin zones. (*i*) Calculated with linear dispersion (the broken line corresponds to 0.5 e.ue.$^{-1}$); (*ii*) calculated with the seven force constants; (*iii*) observed diffuse intensity.

We have seen in Ch. 4 that the DFT function accounted well for the continuous diffuse regions. The dynamic hypothesis of the DFT is one of independent molecular motion. From a vibrational point of view we can speak of a vibrational frequency of the Einstein type (1907). Although that hypothesis is simpler than Debye's, we must accept that the continuous diffuse regions can be calculated within the approximation of the DFT, whereas such a calculation is not possible with the Debye dispersion law.

Figures 42 to 44 show hexamine maps of the part of the I_{TDS} independent of the elastic tensor, as well as maps of the I_{DFT}. Both functions account well for the continuous part. Since the DFT function is easily calculated, while the computation of the diffuse scattering by means of the theory of thermal waves requires a more complex procedure, to recognize the thermal origin of the continuous diffuse regions it is convenient to use the *DFT* function as a first approximation.

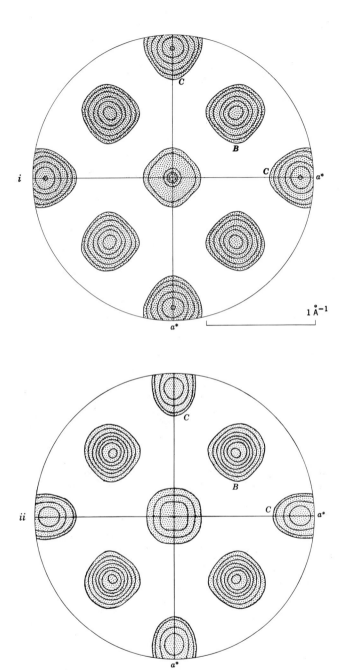

Fig. 42. Hexamine. Level $(001)_0^*$. (i) I_{DFT}; (ii) $I_{TDS_1/\Sigma}$.

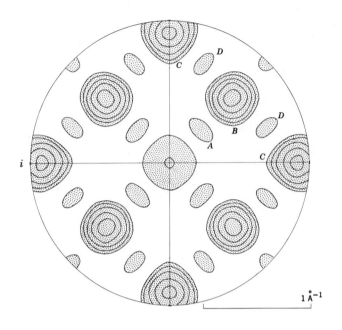

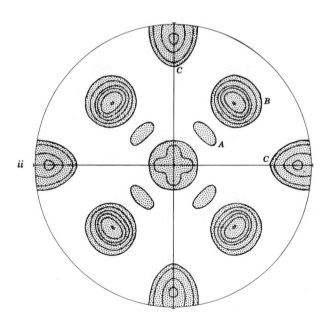

Fig. 43. Hexamine. Level $(001)_{1/2}^{*}$ (i) I_{DFT}; (ii) $I_{TDS_{1/\Sigma}}$.

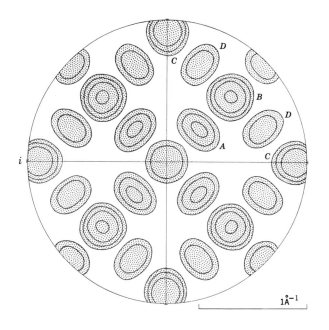

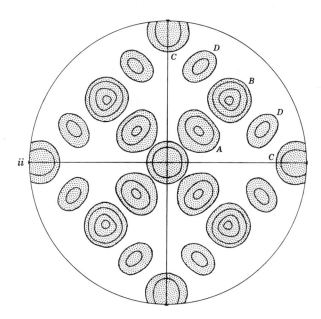

Fig. 44. Hexamine. Level $(001)^*_1$. (i) I_{DFT}; (ii) $I_{TDS_1/\Sigma}$.

6

The temperature dependence of diffuse scattering

It is a well-known fact that the diffraction of x-rays, electrons, and neutrons by crystals is temperature-dependent, so that the scattering is affected by the thermal agitation of the atoms or molecules of the crystal. It has been seen in Ch. 5 that the total intensity scattered by a crystal is, except for the incoherent Compton scattering, the sum of different contributions (Bragg intensities, thermal diffuse scattering of one phonon, of two phonons, etc.), which depend on temperature and on the reciprocal vector in different ways, and is of such a nature that its study can be the key to the discovery of the part that each type of scattering contributes to the observed intensity.

The temperature factor of the Bragg intensities

The theory of the thermal effect on the Bragg intensities is known as the Debye-Waller theory. According to that theory, the intensity of the selective reflections of the crystal planes at a temperature T is diminished with respect to that which they would have if the atoms were at complete rest in such a way that

$$I_T = I_0 \exp\left(-2B(\sin^2\theta)/\lambda^2\right)$$
$$= I_0 \exp\left(-2M\right),$$

$$(1)$$

where $2M$ is the Debye-Waller factor and B is a function of the mean square amplitude of vibration of the atom in the direction normal to

398

the reflecting planes, that is, in the direction of the diffraction vector r^*, and is given by

$$B = 8\pi^2 \overline{u^2}. \qquad (2)$$

The method for calculating M was introduced by Debye (1914) for a monoatomic cubic crystal. Debye suggested as a first approximation the hypothesis that, from a point of view of elasticity, the crystal can be considered an isotropic continuous solid in which all the waves of a given type propagate with the same velocity, although of course the velocities of the longitudinal and transverse waves differ from one another. Although in a crystal such a hypothesis is not obeyed, an approximate value of M can be obtained by supposing the crystal to be elastically isotropic and by choosing conveniently the averages of the velocities of the longitudinal and transverse waves. The mean square amplitude can be expressed as a function of the normal vibration of the crystal, and, therefore, as a function of the energy of the normal-vibration mode of frequency ν.

Debye's spectrum of vibrational frequencies assumes that $\rho(\nu)\,d\nu$, the number of waves whose frequencies are between ν and $\nu + d\nu$, is proportional to $\nu^2 d\nu$. Debye defined a characteristic temperature Θ_D as a function of the maximum frequency ν_m of elastic vibration of the solid such that

$$\Theta_D = \frac{h\nu_m}{k} \qquad (3)$$

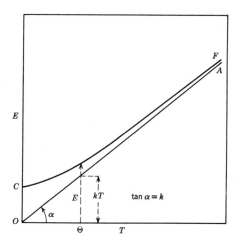

Fig. 1. Thermal wave energy versus temperature. For $T > \Theta$, the equipartition law holds.

In this expression h and k are the Planck and Boltzman constants, respectively. The characteristic temperature determines, in general terms, what temperatures can be considered as high for a given crystal [See (79), (80), Ch. 5]. Thus, if $T > \Theta_D$, quantum phenomena are no longer important and the equipartition of energy between the different modes of vibration of the crystal can be applied (Fig. 1).

James (1954) derived the expression of the Debye-Waller temperature factor, which can be expressed as a function of the diffraction vector $\mathbf{r}^*$, as follows:

$$2M = \frac{3h^2}{km\Theta_M}\left[\frac{\Phi(x)}{x}+\frac{1}{4}\right]|\mathbf{r}^*|^2, \tag{4}$$

where Θ_M is a characteristic temperature defined as a function of maximum frequency of vibration somewhat different from that defined by Debye in the thermodynamic theory, but which is not very different numerically. The term $\frac{1}{4}$ inside the brackets arises from the zero-point energy of vibration of the structure, as a consequence of the quantum theory of the linear oscillator.

The following function was calculated numerically by Debye (1914)

$$\Phi(x) = \frac{1}{x}\int_0^x \frac{\xi\,d\xi}{\exp(\xi)-1}, \tag{5}$$

where

$$\xi = \frac{h\nu}{kT}, \qquad x - \frac{h\nu_m}{kT}. \tag{6}$$

The value of M obtained by Debye was of the same form as (4) but had only half its magnitude. The factor 2 was introduced by Waller (1925) as a consequence of the method used in counting the normal modes of vibration of the structure. For this reason, the temperature factor has since been known as the Debye-Waller factor.

The expression $2M$ consists of two terms: one is independent of the absolute temperature and has its origin in the zero-point energy of vibration that arises from quantum considerations; the other term depends on the absolute temperature through $T\cdot\Phi(x)$. If we call M_0 and M_T, respectively, these two terms, we can write

$$2M = 2M_0 + 2M_T, \tag{7}$$

where

$$2M_0 = \frac{3h}{4m\nu_m}|\mathbf{r}^*|^2,\tag{8}$$

and

$$2M_T = \frac{3kT}{m\nu_m^2}\Phi(x)\,|\mathbf{r}^*|^2.\tag{9}$$

At high temperatures all the possible frequencies of the crystal contribute with approximately the same weight, so the equipartition of energy between the different modes of vibration of the structure is obeyed, while at low temperatures the highest frequencies hardly contribute. Thus the Debye formula for the specific heat is in accordance with experiment at low temperatures since at such temperatures only long waves are excited, and it is appropriate to consider the crystal as a continuum.

For a given temperature, $\Phi(x)$ is inversely proportional to ν_m, that is, to Θ. For example, for hexamine with $\Theta = 116°K$ and $\nu_m = 24 \times 10^{11}$ s^{-1}, at room temperature $\Phi(x)$ is very nearly unity, while for diamond, which has values of $\Theta = 1860°K$ and $\nu_m = 390 \times 10^{11}$, $\Phi(x)$ is considerably smaller than unity at relatively high temperatures.

Since ν_m is directly proportional to the characteristic temperature, comparison of (8) and (9) tells us that, for crystals with high characteristic temperature, a change in temperature has no appreciable effect on the intensity of the Bragg reflections, since in that case M_0 is more important than M_T. The opposite will occur for substances with low Θ_D, for which the Bragg intensity will be temperature-sensitive. We have two extreme cases in the examples cited; diamond with high Θ_D, for which

$$M_0 = 0.031|\mathbf{r}^*|^2,$$

$$M_T = 0.005|\mathbf{r}^*|^2,$$

and hexamine, with low Θ_D, for which

$$M_0 = 0.043|\mathbf{r}^*|^2,$$

$$M_T = 0.368|\mathbf{r}^*|^2.$$

Expression (4) can be written in a more convenient form as

$$2M = \frac{3h^2T}{km\Theta_M^2}\left[\phi(x) + \frac{x}{4}\right]|\mathbf{r}^*|^2\tag{10}$$

since, for values of $x < 1$ (that is, for temperatures T higher than the characteristic temperatures of the crystal) $\Phi(x) + x/4$ is practically equal to unity, and the preceding expression reduces to

$$2M = \frac{3h^2}{km\Theta_M{}^2}T|\mathbf{r}^*|^2, \qquad (T > \Theta_M). \tag{11}$$

Thus, for $T > \Theta_M$, 2M is proportional to the absolute temperature.

Since $M = 2\pi^2 u^2|\mathbf{r}^*|^2$, we obtain the function relating the mean square amplitude of atomic vibration to the absolute temperature

$$\overline{u^2} = \frac{3h^2}{4\pi^2 km\Theta_M{}^2}T\left[\Phi(x) + \frac{x}{4}\right]. \tag{12}$$

For $T > \Theta_M$ this relation is linear, and for the hypothesis that the characteristic temperature is independent of temperature in the temperature range considered, the mean square displacement is

$$\overline{u^2} = \frac{3h^2}{4\pi^2 km\Theta_M{}^2}T. \tag{13}$$

The preceding relations were derived for a cubic monoatomic crystal. It has been seen in Ch. 3 that when the crystal is complicated it is necessary to consider the mean square amplitude of vibration of each kind of atom separately, as well as the anisotropy of its vibration. In that case, M has the properties of a second-rank tensor, and the atomic vibrational ellipsoids can be determined from the temperature factor of the Bragg intensities obtained at a given temperature. For molecular crystals of low symmetry in which there are weak van der Waal's forces between molecules, and much stronger intramolecular forces, in the first approximation the hypothesis of rigid molecules can be made. For a crystal with more than one molecule per unit cell, there is not only an acoustic branch, but also translational and librational optical branches, the optical type of vibrations arising when the molecules in the cell vibrate almost out of phase. For the correct calculation of the rigid-body molecular vibrations in a crystal we must consider the distribution of frequencies in each one of these branches. As a first approximation we can suppose that the frequency is equal and constant in each branch.

For a crystal with two molecules per unit cell, Cruickshank (1956c) has expressed the mean square amplitude of translational vibration of the center of mass of the molecule by

$$(\overline{u^2})_{\text{trans}} = \frac{1}{2}\left\{\frac{3h^2T}{4\pi^2km\Theta_M{}^2}\left[\Phi(x)+\frac{x}{4}\right]+\frac{h}{8\pi^2m\nu_{\text{op}}}\coth\left(\frac{1}{2}\frac{h\nu}{kT}\right)\right\} \quad (14)$$

The first term gives the contribution of the acoustic branches, the second the contribution of the translational vibrations of optical frequencies.

Expression (14) cannot be used to determine the characteristic frequencies since it contains two unknowns, Θ_M and ν_{op}. However, since the characteristic temperatures $h\nu/k$ of the optical translational branches are higher than Θ_M, it is generally adequate to treat the translational motion totally by the Debye-Waller formula (10), using an apparent Θ_M somewhat higher than the actual value for the acoustic branches. Similarly, each of the librational branches can be expressed as a function of two frequencies ν_1 and ν_2 which correspond to the in-phase and antiphase librations with respect to an axis of moment of inertia I, in which case the mean square amplitude of libration (expressed in radians squared) is

$$(\overline{\phi^2})_I = \frac{h}{8\pi^2I}\left[\frac{1}{2\nu_1}\coth\left(\frac{1}{2}\frac{h\nu_1}{kT}\right)+\frac{1}{2\nu_2}\coth\left(\frac{1}{2}\frac{h\nu_2}{kT}\right)\right]. \quad (15)$$

Often there is little difference between ν_1 and ν_2, so that a mean frequency ν_{12} can be taken for the librations about each axis. With this simplification in mind, and at temperatures above the characteristic temperature, we can write

$$(\overline{\phi^2})_I = \frac{kT}{4\pi^2I\nu_{12}{}^2}. \quad (16)$$

Cruickshank (1956c) determined the characteristic temperature of naphthalene, as $\Theta_M = 91°K$, by using expression (10) and the value from x-ray data of $(\overline{u^2})_{\text{trans}} = 4.03 \times 10^{-2}$ Å^2. Following a similar procedure, Canut and Amorós (1961a) determined the characteristic temperature of hexamine, obtaining a value of $\Theta_M = 116°K$, using $(\overline{u^2})^{1/2} = 0.15$ Å from neutron diffraction data of Andresen (1957). Θ_D was also calculated for hexamine from the elastic constants given by Haussühl (1958), by de Launay's method (1959), obtaining $\Theta_D = 116°K$. Likewise, using $(\overline{u^2})^{1/2} = 0.12$ Å, determined from x-ray diffraction data by Phillips (1956) for acridine III, we have calculated the characteristic temperature of that molecular crystal, obtaining $\Theta_M = 71°K$.

Knowledge of Θ is fundamental to the study of the effect of temperature on diffuse scattering, which is now discussed.

The temperature dependence of thermal diffuse scattering

The temperature factors that appear explicitly in the expression for first, second, and third-order diffuse scattering (Laval, 1941) are

$$D_1 = kT \exp\left(-2B_j |\mathbf{r}^*|^2 T\right) \tag{17}$$

$$D_2 = k^2 T^2 \exp\left(-2B_j |\mathbf{r}^*|^2 T\right) \tag{18}$$

$$D_3 = k^3 T^3 \exp\left(-2B_j |\mathbf{r}^*|^3 T\right) \tag{19}$$

when equipartition of energy is applied. Here the B_j's represent coefficients that can be considered as independent of temperature. From the preceding expressions it is seen that the diffuse scattering of first, second, and third-order increases from absolute zero until a maximum value is reached, and then decreases as the temperature is raised further. This behavior was predicted by Laval (1941), who expressed the temperatures at which the maxima of first, second, and third-order diffuse scattering occur as

$$T_1 = \tfrac{1}{2} B_j |\mathbf{r}^*|^2,$$

$$T_2 = 2T_1, \tag{20}$$

$$T_3 = 3T_1,$$

if equipartition of energy is assumed.

If the temperature is not too low $(T > \Theta)$, the diffuse scattering intensity I_{dif} at any given point in diffraction space can be expressed (Born, 1942, 1943) as a first approximation as

$$I_{\text{dif}} \sim T \exp\left(-T/T_h\right). \tag{21}$$

This function has its maximum for $T = T_h$ and so does the diffuse scattering intensity. Born called T_h the inversion temperature of the diffuse scattering associated to the reflection hkl. Nevertheless, as Born indicated, the approximation on which (21) is based, that is, $\exp\left(-2M\right) \simeq 1 - 2M$, is valid only for values of $2M < 1$. Born expressed the inversion temperature for the particular case of cubic crystals as

$$T_h = \frac{T_0}{\Sigma h_i}, \tag{22}$$

where
$$T_0 = \frac{mka^2\Theta^2}{12\pi^2\Sigma h_i^2} = \frac{\Theta}{12\pi^2}\left(\frac{a}{l}\right)^2 \qquad (23)$$

and

$$l = \frac{h}{(mk\Theta)^{1/2}} = \frac{6.96\times10^{-8}}{(\mu\Theta)^{1/2}} \text{ cm.} \qquad (24)$$

Here μ is the atomic mass relative to that of oxygen $= 16$; l is the Born "dynamical lattice constant", a function of the constants of Planck and Boltzman h and k respectively. Born's theory likewise predicts a difference in the temperature dependence according to the order of the reflection. Born and Lonsdale (1942) gave a table of T_0 for some cubic elements.

Theoretically, therefore, the diffuse intensity of first, second, and third orders, but especially of first order, must pass through a maximum as temperature increases. Laval's first experiments with KCl (1941) showed clearly that the diffuse scattering associated with the reflection 600 decreased with increasing temperature, while in all the other cases it increased. However, Laval did not dwell upon the point.

Based on considerations of the low characteristic temperature of lead, Lonsdale (1948) suggested that that metal should show a decrease of diffuse intensity for high-order reflections. Cartz (1955) was able to detect this inversion phenomenon in lead by using the diffractometer technique. Later, Burgers, Kooy, and Tiedema (1956) showed this phenomenon photographically by using back-reflection techniques. More recently, Laberrigue (1959) reported a decrease of the diffuse intensity of the 444 Al reflection with increasing temperature, by using the electron-diffraction technique. Cartz (1955) also gave a list of substances where the effect of temperature on diffuse scattering had been studied. In all cases an increase of diffuse scattering with temperature was reported except for phloroglucinol dihydrate, where no change was observed in the range studied.

From the literature just cited it would appear that the inversion of diffuse scattering is only observable in special cases. However, Canut and Amorós (1961) showed that the phenomenon is general, and that it is only necessary to select appropriate experimental conditions for observation.

Restatement of the problem

Born's formulae are only valid for cubic crystals and their extension to the other crystallographic systems would give a complicated expression in terms of h, k, l, a, b, c, α, β, γ. We can simplify the problem by rewriting the temperature factor of first-order diffuse scattering (17) as follows

$$D_1 = kT \exp\left(-\frac{3h^2}{km\Theta^2}|\mathbf{r}^*|^2 T\right). \tag{25}$$

The maximum of this function satisfies

$$(T_{\max})_1 = \frac{k}{3h^2} m\Theta^2 \frac{1}{|\mathbf{r}^*|^2}. \tag{26}$$

For diffuse scattering close to a reciprocal lattice point we can express (26) in terms of the spacing of the corresponding hkl plane,

$$(T_{\max})_1 = \frac{1}{3}\frac{k}{h^2} m\Theta^2 d_{hkl}^2. \tag{27}$$

Every crystalline substance has a definite temperature range where (27) holds. The upper limit of $T_{\max}$ is obviously the melting temperature, and the lower limit is the characteristic temperature of the substance, because the equipartition law has been applied. These two extreme temperatures define the upper and lower spacings for which (27) applies, or for which the inversion phenomenon should be observable. Since this expression is a function of the crystal space, only certain sets of crystal planes will be potentially able to show the phenomenon.

Experimental conditions impose further limits on the possibility of determining $T_{\max}$. For instance, the x-ray wavelength used defines the limit of the sphere of reflection and therefore the volume of the observable reciprocal space. Also, the value of the structure factor F_{hkl} at rest limits the actual measurements, as TDS_1 is proportional to it. Accordingly, the inversion phenomenon is observable only for diffuse scattering associated with planes having a spacing within the limiting range, $2d_{hkl} > \lambda$, and F^2 big enough to give observable TDS_1.

From (11) and (18) we obtain for the $T_{\max}$ of TDS_2

$$(T_{\max})_2 = \frac{2}{3}\frac{k}{h^2} m\Theta^2 \frac{1}{|\mathbf{r}^*|^2} \tag{28}$$

that is,

$$(T_{\max})_2 = \frac{2}{3}\frac{k}{h^2} m\Theta^2 d_{hkl}^2. \tag{29}$$

In a similar way, from (11) and (19) we obtain for T_{max} of TDS_3

$$(T_{max})_3 = \frac{k}{h^2} m\Theta^2 \frac{1}{|\mathbf{r}^*|^2} \tag{30}$$

$$(T_{max})_3 = \frac{k}{h^2} m\Theta^2 d^2_{hkl} \tag{31}$$

The upper limit is again fixed by the melting temperature of the substance, but as the T maxima of TDS_2 and TDS_3 are, respectively, two and three times the T_{max} of TDS_1 (the formula being valid for $T > \Theta$), the inversion phenomenon for higher orders of diffuse scattering are displaced into the region of increasingly smaller spacings, that is, it soon falls outside the conditions for observation.

Relation between atomic-vibrational amplitude and T_{max}

The atoms in the crystal vibrate with characteristic amplitude for a given structure and temperature. Since the phenomenon of diffuse scattering is a direct consequence of this atomic vibration, there must exist a relation between the atomic-vibrational amplitude and T_{max}.
Letting $T = (T_{max})_1$, we obtain from the Debye-Waller relation (11):

$$\frac{(T_{max})_1}{T} = 1 = \frac{1}{4^2} \frac{d^2_{hkl}}{\bar{u}^2}, \tag{32}$$

and

$$\frac{(\bar{u}^2)^{\frac{1}{2}}}{d_{hkl}} = 0.16. \tag{33}$$

Therefore TDS_1 reaches its maximum value for a given crystallographic plane when $(\bar{u}^2)$ is a definite fraction 0.16 of its spacing.
Similarly, when the maximum of TDS_2 is attained,

$$\frac{(\bar{u}^2)^{\frac{1}{2}}}{d_{hkl}} = 0.22, \tag{34}$$

and for TDS_3,

$$\frac{(\bar{u}^2)^{\frac{1}{2}}}{d_{hkl}} = 0.28. \tag{35}$$

Grüneisen (1925) showed that melting takes place when $(\bar{u}^2)^{\frac{1}{2}}$ is of the order of 0.10 of the shortest interatomic distance.
Our results have a clear physical meaning: the Bragg intensity (corresponding to reflection from ideal planes) decreases with T because thermal vibrations make the plane less and less perfect. Diffuse scattering increases with temperature since thermal disorder increases, but it increases only up to the point where the plane retains

its physical meaning relative to the effect we are considering (one, two, or three phonons). *TDS* begins to decrease when, as the result of thermal agitation, the plane begins to lose its reality, that is, to "melt." Later the whole structure melts, and there ceases to exist a crystal.

The inversion phenomenon as a general phenomenon

In the above we have derived expressions that directly relate the crystal spacings to the temperature of the maximum at which the inversion of the diffuse scattering occurs. These expressions are independent of the type of structure, and are functions only of the mean square amplitude of atomic vibration.

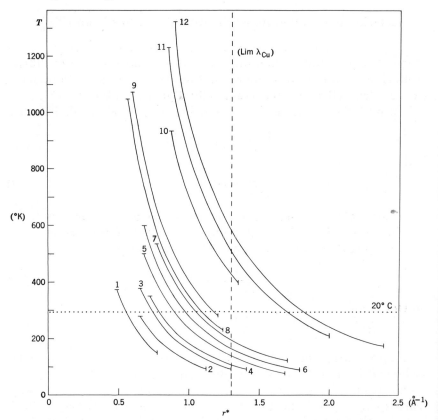

Fig. 2. TDS_1 inversion curves for several molecular, ionic and metallic crystals. Temperature interval: T_m and Θ. (1) Na, (2) benzene, (3) acridine III, (4) naphthalene, (5) anthracene, (6) Pb, (7) hexamine, (8) KCl, (9) NaCl, (10) Al, (11) Ag, (12) Au.

Furthermore, our expression (26) allows us to compute T_{max} for any crystalline substance, since it is likewise independent of the structure. When Θ and m are known, we can plot the inversion curves of TDS_1, if we represent $(T_{max})_1$ as a function of $|\mathbf{r}^*| = 1/d_{hkl}$. Figure 2 shows a set of inversion curves corresponding to different crystal types: metals (Na, Pb, Al, Ag, Au), ionic crystals (KCl, NaCl), and molecular crystals (acridine III, benzene, naphthalene, anthracene, hexamine). Since T_{max} is proportional to d_{hkl}^2, the inversion curves are hyperbolae. If no constancy of Θ is assumed over the interval considered, the curves are only slightly different, so this does not affect the validity of our study.

Figure 2 and Table 1 by no means present exceptional cases. The inversion phenomenon of TDS_1 is universal. In general, the inversion phenomenon is observable mainly at high temperatures in metals,

Table 1   Values of $m\Theta^2$, d_{max}, Θ and d_{min} for several crystalline substances

Crystal type	Substance	$m\Theta^2 10^{-18}$		d_{max}		Θ	d_{min}
		g	T	TDS_1	TDS_2		TDS_1
	Benzene	1.1307°K	278°K	1.54Å	1.09Å	93°K	0.65Å
	Acridine III	1.5506	381	1.49	1.07	71	0.70
Molecular	Naphthalene	1.7699	353	1.38	0.97	90	0.73
	Anthracene	2.2619	490	1.45	1.01	87	0.70
	Hexamine	3.1353	536	1.28	0.91	116	0.78
Ionic	KCl	3.3028	1049	1.74	1.24	231	0.57
	NaCl	3.8313	1074	1.64	1.16	281	0.61
	Na	0.8589	370	2.00	1.44	150	0.49
	Pb	2.6642	600	1.45	1.02	88	0.69
Metals	Al	6.1835	933	1.15	0.80	390	0.88
	Ag	8.2794	1234	1.18	0.82	215	0.86
	Au	9.4529	1336	1.20	0.86	170	0.82

at low temperatures in molecular crystals, and at moderate temperatures in ionic crystals. Of course the curves of Fig. 2 can be extended beyond the lower limit if zero-point energy is taken into account. The values of d_{max} for TDS_1 and TDS_2 define a region in reciprocal space where the inversion phenomenon for a given substance depends only on first-order diffuse scattering.

The fact that organic crystals show high intensity and complex diffuse patterns was to be expected because observation at room temperature is near to their melting points. This can also be an explanation for the intense and complicated diffuse pattern for Na. Comparison between the diffuse scattering of different crystals should be made at temperatures lying at corresponding points of the hyperbola (T_{mp}/Θ). In our opinion, molecular crystals are the substances for which the inversion effect can best be shown experimentally.

Determination of Debye characteristic temperatures from the inversion temperatures

The phenomenon of inversion allows us to determine the Debye characteristic temperatures of a given crystal of any symmetry because, from (27), we obtain

$$\Theta = \left[\frac{3h^2}{km} \frac{(T_{max})_1}{d_{hkl}^2} \right]^{1/2}. \tag{36}$$

Careful measurements with a diffractometer of the diffuse scattering at different temperatures, and very near to a given reciprocal-lattice point (in order to have the maximum contribution of TDS_1) enable one to plot the temperature dependence of TDS_1, and to determine T_{max}. The precision of the method will evidently depend on the precision of the temperature measurements and on the location of the coordinates of the measured point in reciprocal space. Moreover, the variation of T_{max} along different directions in reciprocal space provides the possibility of determining the Θ_{max} and Θ_{min} required when dealing with those crystal structures that are highly anisotropic (Tarasov, 1954).

In order to demonstrate the potentiality of the method we have computed the inversion curves of lead, for which Cartz detected the inversion effect (1955). From Cartz's experimental graphs we have measured the approximate experimental T_{max} for $\overline{4}40$, $\overline{2}4\overline{2}$, $\overline{2}40$, and $33\overline{1}$; these values are plotted in Fig. 3. The corresponding values calculated with our formula are given in Table 2. Two points, $\overline{2}40$ and $33\overline{1}$, lie on the theoretical curve, and the corresponding Θ'_Ds calculated with (36) are in good agreement with the Θ values determined by other methods. The values corresponding to $\overline{4}40$ and $\overline{2}4\overline{2}$ give higher Θ_D values; the reason for this might be that the measurements are made at points where the TDS_2 contribution was high.

The method outlined here can be applied to a crystal of any symmetry. It is not necessary to determine the absolute value of the diffuse scattering. It is only necessary to detect the inversion point.

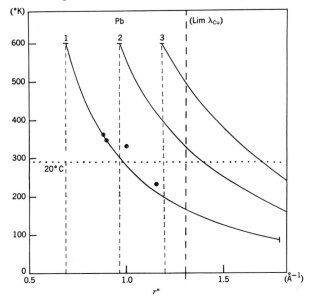

Fig. 3. Lead theoretical inversion curves of TDS_1, TDS_2 and TDS_3 calculated with $\Theta = 88°K$. The values of T_{max} obtained by Cartz are plotted.

Table 2 Θ values of Pb calculated from values of T_{max} given by Cartz

hkl	d_{hkl}	T_{max}	Θ_D
$\overline{4}40$	0.87Å	235°K	92°K
$\overline{2}4\overline{2}$	1.01	330	94
$\overline{2}40$	1.11	345	88
$\overline{3}3\overline{1}$	1.14	360	87

Theoretical prediction of the temperature variation of the diffuse scattering of hexamine and acridine III

Expression (25) for the temperature factor of I_{TDS_1} allows us to show graphically the variation of this function with the temperature T or the reciprocal vector $|r^*|$ when the characteristic temperature of the substance is known. Using the Θ values of hexamine obtained in the preceding section, we have obtained kTe^{-2M} as a function of T and as a function of $|r^*|$ (Figs. 4 and 5). The curves for $T = $ const and $|r^*| = $ const have been calculated assuming equipartition of energy for values of $T > \Theta$ while, for lower temperatures, the zero-point energy

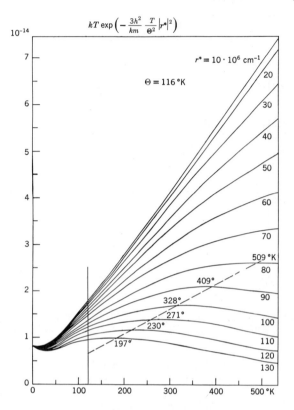

Fig. 4. Hexamine. Temperature variation of the temperature factor of TDS_1 for constant values of $|\mathbf{r}^*|$. The temperature of the maximum is indicated for each iso-$|\mathbf{r}^*|$ curve. The broken line is the locus of the maxima of TDS_1.

of structure vibration has been taken into account by substituting (79) of Ch. 4 and (4) in the expression for kTe^{-2M}. The effect at low temperatures gives a "peacock" shape to the set of curves for $|\mathbf{r}^*| = $ const (Fig. 4). If one restricts consideration to the interval $\Theta < T < T_f$, it is clear that for small values of $|\mathbf{r}^*|$ (that is, at points near the origin of reciprocal space) TDS_1 is a linear function of T. This linearity is lost as $|\mathbf{r}^*|$ increases, and after a certain value of $|\mathbf{r}^*|$ ($\approx 80 \times 10^6$ cm^{-1}) there appears a maximum $(T_{max})_1$ which tends toward lower and lower temperatures as $|\mathbf{r}^*|$ increases. The straight broken line is the locus of $(T_{max})_1$ for each value of $|\mathbf{r}^*|$. There is no doubt that the representation of the variation of the temperature factor by means of curves of $|\mathbf{r}^*|$ constant is very appropriate for the understanding of this effect. Figure 5 shows the isotherms of the temperature factor and their variation with $|r^*|$. The inversion is also clear from this representation.

According to this, the Laue photographs of these crystals taken at low temperatures, when compared with others taken at room temperature but in the same position and conditions, should show, at the lower temperature, a decrease in the diffuse intensity in the central part of the photograph, and an increase (or at least constancy) at the diffuse intensity maxima in the x-ray back-reflection regions.

The inversion of I_{TDS_2} and I_{TDS_3} with temperature obeys a different law. Figure 6 shows the inversion curves of TDS_1, TDS_2, and TDS_3 in hexamine, showing clearly the regions of reciprocal space where the decrease in thermal diffuse scattering is due only to the contribution of one phonon. Finally, the form functions of the diffuse scattering of one, two, and three phonons, as well as the continuous diffuse

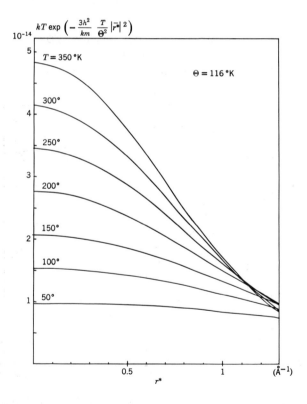

Fig. 5. Hexamine. Variation with $|r^*|$ of the isotherms of the temperature factor of TDS_1.

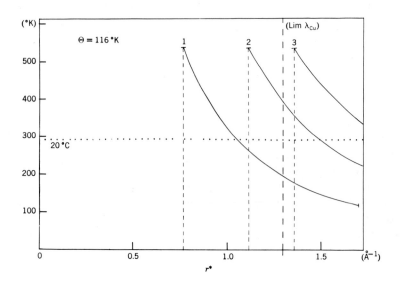

Fig. 6. Hexamine. Variation of the inversion temperature of TDS_1, TDS_2, and TDS_3 as a function of $|\mathbf{r}^*|$.

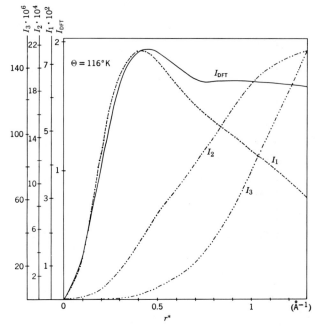

Fig. 7. Hexamine. Form functions of TDS_1, TDS_2, TDS_3, and DFT at room temperature.

414

scattering of the DFT, have been plotted (Fig. 7), using:

$$I_1 \sim f^2 |\mathbf{r}^*|^2 \, kT \exp(-2M), \qquad (37)$$
$$I_2 \sim f^2 |\mathbf{r}^*|^4 k^2 T^2 \exp(-2M),$$
$$I_3 \sim f^2 |\mathbf{r}^*|^6 k^3 T^3 \exp(-2M),$$
$$I_{\text{DFT}} \sim f^2 (1 - \exp(-2M)).$$

The graph allows us to have an idea of the regions of reciprocal space where each type of scattering is preponderant, when we use, for example, $Cu k\alpha$ x-radiation in the experiments.

Similar calculations for acridine III have allowed us to plot the curves of Figs. 8 and 9. In this case the interval of temperatures considered is given by $\Theta < T < T_m$. As can be seen, the phenomenon is similar to that of hexamine. In the case of acridine, we have not considered polymorphism. At room temperatures and higher, the most stable form is phase II, but the region of stability of phase III has not yet been determined (Phillips, 1956).

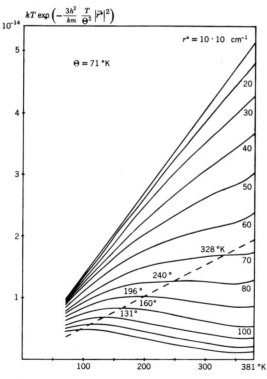

Fig. 8. Acridine III. Temperature variation of the temperature factor of TDS_1 for constant values of $|\mathbf{r}^*|$ for $T > \Theta$. The broken line is the locus of the maxima of TDS_1.

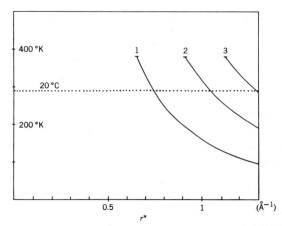

Fig. 9. Acridine III. Variation of the inversion temperature of TDS_1, TDS_2, and TDS_3 as a function of $|\mathbf{r}^*|$.

Variation in the DFT function with temperature

We have seen in Ch. 3 that when the atoms of the molecule are all of the same kind, the difference Fourier transform can be expressed by (64). Likewise, we have demonstrated the good agreement obtained between the continuous diffuse regions observed and those calculated with the DFT for diverse structural types. As a first approximation we have used values of B determined by structural methods that contain implicitly the Debye characteristic temperature (or, more precisely, Θ_M).

The DFT function considers, as an approximation, the independent molecular motion that affects the optical branches. This approximation seems justifiable from the physical point of view since, at temperatures relatively near the melting point where all the frequencies are excited with random phases, it is not incomprehensible that neighboring molecules should vibrate in their positions with a certain independence, with only the influence of their average mutual interaction keeping them in position. It is worthwhile mentioning that the Einstein model of independence of motion should not be rejected at high temperatures (Ziman, 1960), and that room temperature is a relatively high temperature for molecular crystals. Accordingly, in expression (64), Ch. 3 it is more appropriate to use a characteristic temperature based on the independent molecular motion, that is, one of the Einstein type, Θ_E. Taking $\Theta_E = 3\Theta_D/4$ (Mott and Jones, 1958), the Einstein characteristic temperature in the case of naphthalene is $\Theta_E = 63°K$ at room temperature.

The function

$$f_c^2\left[1 - \exp\left(-\frac{3h^2}{km\Theta_E^2}|r^*|^2 T\right)\right] \qquad (38)$$

is the form function of independent molecular motion. The distribution corresponding to this function is isotropic and centered at the origin of reciprocal space. This function is modified, in addition, by the geometrical factor of the molecules at rest $\Sigma_p(A_p^2 + B_p^2)$, and has maxima and minima that depend on the geometry and orientation of the molecules, just as we have found in our systematic study of molecular crystals.

Figure 10 shows the form function of the difference Fourier transform of naphthalene, introducing Θ_E, at absolute temperatures of 100°, 150°,....,350°K. The general appearance of these curves is very similar as that of the cruves plotted with Θ_D (Fig. 11), although the region of the maximum is higher with Θ_E.

The difference Fourier transforms have a value of almost zero in the neighborhood of the origin of reciprocal space and in the case of naphthalene, reach their maxima for all temperatures in the region where $|r^*| = 0.5\,\text{Å}^{-1}$, after which they decrease, but without ever vanishing. The most significant difference between the functions

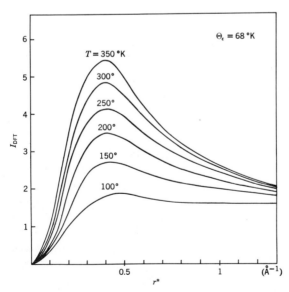

Fig. 10.   Naphthalene. Isotherms of the *DFT* form function calculated from the Einstein Θ_E.

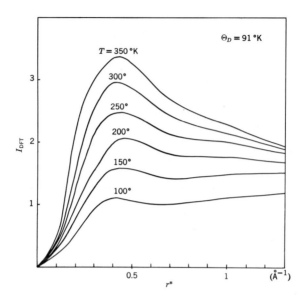

Fig. 11. Naphthalene. Isotherms of the *DFT* form function calculated from the Debye Θ_D.

TDS_1 and DFT is in the fact that the latter increases with temperature throughout reciprocal space although, near the boundary of the sphere of reflection with λ(Cu), the increase is relatively small, while the TDS_1 function shows an inversion such that, at a certain distance from the origin of reciprocal space, the function decreases as temperature increases.

Experimental evidence

Hexamine (Amorós, Carbonell, and Canut, 1962)

In this crystal the inversion has been detected by diffractometer techniques. Figure 12 gives the differences in counts made with a Ross filter at two different temperatures. These measurements correspond to diffuse scattering by longitudinal waves. It is seen how, for reciprocal-lattice points of small diffraction vector, that is, those nearest the origin, the diffuse scattering is most intense at the higher temperature. On the other hand, at the reciprocal-lattice point 800, far from the origin, the diffuse scattering decreased with the increase in temperature. This confirms our theoretical predictions regarding the inversion phenomenon in molecular crystals.

Benzil (Valdés and Canut, 1961)

The diffuse scattering of benzil at a low temperature, 100°K, is markedly different from that which is observed at room temperature. Figure 13 shows Laue photographs obtained at 293°K and 100°K, with the same crystal orientation and identical experimental conditions, except for temperature. From them we deduce:

1. The diffuse scattering associated with nonforbidden reciprocal-lattice points decreases with temperature for small values of the reciprocal vector, but increases with lower temperature for large values of $|r^*|$. Therefore, benzil presents the inversion phenomenon for first-order thermal diffuse scattering.

2. The streaks appear finer at the lower temperature, decreasing in intensity noticeably for small magnitudes of the diffraction vector, while the inversion phenomenon is clearly seen in the appearance of streaks in the region of large $|r^*|$, which did not even appear in the corresponding photograph at room temperature. Nevertheless, in all regions of diffraction space the streaks are very fine.

3. A noticeable effect in the low-temperature photographs with $(11\bar{2}0)$ vertical is the existence of diffuse maxima in the streaks between levels. Maxima of this type have been detected not only in Laue photographs, but also in oscillation photographs, where

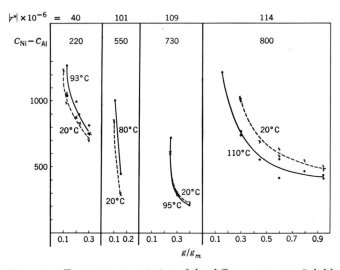

Fig. 12. Hexamine. Temperature variation of the diffuse scattering. Solid line: high temperature. Broken line: room temperature.

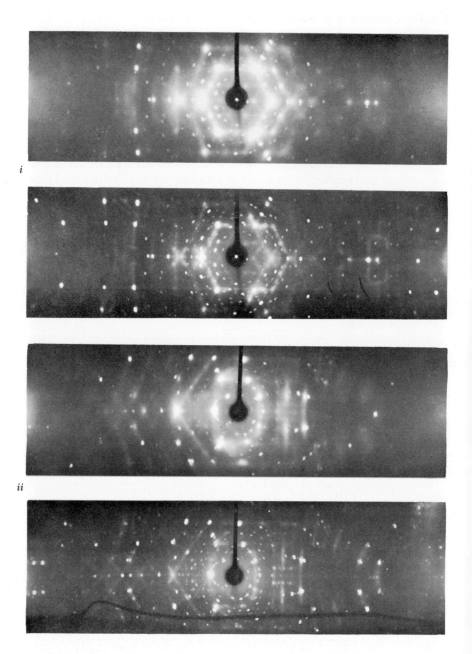

Fig. 13. Benzil. Laue photographs of a crystal oriented with [11$\bar{2}$0] axis vertical, taken in the same position at 20°C and −170°C. (*i*) X-ray beam at 2° to the 3-fold axis; (*ii*) X-ray beam at 50° to the 3-fold axis.

420

there can be no doubt that they appear between levels. Nevertheless, the fact that the Bragg reflections at room temperature decrease noticeably with the modulus of the diffraction vector shows that the mean Debye-Waller factor at room temperature must be quite high, so that the inversion phenomenon should occur at low temperatures. The inversion phenomenon has, in fact, been detected, and the effect extends to the streaks, showing that the fine portion of the streaks corresponds to the diffuse scattering on one phonon.

On the other hand, at room temperature the streaks are much wider, and in addition, there appear continuous diffuse regions. Both components of the total diffuse scattering lack inversion: on the contrary they decrease conspicuously as the temperature is lowered, no matter what the magnitude of the diffraction vector may be. Consequently this kind of diffuse scattering is not scattering of one phonon, but is the contribution of higher orders of scattering, or can be explained in the first approximation as a function of the DFT, taking into account that melting occurs at 96°C, and that near the melting point the Einstein model of independent motion is not physically inconceivable (Ziman, 1960). The fact that some of the continuous regions and the width of the streaks diminish, and even disappear, reveals that at low temperatures the higher frequencies are not excited. The diffuse spots associated with the reciprocal-lattice points at 100°K appear very concentrated about these points. According to the theory of thermal waves, this implies that only waves of very long wavelengths are excited at these temperatures. This applies to longitudinal and transverse acoustic waves, a fact already verified by the comparison of experimental specific heats with theoretical ones based on the Debye model. Order over long distances is preponderant at these temperatures.

In a molecular crystal such as benzil there are, in addition to the acoustic branches, optical branches, librational as well as translational (since there is more than one molecule per unit cell). Based on these branches, Born (1942) predicted the existence of weak maxima of diffuse intensity located at intermediate points of the reciprocal lattice because of the fact that the optical frequencies are minimized when the wave vector is maximized. We have no knowledge to date of any observations of maxima of the type predicted by Born, nor have we observed them in any of the crystals we have studied at room temperature. The fact that they appear at low temperatures seems to indicate that the dispersion curve of optical frequencies is accentuated at low temperatures. However, their final interpretation must await a specific study, since there can possibly be a change of phase near liquid-air temperature.

Naphthalene (Canut and Amorós, 1961)

For this crystal, photographs were selected from the series taken at room temperature in order to repeat them at two different temperatures in the same position. The selection was made in such a way that the temperature dependence could be obtained for the continuous diffuse regions G and C(see Fig. 14i, Ch. 4), and at the same time, the existence of inversion could be checked. Two Laue photographs taken at 300°K and 130°K are shown in Fig. 14.

The temperature dependence of the different kinds of diffuse scattering is reversible with temperature. The Laue photograph taken at low temperature shows that the Laue spots have increased in number and intensity. On the other hand, the diffuse spots associated with reciprocal-lattice points with values of $|r^*|$ between 0 and 70×10^3 cm^{-1} have disappeared, in agreement with the observations

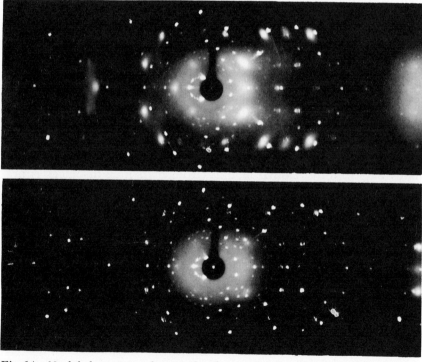

Fig. 14. Naphthalene. Laue photographs of a crystal oriented with [010] vertical and incident beam at 30° to a* in the region of positive β^*. Above, at 20°C; below, at −150°C.

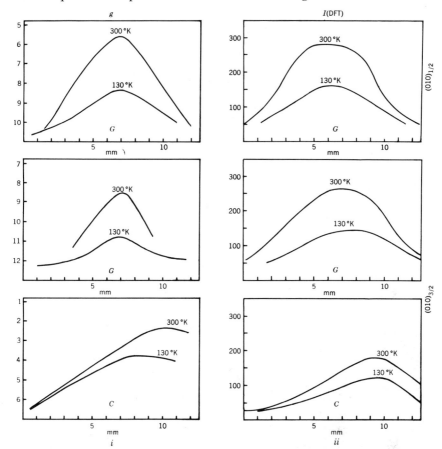

Fig. 15. Naphthalene. Intersections of regions G and C with the Ewald sphere, corresponding to the Laue photographs of Fig. 14. (i) Observed values; (ii) DFT calculated with Θ_E.

of Lonsdale and Smith (1942) in benzil, β resorcinol, and sorbic acid.

The Laue photographs of Fig. 14 also reveal the following:

1. The diffuse spot associated with the reciprocal lattice point 712 ($|\mathbf{r^*}| = 120 \times 10^6$ cm^{-1}) is more intense at the lower temperature, showing the inversion phenomenon in the diffuse scattering near reciprocal-lattice points as temperature decreases.

2. The continuous diffuse regions diminish in intensity as temperature decreases, even in the x-ray back-reflection regions, and therefore do not exhibit inversion.

Figure 15i shows measurements made with a Hilger microdensitometer on both films in regions G and C, in the reciprocal levels

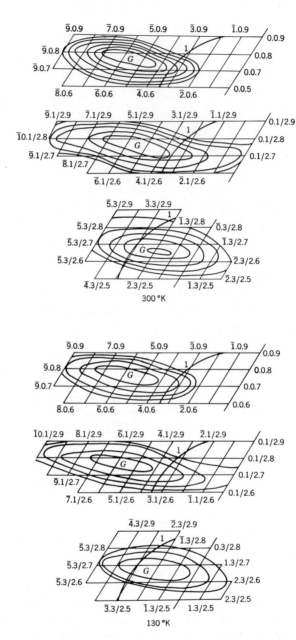

Fig. 16. Naphthalene. DFT isodiffraction curves in the G region for levels $(010)^*_0$, $(010)^*_{1/2}$, and $(010)^*_{3/2}$. Arbitrary contours of 25, 50, 100, 200, ... Arc 1 is the trace of the Ewald sphere as for the Laue photographs of Fig. 14.

$(010)^*_{1/2}$ and $(010)^*_{3/2}$. These measurements are compared with the values with the DFT (Fig. 15ii). For that purpose sections of the diffuse regions G and C were calculated at the reciprocal levels $(010)^*_{1/2}$ and $(010)^*_{3/2}$, at 300°K and 130°K (Figs. 16 and 17). In the temperature factor of the DFT an Einstein characteristic temperature of $\Theta_E = 67$°K was assumed. The isodiffraction contours are for arbitrary values of 25, 50, 100, 200, etc. The arcs marked 1 in the figure mark the Ewald sphere for the position of the crystal in the Laue photographs of Fig. 14; the values along those arcs are those of the DFT that are plotted in Fig. 15i. The experimental values agree quite well with the theoretical ones calculated with the DFT, showing that the continuous diffuse scattering has the same temperature dependence as the DFT.

Pseudoharmonic extension of the theory of diffuse scattering by thermal waves

The theory of the diffuse scattering of x-rays by thermal waves

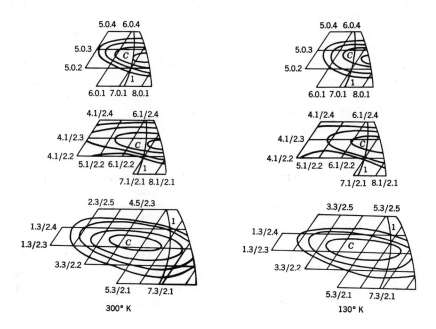

Fig. 17. Naphthalene. DFT isodiffraction curves in the C region for levels $(010)^*_0$, and $(010)^*_{3/2}$. Arbitrary contours of 25, 50, 100, 200, ... Arc 1 is the trace of the Ewald sphere as for the Laue photographs of Fig. 14.

given in Ch. 5 is based on an approximation called the harmonic approximation, according to which, in the series expansion which expresses the potential energy Φ of the crystal as a function of the atomic displacements, the terms of degree higher than second are ignored; this approximation is one whose accuracy increases as the mean square amplitudes of vibration become smaller.

The harmonic approximation implies the following restrictions (Leibfried and Ludwig, 1961): The free energy is the sum of a purely mechanical contribution and a contribution accounting for the vibrations. All the thermal quantities can be obtained from the mechanical part, which is independent of temperature. The equilibrium positions of the atoms are those for which the potential energy of the crystal is minimized. There is no thermal expansion. The adiabatic and isothermal elastic constants are equal, and are independent of temperature and pressure. There is a simple relation between the velocity of sound and the elastic constants of the crystal. The caloric data (derivatives of the free energy with respect to temperature) are consequently calculated from only the vibrational part. The specific heat at temperatures $T > \Theta$ remains constant, and for low temperatures obeys the cube law (Debye, 1912). The Debye characteristic temperature can be calculated for low temperatures from the elastic constants.

It is an experimental fact that crystals show appreciable thermal expansion, that the elastic constants depend on temperature, that the vibrational frequencies are temperature-sensitive, etc., which forces us to depart from the harmonic approximation in considering the thermal effect on physical quantities. A device that allows us to account for some of the thermal effects is the pseudoharmonic approximation. The terms of degree higher than second are again omitted, but the vibrational frequencies are taken to be functions of the lattice parameters, so that part of the anharmonic effects can be explained phenomenologically.

Studies of the variation in Bragg intensities with temperature are usually made under conditions of constant pressure. Under these conditions the volume changes with temperature as a consequence of thermal expansion. Therefore, it should be expected that the characteristic temperature, which depends explicitly on volume, should also vary with temperature. Paskin (1957) obtained the following relation for Θ as a function of volume and the Grüneisen constant γ:

$$\frac{d \ln \Theta(v_T)}{dv} = -\gamma v^{-1}. \tag{39}$$

If we introduce in the Debye-Waller expression the temperature dependence of the characteristic temperature, we obtain

$$2M = \frac{3h^2}{km\Theta_{T_0}{}^2}\left(\frac{v_T}{v_{T_0}}\right)^{2\gamma} T|\mathbf{r}^*|^2. \tag{40}$$

Calling $(v_T/v_{T_0})^{2\gamma}T$ a reduced T', $2M$ is proportional to that reduced temperature:

$$2M = \frac{3h^2}{km\Theta_{T_0}{}^2}T'|\mathbf{r}^*|^2. \tag{41}$$

In this way we compensate for the anharmonic effect reflected in the variation of Bragg intensities with temperature.

First-order diffuse scattering in the pseudoharmonic approximation

The Born and Laval theories of diffuse scattering are based on the harmonic approximation. In order to account for experimentally demonstrated anharmonic effects such as the variation with temperature of the frequency and the elastic constants we shall substitute in Laval's expressions the following: $v(T), \Theta(T)$, and $c_{ij}(T)$ in the places of v, Θ and c_{ij}, respectively. We shall call the result the pseudoharmonic approximation of the diffuse scattering.

If we accept a linear depencence of v on T, that is,

$$v(T) = v_0(1 - aT), \tag{42}$$

we can express the characteristic temperature as a linear function of T:

$$\Theta(T) = \Theta_0(1 - aT). \tag{43}$$

In (42) and (43) v_0 and Θ_0 represent the frequency and characteristic temperature at $0°K$, respectively, and a is an appropriate constant. Substituting (42) and (43) in (99), Ch. 5, we have, as the expression for I_{TDS_1} for longitudinal waves,

$$I_{TDS_1}(\mathbf{g}) = \frac{|R_0(\mathbf{r}^*)|^2|\mathbf{r}^*|^2kT \exp\left[-\dfrac{3h^2T}{km\Theta_0{}^2(1-aT)^2}\right]}{Zmv_0{}^2(1-aT)^2}, \tag{44}$$

a valid expression when there is no structural change in the interval of temperature where it is applied. Under these conditions, the temperature factor for the pseudoharmonic approximation for $T > \Theta$ will be

$$D = \frac{kT \exp\left[-\frac{3h^2}{km\Theta_0{}^2(1-aT)^2}\frac{T}{}\right]}{(1-aT)^2} \tag{45}$$

In this approximation expression (26) is no longer valid for calculating the inversion temperature. In this case, the condition for the maximum of function (45) must satisfy the third-degree equation

$$a^3T^3 - (a^2 + aA')T^2 - (a+A')T + 1 = 0, \tag{46}$$

where

$$A' = \frac{3h^2}{km\Theta_0{}^2}|\mathbf{r}^*|^2. \tag{47}$$

Actually, the inversion curve obtained in this case does not differ much from that obtained under the hypothesis of $\Theta=$ const.

Let us see the effect produced on the diffuse intensities by this variation in the frequencies of the thermal waves with temperature in the concrete case of naphthalene (Canut and Amorós, 1961b).

We do not have at our disposal experimental data on the temperature dependence of the acoustic frequencies in naphthalene, but Ichishima (1950) measured the variation of the Raman frequencies corresponding to the molecular librations between 83° and 298°K, and found it to be linear. Following Cruickshank (1956c) we can assume that the frequencies of the translational branch depend on temperature in the same way. If the librational ν measured by Ichishima are expressed in the form $\nu = \nu_0(1-aT)$, the mean value of a is 0.00067 and $\Theta_D = 113\,(1-0.076T)$. Introducing these values into expression (45) of the temperature factor of TDS_1, the isotherms can be calculated as a function of $|\mathbf{r}^*|$.

Figure 18 shows the variation of the temperature factor of TDS_1 with $|\mathbf{r}^*|$ at absolute temperatures of 100° and 300°. The solid line is calculated with $\Theta = 91°K$ and $\nu =$ const., that is, with expression (45) of the harmonic hypothesis. The shape of the curves is similar, and in both cases the inversion phenomenon occurs between $|\mathbf{r}^*|$ values of 100 and $110 \times$ cm^{-1}. The ratio $I_{300°}/I_{100°}$ of intensities is greater when the variation of frequency is introduced, especially for values of $|\mathbf{r}^*|$ not far from the origin of reciprocal space.

The inversion phenomenon is more marked if the temperature factor of TDS_1 is plotted as a function of T for constant values of

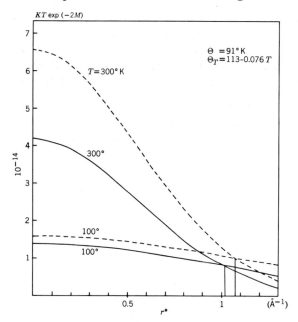

Fig. 18. Naphthalene. 300° and 100°K isotherms of the TDS_1 temperature factor as a function of $|r^*|$. Solid lines: harmonic approximation. Broken lines: pseudo-harmonic approximation. The two pairs of curves exhibit an inversion for $100 < |r^*| < 110 \times 10^6$ cm^{-1}.

$|r^*|$. Figure 19 corresponds to the harmonic hypothesis ($\Theta = 91°$K), while Fig. 20 is for the pseudoharmonic hypothesis ($\Theta = 113 - 0.076T$). We see in both cases that for small $|r^*|$, TDS_1 increases linearly with temperature, this region being the most thermosensitive, but the increase is increasingly smaller, until in naphthalene a value of $|r^*| = 80 \times 10^6$ cm^{-1} is reached, where inversion occurs. Likewise, the form curves for the first-order diffuse scattering can be plotted at different temperatures by means of the first expression in (37). The curves for naphthalene at absolute temperatures of $T = 100°$, 150°,..., 350°K have been calculated with the harmonic approximation ($\Theta = 91°$K) (Fig. 21), as have the curves at the same temperatures with the pseudoharmonic approximation (Fig. 22). The general appearance of the two families of curves is quite similar, which justifies the harmonic approximation used in previous sections. The variation of ν with temperature produces a slight translation of T_{max}, but does not eliminate the inversion. The most important feature of both sets of curves is that the form function of TDS_1 at a given temperature passes through a maximum and then decreases for large values of $|\mathbf{r}^*|$. The maxima of these curves at the different temperatures are located near $|\mathbf{r}^*| = 0.45 \times 10^6$ cm^{-1}. The presence of large maxima of diffuse scattering associated with reciprocal-lattice points in this region has been evidenced by experiments at room temperature.

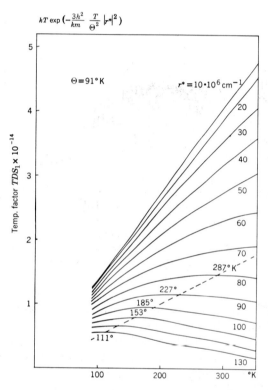

$kT \exp \left(-\frac{3h^2}{km} \frac{T}{\Theta^2} |\mathbf{r}^*|^2 \right)$

Fig. 19.   Naphthalene. Temperature variation of the temperature factor of TDS_1 for constant values of $|\mathbf{r}^*|$, under the harmonic hypothesis.

In Fig. 23 curve 1 is the TDS_1 inversion curve in the region where it is applicable.

The form functions of the second- and third-order diffuse scattering have maxima displaced toward high values of $|\mathbf{r}^*|$, with the displacement greater for the third than for the second order. Figure 24 shows the form functions of the first, second, and third order as well as the continuous diffuse scattering of naphthalene, computed at room temperature. Since the factors k^2T^2 and k^3T^3 appear in the expressions for TDS_2 and TDS_3, respectively, the contribution of the higher orders increases considerably with temperature.

What has just been described is based on the assumption that the functions $\nu(T)$ and $\Theta(T)$ are linear. Thermodynamics tells us that a change of phase produces a discontinuity in many physical properties. If this occurs, the theoretical predictions will be different.

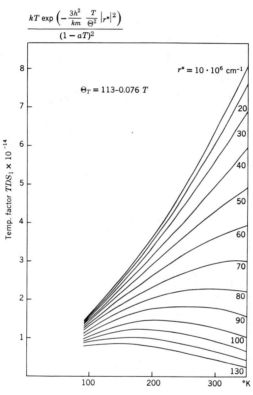

Fig. 20. Naphthalene. Temperature variation of the temperature factor of TDS_1 for constant values of $|\mathbf{r}^*|$, under the pseudoharmonic hypothesis.

Thermal diffuse scattering associated with a change of phase

Thermodynamics of the polymorphic transition

Although the thermodynamic description of changes of phase is a macroscopic phenomenological theory that does not take into account the structure of a crystalline solid, it is useful to define, although ideally, the types of polymorphic transitions. Let us consider the case of transitions at constant pressure. Their thermodynamic

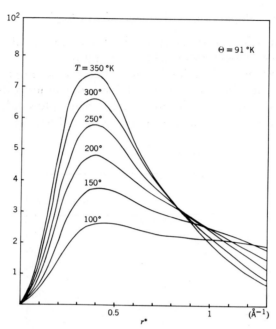

Fig. 21. Naphthalene. Isotherms of the form factor of TDS_1 as a function of $|\mathbf{r}^*|$ under the harmonic hypothesis.

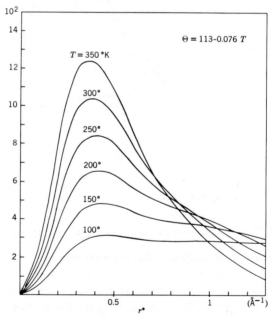

Fig. 22. Naphthalene. Isotherms of the form factor of TDS_1 as a function of $|\mathbf{r}^*|$ under the pseudoharmonic hypothesis.

432

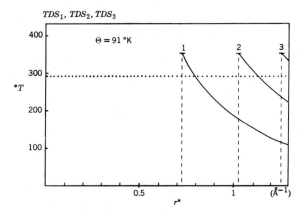

Fig. 23. Naphthalene. Variation of the inversion temperature of TDS_1, TDS_2, and TDS_3 as a function of $|\mathbf{r}^*|$.

description is simple. At constant pressure (e.g., at atmospheric pressure) one polymorph changes to another at a constant temperature. It is known that in systems of a single component, the specific free enthalpy takes the form $g(p, T)$, where p and T are chosen as

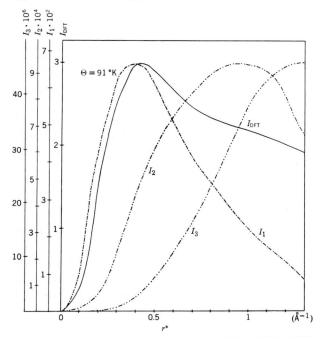

Fig. 24. Naphthalene. Variation of the form factors of TDS_1, TDS_2, TDS_3, and DFT as a function of $|\mathbf{r}^*|$, at room temperature.

independent variables. Gibbs' theorem shows that two phases of the same substance are in equilibrium when the specific free enthalpies of both phases are equal. The equation $g = f(p, T)$ is the equation of a surface. The transition between two phases is then located at the intersection of the two surfaces g_1 and g_2, and the intersection will be at ordinary pressure and at the temperature of transition. Much of the classical discussion of changes in phase was presented in the form of general conclusions about the intersections of independent surfaces of the specific free enthalpy g.

Sometimes it is convenient to consider sections of these g surfaces at $p = $ const. and $T = $ const.. The partial derivatives of g are of great importance, since they refer to experimentally observable quantities such as latent heat, specific volume v, specific heat c_p, the coefficient of isothermal compressibility κ, and the coefficient of thermal expansion α.

The thermodynamic function g is expressed

$$dg = -s\,dT + dp. \tag{48}$$

The entropy and specific volume are the first partial derivatives

$$\left(\frac{\partial g}{\partial T}\right)_p = -s, \qquad \left(\frac{\partial g}{\partial p}\right)_T = v. \tag{49}$$

According to the classical geometrical concepts of a transition between two independent phases 1 and 2, the change from the lower-temperature form 1 to the higher-temperature form 2 takes place with an absorption of latent heat. Curves g_1 and g_2 intersect in an acute angle, and the differences between the slopes of the tangents represent the changes in entropy and specific volume. The effect of pressure on the transition temperature is governed by the Clausius-Clapeyron equation

$$\frac{dp}{dT} = \frac{s_2 - s_1}{v_2 - v_1} = \frac{1}{T(v_2 - v_1)}. \tag{50}$$

In a phase transition that absorbs latent heat, g is continuous at the intersection of the surfaces, but its derivatives $-s$ and v are discontinuous. Transitions of this type are called first-order transitions.

There is another kind of transition in which there is no latent heat of transformation and no change in volume, so that the first derivatives of g are continuous, but the second derivatives

$$\left(\frac{\partial^2 g}{\partial T^2}\right)_p = -\left(\frac{\partial s}{\partial T}\right)_p = -\frac{c_p}{T}, \tag{51}$$

$$\left(\frac{\partial^2 g}{\partial p^2}\right)_T = \left(\frac{\partial v}{\partial p}\right)_T = -\kappa v, \tag{52}$$

$$\frac{\partial^2 g}{\partial p \partial T} = \left(\frac{\partial v}{\partial T}\right)_p = \alpha v, \tag{52a}$$

which are the specific heat c_p, the coefficients of isothermal compressibility κ and of thermal expansion α, are discontinuous. Ehrenfest (1933) has called them second order transitions. In the classification introduced by Ehrenfest the order of the transition is determined by the lowest order of the differential coefficient of the Gibbs function, which is discontinuous at the transition point. The classification can be extended to transitions of third order, and so on, although as the order of the transition becomes higher, the transition itself becomes less clear, since the discontinuity in the physical properties of the substance becomes less and less significant.

For all transitions except first-order, not only g but also s and v are continuous, and the Clausius-Clapeyron equation loses its validity, degenerating into $dp/dT = 0/0$. For transitions of second order, Ehrenfest derived an equation analogous to the Clausius-Clapeyron equation, and later known as the Ehrenfest equation

$$\frac{dp}{dT} = \frac{1}{vT} \frac{c_{p2} - c_{p1}}{\alpha_2 - \alpha_1} = \frac{\alpha_2 - \alpha_1}{\kappa_2 - \kappa_1}. \tag{53}$$

Ehrenfest's thermodynamic derivation in relation to second order transitions was criticized by Justi and Laue (1934) and other authors who affirmed that such transitions could not occur in nature. Putting aside a consideration of these criticisms, this type of classification is of interest to us because it allows us to establish two distinct types of transition, whose essential difference is the following.

In a first-order transition the two phases which are in equilibrium have very different structures, so that they have different potential energies, entropies, and volumes; the first-order transition indicates the point at which a greater difference in properties occurs.

The second-order transition, on the other hand, only marks a point at which a change finishes taking place. The two phases have very similar structures, potential energies, entropies, and volumes, and differ only in the ratios of the variations of these thermodynamic parameters with temperature, pressure, etc.

Landau (1937a,b) restated an important fact about second-order transitions long recognized by crystallographers and mineralogists

(Niggli, 1920). He indicated that, in certain transitions in solids, a number of symmetry elements appear or disappear abruptly, but the density, and more generally the probability distribution in the crystal, differ only slightly after the transition from before the transition. In first-order transitions the change in these quantities is abrupt.

Bauer (1952) notes that although it may be more difficult to know exactly the order of a given transformation, in first-order transitions two distinct phases in equilibrium should be found. According to Bauer, the transformations of second and higher orders are characterized by the fact that the two phases in equilibrium are never found separated in space, and the transition point only signals the end of the transformation. It should be noted that if this transition point is well defined at a certain temperature at a given pressure, it is because the phenomenon is a cooperative one, such that the molecular interactions accelerate the creation of disorder as disorder itself increases.

For transformations of condensed phases, Ubbelohde (1956) suggests a nomenclature of continuous and discontinuous, instead of first- and second-order transformations. According to Ubbelohde's nomenclature, a transformation that behaves experimentally in accordance with classical thermodynamics (that is, the first-order transition of Ehrenfest's classification) is a discontinuous transformation, while transformations that do not exhibit the classical discontinuity are continuous.

These continuous transitions are often of the lamda type, and must be analyzed from a statistical point of view. The value of a statistical theory is that, in principle, it can predict the nature of the phases and of the transitions from the knowledge of molecular properties. Although such a theory may not be perfectly adequate from the quantitative point of view, it is more effective than the purely thermodynamical one, where we must assume the existence of the two phases *ab initio*. From the statistical mechanics point of view, phase transitions are generally considered the results of cooperative interactions among molecules, even though the difficulty in this field arises from the complexity of the mathematical description of the simultaneous cooperation of many molecules.

Experiment has shown that the specific-heat curves of a certain number of molecular and ionic crystals made up of particles of high symmetry exhibit anomalies similar to those observed in order-disorder transitions of alloys. Other physical properties, such as the dielectric constant, exhibit discontinuities at the same temperature at which the specific-heat anomaly appears. To explain this fact theoretically, Pauling, Fowler, and Frenkel have made different hypotheses.

Pauling's hypothesis (1930) assumes that below a certain transition temperature the molecules or atomic groups in the solid state oscillate about equilibrium positions in a potential which, for convenience, is taken to be sinusoidal, but above that temperature the molecules rotate freely. This simple hypothesis accounts for the rise in the dielectric constant and the lowering of the specific heat at the transition temperature. A change from oscillation to free rotation gives rise to a decrease in specific heat by $\frac{1}{2}R$ units per degree of freedom of rotation (R = ideal gas constant), when the temperature increases to surpass the transition point. This decrease occurs because, in classical theory, a freely rotating particle has only half the specific heat per degree of freedom that an oscillating particle has.

Fowler's hypothesis (1935) is an extension of Pauling's concept, in which he introduces the idea that molecular rotation in solids is a cooperative phenomenon. In a molecular crystal diatomic polar molecules are constrained by a sinusoidal potential of magnitude W, but a given molecule can overcome the potential if it has a kinetic energy sufficient to rotate an arbitrary fraction β of 180° from its equilibrium orientation. Calculating the fraction of molecules S that do not rotate, and c_v as a function of the reduced temperature, we have $W = W_0 S$, using Bragg and William's approximation. By this procedure Fowler can determine the type of the transition according to the value of the arbitrary parameter β. The transition which takes place at $T_c = W_0/k$ marks the beginning of completely free rotation. Fowler's theory leads to a decrease in c_v at temperature T_c which reaches values of up to $4R$ according to the value of β. A decrease of $\frac{1}{2}R$ units per degree of rotational freedom is taken as the criterion of free rotation in Pauling's hypothesis, but Fowler's calculations show that the decrease in c_v at the transition temperature will exceed that value in cooperative systems. The common feature of Pauling's and Fowler's theories is that, above the transition temperature, free rotation is assumed.

Frenkel (1935) strongly criticized Pauling's hypothesis, and instead of assuming that the molecules spin freely above the transition temperature, he assumed that the molecules were subject to librations about equilibrium positions distributed more or less at random. He also assumed that the molecules were subject to a potential barrier below the transition point. In Frenkel's hypothesis, the transition point is the temperature at which there is produced a loss of long-range order in the orientations of the molecules with respect to the other molecules and with respect to the crystal axes. In extreme cases all that remains above the transition point is a limited degree of local order. The difference between the process of order-disorder in alloys, and disorder in the Frenkel sense, lies in the fact that, in the first case, certain atoms jump to places in the superstructure originally occupied by other atoms, whereas in the latter case the molecules remain in their positions in the structure, but vibrate about their centers of gravity, taking on new equilibrium orientations. Therefore the process described by Frenkel is called one of rotational and orientational disorder.

Diffuse scattering and discontinuous transitions

Discontinuous transition, which Buerger (1961) calls reconstructive, cannot be studied by diffuse-scattering methods in the temperature interval including the transition point, since a rupture of the original structure is produced, and the original crystal structure is not preserved. From a singly crystal of one phase a polycrystal is obtained, so that, in order to study the diffuse scattering of the phase that is not stable at room temperature, a single crystal of the other phase must be grown at a temperature above or below the transition point. The thermal diffuse scattering of each phase must thus be studied separately.

Since the structures of two phases, I and II, whose transition is discontinuous are, in general, quite different, it is to be expected that the diffuse scattering should be of a different type for each one, so that, in general, we shall have the inequality

$$|F_0^I(\mathbf{r}^*)|^2 \neq |F_0^{II}(\mathbf{r}^*)|^2, \tag{54}$$

and consequently

$$\nu_I \neq \nu_{II}, \qquad \Theta_I \neq \Theta_{II}. \tag{55}$$

Thus, for example, expression (44) for I_{TDS_1} for the two phases I and II in the temperature intervals where each one is stable are

$$I_{TDS_1}^I(\mathbf{g}) = \frac{kT|\mathbf{r}^*|^2 \exp[-(3h^2T/km\Theta_I)]}{Zm\nu_1^2(T)} |F_0^I(\mathbf{r}^*)|^2,$$

$$I_{TDS_1}^{II}(\mathbf{g}) = \frac{kT|\mathbf{r}^*|^2 \exp[-(3h^2T/km\Theta_{II})]}{Zm\nu_{II}^2(T)} |F_0^{II}(\mathbf{r}^*)|^2. \tag{56}$$

The morphologies of the diffuse scattering for phases I and II can be quite different. For example, NH_4NO_3 has five different solid phases at ordinary pressure (Amorós and Canut, 1962); phase III (stable between $+32°$ and $+85°C$) has a structure much different from that of phase IV (stable at room temperature). Alonso, Canut, and Amorós

(1958a) found that the diffuse scattering associated with the high temperature phase III was much weaker and of a different type than that of the room-temperature phase IV. This difference can be explained by (56), since the difference in their structures, from the geometrical and packing point of view, cause their structure dynamics to be different, and it is thus not necessary for the diffuse scattering to be similar.

Diffuse scattering and continuous transitions

In contrast, in a second-order or continuous transition, the transformation is produced by a progressive and cooperative disordering that takes place over a long temperature interval. Thus the vibrational or positional disorder in the low-temperature structure increases until it reaches a maximum at the transition point, without a loss in the continuity of the crystal structure. This continuity allows the study of the variation in the diffuse scattering at the moment of transition. For example, in ferroelectric structures containing polar groups, it is common for an increase in temperature to produce a disordering of a certain per cent of these groups into centrosymmetric position, the percentage increasing gradually up to the transition point, finally reaching 50 per cent when the high-temperature phase is centrosymmetric (paraelectric phase). Thus the centrosymmetric phase is often a disordered phase.

The intensity of the Bragg reflections of the ordered structure is, in general, given by

$$I_{ord}(hkl) = A_{ord}^2(hkl) + B_{ord}^2(hkl). \tag{57}$$

Associated with the Bragg reflections, the ordered structure presents first-order diffuse scattering that is proportional to $I_{ord}(\mathbf{r}^*)$:

$$I_{ord\,TDS_1}(\mathbf{r}^*) \propto A_{ord}^2(\mathbf{r}^*) + B_{ord}^2(\mathbf{r}^*). \tag{58}$$

This diffuse scattering is due to thermal waves and shows strong anisotropy since it is modulated by the elastic tensor.

The disordered phase has an average structure that is centrosymmetric, and therefore, we have

$$I_{dis}(hkl) = \overline{A}_{dis}^2(hkl) \simeq A_{ord}^2(hkl), \tag{59}$$
$$\overline{B}_{dis}^2(hkl) = 0.$$

The intensities of the Bragg reflections of the disordered phase are identical to the square of the real part of the structure factors of the ordered structure, except for a slight variation in the atomic co-ordinates and the variation in the temperature factor. It should be noted that for (59) to hold, the origin for the cell of the noncentro-symmetric phase must be chosen at the point homologous to that center of symmetry that is taken as origin of the cell of the disordered phase.

The disordered phase will also show a thermal diffuse scattering, for which

$$I_{\text{dis } TDS_1}(\mathbf{r}^*) \propto A_{\text{ord}}^2(\mathbf{r}^*) \tag{60}$$

Besides this thermal diffuse scattering, the disordered phase will also show a disorder diffuse scattering given by (110), Ch. 3. The structure of the disordered phase consists of groups of positive or negative polarity with respect to the polar axis, and therefore, in this case, the first term of (110) is given by

$$<F(\mathbf{r}^*)^2> = A_{\text{ord}}^2(\mathbf{r}^*) + B_{\text{ord}}^2(\mathbf{r}^*), \tag{61}$$

and the second term of (110) is

$$<F(\mathbf{r}^*)>^2 = B_{\text{ord}}^2(\mathbf{r}^*). \tag{62}$$

Therefore the disorder diffuse scattering intensity becomes

$$I_{DDS_1}(\mathbf{r}^*) = B_{\text{ord}}^2(\mathbf{r}^*). \tag{63}$$

Expressions (57) and (63) show that Brillouin zones of strong intensity in the ordered phase can have very weak, or almost null, intensity in the disordered phase whenever the chief component of $I_0(hkl)$ is $B_0(hkl)$, for in the disordered phase $B(hkl) = 0$. When correlations are present, the disorder diffuse scattering given by (63) is modulated by the correlation function (115), Ch. 3, of the statistical domains.

It is evident that in the temperature interval of the continuous transitions, the harmonic approximation of the thermal diffuse scattering cannot be applied, since in the thermodynamics of the change of phase there are discontinuities in physical quantities such as the specific heat, thermal expansion, elasticity, electric susceptibility, etc.

The discontinuity in the specific heat is a direct consequence of the vibrational anomaly that occurs in a change in phase, and the same can be said about the anomaly in the elastic tensor. These two quantities are intimately related to the vibrational frequencies, and therefore the thermal diffuse-scattering intensity is directly in-fluenced by such anomalies. Since diffuse scattering permits the study of thermal waves of a given type at special points of reciprocal space, and since sometimes the type of wave is a function of a single elastic constant, it is obvious that if the elastic constant has an anomaly at transition (of the lambda type, for example), the diffuse scattering associated with the corresponding wave vector will exhibit a discontinuity at the same temperature. In this case (44) can be written

$$I_{TDS_1}(\mathbf{g}_l) = \frac{kT|\mathbf{r}^*|^2}{Zm} \frac{I_T(\mathbf{r}^*)}{v_l^2(T)}. \tag{64}$$

A continuous transition is a cooperative phenomenon in which the gradual change in structure, elastic constant, and specific heat sometimes begin at a temperature quite far from the transition temperature. I_T can be a discontinuous function in T in a relatively small temperature interval about the transition temperature, but, due to the anisotropy of the structural change, the variation in $I_T(\mathbf{r}^*)$ depends strongly on the vector $\mathbf{r}^*$. Furthermore, the variation in the vibrational frequency $v(T)$ associated with the variation in the structure throughout the transition process can produce a marked effect on the diffuse intensity. We can say that the anomaly in $I_{TDS_1}(\mathbf{g})$ at each point of reciprocal space is governed by the function

$$I_T(\mathbf{r}^*) \sum_i \frac{\cos^2 (\mathbf{r}^* \cdot \mathbf{e}_i)}{v_1^2(T)}, \tag{65}$$

and therefore the phenomenon is very complex. At certain points of reciprocal space, and along certain directions, there can be an appreciable variation in the diffuse intensity, at others no variation can be detected, and finally, at others there can be discontinuities or well defined peaks.

Critical diffuse scattering and ferro-paraelectric transitions

Landau (1937c) pointed out that in the neighborhood of a polymorphic transition of second order, the presence of fluctuations in the order parameters at large distances gives rise to an anomalously intense diffuse scattering (called critical scattering) near reflections corresponding to superstructures. More recently Krivoglaz (1958) extended Landau's results to cases in which the change in long-range order is described by more than one parameter, and discussed ferro-paraelectric transitions in greater detail. He considers the case in which the long-range order parameters subject to anomalous fluctuations can be expressed by means of the components of spontaneous polarization P_i. According to Krivoglaz, the fluctuations

$P_i - \overline{P}_i$ in the polarization components can be expanded in a Fourier series,

$$P_{il} - \overline{P}_i = \sum_{g}{}' P_{gi} \exp\left[-2\pi i (\mathbf{g} \cdot \mathbf{r}_l)\right] + P^*_{gi} \exp\left[2\pi i (\mathbf{g} \cdot \mathbf{r}_l)\right],$$

where $\overline{P}_i$ is the average value of the equilibrium component i of the polarization vector, while P_{il} is the value of P_i for the crystal cell l, which is at a distance $\mathbf{r}_l$ from the origin. The prime in the summation indicates that it extends over vectors $\mathbf{g}$ of only half the Brillouin zone, excluding the term $|\mathbf{g}| = 0$. The polarization wave for each vector $\mathbf{g}$ is equivalent to a wave of atomic displacements. The direction of displacement of the atoms in the wave $\mathbf{g}$ is given by the polarization vector.

Krivoglaz limits his study to neighborhoods of Bragg reflections, since that is the region where the scattering is anomalously intense. This limitation implies considering only fluctuation waves of long wavelength, so that the only coefficients P_{gi} of the Fourier series of polarization fluctuations which are considered are those corresponding to small $\mathbf{g}$.

A variation ΔP_i in the components of the polarization vector results in a change $d_{hi}\Delta P_i$ in the average structure factor $\overline{F}_h(\mathbf{r}^*)$, so that d_{hi} depends specifically on the reflection h, and therefore, at some reflections it can be zero. Similarly, the deviation of the atomic factor of cell l with respect to the average value in the crystal is given by $(P_{il} - \overline{P}_i)d_{hi}$.

Krivoglaz derives the expression for the critical diffuse intensity, as does Laval in defining the affixes, by considering that the most important part of the summation over the contributions of the different waves is for $\mathbf{g} = \mathbf{r}^*$. The expression for the critical diffuse scattering can be written

$$I_{\text{crit}}(\mathbf{g}) = \frac{kT}{Zm}\left[\overline{F}_h(\mathbf{r}^*)a_{gi}\frac{(\mathbf{r}^* \cdot \mathbf{e})}{|\mathbf{g}|} - d_{hi}\right]\left[\overline{F}_h(\mathbf{r}^*)a_{gj}\frac{(\mathbf{r}^* \cdot \mathbf{e})}{|\mathbf{g}|} - d_{hj}\right]$$
$$(\kappa^{-1} + A_{mn}G_m G_n)_{ij}^{-1}, \qquad (67)$$

where all the quantities are known, except for a_{gi}, d_{hi}, and the last factor. The d_{hi} can be determined experimentally by studying the variation of the structure factors $\overline{F}_h$ with the polarization or the intensity of an applied electric field since, when the components of the polarization P_1 change to $P_i + \Delta P_i$, the average structure factor $\overline{F}_h$ becomes $\overline{F}_h + d_{hi} \cdot \Delta P_i$. In an inhomogeneously polarized crystal there appears a field of stresses and, from the expression for the stress tensor, the quantities a_{gi} can be obtained. Due to the presence of fluctuations δP, the expression for the free energy of the deformed crystal contains the term $-\epsilon_{ijm}U_{ij}\delta P_m$, so that the components of the stress tensor σ_{ij} are given by

$$\sigma_{ij} = \lambda_{ijmn}u_{mn} - \epsilon_{ijm}\delta P_m, \tag{68}$$

where u_{mn} are the components of the strain tensor, and λ_{ijmn} are the components of the elastic tensor. The a_{gm} are obtained by substituting δP_m by a periodic function corresponding to a fluctuation wave g. Likewise, u_{mn} are substituted by the components of the strain tensor that corresponds to the geometrical strain wave produced by the fluctuation wave when the boundaries of the crystal remain stationary. Taking into account that, under these conditions, $\partial \sigma_{ij}/\partial x_j = 0$, Krivoglaz arrives at three equations for $a_{gm}\epsilon_r$

$$\lambda_{ijpr}n_i n_p A_{gm}\xi_r = \epsilon_{ijm}n_j, \qquad (i = 1, 2, 3), \tag{69}$$

where the n_i are the direction cosines of the wave vector g. The third-rank tensor ϵ_{ijm} can be calculated when the variation in the stresses (or strains) with polarization is known. These data can be obtained, for example, by the application of an external electrical field. Thus all the parameters appearing in the expression for the diffuse scattering, except for A_{ijmn}, can, in principle, be obtained by independent experiments. The factor $(\kappa^{-1}+A_{mn}g_m g_n)_{ij}^{-1}$ represents the components of the inverse of the tensor $(\kappa_{ij}^{-1}+A_{ihmn}g_m g_n)$. For small $|g|$ it is simply the dielectric susceptibility k_{ij}. Thus for small $|g|$, all the quantities of (67) can be obtained, and the equation becomes

$$I_{crit}(\mathbf{g}) = \frac{kT}{Zm}\left[\overline{F}_h(\mathbf{r}^*)a_{gi}\frac{(\mathbf{r}^* \cdot \mathbf{e})}{|\mathbf{g}|} - d_{hi}\right]\left[\overline{F}_h^*(\mathbf{r}^*)a_{gj}\frac{(\mathbf{r}^* \cdot \mathbf{e})}{|\mathbf{g}|} - d_{hj}\right]k_{ij}. \tag{70}$$

Then the diffuse intensity in the neighborhood of a Bragg reflection is a function of the second-rank electric susceptibility tensor K_{ij}^{-1}.

Expanding (70), we obtain for the right-hand side a term inversely proportional to $|g|^2$:

$$\frac{kT}{Zm}|F_h(\mathbf{r}^*)|^2 a_{gi}\, a_{gj}\, \frac{(\mathbf{r}^* \cdot \mathbf{e})^2}{|\mathbf{g}|^2}k_{ij}, \tag{71}$$

two others inversely proportional to $|g|$,

$$-\frac{kT}{Zm} F_h\left(\mathbf{r}^*\right) a_{gi} \frac{(\mathbf{r}^* \cdot \mathbf{e})}{|\mathbf{g}|} d_{hj} k_{ij},$$

$$-\frac{kT}{Zm} F_h^*\left(\mathbf{r}^*\right) a_{gj} \frac{(\mathbf{r}^* \cdot \mathbf{e})}{|\mathbf{g}|} d_{hi} k_{ij}, \tag{72}$$

and another independent of $\mathbf{g}$,

$$\frac{kT}{Zm} d_{hi}{}^2 k_{ij}. \tag{73}$$

The term (71) indicates a strong anisotropy in the diffuse intensity, since it is proportional to $\cos^2 \psi$, where ψ is the angle between $\mathbf{r}^*$ and $\mathbf{e}$. The tensor a_{gm} depends strongly on the orientation of $\mathbf{g}$. Thus the intensity distribution of the diffuse scattering can be very complicated. Furthermore (71) is proportional to $|\mathbf{r}^*|^2$, so that it increases as we consider the Brillouin zones farther removed from the origin, in a way similar to Laval's TDS_1 expression. Krivoglaz's equation can be identified with the formula for first-order diffuse intensity, if we take into account that the a_{gi} contain the elastic tensor, which appears explicitly in Laval's formula. The term (72), only being inversely proportional to $|\mathbf{g}|$, will produce a less marked effect that (71), likewise influenced by the factor d_{li}. Finally, the term (73), proportional to $d_{hi}{}^2$, will be important when the $\overline{F}_h(\mathbf{r}^*)$ change with the components P_i.

In the Brillouin zones where $d_{hi} = 0$, (70) reduces to

$$I_{\text{crit}}(\mathbf{g}) = \frac{kT}{Zm} |F_h(\mathbf{r}^*)|^2 a_{gi}{}^2 \frac{(\mathbf{r}^* \cdot \mathbf{e})^2}{|\mathbf{g}|^2} \cdot k_{ik} \tag{74}$$

When the terms of (70) are proportional to k_{ij}, the expression predicts a variation in the diffuse intensity at temperatures where the electric susceptibility tensor varies.

According to the thermodynamic theory of ferroelectricity, in a second-order transition the components of $k_{ij}{}^{-1}$, the inverse of the electric susceptibility tensor, tends to zero. Consequently, (70) predicts an anomalously intense diffuse scattering at the transition temperature, called the critical diffuse scattering. On the other hand, near the transition temperature T_c the second-rank tensor ϵ_{ijm} can be written

$$\epsilon_{ijm} = \overset{0}{\epsilon}_{ijm} + \delta_{ijmn} P_n. \tag{75}$$

In the special case where the transition to the paraelectric structure brings into being a center of symmetry, the ϵ^0_{ijm} vanish identically in the paraelectric phase. In that case $a_{gi} = 0$, so that the terms in $|\mathbf{g}|^{-2}$ and $|\mathbf{g}|^{-1}$, which arise from fluctuations in the polarization, vanish and the critical scattering for $T > T_c$ is due solely to (73).

In the ferroelectric phase, since $a_{gm} \sim \bar{P}$ (spontaneous polarization) the coefficient of $|\mathbf{g}|^{-2}$ is proportional to $\bar{P}^2$. Then for small values of $\bar{P}$, even where $T < T_c$, the term in $|\mathbf{g}|^{-2}$ is not very important. In that case, the term proportional to $d_{hi}{}^2$ accounts for most of the critical diffuse scattering.

The critical diffuse scattering of NaNO$_2$

Since the characteristics of the phenomenon of critical diffuse scattering are dependent on the type of transition and not on whether or not the crystal is molecular, we shall describe the results obtained for NaNO$_2$. This is a ferroelectric of space group $Imm2$ at ordinary temperature, changing to a paraelectric of space group $Immm$, at the Curie point of 163°C. The projections on (100) of the ferroelectric and paraelectric structures are shown in Fig. 25 (Strijk and Mac-Gillavry, 1943, 1946). The average structure of the paraelectric phase results from the possibility that Na$^+$ ions and NO$_2^-$ groups can each occupy one of two positions related by a plane (or center) of symmetry.

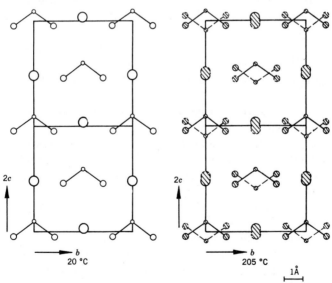

Fig. 25. NaNO$_2$. (*i*) Projection on (100) of the structure of the ferroelectric phase at 20°C; (*ii*) average structure of the paraelectric phase at 205°C.

In reality the structure is a complex one of dynamic antiferroelectric domains called "cigarrillos" by Canut and Hosemann (1964); through this structure there run waves of fluctuations in the orientations of the structural units, which have important correlations along the polar axis of the ferroelectric structure. The disorder diffuse scattering is given by (116), Ch. 3. The structure of statistical domains has been studied in detail by the former authors, and the average disordered structure has been studied by Kay, Frazer, and Ueda (1962). In essence the mechanism of the ferroparaelectric transition is a process that averages the distribution of Na^+ and NO_2^- groups in the two stable positions, and therefore it is to be expected that near the Curie-point fluctuation waves will be important and will give rise to critical diffuse scattering. We therefore consider the study of the critical diffuse scattering made by Canut and Mendiola (1964).

The differences between the two structures is so marked that it clearly affects the variation in the temperature factor B of the Bragg reflections with temperature. The values of B calculated by Wilson's method (1942) from the Bragg intensities measured at different temperatures show (Fig. 26) that the variation of B in the paraelectric phase is practically a linear function of temperature, and that the Curie point marks a discontinuity both in the magnitude and slope of the function. The change is explained not only by the increase in thermal vibration in the high-temperature phase, but also by the appearance of the dynamic disorder characterizing the paraelectric phase.

The structural change is likewise reflected in the variation of the Bragg intensities of the different reflections, according to (57). Figure 27 shows the curves of the peak-intensity variation for the reflections 002, 022, 040, 103, and 004 as a function of temperature. The figure shows how the different Bragg intensities vary with temperature in quite different ways. The origin of the cell in the paraelectric phase is the center of symmetry near the NO_2^- group. If we take as origin of the ferroelectric cell the point homologous to that center, we can interpret the temperature variation of the Bragg intensities at the Curie point as a function of the imaginary part B of the structure factor in expressions (56) and (57). When the imaginary part is zero, as it is at 040, or very small, as at 002 and 004, the variation in the intensity is due, in effect, to the change in the temperature factor. In contrast, when the imaginary part is very significant—as at 103 where the contribution of the imaginary part to the Bragg intensity is 97 per cent—the intensity becomes practically zero in the paraelectric structure, and decreases considerably at 022, where 94 per cent

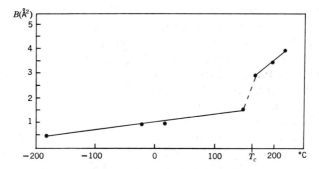

Fig. 26. NaNO$_2$. Temperature dependence of the overall Debye-Waller factor.

is imaginary. Figure 28 shows the points of diffraction space that were investigated and the directions along which the diffuse intensities were measured by Canut and Mendiola (1964) for different reflections.

Figure 29 shows the temperature dependence of the absolute diffuse intensity for given wave vectors $\mathbf{g}_j^i$. These curves show clearly that the variation in the diffuse intensity decreases rapidly with the modulus of the wave vector, that is, as the point of the measurement moves away from the nonforbidden reciprocal-lattice point.

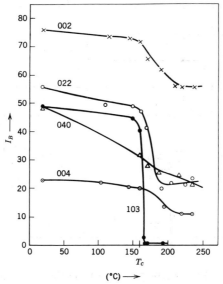

Fig. 27. NaNO$_2$. Temperature dependence of several Bragg intensities showing the anomalies about the transition point.

For wave vectors g_1 and g_7 along [010] perpendicular to the polar axis, and measured from the Bragg reflections 002 and 040, no critical diffuse scattering is observed at the Curie point. The diffuse intensity increases from room temperature to 220°C, and then decreases with an increase in temperature. The anomaly is more intense for smaller wave vectors and practically disappears for $|g| > 3.5 \times 10^3$ cm^{-1}. The intensity-variation curve for a given wave vector does not have the shape of a lambda curve, for its variation is gradual.

On the other hand, when the wave vector is parallel to the polar axis [001] (g_2 and g_6), the critical diffuse-scattering phenomenon appears clearly at the Curie point. The shape of the cruve for g_2 is clearly of the lambda type. The anomaly, however, disappears for $|g| > 3 \times 10^6$ cm^{-1}. Likewise, although less marked than along the [010] axis, there also appears a peak at 215°C.

In directions perpendicular to the polar axis, but parallel to [100], there is another anomaly just above the Curie point. There appear

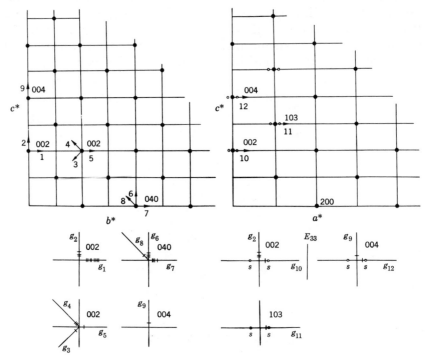

Fig. 28. NaNO$_2$. (*i*) Levels $(100)_0^*$ and $(010)_0^*$ of the reciprocal lattice showing the points studied; (*ii*) positions of the wave vectors. The straight lines extend up to half the distance of the first Brillouin zone.

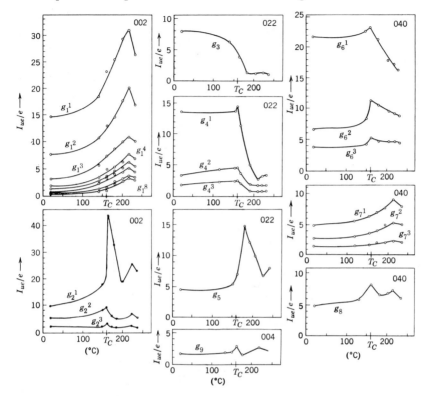

Fig. 29. $NaNO_2$. Temperature dependence of the absolute diffuse intensities for different values of $g_i^j = const$.

well-defined satellites for wave vectors $|g| = 3.0 \times 10$ cm^{-1} on opposite sides of the reciprocal-lattice point. Such is the case, for example, with g_{10}, g_{11}, g_{12} (Fig. 30). These satellites, which were first observed by Tanisaki (1961, 1963), exist only for a short temperature interval (about 2°C), becoming more and more diffuse, until they finally degenerate into diffuse-disorder sheets associated with the paraelectric phase described by Canut and Hosemann (1964) and given by expression (110), Ch. 3.

The temperature variation of the diffuse scattering observed along [010] can be explained by the pseudoharmonic theory of diffuse scattering by thermal waves. In the first approximation, for small wave vectors we can assume that only acoustic waves contribute to the diffuse scattering, and also ignore second-order diffuse scattering. On the other hand, there is experimental evidence that the elastic constants vary with temperature (Hamano, Negishi, Marutake, and

Nomura, 1963). Figure 31, which shows the frequency-dispersion curves for longitudinal waves corresponding to wave vectors $\mathbf{g}_7$, derived from diffuse-scattering measurements at three different temperatures and the corresponding velocity curves. In the velocity curves the limit velocities V_∞ at 20°C and at 220°C calculated from the elastic constant a_{33}, according to the aforementioned authors, have been indicated in the figure. Because the crystal is orthorhombic, the velocity for $\mathbf{g} \to 0$ of the longitudinal waves along [010] is related to the elastic constant a_{33} through

$$V_{l[010]}(\mathbf{g} \to 0) = \frac{\sqrt{a_{33}}}{\rho}. \tag{76}$$

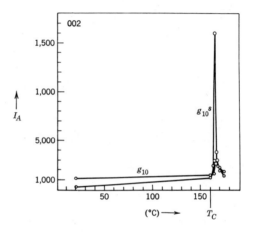

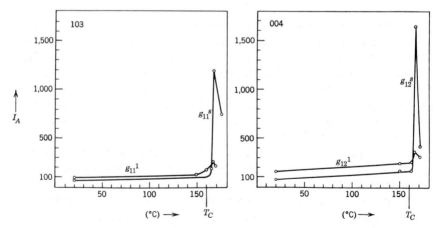

Fig. 30. NaNO$_2$. Temperature dependence of the diffuse intensities and of the satellites for wave vectors parallel to [100]. The intensities are given in arbitrary units.

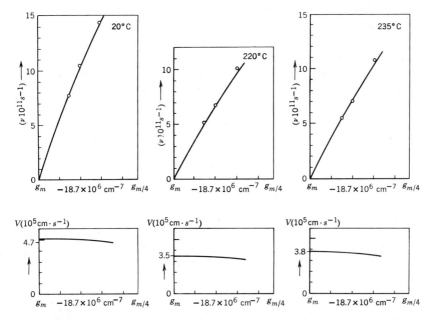

Fig. 31. NaNO$_2$. Dispersion curves of ν and V for longitudinal waves along [010] for small g and at three different temperatures.

There are no data for a_{33} above 220°C. Nevertheless, because Canut and Mendiola's experiments are in good agreement with the results obtained by ultrasonics up to approximately 220°C, it can be concluded that above 220°C the elastic constant a_{33} begins to increase with temperature. Figure 32 illustrates this extreme.

Figure 33i compares the temperature variation of I_{TDS1} ($\mathbf{g}_7$) computed with the pseudoharmonic expression (56), with the iso-$\mathbf{g}_7$ experimental curves. The values of ν_T have been calculated with the hypothesis of linear frequency dispersion from values $V_{[010](T)}$ given by Hamano, Negishi, Marutake, and Nomura (1963). As for the temperature dependence of $I_T(\mathbf{r}^*)$, an experimental variation analogous to that of the Bragg intensity $I_B(040)$ in the figure has been admitted. Figure 33i shows that the pseudoharmonic approximation accounts well for the temperature variation of the diffuse scattering associated with wave vectors along [010], and that precise measurements of the diffuse scattering can detect a new transition or anomaly of the vibrational type.

In the direction of the polar axis the situation is different. Figure 33ii shows that the pseudoharmonic expression (56) does not account

well for the observed diffuse scattering, that is, the temperature variation of the elastic constant c_{22} is not responsible for the diffuse lambda
peak associated with the Curie point. Since, in the direction of the
polar axis of sodium nitrite, the component of the dielectric tensor
k_{ij} exhibits a lambda peak (Sonin and Zheludev, 1963) it is natural to
suppose that Krivoglaz's theory should account for the experimental
results.

In a recent experiment Tanisaki (1963) has shown that, on applying
an external electric field to a sodium nitrite crystal, the satellites
associated with the 042 Bragg reflection, and which are observed only
in a short temperature interval about the Curie point, disappear,
while the Bragg reflection, which had previously disappeared at the
same temperature, again appears as a consequence of the applied
electric field. This shows that the d_{hi} of expression (70) are not zero,
at least for that reflection. Since there are very intense satellites
associated with the 002 reflection (Fig. 30), it seems reasonable to
suppose that for this reflection the behaviour should be similar, that
is, $d_{hi} = 0$.

Since quantitative data for the d_{hi} and the components a_{gm} are lack-
ing, Krivoglaz's theory has not been applied. Nevertheless, we can
say that, in principle, equation (70) predicts the experimental diffuse
scattering shown in Fig. 33ii, and that a quantitative application of the
theory would account well for the critical effect. Experiments of
Shibuya and Mitsui (1961) showed that this critical phenomenon

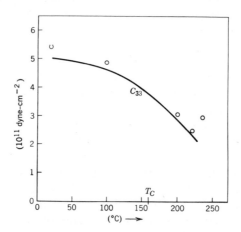

Fig. 32. NaNO$_2$. Temperature dependence of the elastic constant c_{33}, from data of
Hamano, Negishi, Marutake, and Nomura (1963). The circles correspond to the values
obtained from diffuse scattering.

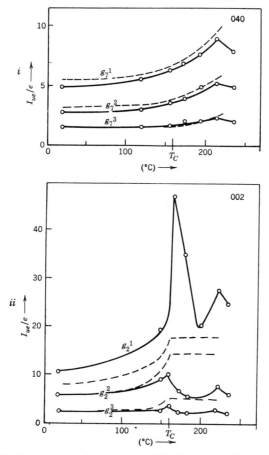

Fig. 33. NaNO$_2$. Temperature dependence of the absolute diffuse intensity corresponding to longitudinal waves of different wave vector. Solid lines: experimental values;
broken lines: calculated values with the quasi-harmonic approximation. (*i*) g[010];
(*ii*) g[001].

appears at the Curie point of a molecular crystal, triglycine sulfate,
although those authors did not study the phenomenon in detail.

In sodium nitrite we can study the lower limits of the wavelengths
of the fluctuation waves that give rise to the critical diffuse scattering
by observing the upper limits of the wave vectors for which the critical phenomenon has been observed. Thus, in the direction of the
polar axis, the lower limit is of the order of 33Å at the Curie point.
Therefore along [001] there are trains of fluctuation waves of wavelengths 33Å and longer. Perpendicular to the polar axis, and in the

[010] direction, at a temperature just above the Curie point, satellites are observed that correspond to waves of 30Å, which occur only in a short temperature range (about 2°C). This tells us that, at the moment of transition, coherent domains of 30Å are generated in the [010] direction, and of 30Å to ∞Å in the polar direction [001]. Since these domains are formed by NO_2^- groups remaining in two antisymmetric positions, they do not alter the periodicity along [100], that is, normal to the layers in terms of which the structure can be described. In the region of stability of the para-electric phase these domains are stable only for dimensions of one or two cells along [010], and therefore the satellites disappear and degenerate into diffuse disorder sheets. Canut and Hosemann (1964) have called these domains elongated in the c direction "cigarrillos." At higher temperatures, the NO_2^- groups begin to rotate about their inertial axes, and it is then that this effect is manifested in the anomalous diffuse scattering observed along the [100] direction at around 220°C. From that temperature to the melting point, the crystal behaves as a plastic crystal, using Timmerman's terminology (1961).

The two measured dimensions of the ordered domain in $NaNO_2$ indicate that the internal field of the substance extends its long-range forces in a sphere of about 15Å. The transition from the ferroelectric to the paraelectric phase is caused by a reversal of the NO_2 groups along the polar axis. This reversal of the NO_2 groups produces a dynamic disorder propagating along the polar axis along which the crystal field is more intense. The reversal of the NO_2 groups along this axis induces the reversal of the groups in the next chain in the structure. Below the transition point the number of NO_2 in the reverse position is small and therefore there is no correlation between the switching of groups in neighboring chains. However, at the transition temperature 50 per cent of the groups are in either extreme position. The crystal field is intense and causes the reversal of the NO_2 groups in the neighboring columns. In the beginning, however, this induced movement occurs only with great histeresis and the whole structure resolves itself into a helicoidal distribution of the NO_2 group in the intermediate positions of the flip-flop along [100], causing the appearance of the satellites. This new phase is stable only in a short range of temperature. After this the whole system is switching rapidly from the two extreme positions and the paraelectric (disordered) phase is obtained. At higher temperatures, the NO_2 probably are freely rotating about [010].

References

Abrahams, S. C., J. M. Robertson, and J. G. White. *The crystal and molecular structure of naphthalene. I. X-ray measurements.* Acta Cryst. **2** (1949) 233–238.

Ahmed, F. R. and D. W. J. Cruickshank. *A refinement of the crystal and molecular structures of naphthalene and anthracene.* Acta Cryst. **5** (1952) 852–853.

Ahmed, F. R. and D. W. J. Cruickshank. *A refinement of the crystal and analyses of oxalic acid dihydrate.* Acta Cryst. **6** (1953) 385–392.

Ahmed, M. S. *Thermal vibrations in cubic crystals.* Acta Cryst. **5** (1952) 587–591.

Airy, G. B. *On the diffraction of an object—glass with circular aperture.* Cam. Phil. Soc. Proc. **5** (1835) 283.

Alonso, P., M. L. Canut, and J. L. Amorós. *Dinámica de redes en cristales iónicos. I. Difracción difusa de las formas polimorfas IV (Entre— 18° C y 32° C) y III (Entre 32° C y 84° C) del nitrato amónico.* Bol. Real. Soc. Espan. Hist. Nat., (G) **56** (1958a) 51–64.

Alonso, P., M. L. Canut, and J. L. Amorós. *Dinámica de redes en cristales moleculares. IX. Difracción difusa térmica en el pentaeritritol.* Bol. Real Soc. Espan. Hist. Nat., (G) **56** (1958b) 379–390.

Amorós, J. L. *Elipsoides de vibración de los átomos y simetria del cristal.* Bol. Real Soc. Espan. Hist. Nat., (G) **57** (1960) 7–16.

Amorós, J. L. and C. Abásolo. *Un nuevo tipo de polimorfismo: Polimorfismo inducido en el aducto urea-subérico.* Bol. Real Soc. Espan. Hist. Nat., (G) **59** (1961) 31–35.

Amorós, J. L., A. de Acha, and M. L. Canut. *L'agitation thermique dans les cristaux moléculaires: la diffusion des rayons X par l'acridine III.* Bull. Soc. franc. Minéral. Crist. **84** (1961) 40–50.

Amorós, J. L., C. Belgrano, and M. L. Canut. *Estudios acerca de la dinámica*

455

reticular en cristales moleculares. V. Determinación directa de la amplitud de la oscilación térmica. P. Dep. Crist. Min. 3 (1957) 5–13.

Amorós, J. L. and M. L. Canut. *Thermal vibrations in dicarboxylic acids.* Acta Cryst. 10 (1957) 794–795.

Amorós, J. L. and M. L. Canut. *Ondas térmicas en cristales en cadenas.* Bol. Real Soc. Espan. Hist. Nat., (G) 56 (1958) 25–50.

Amorós, J. L. and M. L. Canut. *Dinámica de redes en cristales moleculares: Difracción difusa continua y simetria dinámica.* Bol. Real Soc. Espan. Hist. Nat., (G) 58 (1960) 25–41.

Amorós, J. L. and M. L. Canut. *El polimorfismo del nitrato amónico.* Bol. Real Soc. Espan. Hist. Nat., (G) 60 (1962) 15–40.

Amorós, J. L. and M. L. Canut de Amorós. "La difracción difusa de los cristales moleculares." (Consejo Superior de Investigaciones Científicas, Madrid, 1965).

Amorós, J. L. and M. L. Canut-Amorós. *The difference Fourier transform (DFT) method for crystal structure determination.* Z. Krist. 124 (1967) 262–274.

Amorós, J. L., M. L. Canut, and A. de Acha. *Interpretation of the extended continuous diffuse regions of x-ray thermal diffuse scattering of molecular crystals.* Z. Krist. 114 (1960) 39–65.

Amorós, J. L., A. Carbonell, and M. L. Canut. *Un difractómetro de rayos X de dos limbos para altas y bajas temperaturas y su utilización en medidas absolutas de difracción difusa.* Rev. Cienc. Apl. 16 (1962) 385–396.

Andresen, A. F. *Investigation of hexamethylene tetramine by neutron diffraction.* Acta Cryst, 10 (1957) 107–110.

Annaka, S. *Determination of elastic constants of metals and alloys by temperature diffuse scattering of x-rays.* J. Phys. Soc. Japan. 11 (1956) 937–943.

Annaka, S. and J. L. Amorós. *On the x-ray temperature diffuse scattering of anthracene and stearic acid.* J. Phys. Soc. Japan. 15 (1960a) 356–357.

Annaka, S. and J. L. Amorós. *On the x-ray diffuse scattering of anthracene.* Z. Krist. 114 (1960b) 423–438.

Azaroff, L. V. *Polarization correction for crystal-monochromatized x-radiation.* Acta Cryst. 8 (1955) 701–704.

Bacon, G. E. "Neutron Diffraction." (Clarendon Press, Oxford, 1962).

Bauer, E. "Changements de Phases." (Societé de Chimie Physique, Paris, 1952).

Becka, L. N. and D. W. J. Cruickshank. *The crystal structure of hexamethylenetetramine. I. X-ray studies at 298, 100 and 34° K.* Proc. Roy. Soc. (London), Ser. A. 273 (1963a) 435–454.

Becka, L. N. and D. W. J. Cruickshank. *The crystal structure of hexamethylenetetramine. II. The lattice vibrations of a simple molecular crystal.* Proc. Roy. Soc. (London), Ser. A. 273 (1963b) 455–465.

Begbie, G. H. and M. Born. *Thermal scattering of x-rays by crystals. I. Dynamical foundation.* Proc. Roy. Soc. (London), Ser. A. 188 (1947) 179–188.

Blackman, M. *The specific heat of solids*, S. Flugge (ed.), In "Encyclopedia of Physiks. Crystal Physics I." (Springer-Verlag, Berlin, 1955) 325–382.

Born, M. "Dynamik der Kristallgitter." (B. G. Teubner, Leipzig, 1915).

Born, M. *Lattice dynamics and x-ray scattering.* Proc. Phys. Soc. **54** (1942) 362–376.

Born, M. *Theoretical investigations on the relation between crystal dynamics and x-ray scattering,* W. B. Mann (ed.), In "Reports on Progress in Physics. Vol. 9." (Taylor and Frances, Ltd., London, 1943) 294–333.

Born, M. and K. Huang. *Dynamical theory of crystal lattices,* N. F. Mott and E. C. Bullard (eds.). In "The International Series of Monographs on Physics." (Clarendon Press, Oxford, 1956).

Born, M. and Th. von Karman. *Über Schwingungen in Raumgittern.* Physik. Z. **13** (1912) 297–309.

Born, M. and Th. von Karman. *The distribution of the proper periods of a point grating.* Physik. Z. **14** (1913) 65–71.

Born, M. and K. Lonsdale. *Temperature variation of diffuse scattering of x-rays by crystals.* Nature **150** (1942) 490.

Born, M. and E. Wolf. "Principles of Optics." (Pergamon, London, 1959).

Bragg, W. L. *A new type of "x-ray microscope."* Nature. **143** (1939) 678.

Bragg, W. L. *The x-ray microscope.* Nature. **149** (1942) 470–471.

Bragg, L. *Lightning calculations with light.* Nature. **154** (1944) 69–72.

Bragg, L. and H. Lipson. *A simple method of demonstrating diffraction grating effects.* J. Sci. Instr. **20** (1943) 110–113.

Brill, R., H. G. Grimm, C. Hermann, and Cl. Peters. *Anwendung der röntgenographischen Fourieranalyse auf Fragen der chemischen Bindung.* Ann. Phys. **34** (1939) 393–445.

Broadley, J. S., D. W. J. Cruickshank, J. D. Morrison, J. M. Robertson, and H. M. M. Shearer. *Three-dimensional refinement of the structure of β-succinic acid.* Proc. Roy. Soc. (London), Ser. A. **251** (1959) 441–457.

Buerger, M. J. *Optically reciprocal gratings and their application to syntheses of Fourier series.* Proc. Nat. Acad. Sci., U. S. **27** (1941) 117–124.

Buerger, M. J. *Generalized microscopy and the two-wave-length microscope.* J. Appl. Phys. **21** (1950a) 909–917.

Buerger, M. J. *The photography of atoms in crystals.* Proc. Nat. Acad. Sci. U.S. **36** (1950b) 330–335.

Buerger, M. J. "Vector Space and its Application in Crystal-Structure Investigation." (John Wiley & Sons, Inc., New York, 1959).

Buerger, M. J. "Crystal-Structure Analysis." (John Wiley & Sons, Inc., New York, 1960).

Buerger, M. J. *Polymorphism and phase transformations.* Fortschr. Mineral. **39** (1961) 9–24.

Buerger, M. J. *The algebra and geometry of convolutions.* Atti Accad. Naz. Lincei. **6** (1962a) 83–95.

Buerger, M. J. *An algebraic representation of the images of sets of points.* Atti Accad. Sci. Torino. **96** (1962b) 1–18.

Burgers, W. G., C. L. D. Kooy, and T. J. Tiedema. *Thermal diffuse scattering by lead single crystals.* Koninkl. Ned. Akad. Wetenschap. Proc., Ser. B. **59** (1956) 195–203.

Canut-Amorós, M. *On the significance of two new Patterson functions for disordered crystals.* Z. Krist. **124** (1967) 241–261.

Canut, M. L. and J. L. Amorós. *Estudios acerca de la dinámica reticular en cristales moleculares. VI. Difracción difusa de los ácidos dicarboxílicos de la serie par: succínico y adípico.* P. Dep. Crist. Min. 3 (1957) 15–25.

Canut, M. L. and J. L. Amorós. *Dinámica de redes en cristales moleculares. VIII. Difracción difusa térmica de la hexamina,* $C_6H_{12}N_4$. Bol. Real Soc. Espan. Hist. Nat., (G) **56** (1958) 323- 338.

Canut, M. L. and J. L. Amorós. *Difracción difusa térmica del ácido oxálico dihidratado,* COOH-COOH, $2H_2O$. Bol. Real Soc. Espan. Hist. Nat., (G) **58** (1960) 17–23.

Canut, M. L. and J. L. Amorós. *On the inversion temperature function of the first order (one phonon) scattering and the determination of Debye characteristic temperatures.* Proc. Phys. Soc. **77** (1961*a*) 712–720.

Canut, M. L. and J. L. Amorós. *Temperature dependence of the x-ray diffuse scattering of molecular crystals: naphthalene.* J. Phys. Chem. Solids. **21** (1961*b*) 146–155.

Canut, M. L., M. Ayllón, and J. L. Amorós. *Sobre la coexistencia de las fases I y II de* NO_3NH_4 *y la difracción difusa de desorden de la fase I.* Estud. Geol. **20** (1964) 57–64.

Canut, M. L. and R. Hosemann. *X-ray analysis of ferroelectric domains in the paraelectric phase of NaNO₂.* Acta Cryst. **17** (1964) 973–981.

Canut, M. L., M. T. Iceta, and J. L. Amorós. *Subestructura antiferroeléctrica del* NO_3NH_4*–II.* Estud. Geol. **20** (1964) 65–72.

Canut, M. L. and J. Mendiola. *Critical scattering of x-rays in NaNO₂.* Phys. Stat. Sol. **5** (1964) 313–327.

Canut, M. L., L. M. Valdés, and J. L. Amorós. *Empleo de análogos ópticos en el estudio de la difracción difusa de rayos X por los cristales.* Rev. Cienc. Apl. **17** (1963) 199–213.

Carbonell, A. and M. L. Canut. *Determinación del espectro elástico vibracional de un-cristal molecular, la hexamina, por difracción difusa térmica de rayos X.* Rev. Cienc. Apl. **18** (1964) 126–139.

Cartz, L. *Thermal vibrations of atoms in cubic crystals. 1: The temperature variation of thermal diffuse scattering of x-rays by lead single crystals.* Proc. Phys. Soc., Ser. B **68** (1955) 951–956.

Caruso, R. F., G. Richards, and M. Canut-Amorós. *A FORTRAN program for calculating molecular Fourier transforms and difference Fourier transforms.* Report AF-AFOSR-832-65, Southern Illinois University: IBM 7040 program, 1966.

Champier, G. *Étude de la diffusion des rayons X par un monocristal de lithium. I. Théorie.* Bull. Soc. franç. Minéral. Crist. **82** (1959*a*) 61–76.

Champier, G. *Étude de la diffusion des rayons X par un monocristal de lithium. II. Résultats.* Bull. Soc. franç. Minéral. Crist. **82** (1959*b*) 137–150.

Charlesby, A., G. I. Finch, and H. Wilman. *The diffraction of electrons by anthracene.* Proc. Phys. Soc. **51** (1939) 479–528.

Chayes, F. *Order and disorder.* In "Year Book 56." (Carnegie Institute of Washington, Washington, D.C., 1957) 151–156.

Cochran, W. *Lattice vibrations,* A. C. Strickland (ed.). In "Reports on Progress in Physics. Vol. 26." (John Wright and Sons, Ltd., London, 1963) 1–45.

Cochran, W. and G. S. Pawley. *The theory of diffuse scattering of x-rays by a molecular crystal.* Proc. Roy. Soc. (London), Ser. A280 (1964) 1–22.

Cole, H. *Approximate elastic spectrum of acoustic waves in AgCl from x-ray scattering.* J. Appl. Phys. 24 (1953) 482–487.

Cole, H. and B. E. Warren. *Approximate elastic spectrum of β-brass from x-ray scattering.* J. Appl. Phys. 23 (1952) 335–340.

Compton, A. H. and S. K. Allison. "X-rays in Theory and Experiment". (D. Van Nostrand Company, Inc., New York, 1954).

Cox, E. G., D. W. J. Cruickshank, and J. A. S. Smith. *The crystal structure of benzene at −3° C.* Proc. Roy. Soc. (London), Ser. A 247 (1958) 1–21.

Cruickshank, D. W. J. *The analysis of the anisotropic thermal motion of molecules in crystals.* Acta Cryst. 9 (1956a) 754–756.

Cruickshank, D. W. J. *A detailed refinement of the crystal and molecular structure of anthracene.* Acta Cryst. 9 (1956b) 915–923.

Cruickshank, D. W. J. *The variation of vibration amplitudes with temperature in some molecular crystals.* Acta Cryst. 9 (1956c) 1005–1009.

Cruickshank, D. W. J. *A detailed refinement of the crystal and molecular structure of anthracene: Corrigenda.* Acta Cryst. 10 (1957a) 470.

Cruickshank, D. W. J. *A detailed refinement of the crystal and molecular structure of naphthalene.* Acta Cryst. 10 (1957b) 504–508.

Cruickshank, D. W. J. *Notes for authors: anisotropic parameters.* Acta Cryst. 19 (1965) 153.

Curien, H. *Étude des ondes élastiques dans le réseau cubique centré du fer α.* Bull. Soc. franç, Minéral. Crist. 75 (1952a) 197–230.

Curien, H. *Étude des ondes élastiques dans le réseau cubique centré du fer α. II.* Bull. Soc. franç. Minéral. Crist. 75 (1952b) 343–384.

Debye, P. *Zur Theorie der spezifischen Wärmen.* Ann. Phys. 39 (1912) 789–839.

Debye, P. *Interferenz von Röntgenstrahlen und Wärmebewengung.* Ann. Phys. 43 (1914) 49–95.

Dickinson, R. G. and A. L. Raymond. *The crystal structure of hexamethylenetetramine.* J. Am. Chem. Soc. 45 (1923) 22–29.

Doetsch, G. "Guide to the Applications of Laplace Transforms". (D. Van Nostrand and Co., Ltd., London, 1961).

Donnay, J. D. H. and W. Nowacky. "Crystal Data. Classification of Substances by Space Groups and their Identification from Cell Dimensions." (Geological Society of America Memoir 60, New York, 1954).

Dunkerley, B. D. and H. Lipson. *A simple version of Bragg's x-ray microscope.* Nature. 176 (1955) 81.

Ehrenfest, P. *Phasenumwandlungen im ueblichen und erweiterten Sinn,* classifiziert nach den entisprechenden Singularitäten des thermodynamischen Potentiales. Koninkl. Akad. Wetenschap., Proc. Ser. B. **36** (1933) 153–157.

Einstein, A. *Die Planchsche Theorie der Strahlung und die Theorie der spezifischen Wärme.* Ann. Phys. **22** (1907) 180–190.

von Eller, G. *Sur un nouvel appareil pour le développement par voie optique des séries de Fourier à plusieurs dimensions.* Compt. Rend. **232** (1951a) 1122–1124.

von Eller, G. *Deux utilisations de la machine optique pour le calcul des séries de Fourier.* Compt. Rend. **232** (1951b) 2333–2335.

von Eller, G. *Le photosommateur harmonique et ses possibilitiés.* Bull. Soc. franç. Minéral. Crist. **78** (1955) 157–213.

Ewald, P. P. *Das "reziproke Gitter" in der Strukturtheorie.* Z. Krist. **56** (1921) 129–156.

Ewald, P. P. *Elektrostatische und optische Potentiale im Kristallraum und im Fourierraum.* Nachr. Ges. Wiss. Göttingen, Math-physik. Klasse. **3** (1938) 55–64.

Ewald, P. P. *X-ray diffraction by finite and imperfect crystal lattices.* Proc. Phys. Soc. **52** (1940) 167–174.

Fairbairn, H. W. *Packing in ionic minerals.* Geol. Soc. Am. Bull. **54** (1943) 1305–1374.

Felix, A., M. L. Canut, and J. L. Amorós. *Dilatación térmica y desorden de apilamiento en cristales moleculares. I. 2,2'-piridil.* Bol. Real Soc. Espan. Hist. Nat. (G) **62** (1964) 187–197.

Fowler, R. H. *A theory of the rotations of molecules in solids and of the dielectric constant of solids and liquids.* Proc. Roy. Soc. (London). Ser. A. **149** (1935) 1–28.

Françon, M. "Diffraction Cohérence en Optique." (Gauthier-Villars, Paris, 1964).

von Frenkel, J. *Über die Drehung von Dipolmolekülen in festen Körpern.* Acta Physicochimica URSS 3 (1935) 23–36.

Gonell, H. W. and H. Mark. Röntgenographische Bestimmung der Strukturformel des Hexamethylentetramins. Z. Phys. Chem. **107** (1923) 181–218.

Grüneisen, E. *Zustand des festen Körpers.* In "Handbuch der Phys." **10** (1925) 1–52.

Guinier, A. "Théorie et Technique de la Radiocristallographie." (Dunod, Paris, 1956).

Hamano, K., K. Negishi, M. Marutake, and S. Nomura. *Electromechanical properties of $NaNO_2$ single crystals.* Japan J. Appl. Phys. **2** (1963) 83–90.

Hanson, A. W. and H. Lipson. *Optical methods in x-ray analysis. III. Fourier synthesis by optical interference.* Acta Cryst. **5** (1952) 362–366.

Harburn, G. and C. A. Taylor. *Optical Fourier synthesis for noncentrosymmetric projections of crystal structures.* Nature **194** (1962) 764.

Haussühl, S. *Elastische Konstanten von Hexamethylentetramin.* Acta Cryst. **11** (1958) 58–59.

Henry, N. F. M. and K. Lonsdale. "International Tables for X-ray Crystallography. Volume I. Symmetry groups."(The Kynoch Press, Birmingham, Eng., 1952).

Hettich, A. *Beiträge zur Methodik der Strukturbestimmung*. Z. Krist. **90** (1935) 473–492.

Higgs, P. W. *Vibrational modifications of the electron distribution in molecular crystals. II. Mean square amplitudes of thermal motion.* Acta Cryst. **8** (1955) 99–104.

Hirokawa, S. *The crystal structure of adipic acid.* Bull. Chem. Soc. Japan, **23** (1950) 91–94.

Hoppe, W. *Die diffuse Röntgenstreuung an elasticshen Wärmewellen in Kristallen als neue Methode zur Strukturanalyse starrer Atomgruppen (Moleküle). Der pseudoakustische Fall.* Z. Krist. **107** (1956a) 406–432.

Hoppe, W. *Strukturanalyse starrer Atomgruppen (Moleküle) durch Untersuchung der diffusen Röntgenstreuung an elastischen Wärmewellen in Kristallen. Die diffuse Streuung des Anthrachinonmoleküls.* Z. Krist. **107** (1956b) 433–450.

Hoppe, W. *Die Orientierung des aromatischen Ringsystems in Phyllochlorinester.* Z. Krist. **108** (1957) 335–340.

Hoppe, W. and F. Baumgärtner. *Nachweis der Stäbchengestalt und Orientierungsbestimmung des organischen Kations in 1,5,N-N'-Dipyrrolidylpentamethinperchloratkristallen mit diffuser Röntgenstreustrahlung.* Z. Krist. **108** (1957) 328–334.

Hoppe, W., H. U. Lenné, and G. Morandi. *Strukturbestimmung von Cyanursäuretrichlorid $C_3N_3Cl_3$ mit Verwendung der diffusen Röntgenstreustrahlung zur Bestimmung der Molekülorientierungen.* Z. Krist. **108** (1957) 321–327.

Hosemann, R. and S. N. Bagchi. "Direct Analysis of Diffraction by Matter." (North-Holland Publishing Co., Amsterdam, 1962).

Housty, J. and M. Hospital. *Localisation des atomes d'hydrogéne dans l'acide adipique COOH $(CH_2)_4$ COOH.* Acta Cryst. **18** (1965) 693–697.

Hvoslef, J. *A neutron diffraction study of pentaerythritol.* Acta Cryst. **11** (1958) 383–388.

Ichishima, I. *The specific heat and entropy of crystalline pyridine and naphthalene.* (In Japanese). J. Chem. Soc. Japan (Pure Chem. Sec.) **71** (1950) 607–608.

Jacobsen, E. H. *Elastic spectrum of copper from temperature-diffuse scattering of x-rays.* Phys. Rev. **97** (1955) 654–659.

Jahn, H. A. *Diffuse scattering of x-rays by crystals. The Faxén-Waller theory and the surfaces of isodiffusion for cubic crystals.* Proc. Roy. Soc. (London). Ser. A **179** (1942) 320–340.

James, R. W. "The Crystalline State. Vol. II. The Optical Principles of the Diffraction of X-rays." (Bell, London, 1954).

Johnson, C. K. "OR TEP: A FORTRAN Thermal-ellipsoid Plot Program for Crystal Structure Illustrations." (Oak Ridge National Laboratory, Oak Ridge, Tenn, 1965).

Joynson, R. E. *Elastic spectrum of zinc from the temperature scattering of x-rays.* Phys. Rev. **94** (1954) 851–855.

Justi, E. and M. v. Laue. *Phasengleichgeuichte dritter Art.* Z. Tech. Phys. **15** (1934) 521–529.

Kay M. I., B. C. Frazer, and R. Ueda. *The disordered structure of $NaNO_2$ at 185° C.* Acta Cryst. **15** (1962) 506–508.

Keating, D. T. and G. H. Vineyard. *The complete incoherent scattering function for carbon.* Acta Cryst. **9** (1956) 895–896.

Kitajgorodskij, A. I. "The Theory of Crystal Structure Analysis." (Consultants Bureau, New York, 1961*a*).

Kitajgorodskij, A. I. "Organic Chemical Crystallography." (Consultants Bureau, New York, 1961*b*).

Kitajgorodskij, A. I. *The principle of close packing and the condition of thermodynamic stability of organic crystals.* Acta. Cryst. **18** (1965) 585–590.

Kittel, C. "Introduction to Solid State Physics." (John Wiley & Sons, New York, 1956).

Knott, G. *Molecular structure factors and their application to the solution of the structures of complex organic crystals.* Proc. Phys. Soc. **52** (1940) 229–238.

Knox, R. S. and A. Gold, "Symmetry in the Solid State." (W. A. Benjamin, Inc., New York, 1964).

Krivoglaz, M. A. *On the scattering of x-rays and thermal neutrons by single-component crystals near phase-transition points of the second kind.* Soviet Phys. JETP. **7** (1958) 281–285.

Laberrigue, A. *Diffusion des électrons par l'agitation thermique des atomes d'un cristal.* Ann. Phys. Paris. **4** (1959) 385–433.

Landau, L. *Zur Theorie der Phasenumwandlungen. I.* Physik. Z. Sowjetunion. **11** (1937*a*) 26–47.

Landau, L. *Zur Theorie der Phasenumwandlungen. II.* Physik. Z. Sowjetunion. **11** (1937*b*) 545–555.

Landau, L. *Streuung von Röntgenstrahlen an Kristallen in der Nähe des Curie-Punktes.* Physik. Z. Sowjetunion. **12** (1937*c*) 123–137.

de Launay, J. *Debye characteristic temperature at 0°K of certain cubic crystals. II.* J. Chem. Phys. **30** (1959) 91–92.

Laval, J. *Étude expérimentale de la diffusion des rayons X par les cristaux.* Bull. Soc. franç. Minéral. Crist. **62** (1939) 137–253.

Laval, J. *Diffusion des rayons X par les cristaux.* Bull. Soc. franç. Minéral. Crist. **64** (1941) 1–138.

Laval, J. *Théorie de la diffusion des rayons X par les cristaux (première partie).* J. Phys. Radium. **15** (1954*a*) 545–558.

Laval, J. *Théorie de la diffusion des rayons X par les cristaux (deuxiéme partie).* J. Phys. Radium. **15** (1954*b*) 657–666.

Leela, M. and K. Lonsdale. *Temperature dependence of the diamagnetic anisotropy of benzil.* Proc. Natl. Acad. Sci., India, Sect. A. **25** (1956) 68–73.

Leibfried, G. and W. Ludwig. *Theory of anharmonic effects in crystals,* F. Seitz and D. Turnbull (ed.), In "Solid State Physics, Vol. 12." (Academic Press, New York, 1961) 275–444.

Lipson, H. and W. Cochran. "The Crystalline State. Vol. III. The Determination of Crystal Structures." (G. Bell and Sons, Ltd., London, 1957).

Lipson, H. and W. Cochran. "The Crystalline State. Vol. III. The Determination of Crystal Structures." (Cornell University Press, Ithaca, New York, 1966).

Lipson, H. and C. A. Taylor. "Fourier Transforms and X-Ray Diffraction." (G. Bell and Sons, Ltd., London, 1958).

Llewellyn, F. J., E. G. Cox, and T. H. Goodwin. *The crystalline structure of the sugars. Part IV. Pentaerythritol and the hydroxyl bond.* J. Chem. Soc. (1937) 883–894.

Lobatchev, A. N. *Electronographic determination of the position of the hydrogen atoms in the crystal structure of urotropine.* Trudy Inst. Krist. Akad. Nauk SSSR. **10** (1954) 71–75. (In Russian).

Lonsdale, K. *X-ray study of crystal dynamics: An historical and critical survey of experiment and theory.* Proc. Phys. Soc. **54** (1942) 314–353.

Lonsdale, K. *Experimental study of x-ray scattering in relation to crystal dynamics,* W. B. Mann (ed.), In "Reports on Progress in Physics, Vol. 9." (Taylor and Francis, Ltd., London, 1943) 256–293.

Lonsdale, K. "Crystals and X-Rays." (G. Bell, and Sons, Ltd., London, 1948).

Lonsdale, K. *Experimental studies of atomic vibrations in crystals and of their relationship to thermal expansion.* Z. Krist. **112** (1959) 188–212.

Lonsdale, K. and J. Milledge. *An x-ray study of rigid-body and internal vibrations of organic molecules.* Nature. **184** (1959) 1545–1549.

Lonsdale, K. and J. Milledge. *Analysis of thermal vibrations in crystals: a warning.* Acta Cryst. **14** (1961) 59–61.

Lonsdale, K., J. Milledge, and K. El Sayed. *The crystal structure (at five temperatures) and anisotropic thermal expansion of anthraquinone.* Acta Cryst. **20** (1966) 1–12.

Lonsdale, K., J. M. Robertson, and I. Woodward. *Structure and molecular anisotropy of sorbic acid, $CH_3.CH:CH.CH:CH.COOH$.* Proc. Roy. Soc. (London) Ser. A **178** (1941) 43–52.

Lonsdale K. and H. Smith. *An experimental study of diffuse x-ray reflexion by single crystals.* Proc. Roy. Soc. (London), Ser. A **179** (1942) 8–50.

Ludwig, W. *Dynamics of a crystal lattice with defects,* B. Gruber (ed.), In "Theory of Crystal Defects." (Publishing House of the Czechoslovak Academy of Sciences, Prague, 1966) 57–165.

MacGillavry, C. H. *The crystal structure of adipic acid.* Rec. trav. chim. Pays Bas. **60** (1941) 605–617.

MacGillavry, C. H. and G. D. Rieck. "International Tables for X-Ray Crystallography. Vol. 3. Physical and Chemical Tables." (The Kynoch Press, Birmingham, Eng., 1962).

Mackay, K. J. H. *Deductions from the molecular transform of 9:10-anthrahydroquinone dibenzoate.* Acta Cryst. **15** (1962) 157–160.

Maradudin, A. A., E. W. Montroll, and G. H. Weiss. *Theory of lattice dynamics in the harmonic approximation*, F. Seitz and D. Turnbull (ed.), In "Solid State Physics, Supp. 3." (Academic Press, New York, 1963).

Mason, R. *The crystallography of anthracene at 95°K and 290°K.* Acta Cryst. **17** (1964) 547–555.

Mathieson, A. M., J. M. Robertson, and V. C. Sinclair. *The crystal and molecular structure of anthracene. I. X-ray measurements.* Acta Cryst. **3** (1950) 245–250.

McWeeny, R. *X-ray scattering by aggregates of bonded atoms. I. Analytical approximations in single-atom scattering.* Acta Cryst. **4** (1951) 513–519.

Morrison, J. D. and J. M. Robertson. *The crystal and molecular structure of certain dicarboxylic acids. Part IV. β-succinic acid.* J. Chem. Soc. (1949a) 980–986.

Morrison, J. D. and J. M. Robertson. *The crystal and molecular structure of certain dicarboxylic acids. Part V. Adipic acid.* J. Chem. Soc. (1949b) 987–992.

Mott, N. F. and H. Jones. "The Theory of the Properties of Metals and Alloys." (Dover Publications Inc., New York, 1958).

Müller, A. *The crystal structure of the normal paraffins at temperatures ranging from that of liquid air to the melting points.* Proc. Roy. Soc. (London), Ser. A **127** (1930) 417–430.

Niggli, P. "Lehrbuch der Mineralogie." (Verlag von Gebrüder Berntraeger, Berlin, 1920).

Nitta, I. and T. Watanabe. *Hydrogen bridges in solid pentaerythritol.* Nature, **140** (1937) 365.

Olmer, P. *Interactions photons-phonons et diffusion des rayons X dans l'aluminium.* Bull. Soc. franç. Minéral. **71** (1948) 145–258.

Paskin, A. *A reformulation of the temperature dependence of the Debye characteristic temperature and its effect on Debye-Waller theory.* Acta Cryst. **10** (1957) 667–669.

Pauling, L. *The rotational motion of molecules in crystals.* Phys. Rev. **36** (1930) 430–443.

Pawley, G. S. *On the least-squares analysis of the rigid body vibrations of non-centrosymmetrical molecules.* Acta Cryst. **16** (1963) 1204–1208.

Pearson, W. B. *Thermal expansion of lithium, 77° to 300°K.* Can. J. Phys. **32** (1954) 708–713.

Pepinsky, R. *An electronic computer for x-ray crystal structure analyses.* J. Appl. Phys. **18** (1947) 601–604.

Pepinsky, R. "Computing methods and the phase problem in x-ray crystal analysis." Report of a conference held at the Pennsylvania State College, April 6–8, 1950. (The X-ray Crystal Analysis Laboratory, Dept. of Phys., Pa. State College, State College, Pa., 1952).

Phillips, D. C. *The crystallography of acridine. Part II. The structure of acridine III.* Acta Cryst. **9** (1956) 237–250.

Prasad, S. C. and W. A. Wooster. *The determination of the elastic constants of silicon by diffuse x-ray reflexions.* Acta Cryst. **8** (1955a) 361.

Prasad, S. C. and W. A. Wooster. *The determination of the elastic constants of germanium by diffuse x-ray reflexion.* Acta Cryst. **8** (1955*b*) 506–507.

Prasad, S. C. and W. A. Wooster. *The study of the elastic constants of white tin by diffuse x-ray reflexion.* Acta Cryst. **8** (1955*c*) 682–686.

Prasad, S. C. and W. A. Wooster. *The elasticity of single crystals of lead.* Acta Cryst. **9** (1956*a*) 38–42.

Prasad, S. C. and W. A. Wooster. *The elasticity of iron pyrites, FeS_2.* Acta Cryst. **9** (1956*b*) 169–173.

Prince, E. and W. A. Wooster. *The elastic constants of zincblende, determined from thermal diffuse scattering of x-rays.* Acta Cryst. **4** (1951) 191.

Prince, E. and W. A. Wooster. *Determination of elastic constants of crystals from diffuse reflexions of x-rays. III. Diamond.* Acta Cryst. **6** (1953) 450–454.

Ramachandran, G. N. and W. A. Wooster. *Determination of elastic constants of crystals from diffuse reflexions of x-rays. I. Theory of method.* Acta Cryst. **4** (1951*a*) 335–344.

Ramachandran, G. N. and W. A. Wooster. *Determination of elastic constants of crystals from diffuse reflexions of x-rays. II. Application to some cubic crystals.* Acta Cryst. **4** (1951*b*) 431–440.

Rayleigh, Lord. *On images formed without reflection or refraction.* Phil. Mag. Ser. 5 **11** (1881) 214–218.

Robertson, J. M., H. M. M. Shearer, G. A. Sim, and D. G. Watson. *The crystal and molecular structure of azulene.* Acta Cryst. **15** (1962) 1–8.

Robertson, J. M. and I. Woodward. *The structure of the carboxyl group. A quantitative investigation of oxalic acid dihydrate by Fourier synthesis from the x-ray crystal data.* J. Chem. Soc. (1937) 1817–1824.

Sándor, E. *Lattice vibrations of molecular chains.* Acta Cryst. **15** (1962) 463–473.

Sándor, E. and W. A. Wooster. *The elastic constants of vanadium single crystals.* Acta Cryst. **12** (1959) 332–336.

Sayre, D. *The calculation of structure factors by Fourier summation.* Acta Cryst. **4** (1951) 362–367.

Schwartz, M. "Approximate Elastic Spectrum of β-AuZn from Temperature Diffuse Scattering of X-Rays." (Pitman-Dunn Laboratories Group, Philadelphia Frankford Arsenal, 1957).

Schwartz, M. and L. Muldawer. *Approximate elastic spectrum of β-AuZn from temperature diffuse scattering of x-rays.* J. Appl. Phys. **29** (1958) 1561–1568.

Shaffer, P. A. *Anisotropic oscillations in the hexamethylenetetramine crystal.* J. Amer. Chem. Soc. **69** (1947) 1557–1561.

Shibuya, I. and T. Mitsui. *The ferroelectric phase transition in (glycine)$_3$· H_2SO_4 and critical x-ray scattering.* J. Phys. Soc. Japan. **16**(1961) 479–489.

Shiono, R., D. W. J. Cruickshank, and E. G. Cox. *A refinement of the crystal structure of pentaerythritol.* Acta Cryst. **11** (1958) 389–391.

Sinclair, V. C., J. M. Robertson, and A. M. Mathieson. *The crystal and molecular structure of anthracene. II. Structure investigation by the triple Fourier series method.* Acta Cryst. **3** (1950) 251–256.

Slater, J. C., *Interaction of waves in crystals*. Revs. Modern Phys. **30**, (1958) 197–222.

Smith, A. E. *The crystal structure of the urea-hydrocarbon complexes.* Acta Cryst. **5** (1952) 224–235.

Sonin, A. S. and I. S. Zheludev. *Some dielectric properties of sodium nitrite single crystals.* Sov. Phys. Cryst. **8** (1963) 41–44.

Strijk, B. and C. H. MacGillavry. *A high temperature modification of NaNO₂.* Rec. trav. chim. Pays Bas. **62** (1943) 705–712.

Strijk, B. and C. H. MacGillavry. *Rectification of "A high temperature modification of NaNO₂".* Rec. trav. chim. **65** (1946) 127.

Tanisaki, S. *Microdomain structure in paraelectric phase of NaNO₂.* J. Phys. Soc. Japan. **16** (1961) 579.

Tanisaki, S. *X-ray study on the ferroelectric phase transition of NaNO₂.* J. Phys. Soc. Japan. **18** (1963) 1181–1191.

Tarasov, V. V. *Chain and layer structures in crystals and glasses and the quantum theory of heat capacity.* Trudy Inst. Krist. Akad. Nauk SSSR. **10** (1954) 136–148. (In Russian).

Taylor, C. A., R. M. Hinde, and H. Lipson. *Optical methods in x-ray analysis. I. The study of imperfect structures.* Acta Cryst. **4** (1951) 261–266.

Taylor, C. A. and H. Lipson. "Optical Transforms. Their Preparation and Application to X-ray Diffraction Problems." (Cornell University Press, Ithaca, New York, 1965).

Timmermans, J. *Plastic crystals: A historical review.* J. Phys. Chem. Solids. **18** (1961) 1–8.

Trueblood, K. N. *Symmetry transformations of general anisotropic temperature factors.* Acta Cryst. **9** (1956) 359–361.

Ubbelohde, A. R. *Crystallography and the phase rule.* Brit. J. Appl. Phys. **7** (1956) 313–321.

Vainshtein, B. K. *The contribution from orientation in the scattered intensity from a molecular crystal.* Sov. Phys. Cryst. **9** (1964) 129–131.

Valdés L. M. and M. Canut. *El fenómeno de inversión en la difracción difusa del bencilo a baja temperatura.* Bol. Real. Soc. Espan. Hist. Nat., (G)**59**(1961) 41–48.

Velasco, M., M. L. Canut, and J. L. Amorós. *Estudios acerca de la dinámica reticular en cristales moleculares. II. Diffracción difusa del ácido adipico.* P. Dep. Crist. Min. **1** (1954) 165–171.

Verweel, H. J. and C. H. MacGillavry. *The crystal structure of succinic acid. (COOH-CH₂-CH₂-COOH).* Z. Krist. **102** (1940) 60–70.

Walker, C. B. *X-ray study of lattice vibrations in aluminum.* Phys. Rev. **103** (1956) 547–557.

Waller, I. *Zur Frage der Einwirkung der Wärmebewegung auf die Interferenz von Röntgenstrahlen.* Z. Phys. **17** (1923) 398–408.

Waller, I. "Theoretische Studien zur Interferenz-und Dispersionstheorie der Röntgenstrahlen." (Appelbergs Boktryckeri Aktiebolag Lundequistska Bokhandeln Uppsala, 1925).

Waser, J. *The anisotropic temperature factor in triclinic coordinates.* Acta Cryst. **8** (1955) 731.

Wentzel, G. *Zur Theorie des Comptoneffekts.* Z. Phys. **43** (1927) 1–8.

Wilson, A. J. C. *Determination of absolute from relative x-ray intensity data.* Nature. **150** (1942) 152.

Wooster, W. A. *Diffuse x-ray scattering and the physical properties of crystals.* Brit. J. Appl. Phys. **5** (1954) 231–237.

Wooster, W. A. "Diffuse X-Ray Reflections from Crystals." (Clarendon Press, Oxford, 1962).

Wrinch, D. *Fourier transforms and structure factors.* American Society for X-ray and Electron Diffraction, Monograph number 2 (1946) 1–96.

Wyckoff, R. W. G. and R. B. Corey. *Spectrometric measurements on hexamethylene tetramine and urea.* Z. Krist. **89** (1934) 462–468.

Yagi, M. *Structural investigations on urea and hexamethylenetetramine by proton magnetic resonance.* Sci. Rep. Tohoku Univ. Ser. I, **42** (1958) 182–189.

Yardley, K. *The crystalline structure of succinic acid, succinic anhydride, and succinimide.* Proc. Roy, Soc. (London), Ser. A **105** (1924) 451–467.

Zachariasen, W. H. "Theory of X-Ray Diffraction in Crystals." (John Wiley & Sons, Inc., New York, 1945).

Zhdanov, G. S. "Crystal Physics." (Academic Press, London, 1965).

Ziman, J. M. "Electrons and Phonons. The Theory of Transport Phenomena in Solids."(Clarendon Press, Oxford, 1960).

Index